THE
MALMESBURY
BRANCH

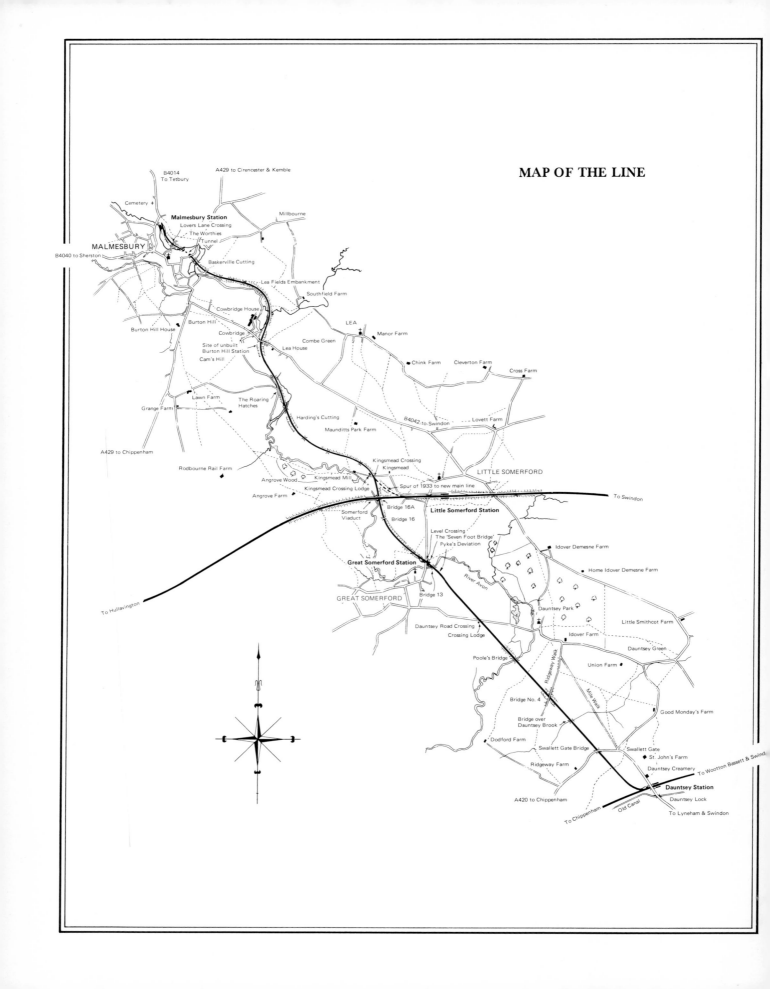

MAP OF THE LINE

B4014
To Tetbury

A429 to Cirencester & Kemble

Cemetery

Malmesbury Station
Lovers Lane Crossing
The Worthies
Tunnel

Millbourne

MALMESBURY

B4040 to Sherston

Baskerville Cutting

Lea Fields Embankment

Southfield Farm

Cowbridge House

LEA

Manor Farm

Burton Hill

Burton Hill House

Cowbridge

Combe Green

Chink Farm

Cleverton Farm

Cross Farm

Site of unbuilt
Burton Hill Station

Lea House

Cam's Hill

Lawn Farm

The Roaring
Hatches

Grange Farm

Harding's Cutting

B4042 to Swindon

Lovett Farm

A429 to Chippenham

Maunditts Park Farm

Rodbourne Rail Farm

Kingsmead Crossing
Kingsmead

LITTLE SOMERFORD

Angrove Wood

Kingsmead Mill

Spur of 1933 to new main line

Kingsmead Crossing Lodge

Angrove Farm

Somerford
Viaduct

Bridge 16A

Bridge 16

Little Somerford Station

To Swindon

Level Crossing
The 'Seven Foot Bridge'
Pyke's Deviation

Idover Demesne Farm

Great Somerford Station

Home Idover Demesne Farm

River Avon

GREAT SOMERFORD

Bridge 13

Dauntsey Park

Little Smithcot Farm

To Hullavington

Dauntsey Road Crossing

Crossing Lodge

Idover Farm

Dauntsey Green

Poole's Bridge

Ridgeway Walk

Union Farm

Bridge No. 4

Mile Walk

Good Monday's Farm

Bridge over
Dauntsey Brook

Dodford Farm

Swallett Gate Bridge

St. John's Farm

Swallett Gate

To Wootton Bassett & Swind

Ridgeway Farm

Dauntsey Creamery

A420 to Chippenham

Dauntsey Station

To Chippenham

Old Canal

Dauntsey Lock

To Lyneham & Swindon

THE
MALMESBURY
BRANCH

MIKE FENTON

WILD SWAN PUBLICATIONS LTD.

'There is a market cross in this town, the sight of which is worth a journey of hundreds of miles.' (William Cobbett, *Rural Rides*, 1826.)

Collection Oliver Pike

CONTENTS

FOR TRICIA
A Malmesbury girl

With special thanks to Gerald and Shirley Cooper

© Wild Swan Publications Ltd. and Mike Fenton 1990
ISBN 0 906867 88 6

Designed by Paul Karau
Printed by Amadeus Press Ltd., Huddersfield

Published by
WILD SWAN PUBLICATIONS LTD.
1—3 Hagbourne Road, Didcot, Oxon OX11 8DP

Malmesbury.

An old postcard view, looking down the Tetbury Road during the early years of the century, with Malmesbury Abbey still managing to dominate the skyline through the foliage.
Author's collection

INTRODUCTION
A CHAPTER OF ACKNOWLEDGEMENTS

IN 1951, when the passenger service ran from Malmesbury for the last time, I was a three year-old living within earshot of Dick Cooper's train as it entered the anonymity of the Swindon yard. Twenty years later, the Malmesbury girl whom I was to marry conducted me on guided tours of her hometown, and my interest in the old railway line was aroused by the mysterious tunnel under Holloway Hill, the steeply excavated cutting at Baskerville and the redundant engine shed still presenting its defiant appearance of rough-hewn Victoriana to the car-orientated modern world. Encouraged by Tricia's uncle, E. K. 'Paddy' Lockstone, the town's principal railway enthusiast and modeller, and sparked by reading two interesting articles about the line (in *Trains Illustrated*, October 1956, by Colin Maggs, and *The Railway Magazine*, June 1933, by C. L. Mowat), I spent two years of relatively modest research producing a small paperback for Oakwood Press in time for the branch's centenary in 1977. EKL was, as he has been all along, an enthusiastic backer of the project at all times, putting his local connections and his work as an SEB installations inspector to good use in the search for photographs, relics, railwaymen who worked the Malmesbury branch and any related material which would help me in my quest.

After the publication of my first rather modest little work, the preparation for which was complicated by the need to meet the 1977 centenary deadline and by my being abroad during 1976–77, I found that, far from, as it were, closing the chapter on the Malmesbury railway, the booklet stimulated vast new areas of research, more photographs coming to light, many new contacts with information to contribute, not to mention a greater awareness in me of the need for undertaking the work with a greater depth and accuracy. These factors, combined with an increased knowledge of the amazing wealth of material available in the transport records at the Public Record Office, Kew, led me to the decision that I should chronicle the history of the branch in greater detail.

My first meeting with Paul Karau early in 1978 gave me the inspiration to go ahead on a fresh attempt at the project, as it was now possible to lean on someone who could provide much needed help with locomotive working and a detailed knowledge of publishing and the production of plans and maps. Thus assured of a publisher who could present the work in the manner I felt the subject deserved, I embarked upon a further eight years of research in which I was able to use my increased knowledge of the local area and the archives at Kew, and in which staff interviews, lengthy recorded conversations with many ex-GWR people who had worked the branch, became a feature of the project which I believe has added an invaluable depth and richness to the work.

Despite the line being finished as a passenger service for thirty years by 1981, at this time I was still finding ex-GWR men who not only had first-hand experience of life and work on the branch but were pleased to see us (Paul gave me valuable support with several excellent staff interviews) and

The building that first stirred my interest in the Malmesbury line — the branch engine shed, seen here in 1958. It can still be seen there today.
I. D. Beale

1

Edgar Cross, 1896–1989, seen during his days as station master at Patney & Chirton, junction for the Devizes line.
Courtesy Edgar Cross

eager to contribute. How thrilling it was, how revealing, to listen to Arthur 'Buller' Reeve describing a night as engine cleaner of Malmesbury shed in 1917 – moreover, I discovered that he had married a daughter of the family who inhabited the crossing cottage at Kingsmead for nearly fifty years from the opening of the line, and this knowledge opened up a whole new area of enquiry. Edgar Cross, whom I visited many times at Patney, not far from the site of the old junction at Patney & Chirton where he was station master for 15 years, described a similar period as porter at Dauntsey from 1923 as the time and place 'where I really learned to be a railwayman'. From Charlie Hurley, one of many people with Malmesbury railway connections whom I found retired in the Swindon area, I learned much valuable information about the changes in signalling when the branch was diverted to Little Somerford in 1933. Former crossing keeper Bill Archard held me enthralled as he described how he had to chip ice off the padlocks on Kingsmead Crossing gates before dawn on winter mornings in the '20s. These were memories of life in a different age which I have been privileged to preserve with my research and writing.

In 1978 I was surprised and delighted to locate Malmesbury's last station master, Percy Wood, alive and well near Barmouth on the Cambrian coast, having been retired there for almost a quarter of a century. Although we never met, our correspondence during the last three years of his life and the photographs he provided yielded valuable information about the line's last years. Mr. Wood's contribution also echoes for me a sad note, in that during the years I have been involved with the work several people whose help was immeasurable have passed on without seeing the book come to fruition – to men like Percy Wood, Bill Archer, Ron Thomas and Bill Archard, both I and my readers owe a great

deal. Remembered with a gratitude, too, is a lengthy tape of memories sent to me from South Wales by a former resident of Malmesbury, Roy Eattell, whose death occurred even before the publication of my Oakwood volume. How we therefore must value the contribution of the older generations – their aid must be sought with care, respect and consideration, whether it be in first approaches, arranging meetings, borrowing photographs or interviewing and recording. In the researching of railway history, we are very concerned with the human element – the information imparted is a very precious link with the past, which we have a duty to record with sympathy and understanding. Many meetings have produced lasting friendships, and I treasure greatly the hospitality, sincere interest and genuine kindness shown to me by many railwaymen, past and present, and their families.

Many historians in all fields, I am sure, will echo these feelings, where one not only establishes a useful contact but also forges a friendship which means that visits to undertake staff interviews become so much more than mere fact-finding missions. How delightful it was to share a roast lunch with Mr. & Mrs. Edgar Cross at their home deep in the Wiltshire countryside near Devizes, where I was able to admire Mr. Cross's talent as an artist as well as discuss branch operations at Dauntsey. Mr. & Mrs. Ken Stoneham were so interested in the work that they accompanied me on one visit to the old engine shed in Malmesbury, Ken's first time in there since his days as a Malmesbury fireman thirty years before. John Barnby, for eleven years the clerk at the terminus, not only kindly read manuscripts and offered the work the benefits of his immense administrative experience on the GWR, but even marked some of the provisional text with all the zeal of a school teacher, quite an experience for the headmaster I then was!

One of my most moving experiences was listening for hours to the memories of Bill Archard, who lived for nearly 60 years in the crossing cottage at Kingsmead, and who told me that if I could print him enlargements of two of the photographs he was loaning me, it would, he said, 'make my life for me'. I was only too happy to oblige, and it was a source of pleasure to me on subsequent visits to see those same enlarged copies framed and standing on a bedside cabinet. On many such visits, there was a special sense of reward in feeling that through my interest in their work and times, through my wish to listen and record, a fresh new interest and purpose was added to their last years. From such people, I came to picture the Malmesbury line as a personal service, undertaken by men with a great pride in and a great love for their work, with a diligence and devotion which remained a feature of the branch even after it ceased to serve the town adequately after the Great War, even during the final years of the passenger service when it was evident that the new nationalised railway had no intention of keeping it open.

The Malmesbury branch was unique in that it changed its junction from one main line to another of equal stature during its life, a fact that has presented some organisational hurdles to this study, and it also possessed many delightful features which will unfold to the reader throughout the course of the book. Most especially notable was the amount of heavy earthworks and the extremely large number of bridges for so short a branch, these characteristics a result of both the terrain and the circuitous River Avon and its tributaries. Worth

E. K. ('Paddy') Lockstone is at the front of this interested group at Lovers Lane Crossing on 18th August 1957, as an RCTS special train runs bunker-first out of Malmesbury.

recalling is a reference to the branch made in 1948 in *The Story of the Settle-Carlisle Line* by Frederick W. Houghton and W. Hubert Foster, published by Arch Books. In referring to the massive engineering features of the S & C, it read:

> 'Today the consolidation of railways in Britain is complete, and the Settle-Carlisle is at one with the Bristol to Paddington, the York to Newcastle, the Glasgow to Aberdeen and the Little Somerford to Malmesbury lines.'

If the inclusion of the Malmesbury branch seems somewhat unusual in such a context, this reference was included especially for our stalwart EKL, who had been introduced to Hubert Foster in Foster's model railway shop in Bradford, Yorkshire, just after the last war. During their friendship, no doubt EKL's home-town branch came up frequently in conversation, thereby prompting Mr. Foster to put the reference to the little Wiltshire branch amongst such eminent company!

A large collection of photographs has been assembled over the years involved on the project, now running into several hundred. EKL provided many fine photographs of his own, but the hunt saw many old prints being unearthed in places well away from Malmesbury and in unexpected locations. If I expected to trace photographic material in the Swindon, Chippenham and Bristol areas, which I often did, it was rather more surprising to receive it from less predictable places and as far afield as Otley, Dartford, Axminster, Quebec and Perth, Australia! I even found myself making successful forays into the Science Museum in Kensington and the Wiltshire Department of Highways and Transportation in Trowbridge!

Often a little 'detective' work was involved in tracing people whom I thought might be able to assist. Having traced the family of Malmesbury station master Edgar H. Doswell to the Kingswood district of Bristol, via a retirement notice in

the *GWR Magazine* and the telephone directory, I spent a very pleasant morning and enjoyed a satisfying lunch whilst hearing of a Malmesbury boyhood of sixty years before, then left with the mounted original of the photograph which now forms the cover of this volume. Such success does compensate for the number of blank avenues ('Oh yes, we had a lovely photo of the bridge, but it was thrown out when Dad moved house') and the frustration of having to leave certain areas unrepresented by some form of illustration – there is an annoying lack of photographs of the old Dauntsey-Great Somerford section of the branch, partly as a result of its being closed so long ago. There will always be photographic gaps in such a work, of course, but how priceless it would have been to have located a view of Dauntsey before 1900, Great Somerford before enlargement of the station house, Swallett Gate bridge before demolition, the evacuee train on the branch in 1939, not to mention an opening day view at Malmesbury – such a great day in the history of the town simply must have been photographed! No doubt there are still priceless photographs lying undiscovered in drawers,

Station keys.　　　　　　　　　　　　*Athelstan Museum*

attics and old albums which may yet surface after the publication of this book.

Although some of my research was undertaken while the BTHR material was housed at Porchester Road, the bulk of the archive work, apart from visits to the local newspaper offices in Swindon and Cirencester, has been at the Public Record Office, that magnificent building at Kew in which I would have preferred to have been turned loose for a month rather than make regular expensive trips to London to be governed by office hours and computers that would not order me more than three documents at a time, a frustrating limitation on the work I was able to get through in a day, although the staff were always most helpful.

Occasionally, I came across annoying gaps in the records, such as the 1933 GWR locomotive allocations and a vital Uniformed Staff volume (RAIL 264/344) which would have yielded crucial information, and beyond that I wonder just what references still lie missed and overlooked in the records, through the sheer weight of potentially revealing material to be relentlessly combed, with time always my enemy. As Adrian Vaughan rightly says, though, in his book about the Faringdon branch, one cannot know all that happened to a branch railway throughout a century of history. The minor references we do glean from the records and the contemporary press, the sometimes seemingly trivial stories and incidents, often correlate quite excitingly and significantly with other evidence and assist in providing a flavour and atmosphere of times long past. How frustrating it is, though, to think of what we missed by not being there, to experience the desolation of standing at the site of what once was Dauntsey station, once the junction for Malmesbury, to look upon its pathetic denuded remains and forlornly wish that a time machine could whisk one back sixty years or more!

Over the years I have tried several appeals in newspapers for material and contacts, and although I have found that such publicity usually inspires only limited response, on occasion a helpful reply can bear fruit and uncover a new trail of research, and in this respect two positive results were quite memorable. Via such an appeal, an address given and some correspondence, I visited Mr. & Mrs. Maurice Drinkwater, just thirty minutes from my then home in Kent. Mrs. Drinkwater's grandfather was William Hine, the last crossing keeper at Dauntsey Road Crossing before it closed with the switch of junction in 1933. She produced superb views of the crossing and cottage (pp. 60 & 89), and the GWR connection was even deeper than I expected! It is Mr. Drinkwater as a young man who is seen seated on the crossing gate on page 89, and his father was the railway's chief First Aid man at Swindon, who attended to George Churchward at the fatal accident in December 1933, in which the retired GWR Superintendent was killed early on a foggy morning by a South Wales express.

Mrs. Grace Whiteside of Reading was thrilled to assist with the project. Her grandfather, John Quarrell, was at Malmesbury at the very opening of the line and gave the branch nearly half a century of service. One morning an envelope arrived from Reading amongst my Christmas mail containing a faded 1906 postcard showing a small staff group on Malmesbury platform, together with a charming letter, from which I quote this memorable extract;

'From about the age of five I was often put in charge of the guard of the train to the West Country at Reading, who was given instructions that "the child's grandfather will meet her at Dauntsey". It was a dear little branch line to Malmesbury, the highlight of the journey being the tunnel. You could hang out of the window to catch your first glimpse of the station and my waiting grandmother on the platform.'

I owe a great debt to many railway photographers who visited the branch through the years and recorded the scenes of change before steam and the line itself were lost forever – to the late Professor C. L. Mowat whom we have to thank for the only view so far traced of the actual junction and branch curve at Dauntsey, to Bill Camwell, who not only took some excellent views but was prepared to loan his original negatives, so much better for real clarity than merely making a copy of an old print, and to John Barnby, who often took his camera to work with him during his days as clerk at Malmesbury, and took some quite beautiful and unusual views.

Much is owed to the interest and vision of Bertram Farmer, today a professor at Cambridge University. In the early '30s he was a local schoolboy, living in a house overlooking the terminus at Malmesbury, and his interest and his realisation that times were irrevocably changing produced the many excellent photographs he took both in the early '30s and later – as a teenager he was the only person known to have recorded on camera the departure of the first public train to leave Malmesbury for the new junction at Little Somerford, early one July morning in 1933. In 1977, at a model railway exhibition co-ordinated by EKL in Malmesbury Town Hall as part of celebrations of the old branch's centenary, Mr. Farmer was a welcome visitor, bringing with him two old destination boards from the old Malmesbury carriages together with the number plate from Collett 0–4–2T No. 5802, the first locomotive of the '58XX' class to work the line.

Having stressed the rewarding relationships developed on such a project, one must not forget the camaraderie which can exist between historians and researchers with similar goals. In this respect, much is owed to Chris Turner of Dartford, whose work at the PRO, often at the expense of his own study time, saved me a good few trips and much time and money. Portia Hobbs, retired headteacher of Great Somerford village school, who spent several years researching the history of her village, would frequently trade gobbets of information with me – her work has since been published – *Somerford Magna – the history of a village in north Wiltshire* (Alan Sutton Publishing). I am grateful to Peter Wells and Richard Croucher of the Great Western Society for entrusting me with large chunks of their collections of *Great Western Railway Magazines*, allowing me to borrow them and comb them in depth at my leisure. Bath schoolteacher Colin Maggs, having provided me with an initial impetus with his 1956 article, proving to me that research upon a then seemingly-obscure branch subject was possible, maintained his interest and assisted with his photographs and constructive comments, drawing upon his vast experience in railway writing. It would have been impossible to make any serious attempt at delving into the minefield of the subject of railway signalling without the invaluable assistance of Signalling Record Society members John Morris, Adrian Vaughan and Reg Instone, and especially Mike Christensen, with whose help and patience I managed to put together a full signalling chapter after many attempts! Even with a branch on which the signalling was relatively simple, there were a lot of complexities, not to mention the mysteries of pre-1900 signalling, which I should have found impossible to write up without being able to call on such expert help. Mention must be made of GWR historian Eric Mountford, who would always reply to a query with a very full and enthusiastic letter, and Malmesbury's Bert Vizor, who has always showed great interest in the project and been of great help in tracing contacts and drawing on his own memories of the line going back to his childhood in the late '30s.

In attempting to trace families of former railwaymen associated with the branch, it was pleasing to receive a great deal of co-operation from various administrative personnel in several British Rail Area Manager's Offices, in particular Mr. H. R. Hayden of the Swindon office who proved to be very helpful in providing me with addresses of former employees, often creating very productive avenues of investigation. Peter Weston, today in the Swindon BR Travel Office, was Dauntsey's last station master, and showed great interest in the work, even to the extent of nearly cutting himself shaving one morning when he suddenly recalled a piece of information which I needed whilst over the sink and rushed from the bathroom to write it down for me before forgetting it!

The irony in producing a work of this nature is that, in recognising that the demise of many rural lines was brought about largely by the development of the private car, so it is the private car which makes possible much of my research. How much poorer the work would have been without the

contributions of Albert Stanley (Challow, Berks), Doreen Hicks (Amberley, Glos), Hubert Spencer (Brinkworth, Wilts) and Len Hillman (Swindon). Mr. and Mrs. K. E. Iles of Goatacre, Wilts, kindly loaned a wonderful old album containing superbly clear photographs of her grandfather, Malmesbury engineman Ted Jones, one of which was conveniently dated on the back. Without a reliable motor to facilitate convenient arrangements for visits, reaching such helpful people would have been very difficult.

Very often a day's research would involve one of my many morning visits to Edgar Cross at Patney, then maybe a call at Devizes Library or Museum, or to Swindon to use microfilmed newspapers at the Library there (not an enjoyable task – I could only manage an hour at a time before my eyes could take no more). A visit to Swindon would also probably include a call on any one of numerous helpful contacts in that town, before going back to Malmesbury or the Somerfords for an evening appointment. I was fortunate in being able to be regularly put up for the night by my in-laws, Mr. & Mrs. Lockstone of Malmesbury. For arranging such research schedules to scattered venues, being mobile was vital.

I have taken great pleasure in including a chapter of staff portraits focusing on the uniformed staff based at Malmesbury itself, and a chapter based on the work of the crossing keeper, the work of the permanent way men being covered as appropriate in the general history. The lives and work of the

An evocative branch line scene in Malmesbury yard in 1955. Bill Archer is seen with shunting pole while Masters David and Hugh Farmer are seen on the footplate of No. 5802. No wonder boys of that era grew up wanting to be engine drivers! *Bertram Farmer*

men of Malmesbury's locomotive department are covered in detail in the 'Locomotive Department' chapter. It is the purpose of the staff profiles chapter to give some insight into the working of Malmesbury station through chronicling the careers of several of the station staff and the duties they performed. If this chapter appears uneven in content, it is simply because I naturally obtained a fuller description of the life and times of the people concerned when I was able to speak to them personally, as in many interviews with John Barnby and Bill Archard. Where this was not possible, the information has been collated from GWR staff records and from talking with members of their families who were directly involved with the railway work. Through such contact, with ex-employees and with family surviving staff from earlier times, a very clear picture emerged of everyday life on the branch, supplemented by the facts gleaned from the records. The selection of the portraits for this section has been on the basis of obtaining as first-hand a contact as possible with the person concerned, the one thing they all have in common being their long association with the branch, and certainly no denigration is intended of anyone seemingly omitted from this section, there being staff references wherever relevant throughout the book.

Bert Vizer's interest in this book was directly responsible for one of the most memorable finds on the whole project. In 1979 a conversation with Bert in Malmesbury Library led me via a High Street shop to a farm at Goatacre where I was made welcome by Mr. & Mrs. K. Iles. Mrs. Iles's grandfather was branch engineman during the early years of the century, and the family album she kindly loaned was packed with railway treasures which have particularly enhanced the 'Loco Department' chapter. Above, seen on Malmesbury platform c.1912, are driver Jones's daughters and son-in-law, Mrs. E. Trow, Mr. J. Trow, Mrs. K. Fountain. *Courtesy Mr. & Mrs. K. Iles*

To begin a branch line study is to realise that a railway was so much more than mere hardware, that even a short line which existed as a working presence for well under a century would not only leave its almost indestructible self on the landscape in many forms, but would generate a vast amount of material, memories, records and emotions scattered over a wide area, and I found that the pieces were simply waiting to be brought together to assume a corporate and meaningful identity. Although I explored remains of the line at length, in

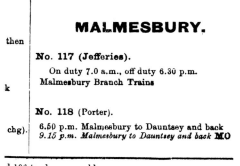

MALMESBURY.

then

No. 117 (Jefferies).

On duty 7.0 a.m., off duty 6.30 p.m.
Malmesbury Branch Trains

k

No. 118 (Porter).

6.50 p.m. Malmesbury to Dauntsey and back
9.15 p.m. Malmesbury to Dauntsey and back **MO**

chg).

d 106 to change weekly.

All snippets found were important, waiting to be brought together to form a 'corporate and meaningful identity' in the work — this is a guard's duty roster from a Working Time Table Appendix of 1902.

order to attempt to absorb some of the feeling of the old line and to know exactly where things were, there was always a certain anger, a definite sadness, in exploring the course of a defunct railway, which renders it an unrewarding exercise if you prefer to recall the way things were in former days. I came to feel on such fieldwork that the desecrated remains of an old railway were quite unworthy of the camera, and therefore we have avoided presenting modern photographs of what is left — why do so anyway, when the space can be given to excellent views of the railway as it was? In the search for relevant material, the researcher does go down many blank paths, and may even just occasionally encounter apathy or even refusal to co-operate, but nevertheless the journey is an exciting one, made all the more rewarding by the relationships which develop and the thrill of stumbling on rare photographs, those priceless windows on the past which serve to bring the whole story alive.

Malmesbury's branch line appears to have been built, staffed and run without ever really evolving, and, with its two junctions being at minor stations, could never really adjust to the needs of a rapidly changing world during this century, particularly in a locality where prosperous aristocracy, businessmen and farmers could afford other means of transport to the detriment of a local line with a limited train service which, in the words of a local correspondent writing in 1951, 'went nowhere and met nothing'. With the exception of major alterations such as that at Somerford in 1893 and the change of junction in 1933, the line appears to have come into existence, constructed somewhat optimistically with room for doubling of the track, and remained relatively unchanged from earliest times, most of the changes being in the form of economies, such as reduction of signalling. Aside from basic maintenance,

very little appears to have been done — short sections of line were re-sleepered and track replaced as required, but references in the records are rare and devoid of detail. There are occasional mentions in the General Manager's Fortnightly Reports to the GWR Board, but references to the branch in Engineering Committee and Signalling Committee Minutes are rare. Certainly the character of the line altered drastically with the major changes of the 1930s and World War II, but these had more to do with atmosphere and changing times in the country generally rather than positive additions which might have benefited the service, the switching of the junction to Little Somerford itself being an economy. Traffic never really merited any major additions to facilities on the branch, and even the arrival in later years of major providers of traffic, such as E. K. Cole and A. B. Blanch, came too late to arrest decline, although the business they provided was substantial.

In piecing together the history of a defunct branch line, my overriding feeling is that no matter how much time is spent delving through the records, whether combing bound volumes of newspapers or poring over plans and maps, the richest source of information and the real atmosphere of a bygone era is only truly secured through talking with the people themselves. While it is true that facts vary from person to person, memories may be dimmed by passing years, and exaggeration is an undeniable characteristic of human nature, it is also true that in the people one finds the humour, the tolerance, the understanding, and above all the first-hand experience of a way of life which we can never know — a pattern of life in which the branch line was a town's contact with the world beyond, with which it existed in a state of mobile interdependence, until the Great War and the development of road transport changed that way of life forever, long before the Malmesbury line's final demise. It was always very rewarding and exciting also when a human source would correlate closely with or confirm facts which existed in the records, and this would often work to good effect in reverse

For many years the postbox from Malmesbury station survived on the car park wall outside the old Railway Hotel. *Author*

and ensure accuracy in the final write-up. Presented here in this document is the result of fifteen years' work, intended not simply as a railway history, but a social study, an account of life and times as they once were. When we are interested in things which are no longer the same or no longer exist, the writer takes on the responsibility to preserve them in a form which can be enjoyed, appreciated and understood by present and future generations, and it is this I have attempted to do, not just for railway enthusiasts and modellers, not just for Wiltshire folk and the people of Malmesbury, but for all who treasure the memories I trust are enshrined in this collection.

In acknowledging the assistance of all who have contributed to this branch line history, I would like to record special thanks to Jim Thornbury, once Malmesbury's 'Jack-of-all-Trades' on the railway, who always showed interest in the work and was never too busy to receive a visit whenever I needed clarification or help in identifying a feature or people on a photograph. Mention must also be made of Mr. W. A. Thompson, a Malmesbury agricultural contractor, who owned the old engine shed for many years after final closure of the line – he used the building to keep his machinery and might have made a fortune had he decided to charge the many enthusiasts who called on him requesting permission to visit, photograph or measure it for modelling purposes. It must be recorded that Mr. Thompson was always most accommodating. I would also like to give special mention to my wife Tricia, who has lived through the years involved on this work and my other projects with an appealing mixture of patience and interest, even coming on some of my trips to Kew to see what I was up to and give me a hand with the seemingly never-ending combing of documents. We both know, of course, that I would never have produced this work had she not come into my life, so it is she who is really the principal reason for the book, therefore to her it is dedicated, as well as to all those railwaymen who gave me their time and their expert knowledge based upon their own working lives.

In addition to those mentioned previously in this chapter, I would also like to acknowledge the help of the following: K. Barnes, Ron Barnicoat, Philip Basevi, Ralph Biggs, A. Blanch, Sean Bolan, J. Britton, Mrs. F. Bubb, Fred Canter, C. Carr, C.J. Carr (Traffic Officer, Bristol Omnibus Company), Mr. & Mrs. Les Carter, H. C. Casserley, D. Castle, Rose Clark, Mr. & Mrs. D. Cole, R. Coles, Peggy Connolly, L. J. Cook, David Cooper, Gerald Cooper, John Cooper, Don Cross, W. G. Dinham, Mr. & Mrs. C. J. Doswell, Mr. & Mrs. W. G. Down, Mrs. Edna Evans, Mrs. Nancy Fowler, D. Garnett, Mrs. George Gibbs, Dr. Richard Gulliver (Custodian of the Mowat Collection), R. Hatchwell, Derek Hayes, Gerald Hill, Henry Hill, Mrs. Ruth Hill, Brian Hilton, Gordon Hoare, David Hodgson, Mr. & Mrs. Stan Hudson, David Hyde, Iris Jones, Syd Jones, Mrs. M. R. King (Personnel Officer, Linolite Ltd.), Kenneth Leach, John Lewis, Robin Littlewood, Mr. & Mrs. Doug Lockstone, Jim Long, Richard Martin, Jock Mearns, J. Mills, Keith Montague, Gilbert Moore, Mark Moore, Stanley Mulcock, Bob Neal, Jack Neale, Stanley New, Ian Nulty, Lionel Padin, J. Pike, Oliver Pike, Don Pritchard, K. Ratcliffe, R. L. Ratcliffe, Jessica Reeve, Mrs. Bert Reynolds, Joe Reynolds, Mrs. Betty Richards, R. C. Riley, John Robinson, Mrs. J. Rogerson, Horace Scott, Mrs. Mary Sharpe, Maurice Skull, Mrs. A. Smith, Frank D. Smith, George Sterne, Mike Stewart, Philip Sturgess, Norman Thornbury, Mrs. Percy Wakefield, Walter Wakefield, Peter Webber, Derek White, and other railway photographers.

My thanks are due to the staff of the following archives and institutions: Swindon Library; *Swindon Advertiser*; *The Wiltshire Gazette & Herald*, Swindon; *The Wilts & Glos Standard*, Cirencester; Wiltshire County Record Office, Trowbridge; Wiltshire Library & Museum Service, Trowbridge; Gloucestershire County Record Office, Gloucester; Gloucester Carriage & Wagon Works; Malmesbury Library; Athelstan Museum, Malmesbury; The Public Record Office, Kew; The Science Museum, Kensington; Devizes Museum & Library; British Rail Public Relations, Paddington (WR); Great Western Society, Didcot; Locomotive & General Railway Photographs; Photomatic Ltd; The National Monuments Record, Savile Row, London; The Society of Royal Engineers; The Bristol Omnibus Company, Ltd; Pye TMC, Malmesbury; Linolite Ltd, Malmesbury; Lens of Sutton; Railway Correspondence & Travel Society; *The Western Daily Press*; Great Western Railway Museum, Swindon; National Railway Museum, York.

Finally, I would like to express my sincere thanks to my publisher Paul Karau, for his knowledge, expertise and efforts to give this work the best possible presentation, and to June Judge, for her work on the manuscript.

Mike Fenton
Whittington
Worcester
1990

Bibliography
The following publications have been consulted in the preparation of this book. Major Kew group & class reference numbers are given.
Malmesbury Railway Act 1872 – Malmesbury Town Hall
Documents of the Malmesbury Railway 1872–1880
McDermot/Clinker *History of the Great Western Railway Vols I & II*
The Railway Magazine
Victoria County History of Wiltshire, Vol IV
Locomotives of the GWR Part 6 – Four-Coupled Tank Engines (RCTS)
Kelly's Directories
Malmesbury Almanacks
Clinker's Register of Closed Passenger Stations & Goods Depots in England, Scotland and Wales 1830–1970.
Working Timetables of the GWR (RAIL 937)
Bradshaw Railway Timetables
The Faringdon Branch by Adrian Vaughan (OPC)
Great Western Signalling by Adrian Vaughan (OPC)
The Great Western Railway Magazine
GWR Staff Records, Kew (RAIL 264)
GWR Shed Allocations, Kew (RAIL 254)
GWR Operating Instructions, Kew (RAIL 279)
GWR Board Meetings, Fortnightly Reports, Engineering Committee, Traffic Committee, Signalling Committee Minutes (RAIL 250)
Station Traffic Receipts, Kew (RAIL 266)
Excursion Handbills, Kew (RAIL 253)
MT6 Files, Kew (Board of Trade)
Great Western Stations Vol IV by R. H. Clark (OPC)
Great Western Coaches by Michael Harris (Ian Allan)
The Malmesbury Railway by D. M. Fenton (Oakwood Press)

CHAPTER ONE

SETTING THE SCENE

'What with the water, the meadows, the fine cattle and sheep, and, as I hear, the absence of hard-pinching poverty, this is a very pleasant place.'
William Cobbett, 'Rural Rides', September 1826

THE ancient town of Malmesbury, claimed to be England's oldest borough, is situated on a narrow hilltop between two rivers which meet on the town's eastern side to form the River Avon. The presence of these rivers had a substantial effect upon the construction of Malmesbury's railway, the more northerly of the streams, the Inglebourne, forming the western boundary of the town's

names flowed much more easily in the process of natural derivation from Malmud, thence to Malmeesdburg to Malmesbury, rather than from a Maildulph/Aldhelm combination.

Malmesbury must have been the ideal defensive site, the loop of water forming a natural defence, with a barricade necessary only at the western approach on a narrow escarp-

J. C. Varrall's 1829 engraving of Malmesbury Abbey based on Turner's 1791 romantic view. With some allowance for artistic licence, the direction from which the Abbey is viewed here indicates that this is the valley of the Inglebourne in which the railway terminus was built. *Collection Robin Littlewood*

station yard. Whichever way the motorist approaches the town, only by the B4040 from the Sherston direction is it possible to enter Malmesbury without crossing water.

Malmesbury is ten miles north of Chippenham, fifteen miles west of Swindon, and twelve miles south-west of Cirencester. To the south lie the Wiltshire Downs and the flat country of the Avon Valley, while to the north across the Gloucestershire border lie the high pastures and stone walls of Cotswold country. Indeed, Malmesbury has a Cotswold air about it – from the roof of the Abbey one can look down over grey, stone-tiled roofs, with terraced Bath stone dwellings in varying shapes and sizes built long before anyone ever thought of town planning – these houses were built with an eye for privacy, unlike the newer estates out on the Bristol road. Like many of its Gloucestershire neighbours, the town had a long historical association with the production of wool. The population of the Borough in April 1984 was 3,276.

The name Malmesbury is a confusion between Maildulph, an Irish monk who arrived in the 7th century, Aldhelm, saint and bishop who ruled the Benedictine Abbey for 33 years, and Malmud, a chieftain who fortified the hill on which the town stands around 400 years BC. Malmesbury's great historian, the late Stan Hudson, was of the opinion that the

ment. Its position was no doubt held in awe by the Roman invaders – no Roman remains have ever been discovered on the site, the nearest encampment being at White Walls, $2\frac{1}{2}$ miles away on the Fosse Way.

With the founding of the kingdom of Mercia, to the north of Wessex, in 587 AD, the Saxons used Malmesbury as their nothern frontier stronghold to guard against attack from the north. The arrival of Maidulph saw Malmesbury become a centre of learning, and Aldhelm, one of his pupils, became Abbot of Malmesbury in 672. When Aldhelm died in Dorset in 705 his remains were brought to Malmesbury and his canonisation greatly enhanced the town's fame. After being taken and burnt by the Danes in 872, the town was retaken by Alfred the Great in 880, at which time its Borough Charter was granted, the 11th centenary of which was celebrated by Malmesbury in 1980.

Alfred's grandson, Athelstan, the first king of all England, in gratitude to the town's inhabitants for the way they fought against the Danes, granted a large piece of land, Malmesbury Common, and also a Charter conferring the right of being 'commoners' to those living within the town walls and to their sons and sons-in-law. Athelstan died at Gloucester in 941, and at his own request was buried beneath the altar of the

9

monastery in Malmesbury. Today, the town still reflects his presence, with a road, school, garage, fire engine, coach service, cinema, museum and amateur drama group named after him.

During the Middle Ages, Malmesbury maintained its place as a centre of learning with William of Malmesbury, the famous medieval historian, being librarian to the Abbey during the first half of the 12th century. The present abbey building dates from the late 12th century – it dominated the surrounding countryside, owning the land, teaching, providing employment, succouring the poor. In 1545, the monastery site was sold off during the Dissolution to William Stumpe, the buildings being turned into workshops for cloth. Malmesbury's trade prospered from this time, with much of the populace being employed in cloth weaving, sheep rearing for wool, and tanning of hides. The Abbey remains today as a beautiful church, its Norman architecture the finest existing anywhere, and many photographs of the branch railway show the Abbey dominating the scene, quietly observing from its position of centuries the little line which came and went in just 85 years.

Malmesbury has numerous distinctions, in particular several attributes concerned with the development of transport and communications, notably in the air. It was the site of the first known attempt to fly, when a monk named Elmer jumped from the Abbey roof equipped with wings, more than eight centuries before the railway arrived in the town. He broke both legs for his pains, and was restrained from further attempts by the Abbot. The connection with flight was furthered by the MP, Walter Powell, who was not only deeply involved in bringing the railway to the town but also made several trips from the town by balloon. His hobby provided his undoing, as he was lost over the Channel off Bridport in 1881, his balloon drifting out over the sea and never being seen again. During this century, it was a Malmesbury firm, Ekco (E. K. Cole), who assisted in the growth of radar.

If Malmesbury was not a route centre on the old Roman network, it was certainly of strategic importance in this respect by the time of the Civil War, the town changing hands seven times between 1642–4 as the Royalists and Roundheads fought for command of the Oxford-Bristol road. The town's contribution to driving could be argued – it remains an ideal place to learn to drive, containing just about every conceivable traffic hazard, being particularly suitable for practising hill starts!

In addition to its association with Athelstan and its claim to the oldest Borough Charter, it possesses one of only three market crosses of similar design in the whole country, this being built in 1490 to provide shelter from the elements for marketgoers. The Abbey was once the possessor of the highest spire in all England, even higher than Salisbury Cathedral, until it came crashing down one night in 1479. John Wesley preached in the town on several occasions in the mid-18th century, the agricultural land of the area was praised by William Cobbett in 'Rural Rides', and the Abbey was painted by no less an artist than Turner in 1791. When the railway eventually arrived, it, too, lent its own touches of uniqueness to the town – its construction and earthworks were extremely heavy for so short a line, including the only tunnel between Malmesbury and Paddington, and the switching of the branch junction in 1933 holds a place as the only time a branch of

the GWR was altered in this way, from one main line to another of equal stature.

During coaching days in the 18th century and the first half of the 19th, Malmesbury was an important call on coach routes between London and Bristol and the West, the King's Arms Hotel on the High Street being as good an example as one will find anywhere in England of a coaching inn and yard. Where Malmesbury Post Office stands today was once the White Swan Inn, and it is recorded that in 1773 a coach left this inn for Holborn Bridge every Wednesday.

In order to fully understand the Malmesbury of Victorian England, which spent some thirty-plus frustrating years in trying to obtain rail connection, it is necessary to chronicle the important developments in the town dating from the turn of the 19th century. The insanitary conditions of the old town were swept away when the first drains were laid in 1799, street cleaning beginning soon afterwards. Pavements were first laid in January 1800, and the streets saw gas lighting in 1836. The workhouse was erected on the Sherston road in 1834. In 1837, January 28th saw the founding in Malmesbury of the *Wiltshire & Gloucestershire Standard*, which still serves the area today, the bound volumes of this newspaper, housed at Cirencester, being very helpful in providing precise details about the history of the branch railway.

The town hall was built overlooking the central Cross Hayes square in 1854, and the Malmesbury Water Company was formed in 1864. During the years of struggle to bring rail service to the town, an important development in the mid-19th century was the purchase of an old cloth mill by a Derby firm – this building was turned over to silk production, an industry which lasted until the outbreak of the 1939 war and provided the railway with much business. From the early 18th to the late 19th century Malmesbury was famous for its clockmaking, but the chief industry during the 18th century had been lace. Originally started by Flemish weavers who came over at the time of William of Orange, the industry was gradually killed off by machine-made lace from elsewhere. It was revived briefly in 1908 by Lady Suffolk of nearby Charlton Park, although it soon died out again.

When the first railways through Wiltshire were built, Malmesbury missed out, as the first main lines passed to the north and south of the town. The GWR main line reached Swindon in 1840, and from here the line to Bristol passed through Chippenham, ten miles south of Malmesbury, whilst that from Swindon to Gloucester, opened throughout in 1845, also bypassed the town by some ten miles. Efforts were made locally to link the town with the new lines by horse omnibus, and during the 1860s three local proprietors ran daily services out of Malmesbury. One John Beames ran an omnibus to Chippenham daily, leaving Malmesbury at 7.45 a.m., arriving in Chippenham at 9.30 a.m., via Little Somerford, Great Somerford, Sutton Benger, Draycott and Langley Burrell. A return trip left Chippenham at 4 p.m., arriving back in Malmesbury at 5.30. Beames, who owned livery stables in Westport, was also the proprietor of the 'Railway Inn' at 107 Gloucester Road in Malmesbury. This hostelry is known to have existed there in the mid-1860s, and may well have been in anticipation of the expected Wilts & Glos Railway which was being projected at that time. Indeed, in neighbouring Tetbury, there still exists a house which was built as an intended Midland 'Railway Hotel'. The failure of the Wilts &

Across Malmesbury rooftops c.1862, with the Market Cross of 1490 and, of course, the Abbey with its fine flying buttresses and Norman entrance porch. Directly behind the Market Cross is the Green Dragon Inn, from which pre-railway horse-bus services ran to Chippenham and Cirencester.
Collection E. K. Lockstone

Glos Railway scheme is detailed in Chapter 2. By 1880 the Gloucester Road establishment was under the landlordship of Henry Jones and known in full as the 'Railway Commercial and Farming Hotel and Posting House'. In the opposite direction to Chippenham, carrier John Machin ran an omnibus from Malmesbury High Street to the GWR station at Minety, seven miles away on the Swindon-Kemble line, which in those days provided Malmesbury's most direct service to London. The MP, Walter Powell, who resided at Dauntsey House, used Minety station to meet guests from London.

The main local operator in the Malmesbury area pre-railway was Henry Long, who in 1865 ran a daily omnibus service from the 'Green Dragon' public house, of which he was also the proprietor, to Chippenham, leaving at 8.00 a.m. and arriving at 9.30. The return trip was made from Chippenham at 4.00 p.m., arriving back at 5.30. Long also worked a service to Cirencester, which departed at 8.15 daily, calling to meet trains at Tetbury Road station *en route*. The return journey left Cirencester at 4.00 p.m. and met the 5.00 p.m. 'up' and the 5.05 'down' trains at Tetbury Road, before returning to Malmesbury. This Cirencester service was discontinued when tolls were introduced in both directions, as Mr. Long stated that the amount of traffic using the run would not enable him to afford tolls both ways. High Street furniture dealer, Joseph Angel, took over the run, but only on Mondays and Fridays. After 1882 this included calls at Kemble, by then a fully-fledged station, and this Cirencester service was maintained under various operators until the beginning of the Great War.

In 1875 Long's Chippenham service was known as 'The Volunteer Omnibus', presumably being named after the Great Somerford public house which was one of its calling points.

This service also left Malmesbury at 8.00 a.m., returning from the Great Western station at Chippenham at 4.00 p.m., Sundays excepted. By 1875, there was also a run by carrier Enos Evans to Bristol, departing each Monday and Thursday, returning each Wednesday and Saturday.

The improvements in railway communications in north Wiltshire by 1852 came too late to arrest the decline of the west Wiltshire woollen industry, and Malmesbury continued to be ignored during this period. The town's long established market had stagnated and was in need of the stimulus which it was believed rail service would give, as indeed it would to business in town generally. By 1875, Malmesbury possessed around 240 commercial businesses and enterprises, including three breweries, a silk manufactory, 23 public houses, a coach builder, 20 insurance agents, various grocers, chemists, footwear makers, carpenters and milliners, and an iron foundry (Ratcliffe's Westport Iron Works, established c.1870). The town therefore possessed diverse concerns and there existed a real need for Malmesbury to have its own railway. If, in retrospect, the provision of a branch line which survived nationalization by only three years seems a failure, a costly anachronism which the town never appreciated in the present century, it must be remembered that the success of railways could never be judged adequately in terms of the actual costs/ profits of the operation, but rather in the prosperity and beneficial changes they helped bring to towns and their environs, especially in the context of the 19th century. However, for Malmesbury, its efforts to obtain its own railway provided many years of impediments and frustrations, through problems of backing, finance, construction and the battleground of 'railway politics', as we shall see.

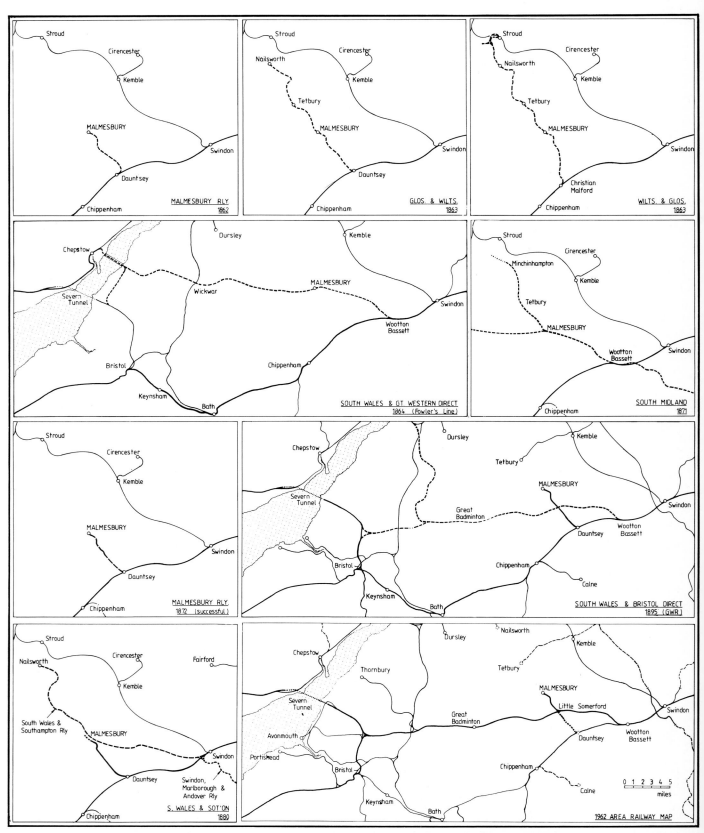

Drawings based on original plans for the various schemes which involved providing a railway at or near Malmesbury. *Monty Wells*

CHAPTER TWO

LOSING OUT TO RAILWAY POLITICS

ALTHOUGH Malmesbury missed out on the early development of railways, the town was a main consideration in many schemes which failed to materialize. Many of these plans had a certain north-south emphasis, very different from the plan for which Malmesbury eventually settled. In the 1840s, railways were still in their infancy, and many schemes during the early 'mania' tended to aim at linking major centres. Therefore Malmesbury figured as just one potential station, admittedly not very major, on large ambitious projects, often very grandly named, which would naturally include the town with its historical eminence and its commanding position between the Marlborough Downs and the Cotswolds.

Schemes have been mentioned concerning Malmesbury as early as 1839, although no documentary evidence has come to light during this study. The first documented scheme to mention Malmesbury specifically was brought forward by an influential Chippenham solicitor (and later its MP), Gabriel Goldney, in 1843, and was intended, in its widest sense, to connect Malmesbury with Southampton and Plymouth in the south, Bristol and Bath to the west, and the Midlands and North via Gloucester and Birmingham. This was projected as the Wilts & Gloucester Junction Railway of 1845, which was to run from Stonehouse, on the Bristol & Birmingham Railway, via Stroud, Woodchester, Minchinhampton, Tetbury, Malmesbury, Hullavington and Kington St. Michael to Thingley Junction near Chippenham, where it was to form a junction with the Wilts & Somerset Railway.

This plan was abandoned on account of powerful opposition from landowners, particularly in the Malmesbury area. The line was surveyed throughout, but the surveyors, Messrs, Low & Reid, ran into trouble in the fields, where, it is said, when the farmers saw them at work with their theodolites, they turned their bulls loose on them. Farmers and huntsmen at the time were against the railway as they believed that the new railways would drive horses off the roads. The line would have passed across Malmesbury Common, to the south-west of the town, which would have benefited many towns, such as Melksham, Trowbridge, Bradford-on-Avon, Nailsworth and Stroud, all of which relied upon the Common for fine garden produce, especially potatoes, which could have been supplied much more cheaply and quickly via the projected railway. The commoners, referred to in Chapter 1, grew whole fields of potatoes, carrots, cabbages and turnips for a wide area, ranging as far away as South Wales.

On 18th October 1845 the *Gloucester Journal* referred to an ambitious scheme called 'The Direct Northern, Eastern & Western Junction Railway', which proposed a line from Bristol by way of Malmesbury, Cirencester, Burford and Chipping Norton to Banbury to join with the proposed line from Northampton to Ashchurch, thus forming 'an unbroken line of communication between the Northern, Eastern and Western coasts of England'. However, despite this being the period when 'railway mania' was at its height (or maybe because of this), it appears that the share issue was not successful, despite the publication of a long list of the names of the very influential supporting committee, and of the thirty-three railway schemes deposited with the Clerk of the Peace in 1845 in Gloucester alone, the DNEWJR was not among them. Clearly the estimated cost of £1,250,000, to be raised in 50,000 £25 shares, did not appeal to enough potential subscribers, and the plan never reached Parliament.

Another abortive project of 1845 was the Gloucester & Southampton Junction Railway, the preliminary advertisement for this appearing in the *Gloucester Chronicle* of 8th November 1845. It specifically referred to Malmesbury, and was to form, in conjunction with existing and projected lines 'the most preferable and direct communication between Southampton and the south coast and Gloucester, Cheltenham, Worcester, Birmingham, Manchester, Liverpool, the whole of the NW counties of England together with Wales and Scotland'. The proposed line was to run from Gloucester via Nailsworth, Tetbury, Malmesbury, Devizes and Salisbury to Southampton, but no Act was passed – this widely pretentious scheme seems to have disappeared without trace.

THE WILTSHIRE & GLOUCESTERSHIRE RAILWAY

After the veritable jungle of railway schemes of the 1840s, the 1850s were something of a barren period for Malmesbury, but the 1860s saw concentrated efforts to put the town on the railway map. In 1861 there were moves to promote a Bill in the ensuing session of Parliament for a line between Malmesbury and Tetbury. The idea had the support of several influential local gentlemen, and basically proposed a branch from Dauntsey to Tetbury; the eventual branch, of course, did form a junction with the Swindon-Bristol main line at Dauntsey. An engineer was appointed and the agreement of all the landowners involved was obtained. The ten mile line was estimated to cost £100,000, of which £40,000 was to be raised locally. The *Wilts & Gloucester Standard* of 19th October 1861 referred to the need for towns such as Malmesbury and Tetbury to have rail service in order to revive their markets. However, less than a week later, this project was abandoned, for at a meeting to discuss the line held in Tetbury, the general opinion was that a through line was required.

The idea of a Dauntsey-Tetbury branch serving Malmesbury gave rise to a new scheme which was to occupy the horizons of Malmesburians for the next decade, arising from a meeting held in the White Hart Hotel in Tetbury on 8th November 1861, to discuss reviving the Chippenham-Stroud idea of the 1840s. The meeting was attended by Lord Suffolk, from Charlton Park, near Malmesbury, and also by T. Sotherton-Estcourt, MP for North Wilts. Mr. Richard Ward was engaged as civil engineer, and the MP contracted both the GWR and the Midland Railway on the subject of working the line. After his survey, Ward recommended that the through line run from Christian Malford on the GWR, via Malmesbury, Tetbury and Nailsworth, to a junction with the Midland at Stonehouse. The line was to be broad gauge from Christian Malford to Nailsworth, and mixed gauge from Nailsworth to Cainscross on the Midland.

Malmesbury from Holloway

Malmesbury seen from Blicks Hill. The building nearest the camera by the Cirencester Road is the old pump house which supplied water to the tower seen on the hilltop to the right of the church spire. To the right, enclosed by the hill, the river and the road, is the triangular field where the 1865 ceremony of the cutting of the first sod of the Wilts & Glos Railway took place.

Collection Tricia Fenton

However, although this scheme was public knowledge, no company had as yet been formed. During 1862, Mr. Sotherton-Estcourt suffered from ill-health, and, as he was such a dominant figure in the scheme, negotiating with the GWR, the business was postponed for a year. This delay prompted two rival schemes, both promoted by outside interests, under the erroneous impression that the plans for a through line had been abandoned. The first of these was a plan for a broad gauge branch from Dauntsey, which was to have left the main line near mile post 88 and run east of Dauntsey House (unlike the eventual line, which ran to the west of it), between the villages of Great Somerford and Little Somerford, terminating at Malmesbury where the turnpike road to Cirencester bridged the River Avon near the Duke of York public house. Deposited on 29th November 1862, the Bill came before Parliament in 1863, with James Burke listed as its engineer. Burke was also engineer to the Abingdon and Calne branches and the Wallingford and Watlington Railway. However, the scheme lacked support from both the GWR and the area it purported to serve, so there was therefore little hope of it being authorised, and it lapsed into oblivion.

A more mysterious infiltrator into the story in 1863 was the Gloucestershire & Wiltshire Railway, the initials of which could have caused some confusion in later railway history had it survived. This plan was submitted to Parliament on 30th November 1863. Again, the scheme was for a line emanating from the Midland, passing Malmesbury just north of the Duke of York Inn, and thence to Cowbridge Mill on a falling 1 in 100, eventually linking up with the GWR at Christian Malford. There is some doubt as to whether this line was intended to be broad or narrow gauge (while the broad gauge still existed, in the last century all lines built as what we know as the standard 4′ 8½″ gauge were called 'narrow gauge'), although it was reported in the *Wilts & Glos Standard* as being narrow. Again, it was a purely speculative effort without local interest, but its very existence raised an interesting question – who was backing it? The *Standard* reported that this scheme was supposedly under the auspices of the Midland Railway, but, more mysteriously, there was 'reason to believe this was

not the case'. The fact that the paper reported the line as a narrow gauge railway does tend to suggest that the Midland would have been involved, as they would have been less likely to want to have anything to do with a broad gauge scheme, but more interesting is a fact concerning the North & South Wiltshire Junction Railway of 1865. Much has been written about the Midland's attempts to infiltrate GWR territory in the 1860s, and it was precisely via the NWSJR that the Midland hoped to strike southwards towards Salisbury when the Wilts & Glos Railway project got under way. Significantly, both the NSWJR and the Gloucestershire & Wiltshire schemes employed a George Bruce as engineer, and the same London solicitor, Henry Carnsew. With the 1863 Glos & Wilts scheme, maybe the Midland were trying to sneak a narrow gauge line into Great Western country, keeping the NSWJR in the wings until such time as was desirable for their own ends?

Whatever the Midland's interest in this project, however, it was doomed to failure. An amended deposit of 1st March 1864 altered the course so that it was to run further eastwards from Great Somerford, but on 12th March the *Wilts & Glos Standard* reported that 'the rival Gloucestershire & Wiltshire Railway has been thrown out by the Lords' Committee on standing order'.

On 12th September 1863 a meeting was held in Malmesbury Town Hall to discuss the best route for the through line envisaged by the Wilts & Glos railway scheme. The broadcast intent of the project aimed to link the north and south of the country and place South Wales in connection with Southampton, running from the GWR at Christian Malford to the GWR at Stroud, with arrangements with the Great Western and the Midland companies for running powers over their lines, linking with the Midland at Stonehouse as an extension of the Stonehouse and Nailsworth Railway of 1863. The Midland, who had promoted the Nailsworth branch scheme, and maybe anticipating the failure of their Gl. & Wilts scheme in the Lords, gladly seized the opportunity and agreed to work the proposed new line as an extension of the Nailsworth line. From Christian Malford the route to Stroud was via Broad (Great) Somerford, Little Somerford, Rodbourne, Burton Hill, Malmesbury, Brokenborough, and thence to Long Newnton, Tetbury, Avening, Nailsworth, Dudbridge and Kings Stanley, with branches to the GWR at Stroud and the authorised line of the Stonehouse and Nailsworth Railway.

While the rival Gl. & W. scheme was being rejected by the Lords, the WGR Bill received its second reading, being finally sanctioned in the House of Commons on 21st June 1864. Since the depositing of the WGR plans, there had been negotiations with the GWR and the Midland with a view to constructing the line using both broad and narrow gauges, but it was unfortunately clear very early on that the intransigent and hostile attitude of the two major companies towards each other was going to hinder the progress to reality of the WGR. The intention was to construct a broad gauge route from one end to the other, and put in a mixed gauge if it was certain that the Midland would use it. It was originally intended that the narrow gauge would stop short at Malmesbury, but the GWR objected to any narrow gauge at all. A further speculation was to extend the East Gloucestershire line from Fairford to join the WGR at Malmesbury – known as the East Gloucestershire & Wiltshire Railway. This short-lived plan would have provided a link in the east-west communications of the GWR system that never did materialise. Involving land purchase mainly from the Earl of Suffolk & Berkshire's estate, and planned to form a triangular junction with the WGR at Brokenborough, north of Malmesbury, the line was granted by the Commons, but rejected by the Lords in 1865.

Despite the ominous portents of intractable problems ahead, all practical problems were forgotten in the euphoria of the cutting of the first sod of the WGR at Malmesbury on 1st July 1865. At least something tangible was happening to bring rail service to the town, and the townsfolk made the most of the occasion. Business was suspended and flags and bunting were everywhere in evidence. A vast procession formed in the Cross Hayes, including the Malmesbury Rifle Corps, children of various schools with their teachers, factory hands, and members of the Corporation, directors, contractors, shareholders and the Malmesbury Court of Ancient Order of Foresters. Flags and banners were carried, and the procession wound its way round into the High Street, then down Oxford Street and Holloway Hill to a triangular field near the Duke of York Inn on the Cirencester Road, the enclosure bounded on one side by the river, on another by the road, and the other by the steep hill on which the town is built.

After prayers to solemnize the occasion from the Reverend Canon Estcourt, and a speech from the WGR Chairman, Samuel Marling, Lady Suffolk was requested to turn the first sod. One of the contractors, Mr. Chambers, handed her the ceremonial spade, of a twisted oak handle mounted with silver, and she proceeded as requested, 'gracefully amidst cheers and music'. The spade and barrow were given to the Suffolk family, and are today preserved in the Athelstan Museum in the Town Hall. A sumptuous meal was provided for the occasion for up to 400 persons, in a marquee, complete with boar's head and wines supplied by Mr. Jones of the King's Arms Hotel. The half-yearly meeting of the WGR Board in August 1865 made mention of the ceremony, and stated that negotiations had been entered into for land

purchase, stating further that the draft of the agreement between the WGR and the Midland had been approved by the Boards of each company. Unfortunately, this agreement did not include the Great Western.

Although there had been an Amalgamation Act of 1863 between the GWR and the Midland, by which the latter had secured many advantages, the director of the Midland Railway, James Allport, was always most hostile towards the

The silver-mounted ceremonial spade and wheelbarrow used for the cutting of the first sod of the Wilts & Glos Railway, Malmesbury, 1st July 1865.   *Athelstan Museum*

Malmesbury High Street, lower end, looking south towards Chippenham in the 1890s.   *Collection Oliver Pike*

GWR, and whatever the Midland's involvement in the short-lived Glos & Wilts scheme, its participation in the WGR project was not only the way it saw to infiltrate GWR territory, but also to reach Salisbury, which they proposed to reach via the North & South Wilts Junction Railway to link up with the Berks & Hants Extension Railway (worked by the GWR) between Woodborough and Devizes, and the Wiltshire Railway across the Salisbury Plain to Porton on the LSWR, five miles east of Salisbury.

By February 1866, at the half-yearly meeting of the WGR in Malmesbury, the writing was really on the wall for this scheme, when the company's report was read by Mr. Charles Hart, the secretary, stating that the arrangements made for the execution of the works of the railway with the contractors, Messrs. Chambers and Wrigley, had been terminated owing to the unexpected (one finds it hard to believe that this was such a surprise) objection of the GWR to the WGR's Agreement with the Midland for working the line when completed. Dealings between the GWR and the Midland at Gloucester, where the two companies had separate stations, had never

been harmonious, and indeed it had been at Gloucester just over a decade previously where the initial death-knell of Brunel's broad gauge had been sounded, so it was highly unlikely that they should settle their differences over the questions of break of gauge and running powers through Malmesbury. Under the 1863 Act, complete accord was required between the two companies as to the construction, leasing, working and subscribing to of any new line necessary for giving proper accommodation to the districts in which they were both directly interested. Any difference of opinion was to be settled by arbitration. The GWR alleged that the agreement on the part of the Midland to work the new line was at variance with the spirit of the 1863 Act. An enquiry into the matter took place on 12th May 1866, under Captain Galton, who had been appointed arbitrator by the Board of Trade in pursuance of the Act. His decision, made public on 4th July, ruled against the Midland's right to work the line, and was a bitter deathblow to the WGR directors and to Malmesbury in particular, barely a year after the joyous and lavish ceremony of 1865. Many of Malmesbury's local dignitaries had put money into the scheme, and Jones & Forrester of Malmesbury had been solicitors for the 1864 Bill.

Despite the hopeless nature of the situation, the WGR saga dragged on for five more years. At the company meeting in Tetbury in February 1868, the chairman reported that there had been no progress in the state of affairs between the GWR and the Midland. He further added a significant comment, which does give food for thought, concerning the work that has often been believed was started on the project, saying that had they begun the work twelve months previously the position would be much worse, and that they 'should oppose commencing the works unless they could see the way clearly for finishing the line as far as it was proposed to extend it'.

Even more significantly, the Chairman, Mr. Marling, continued:

'It is most unfortunate that we should have gone to so large an expense and yet not be able to complete or even commence the scheme, which was simply impossible to do while there was such a state of things in the railway world.'

These comments tend to indicate that no work on the railway was actually started, that any such assumed work may simply have been confused with the turning of the first sod in 1865. A great deal of money was spent on the WGR scheme, certainly on surveying, planning, legal and Parliamentary fees, not to mention the revels of 1st July 1865. Previous belief that the tunnel, which still exists under Holloway Hill, was begun by the WGR and used by the later company during the construction of the branch, is probably ill-founded. No documentary proof has been found to substantiate WGR construction work of any kind, either in July 1865 or at any other time. It is often thought too that the position of the eventual Malmesbury station, beyond the town rather than short of it, could be explained by the town's projected situation on the through route of the WGR and the making use of a tunnel which already partly existed. Subsequent research has shown that the independent company which began building the Malmesbury branch in 1874 had no plans for a tunnel at Malmesbury, the engineer later re-routing the line and constructing the tunnel at the request of the GWR.

Meetings of the WGR in 1868 and 1869 discussed ways in which they might go ahead on their own means to build the line. Efforts were made to stimulate finance for the Nailsworth-Tetbury portion, but without success. Eventually, it was recognised that the only solution was to wind up the company's affairs, and further meetings of the WGR, held in Tetbury Town Hall, were short and rather depressing affairs, very thinly attended. Following the meeting of August 1870, an application was put in to the Board of Trade for a warrant of abandonment, the final meeting taking place in London on 28th February 1871, the petition for winding up being presented at the Court of Chancery in London on 17th March 1871, on which date the Wilts & Glos Railway ceased to exist.

'FOWLER'S LINE'
During the time the WGR project was taking shape, another scheme, with an east-west emphasis this time, was passing almost unnoticed. This was the South Wales & Great Western

Direct Railway, authorised in 1865, and known as 'Fowler's Line' after the GWR's consulting engineer. This was to have been a 41 mile, mixed gauge line, double track, from Wootton Bassett to Chepstow, bridging the Severn at Oldbury Sands. It was planned to run it via an overbridge over the authorised WGR line, and pass close to the southern edge of Malmesbury – the town is mentioned in the Act, and would probably have had a main line station. The scheme was not followed up even though the Bill was passed.

THE SOUTH MIDLAND RAILWAY
On 11th November 1871 a meeting was held at Gloucester to consider a new scheme which proposed to bridge the Severn and link the South Wales coalfields with Southampton. A large and influential attendance heard the promoters outline a plan from Lydney station along the GWR to Purton Passage, crossing the Severn via a bridge near Sharpness, progressing via Wotton-under-Edge to Malmesbury where there was to be a branch to Tetbury and Nailsworth. From Malmesbury the line was to continue eastwards to Wootton Bassett, Hungerford, Andover, thence to Southampton and London. Deposited in November 1871, the SMR Bill involved the construction of seven lines, an ambitious scheme which would have, therefore, placed Malmesbury as a junction. The actual junction was to have been in a meadow known as the 'Two Acre Field', belonging to one Daniel Beak. The plan to establish the branch to Nailsworth was to have involved land purchase from the author's wife's family, the Lockstones.

During December 1871 the promoters of the SMR were busy in Malmesbury trying to enlist support for their railway, but as this was yet another application to Parliament for a Bill involving a junction with the Midland Railway (at Nailsworth and Stroud), the visitors, hardly surprisingly, encountered feelings of apathy and not a little suspicion. Meetings were held in Malmesbury and Stroud, chaired by Samuel Marling, late of the ill-fated WGR. The Malmesbury meeting was addressed by corn dealer Joseph Reynolds of Gloucester, formerly of Burton Hill, Malmesbury. There was not a single landed proprietor present, and, although there was a general feeling of favour towards a through route if it were practicable, the experience with the WGR was too recent and too bitter for anyone to have any confidence of it ever being carried out.

By December 1871, also, the Malmesbury Railway project to give the town its own branch line, was being assembled with the support of all the leading dignitaries and landowners of the area, and bearing in mind the fate of the other through-line schemes, it is not surprising that the *Wilts & Glos Standard* commented:

'The people of Malmesbury prefer the bird-in-the-hand which is secured for them to the two-in-the-bush promised by the gentlemen from Southampton.'

Nor was it unexpected when the *Standard* of 20th January 1872 reported the withdrawal of the SMR project, stating that the Bill would not come before Parliament owing to lack of support. A pity, for had this scheme come to be, then it is highly possible that Malmesbury might still be on the railway map today, as Malmesbury Junction at that.

'This town, though it has nothing particularly engaging in itself, stands upon one of the prettiest spots that can be imagined . . . there is a pretty ridge of ground, the base of which is a mile to mile and a half wide. On each side of this ridge a branch of the River Avon runs down, through a flat of very fine meadows. The town and the beautiful remains of the famous old Abbey stand on the rounded spot which terminates this ridge . . . and just below, nearly close to the town, the two branches of the river meet, and then they begin to be called the Avon . . . the land round about the town is excellent and of a great variety of forms . . . (William Cobbett, Rural Rides, September 1826)

Collection Tricia Fenton

CHAPTER THREE

THE MALMESBURY RAILWAY COMPANY

FOLLOWING the final demise of the Wilts & Glos Railway in March 1871, determination was high that Malmesbury should have its own railway, and the first moves were made in London in the summer when Mr. James Grierson (GWR general manager 1866–87) met with Mr. W. S. Jones (of solicitors Jones & Forrester, Malmesbury) and Colonel Miles of Burton Hill, Malmesbury, to discuss a branch to the town from the Great Western at Dauntsey, where a station had opened in 1868. Financing the project was discussed, it being estimated that the line would cost £60,000, of which the GWR would subscribe half, the rest to be raised locally in Malmesbury and its neighbourhood, although Jones and Miles expressed the view that probably an amount around £14,000 was a reasonable estimate of the money Malmesbury could expect to find.

A preliminary meeting, summoned by circular, took place in Malmesbury Town Hall on 16th October 1871, and was attended by landowners through whose properties the line was projected, and many dignitaries and businessmen of the Malmesbury area. Chaired by Colonel Charles Miles, those present included Sir Walter Powell, MP, Sir Richard Hungerford-Pollen, Bart., the Rev. W. Andrews, agents acting on behalf of Lord Northwick, Lord Pembroke and the Earl of Carnarvon, Mr. Butt of Messrs. Davenport & Co. (silk manufacturers), Mr. W. S. Jones and Mr. C. F. Hart. Convened by Mr. Jones, who opened the business of the meeting, two resolutions were carried – the course of the railway was approved, although it was stated that the GWR proposal for working the line for 50% of the receipts should be more clearly defined, and a provisional committee was formed comprising Mr. T. D. Hill (chairman), Colonel Miles, Sir Hungerford-Pollen, Mr. W. Hollis Luce, Mr. Charles R. Luce and Mr. W. Panting, with power to add to their number if required. First official notice of the new company's application to Parliament for a Bill for 1872 appeared in the *Wiltshire and Gloucestershire Standard* of 11th November 1871, the first public meeting for the project taking place on 5th December following this announcement:

```
      Super-Mare.
      MALMESBURY RAILWAY.
  A PUBLIC MEETING will be held at the Town
      HALL, MALMESBURY, on TUESDAY NEXT, 5th
  December, in support of this undertaking.
      The Chair will be taken at Three o'clock in the
  Afternoon precisely.
      Malmesbury, 28th November, 1871.
```

There was a large and influential attendance at this meeting, the landowners, businessmen and dignitaries present including the Right Hon. T. H. Sotherton-Estcourt, former MP for North Wilts and for so long a champion of Malmesbury's railway cause. The chairman, Mr. Hill, reminded the meeting of the failure of previous schemes to connect Malmesbury with the railway network, but he stressed that the present idea of a branch from the Great Western had the support of that

company's board at Paddington, they having agreed to find half the capital and work the line for half the gross receipts. MP Walter Powell showed that Malmesbury's population had been at a standstill since 1861 (6,880 in the full Parliamentary Borough in 1871) and many locals spoke of the state of the town's market, which had once been very prosperous but had dwindled in importance because dealers had moved to places which had rail connection. The provision of rail service, it was felt, would give a great boost to trade in the town. One of the great benefits would be cheaper coal – at that time Radstock coal was coming into Malmesbury via Chippenham by horse and cart. With Colonel Miles emphasising the importance of GWR aid, and an enthusiastic address by Sotherton-Estcourt, the meeting unanimously decided to press ahead with the Dauntsey project, and the scheme's engineer, Richard Ward, was introduced to describe the line and the route that was envisaged.

Richard James Ward was born in Bristol in 1817. His background was impressive – in 1836 he had been articled for four years to I. K. Brunel himself at Paddington, and he had charge of the Thames bridges at Moulsford and Basildon, and the erection of Swindon locomotive shed. He was appointed resident engineer to the Oxford line of the GWR and later the Wilts, Somerset & Weymouth Railway. During work on the Berks & Hants Extension Railway he took over the post of chief engineer on the death of Brunel in 1859. Several GWR branches came under his supervision, including those at Marlborough, Aylesbury and Portland, and he was also involved in the construction of Clevedon Pier in 1868 and several water-works. After his appointment to the ill-fated Wilts & Glos project, his engagement to the Malmesbury Railway was his last in England – he died in May 1881 whilst working on the Wexford & Rosslare Railway in Ireland.

Describing his projected route, Mr. Ward explained that it was to pass over flat land near Dauntsey House, between the villages of Great Somerford and Little Somerford and thence to Cowbridge, from there it would follow the River Avon to the Cirencester Road, between the Duke of York public house and the pumping station. The *Wiltshire Gazette & Herald*, in describing the meeting, stated that:

'The line traces the course of the river to a portion of the Tetbury Road, which point was selected for termination because it is a place where a station could be cheaply made.'

The site chosen afforded the largest expanse of flat land suitable for a station and yard in the town, and the newspaper also alluded to the site's proximity to Tetbury, where residents of that town would be brought four miles closer to a railway than previously (the branch from Kemble to Tetbury was not opened until 1889). The view was expressed that for people on the Burton Hill side of town the terminal station in Westport would not be so convenient, so it was suggested that the GWR agree to a small stopping place with a siding for coal close by Winniatt's Mill, but this never materialised as a result of a later re-routing of the line at this point, with the consequence that representations for an extra station close to Malmesbury

Malmesbury High Street, looking north in the early 1880s. The Abbey appears to form a stone curtain across the end of the street behind the Market Cross. The horse-bus is waiting outside the Kings Arms, the main commercial hotel of the town, where several of the Malmesbury Railway Company meetings took place.
Collection Oliver Pike

were to centre on Cowbridge. Reference was also made on this occasion to the South Midland Railway proposed by interests from Southampton, but by this time everybody was firmly against a through route in the light of previous bitter and expensive experience. The meeting closed with a greater feeling of optimism than had been present in Malmesbury for many years.

The following week, the Malmesbury Railway's prospectus appeared in the *Wiltshire & Glos Standard* for the first time, inviting the public to purchase £10 shares upon which shareholders were 'certain of a minimum dividend of $2\frac{1}{2}$%'! Such optimism so late in the last century seems incredible now, and gave no indication of the six years of troubles that lay ahead for the new company.

At the 73rd half-yearly meeting of the GWR Board of Directors at Paddington on 28th February 1872, the GWR chairman, Sir Daniel Gooch, averted to the proposed Malmesbury line and expressed the view that the Malmesbury district had been somewhat ill-used by both his and the Midland companies. Because of the 1863 agreement, neither his company nor the Midland could work such a through line as had then been proposed, and a great deal of local money had been lost on the venture, but with the new branch scheme the Midland were not involved. Sir Daniel further remarked that the revenue from the new line would not be large, but the branch would connect a large country town with their

MALMESBURY RAILWAY.

CAPITAL £60,000, IN 6,000 SHARES OF £10 EACH.

Deposit 10s. per Share, to be Paid on Application.

Provisional Committee.

THOMAS DANIEL HILL, Esq , 30, Grosvenor Place, and 4, Mincing Lane, London, *Chairman.*

SIR RICHARD HUNGERFORD POLLEN, Bart , Rodbourne, Malmesbury.

CHARLES WILLIAM MILES, Esq., Burton Hill, Malmesbury.

WALTER POWELL, Esq., M.P., Dauntsey House, Malmesbury.

WILLIAM HOLLIS LUCE, Esq., Burton Hill, Malmesbury.

CHARLES RICHARD LUCE, Esq., Halcombes, Malmesbury.

WILLIAM PANTING, Esq., Auctioneer and Estate Agent, Malmesbury.

Banker.

THE WILTS AND DORSET BANK, Malmesbury.

Engineer.

R. J. WARD, 11, Great Queen Street, Westminster.

Solicitors.

JONES and FORRESTER, Malmesbury.

Secretary.

CHARLES F. HART (Berks and Hants Extension Railway), Devizes.

PROSPECTUS.

THE Malmesbury Railway Company is intended to be incorporated for the purpose of constructing a Railway from the Dauntsey Station, on the Main Line of the Great Western Railway, to Malmesbury,

main line, and he authorised the necessary capital for the scheme to go ahead.

During February 1872 another important development was taking place along the main line through Dauntsey, as the GWR route here was being converted from broad to mixed gauge, although not for another 20 years did the broad gauge finally disappear from the GWR system. On 17th February 1873 the GWR secretary, Mr. Saunders, wrote to the Malmesbury Railway Company concerning the question of gauge:

'No decision has yet been come to as to the alteration of the gauge on the lines of this Company west and south-west of Swindon, but assuming that the purchase of the land is the matter upon which action must first be taken I am authorised to say that my Board concurs in the course which it is understood your Directors propose to take of purchasing the land of sufficient width for a double narrow gauge line – this will of course admit either of a double line of narrow gauge or of a single line of Broad gauge being laid in the first instance as circumstances may render most expedient.'

At a meeting of shareholders in the 'King's Arms' in Malmesbury in March 1873, Richard Ward recommended the use of the narrow gauge and this was accepted. It should be remembered that at this time, with both gauges still in use on the GWR, the term 'narrow' refers to the now standard gauge of 4 ft $8\frac{1}{2}$ ins.

Malmesbury Railway Company seal.
(Great Western Railway Magazine)

Following its second reading in the House of Commons on 6th March 1872, the Malmesbury Railway Bill went before the Lords' Committee on 3rd July. The only question for consideration related to the level crossings on the proposed line at Dauntsey and Somerford. They were to be allowed on condition that the company were to provide a subway ten feet wide and seven feet high under the railway at Somerford – this was to allow farmers to continue cattle driving at this point when the crossing gates were shut across the road. The undertaking was well and truly under way when the Bill received the Royal Assent and was incorporated by an Act of 25th July 1872, which authorised the Malmesbury Railway Company to construct a branch railway '. . . six miles and four furlongs in length, commencing by a junction with the Great Western Railway, near the Dauntsey Station of that railway, and terminating in a meadow in the parish of Malmesbury the Abbey . . .'. The capital was an authorised £60,000 in 6,000 shares of £10 each. As the MRC doubted that as much as half of this could be raised locally, it was agreed with the GWR that the MRC would borrow £5,000 in debenture loans at their own expense, and also capitalise the rent charges for which land was bought, thus raising another £6,000 and

thereby leaving £19,000 to be raised in the Malmesbury area. At the first meeting of shareholders in Malmesbury Town Hall on 21st October 1872, it was reported that sanction had been obtained from Parliament to the agreement between the MRC and GWR for the maintenance, working and use of the line, and the subscribing of £30,000 by the GWR towards the building of the branch was confirmed. Charles F. Hart was confirmed as secretary for the Malmesbury Railway Company, based at his Devizes office from where he had for several years been employed in a similar capacity to the Berks & Hants Extension Railway, and local firm Jones & Forrester of Malmesbury were to be solicitors to the company. The MRC office in Malmesbury was located in a building dating from the turn of the 19th century in St. Dennis Lane, between the Cross Hayes and the High Street, later the printing works of J. T. Bird.

Despite the encouragement of receiving its Act, and depite Malmesbury and environs being a prosperous area of landed gentry and an affluent agricultural economy, the subscription list for shares in the new line made slow progress. In March 1873 concern was expressed at the slow start, and it appears that there was apparent GWR countenance for agitation for a line between Tetbury and Kemble. This had a serious effect on the Malmesbury share issue as people had backed off to reserve their support for the Tetbury project. The MRC sent a letter to Paddington pointing this out, and the GWR agreed to increase the debenture loans from £5,000 to £12,000 if it should prove necessary. During February and March, MRC engineers were seen at work staking out the course of the line, but successful completion of this work was hindered by slowness in agreements for some of the land purchase, with the result that autumn was the earliest possible time when the work of building the line could be put out to tender.

In March 1873, the GWR asked Richard Ward to make a substantial deviation from the original plans of the railway, in order to provide a more direct course with better gradients. Having undertaken to work the branch when completed, they were clearly worried about the line following the course of the river so closely from Cowbridge, as the Avon had a known tendency to flooding in this area. The original plans of the railway and Clause 23 of the Malmesbury Railway Act show clearly that it was to have approached the town close to the river all the way from Cowbridge, crossing both a branch of the river and the main road to Cirencester on a bridge of fifteen feet in height. In order for the line to skirt Holloway Hill and at the same time maintain a reasonable height above the river, a large S-curve would have been necessary, as well as substantial embankments on a line already planned to be heavily earthworked. An important consideration was the avoiding of extra expense on land purchase by keeping the couse of the railway within the original limit of deviation, something Ward had to bear in mind when revising the route.

After Ward had surveyed the alternatives, he re-routed the course by moving it further northwards from Cowbridge House and the river, thus avoiding the easily-flooded meadows of Lea fields and Baskerville, then straightened it by planning a deep cutting through Baskerville Hill, crossing two channels of the Avon via bridges numbered 33 and 34, with a tunnel through Holloway Hill to take the line through to the terminus via yet another bridge, No. 36, across the river. Ward's Bill of Quantities for the tunnel was produced in April 1873, showing a 105 yard tunnel with specific references to brickwork, recesses and drainage, with 4,760 cubic yards of earth to be excavated, which, when added to the 29,800 to be taken from the cutting at Baskerville, would provide useful spoil for keeping the railway above the floor plain, the 49 chain embankment in the Lea fields alone requiring 21,240 c. yards of earth. Ward's amended plans produced a falling gradient of 1 in 410 from Baskerville to the edge of the station yard at Malmesbury, thereby producing a more direct and less steeply-graded route for the GWR to work, although, in so doing, the original costing of the construction was going to be affected, causing conflict with the contractors and contributing towards serious financial difficulties for the company, as we shall see.

During the autumn of 1873, upon completion of the permanent survey and land plans, tenders for the work of building the line were obtained from five contractors. A firm based in Westminster, Budd & Holt, came just inside Ward's estimate of £40,000 with a figure of £39,960, but before a contract could be awarded there was still concern over the share issue. In September 1874 the MRC directors assured shareholders:

> 'The deficiency in the amount of Subscriptions must be made up before the line can be commenced. Your Directors do not entertain any doubt that Malmesbury and the district will provide the further sums required.'

By January 1874, the shares totally £18,000, leaving the MRC still £1,000 short of its revised target, but in February the directors themselves, setting a good example, agreed to take ten shares each, and with the engineer, secretary and solicitors each promising to subscribe, the deficit was reduced to £170. The directors now felt safe in signing the undertaking to build the line, and this was duly done on 26th February 1874, Budd & Holt being awarded the contract on 24th March at a meeting in the Malmesbury office of Jones & Forrester

at which they were present with the directors. Budd & Holt's contract was confirmed on 20th May, they agreeing to receive shares as 5% payment, and the stage was set for constructing the line.

With the initial financial crisis over, however, money was still in short supply for a project which it was clear was going to cost well above its original estimate. Many shares had been taken out with 10 shilling deposits, so on 20th May, at a meeting of directors at the Great Western Hotel, Paddington, it was decided that for purchase of land and construction of works a call upon all the shareholders of £2 per share should be made – this was duly implemented, and by 19th June had produced £10,226.

Unlike the Wilts & Glos Railway, when much money had been lavished upon the ceremony for the cutting of the first sod, only to see the scheme come to nothing, there was no glittering social occasion recorded to herald the coming of the Malmesbury Railway. A hard lesson had been learned, the money gained for the new project had not been easily found, and people preferred to save celebrations for when the trains became a reality. Work finally began on the new railway on Wednesday, 8th July, 1874, at Cowbridge, where some forty navvies diverted a tiny loop of the Avon, which involved digging a cutting about 50 yards long, in order to save the expense of putting in two bridges within this distance. The work was completed by the 17th, by which time similar attention was being given to the drainage at the terminus site in Westport. Here the Inglebourne was widened several feet in order to dispense with a backstream which intervened between the river and railway route, thus averting a possible large flux of water onto the site in the rainy season. Even if these activities were somewhat prosaic in the context of railway engineering, they still drew many interested spectators, who no doubt found it hard to believe that their long-awaited

Malmesbury Railway Company share certificate issued to Charlton schoolmaster Bradley Bartlett.
Athelstan Museum

Burton Hill House, Malmesbury.

Burton Hill House, Malmesbury, home of Col. C. W. Miles, one of the Directors of the Malmesbury Railway Company.
Collection Robin Littlewood

railway was about to materialise! However, an early problem arose over this work, as an ominous foretaste of the acrimony to come, when Richard Ward decided that the contractors' estimate of £213 for widening the mill dam in Westport was far too high. The work was sub-contracted to a Mr. Middleton for £45, and the job was done with no apparent lack of quality. Thus were the seeds of bad feeling between engineer and contractors sown.

In July 1874 contractor Holt informed the GWR Board that work would soon start on Ward's projected tunnel. On the 18th the *Wilts & Glos Standard* reported enthusiastically: 'We hear that the tunnelling at Holloway will shortly commence'. However, by the end of August, nothing had happened. If there was great pride in Malmesbury at the thought of having the only tunnel between Malmesbury and Paddington, it is quite likely, although no recorded evidence has been found, that Budd & Holt were less than enthusiastic about it. Over what such a discord centred is not clear, although no doubt the contractors still resented the incident of the mill stream damming, but it may be that the contractors were trying to save money by building a cutting though Holloway rather than boring a tunnel. They claimed, with some justification, that mixed gauge work on the main line had hindered the delivery of their plant, a great deal of which was purchased from the construction of the Somerset & Dorset Railway's Bath line. Budd & Holt needed the equipment to start on the heavier portions of the work near Malmesbury, but much of it did not arrive at Dauntsey until September 1874, along with vast quantities of fencing and other materials. Such delay was costing both contractors and MRC a great deal of money. Ward's Engineer's Report of 10th September referred to little other work being accomplished than the drainage modifications mentioned and the arrival of the fencing, the first of several depressing progress reports he was to make during the next three years. The shareholders meeting at Malmesbury Town Hall on 21st September was informed that the line would be ready for traffic in 16 months.

In September 1874, with funds again dwindling and more cash needed to pay for land and works, the Directors proposed: 'That a Second Call of £2 per Share be made upon the respective Shareholders of the Company, payable at the Malmesbury Branch of the Wilts & Dorset Banking Company on Monday 19th October, 1874.' The well-preserved volumes

of the Malmesbury Railway Company, bound in maroon covers with golden-imprinted letters, record that by December this appeal had yielded £18,514.

The navvies who built the Malmesbury branch do not appear to have brought with them the reigns of terror and debauchery which they inflicted on other areas in the history of railway construction. Misdemeanours were, it seems, only minor, and some emerged as heroes. On 10th September 1874, whilst in charge of a team hauling a wagon of two tons of railway metals from Chippenham to Dauntsey, an excavator named Taylor, a huge man formerly employed on the Midland Railway, was called upon to perform a great feat of strength when a lynch pin came out and a wheel came off the wagon. Taylor laid on his back and lifted the load with his legs so that nearby workmen could slip the wheel back on when the axle was raised high enough.

On 14th November 1874, the Market Committee met in the King's Arms to discuss changing the day on which the market was held each month, but the matter was postponed as it was decided to wait until after the railway had opened.

Meanwhile, back at the tunnel site, after some disagreement over procedure, Ward allowed the contractors to attempt to drive an open cutting through Holloway Hill. Referred to in the *Wilts & Glos Standard* of 17th October 1874, as 'The Great Cutting at Holloway', it was intended to be more than 40 feet in depth, but how much of it was accomplished as a cutting is uncertain. On 26th December 1874, the *Standard* reported:

"Messrs Budd and Holt are vigorously pushing on with the line. At several points the road is nearly ready for laying of the metals. Vast quantities of materials and concrete for the base work of several bridges across the Avon are in course of preparation. When the two great cuttings at Holloway and Baskerville's Hill are completed, it will be but a matter of time before we shall have our first sniff of the breath of the 'iron horse.'"

Trouble again reared its head over sub-contracting in December. A George Chapman had agreed to execute certain works for Budd & Holt, this·without the knowledge of either Ward or the MRC, and had also undertaken certain works in addition. An action was brought against Chapman by the contractors for not fulfilling contractual obligations. The case was referred to arbitration and was heard in the King's Arms Hotel in Malmesbury on 19th December and though faults were found on both sides, Budd and Holt were awarded £24 4s 9d owing from Chapman. Although this was a relatively minor difficulty, the direct result of this was that in January 1875 the GWR exercised its right to bring in their own nominees on the MRC Board. Two GWR Directors, Sir C. Alexander Wood and John W. Miles, Esq., joined the little company's board in an effort to ensure that all subsequent transactions of the MRC were under the direct supervision of the Great Western Railway.

On 28th January 1875, a serious accident befell Thomas Hitching, an excavator, who was wheeling a barrow of stones along a narrow plank serving as a temporary bridge, 14 feet high above a brook at Holloway, for the purpose of filling up a hollow between two streams. Slipping, he sustained a bad injury to the head and was taken to a local doctor who removed a piece of his skull. Dr. C. W. Pitt, the appointed surgeon to the line, attended the injured man daily, and a week afterwards Hitching was reported as recovering.

Some of Malmesbury's railway builders with their 'coffee-pot' engine seen during construction in 1875. Who was the smartly dressed boy seen standing behind the horse?
Collection D. Garnett

On 30th January, at some depth below the surface, the jawbone of a man, with teeth perfectly preserved, was found in a garden at Holloway. During the same period, two navvies found themselves in court – John Hooper was convicted in February of cruelly beating a horse near the Duke of York, and one John Oatley of Melksham was convicted of shirt stealing in March. Later in the year, the only other reported indiscretion of a Malmesbury railway navvy occurred when two men were charged with stealing money from the Great Somerford shopkeeper with whom they were lodging, having made their situation rather worse by giving false names when first apprehended.

Richard Ward's Engineer's Report, presented at the 5th half-yearly meeting of the MRC in March 1875, stated rather pedantically that whereas the line should be half complete, only four-ninths was done! Rails had been delivered sufficient for $4\frac{1}{2}$ miles of single track, but the supply of stone, gravel and sleepers for the permanent way was far less. He admitted that progress had been slowed by some severe winter weather which at times had halted the work completely, and also by the dispute over Mr. Chapman. Far from the optimism of the *Standard's* December report, it was still nearly three years before Malmesbury would have its 'first sniff of the breath of the iron horse'.

On 23rd March 1875, a dreadful accident befell one of the navvies, Bill Ponting. A week previously, he had been a hero when he rescued a local girl, Mary Box, from drowning near where he was working. On the 23rd, whilst working in Baskerville Cutting, he jumped off a loaded truck while it was moving and fell under the wheels. Dr. Pitt was summoned to the scene and found it necessary to amputate Ponting's right arm. With the left arm badly broken in two places, his left thumb gone, and with head, chest and face severely bruised, he was not expected to survive. However, survive he did, taking the job of gateman at Kingsmead Crossing when the line opened and remaining there until his death in 1920. In

June 1876 he married the girl he had rescued a week previous to his accident!

As only one-third of the masonry work was complete by March 1875, instead of the expected two-thirds, Budd & Holt incurred a penalty of £500. An indication of the worsening relations between the railway company and the contractors was contained in a Report at the Meeting of Directors on 22nd May at the office of Jones & Forrester, in which the Board proposed to give notice that: 'In the event of non-performance of the quantity of work expected to be done, the Company may be in a position to take the works into their own hands.'

Ward's chief complaint at the contractors' slow progress was mainly in respect of Cutting No. 17, that at Baskerville. No doubt there was still some bad feeling over the disagreement concerning Holloway Hill, but if that still rankled, he regarded Baskerville as very much the 'key to the work', and was angry at the wasted time over its construction, seeing its excavation taking ten months at the current rate of progress.

In March 1875, with a seat on the MRC Board becoming vacant upon the standing down of Mr. William Luce, the GWR took the opportunity to bring in a third representative of their own, F. N. Micklethwaite, Esq., giving the GWR 50% representation on the Malmesbury Board. This was a very typical situation where a large railway company was overseeing small concerns with financial and other difficulties, usually being the first steps towards complete take-over.

The newspapers and MRC Minutes are silent on the subject of the work at Holloway during the first months of 1875, but in May the *Wilts & Glos Standard* reported that the contractors had abandoned the idea of making an open cutting through Holloway Hill and had commenced tunnelling. It is not known for certain why Ward's tunnel was re-adopted as the best means of taking the line through Holloway Hill, but the following are possible reasons:

1. The plan to dig a cutting may have proved difficult in view of the proximity of the remains of the old town walls. On this hilltop location landslips could have caused problems with the old foundations.
2. Outcry from inhabitants about the spoliation of valuable garden property by a cutting as large as was needed.
3. Possible objections to smoke rising from passing locomotives in a cutting, local gentry preferring engines to pass more discreetly in a tunnel, as in the case of the 'roofed-in' tunnel at Kemble on the GWR ten miles away.
4. Land purchase difficulties with owner of Abbey House above the tunnel.

In any event the cutting never came about, but the tunnel did, and still survives in Malmesbury today. As digging operations on the cutting had been directed at opposite bases of the hill on each side, it is clear that the eventual tunnel was constructed shorter than the one Ward had first intended.

During June and July, several factors conspired against the contractors to hinder progress. A wet summer produced a great deal of flooding, and whilst this provided useful information as to the requirements and levels of waterways and ballasting, it was also very costly in terms of wasted time and effort and damage done. Mr. Mackenzie, the contractors' site engineer, was ill and absent from work for a time, and Budd & Holt also brought a case to court against four local lads who had caused damage on the railway workings at Somerford. On 16th July, the one fatality which occurred during the railway's construction took place – a donkey was crossing the tracks (unknown to its excavator owner) at the mouth of Baskerville cutting, and was killed by a ballast engine emerging from the cutting with four loaded trucks.

Although only one intermediate station was ever built on the branch, that at Great Somerford, another was planned and some work actually carried out on it. Mention has been made of the early suggested station at Winniatt's (Wynyard's) Mill, but nothing ever came of this owing to the re-routing of the line, thus rendering a station impractical in that locality. Attention then switched to a site at Cowbridge, where the branch passed under the Swindon road. Earthworks were carried out here in the cutting just south of the road bridge in June and July of 1875, costing £140. The intended station was to have been named Burton Hill, somewhat inappropriate in view of the site being at Cowbridge, nearly a mile from Burton Hill, but possibly explained by the fact that two of the Directors lived at Burton Hill! There were three mills at Cowbridge which would have put a large volume of traffic on the line, but, despite the prevalent feeling amongst shareholders that the station had been promised, it was never built. With the MRC in financial difficulties, there was never going to be enough money to complete the station, and even the station at Somerford was incomplete when the line eventually opened. Predictably, response to the share issue had been low in the Somerford and Cowbridge areas, and this may also have been a factor in the non-appearance of Burton Hill station. Even today, the fencing contractor's yard adjacent to the site of the projected station has the air about it of a station yard and approach that never came to be.

The same group and engine, with wagons of hard core. Again, the young boy with boater (see text, page 26). *Collection Oliver Pike*

The Volunteer public house, Great Somerford, one of the calling points of pre-railway horse-omnibus services.   *Courtesy Mrs. F. Bubb*

In July 1875 a separate contract was made with Budd & Holt for excavation of the station ground at Malmesbury, a necessary job if the Bristol firm of Brock & Bruce were to go ahead with the station buildings, a contract awarded them in July at a costing to the MRC for the station of £3,248 15s.0d. Cowbridge (Burton Hill) had also been included in Brock & Bruce's contract, but, as we have seen, the site never saw any more than the tentative earthworks accomplished by Budd & Holt.

During the summer of 1875 work progressed on the tunnel. On 29th June one John King of Chepstow, a 'miner', as tunnel excavators were known, suffered a broken leg when a large stone, under which he was digging, fell on him. He was carried to the sustaining atmosphere of the Duke of York public house nearby, where Dr. Pitt attended to him. On 5th August the tunnel was at last pierced through, the men from each side shaking hands through the hole. The chief of the gang, Henry Haden, sent his son through first, then the whole group passed through as the aperture widened, all repairing immediately to the Duke of York for a celebration beer! Apart from the broken leg, the only other injury sustained in the building of the tunnel occurred three weeks later, when Mr. Whiting, the tunnel masonry contractor, was assisting one of his men in fitting a $1\frac{1}{2}$cwt stone into the crown of an arch. Whiting slipped and fell across a beam, dislocating two ribs and suffering severe bruising to a hand as a result of the stone falling on it. However, he remained at work. This accident happened at midnight, at a time when both miners and masons were working through the night to speed up the work. The tunnel was finally completed on 17th October 1875, with the last keystone being put in place at the Malmesbury end. The day after, two of the tunnel navvies earned a town's gratitude when they were interrupted from the job of clearing the site at the Baskerville end of the tunnel by the sound of boys playing on the line. One of the boys fell into the river but the two workmen both went in after him and rescued him from drowning.

Sometime during late summer in 1875 a group of Budd & Holt's workmen were photographed on the line with a 'coffee-pot' engine, a small vertical-boilered locomotive used for hauling sleepers and hard core to required sites. Two photographs of this group are known to have survived, and both are curious in that each is dominated by a bearded man on the footplate bearing an anonymous insignia on a beret, this man possibly being the contractors' site engineer, Mr. Mackenzie. Also present on each photo is an incongruously smartly-dressed boy of about eight or nine wearing a boater. Major-General Sir Richard Luce (1867–1952), in his book *The History of the Abbey and Town of Malmesbury*, recalled how the railway was brought to Malmesbury 'after considerable financial difficulties in 1877'. As a small boy he remembered climbing through the narrow passage formed when the tunnel under Holloway was first pierced. It is highly likely that the boy in the group of navvies is Richard Luce, he perhaps even being the reason for the photo being taken, to depict a child of local aristocracy with the railway builders.

Ward's Report to the Board sounded more promising in August, when he described the heavier portions of the line as virtually complete, as also were the junction works and signals at Dauntsey. He pointed out that he had drawn the contractors' attention to various points concerning the summer flood damage to the workings, involving repair work which was provided for in their contract. October saw good progress, with the cuttings at Baskerville and Harding's Hill (between Cowbridge and Kingsmead) being completed, and the permanent way being finished from Dauntsey to Baskerville. Financially, however, the situation did not look good, as figures presented at the September Directors Meeting showed the total cost of completing the line to be £71,886 if the stations at Somerford and Cowbridge were included. Clearly the line was going to cost an amount way beyond its original estimate, and the Malmesbury Railway Company now sought more capital, exercising its borrowing powers to the tune of £14,500 from the GWR.

At the beginning of November, Ward maintained 'three months to complete'. With the tunnel and major cuttings finished, things looked better when in the first week of November iron girders were brought along the line for completion of the last three river bridges. There had been some delay to this work because of flooding, but the two bridges between Baskerville and the tunnel were completed by the 10th. Unfortunately, things took a turn for the worse on the weekend of the 11/12th, when heavy continuous rain made the workings a muddy morass and delayed completion of the final bridge, the 60 ft span on the Inglebourne just outside Malmesbury terminus, the largest span on the line. The resulting floods did substantial damage elsewhere, notably at Kingsmead and Dauntsey, where large amounts of ballast were washed away, leaving nothing but the tracks. The situation worsened with more wet weather towards the end of 1875, causing flooding which seriously damaged the works at Malmesbury and Cowbridge, but it was felt that all repairs should be done by Budd & Holt within the terms of the contract. In January 1876 the cutting at Cowbridge was widened ready for the station there, but this was the last work accomplished in respect of Burton Hill station. Further flooding at Kingsmead in February was followed by a complaint from the contractors regarding insufficient payments, despite an advance of £500 from the MRC to cover this damage. Bad feeling increased when Budd & Holt's men removed some wagons from the works without having received Ward's authority to do so.

In January 1876 John Evans, a carpenter employed by Brock & Bruce on the work at Malmesbury station, suffered compound fractures of the thigh and serious internal injuries when he fell from the scaffolding in wet, foggy conditions. This was also a sad month for those who had worked for many years to bring the railway to Malmesbury, as the death occurred of T. Sotherton-Estcourt, former MP for the area and long-time champion of the railway cause. He therefore did not see the line become a reality, as opening was still almost two years away.

The year continued to be a bad one for progress on the branch. The damage caused to the workings by the weather, and disagreements between contractors and engineer over standard of work and general progress, culminated in Budd & Holt filing a claim against the Malmesbury Railway Company for £5,000 for alleged extra works in February 1876. The contractors detailed this claim as being for 'delays and impediment occasioned by default of the Company, the line being laid out below flood level [this a clear condemnation of Ward's plans], non-payment of money on Engineer's certificate, ordering of extra works, salaries of staff, cost of horses for haulage, depreciation of plant and rent of offices and stables'. This included a claim that works on Contract No. 1 were paying them £500 less than they were entitled to. Without Ward's authorisation, alterations had been made to the wings of three bridges, for which £100 was being claimed. A retaining wall had been put in at the south end of Malmesbury tunnel, costing £223 and still there today – the MRC deemed this unnecessary, and so it would have been, Ward claimed, had Budd & Holt proceeded with the tunnel from the very beginning. The contractors' claims were resisted by the MRC, and they brought a counter claim against Budd & Holt, but this injunction was dissolved by the Master of the Rolls on 10th February, costs being awarded against the railway company to the tune of £200. By this stage, work had ceased altogether, a particularly frustrating state of affairs for the MRC and the people of Malmesbury, as their railway was almost complete, with all bridges and track being in position.

In March 1876 the Report of the Malmesbury Railway Company informed its shareholders:

Your Directors greatly regret that the contractors have not proceeded with the completion of the line in a manner that has been either satisfactory to them, or in accordance with the time obligations of their Contract, but they forbear to remark further on this subject, as arrangements have now been made under which the contractors have pledged themselves to proceed with the Works as quickly as possible. A claim for some alleged Extra Works, amounting to nearly £5,000, has been made upon the Company by Messrs Budd & Holt, which your Directors, after due deliberation, have felt in the protection of your interests, bound to resist. The Contract provides for the adjustment of such differences by an appeal to an Arbitrator, and under its authority the Contractors have made such appeal. Mr Gregory, the Arbitrator agreed upon, has partly heard the evidence of Messrs Budd & Holt, and has yet to hear the case of the Company on the several items of claim, and your Board await his decision, believing that his award will justify the course they have taken.

The Engineer's Report on 29th March, 1876, ran as follows:

ENGINEER'S REPORT.

8, Queen Anne's Gate, Westminster, S.W., 29th March, 1876.

To the Directors of the Malmesbury Railway Company.

GENTLEMEN,—

The progress of the Works undertaken by Messrs Budd and Holt has been exceedingly small during the half-year. At present, and for the past two months they have been practically suspended.

The Contractors have justified their delay on the grounds that the Company declined to make them advances on Claims which are at present, as you are aware, under the consideration of the Arbitrator, but an arrangement has been lately arrived at, which will, it is hoped, provide for their proceeding at once with, and completing the Work.

The Contract for the Station Building at Malmesbury is being satisfactorily executed.

The Passenger Building and Engine House are roofed in. The Goods Shed walls are up to the level of the wall plate.

I have the honour to remain,

Your obedient Servant,
R. J. WARD.

Budd & Holt's claim upon the MRC came up before the Arbitrator, Mr. Charles Gregory, in London on 29th April who decided in favour of a payment of a compromise amount of £3,000 to the contractors, of which £1,000 was to be advanced immediately on condition that they proceeded with the works forthwith. Ward about this time asked the GWR for an independent engineer to assess the cost of completing the railway. He was worried now by the financial difficulties of the MRC, as they were behind on their payments to him. Work on the line resumed in May, priority being given to the raising of the line above flood level in the meadows near Dauntsey, where much damage had been done to the ballasting by the flooding of the previous November. Expected work on the crossing lodges had not started, though, and Ward complained that the contractors were 'proceeding in a manner almost defiant'. Fortunately, as reflected in Ward's March Report, the work on the buildings at Malmesbury was going well, being under the separate contract with Brock & Bruce. Payments were made in April to the Bristol firm for their work on the station and the river bank at Malmesbury, and Budd & Holt duly received their money awarded in the Arbitration, leaving the MRC's account overdrawn by £1,379. However, by this time, the GWR had given assent to further borrowing of £9,500 in debenture loans, which arrived in the MRC account in time to satisfy the company's bankers.

In June 1876 the costing requested by Ward, and a fixing of the amount of work due to be undertaken by the contractors, was received from the GWR's Engineer, Mr. Lancaster Owen, son of William Owen, the GWR's Chief Engineer from 1868–85. £19,472 was still required to meet the MRC liabilities and complete the line. The GWR Minutes of 8th June stated:

'Having regard to the liability already incurred by the Malmesbury Railway Company, the Board authorises arrangements to be made for providing through the agency of this company the amount which may be required to secure the completion of the line, either by taking up Lloyds Bonds by way of security, or in such other manner as may be thought expedient, but only on condition that all payments may be entirely under the control of the Directors of the Great Western Railway Company, and be carried out by officers named by them.'

At this time there was also the first hint of the later absorption of the MRC by the GWR:

'The Board however would prefer that an arrangement be entered into by which the undertaking of the Malmesbury Company should become vested in the Great Western Company.'

In June a further problem arose from an unexpected quarter when a Captain Wiltshire of the 3rd Wiltshire Rifle Volunteer Corps complained to the MRC that railway construction at Cowbridge had destroyed their shooting range so that ranges up to only 600 yards could be used. The Captain asked that the company should restore the long range and provide an additional 1st Class target for the Corps, obtainable second-hand for £6. The MRC Board were unable to agree to this, however, as restoration of the long range would involve shooting across the railway!

At an Extraordinary General Meeting of the GWR Board of Directors at Paddington on 6th July 1876, an Agreement was submitted for £19,000 to complete the line. Ward's position as Engineer had to be considered, as the Agreement was intended to give the GWR complete control of the expenditure of the money they provided, and therefore their own engineer

had to be in charge, but Ward had indicated that although he was prepared to work with the GWR Engineer, he was not prepared to work under him. It was diplomatically decided to keep Ward on to work with Lancaster Owen as Joint Engineers, with Owen in charge of the works but without Ward having to relinquish his position as MRC Engineer. With the resignation of one of the GWR representatives from the MRC Board, John W. Miles, the Paddington Board used the opportunity to replace him with Captain Thomas Bulkeley, who had been on the boards of several other minor railway companies in which the GWR had a vested interest, being very much their 'troubleshooter' where such railway problems were concerned.

On 19th July, the organisers of Malmesbury market, Messrs. Goulter and Rich, went ahead with their proposed switch to a Wednesday market, no doubt very impatient at the delay over the railway. It was a very successful occasion, the spacious cattle market in the Cross Hayes being full. Free conveyance was put on between Malmesbury and the GWR's Chippenham station for all who required it. With the railway being built, the market now promised to prosper as of old, and the opening of the branch was eagerly awaited, although it is probably true to say that the change of day had a greater and more lasting effect on the state of the market than did the eventual opening of the railway.

In mid-July 1876 Ward reported to the Board that Budd & Holt were not proceeding with the earthworks at Malmesbury station. The extra excavation of the station site had been arranged in a supplementary contract with Budd & Holt, and, with the line itself virtually finished, these works were very much the key to completion. As more loss would be sustained through the stoppage, Ward gave the contractors notice that if the works were not resumed within a week, and carried on at a rate of at least 300 cubic yards per day, then their contract would be terminated. Budd & Holt were again complaining of insufficient payments – a cheque for £122 for work already performed was paid on solicitor's advice, and was enough to restart the work, but on 26th July a letter to the company from the contractors objected further to lack of funds and of too great a deduction in respect of calls due to their own shares in the MRC. They began pressing Ward to go to Mr. Gregory again to try to determine some of their claims, but the GWR intervened and advocated postponement of this until a new arrangement on financing could be worked out.

At the September 1876 Meeting of the MRC Directors in Malmesbury, the Board were astounded to learn from Charles Luce that Budd & Holt were making use of the line by carrying goods and coal upon it for the public! When this was investigated it transpired that on 12th August the 3rd Wilts Rifle Corps had been conveyed along the line to Dauntsey on their way to Aldershot, this being quite illegal on a line not passed for passenger conveyance by the Board of Trade! On 17th August, the Malmesbury Floral & Horticultural society had used the line for carriage of all foreign poultry exhibits for their Flower Show Day – having been unable to arrange for passenger excursions with the railway company, the Flower Show Secretary had managed to negotiate a deal for the poultry with Budd & Holt's Engineer, Mr. Mackenzie. It is not known whether Budd & Holt were aware of what their engineer was up to! The MRC Board instructed their solicitors to write to the contractors instructing them to cease using the line in this manner (no doubt someone was making a fair

Malmesbury's Cross Hayes square on a market day in the 1860s. The town museum, which supplied the original photograph, is now housed in the Town Hall, in the section behind the left-hand of the three large arches at left. *Athelstan Museum*

amount of money) and that the MRC would hold Budd & Holt responsible for their acts in the matter. As ballasting formed the major part of the work remaining to be completed, one wonders how smooth a ride was achieved on these illegal trips?

By September some progress was reported in the enlargements and additions to waterways affecting the line, shown to be necessary by the 1875 floods. The line had been partially raised in the Dauntsey meadows but there were still about 1000 cubic yards of filling and considerable amounts of reballasting throughout the line to be done. Work at Malmesbury station was well-advanced, the chief work remaining being floors, doors and cranes for the goods shed, and the paving of the engine shed.

In December, 1876, five years since the formation of the MRC and still without a line open, Budd & Holt put in another claim on the company, this time for £9,224. Ward considered this claim highly extravagant, founded chiefly on a misunderstanding of the requirements of the contract. Ward now requested from the company the late payments which were due to him, which had been overlooked in the line's slow progress and the continuing disputes. This matter was postponed, but a chagrined Ward informed the Board that he could not continue to give his services gratuitously after the end of the year, upon which it was then agreed to pay Ward 50 guineas for the extra work an Abritration over the £9,224 would force on him, to be paid at the next meeting. Budd & Holt's new claim included money for loss from flood damage, stripping of ballast, drawings and tracings supplied to Ward, and for extra work on Pyke's Deviation. This last was an alteration to the route carried out at Great Somerford on the request of farmer Henry Pyke in order to move the tracks farther away from the buildings at Brook Farm, just

south of the River Avon. Ward had estimated £100 extra in costs to divert the line about 15 yards. Extra lengths of permanent way were required, and although Ward considered that the appearance of the line would suffer, the job was carried out.

The continued problems between company, contractors and engineer were a salutary example of what could happen in situations where bland optimism for a project was not matched by appropriate funding, certainly in an area where such difficulties were easily exposed by adverse weather and by the geography of the line. The MRC Minutes recorded that the inability of the company to complete the works for the amount originally estimated arose from circumstances beyond its control, namely;

1. the contract with Budd & Holt being construed by the arbitrator in a sense widely different from that which both parties intended, whereby the company sustained a loss of £3,000 plus costs.
2. rise in prices of materials for station buildings.
3. increased requirements of the Board of Trade in respect of signals and interlocking at the branch junction.*
4. from carrying out the wishes of the GWR in making the line more direct with better gradients by a tunnel near the town.
5. general charges attributable to the delay in completing the line.

Faced with Budd & Holt's new litigation, the MRC's first move of 1877 was to prepare a Bill for depositing in Parliament for further powers to raise more capital to finish the line; this was not proceeded with, however, as the GWR decided that

---

* Due to an alarming increase in accidents in the 1860s, the Railway Regulation Act of 1871 gave further powers to the Board of Trade which resulted in an Act of 1873 which required all railway companies to make returns showing progress made with interlocking signalling and the block telegraph. Special machinery was provided at Swindon Works for the rapid manufacture of locking gear in February 1873.

no more expense could be risked on Parliamentary application. In the event, the GWR persuaded the MRC to raise the required capital via Lloyds Bonds, and, as the MRC records show, a substantial amount of money came direct from the pockets of the affluent GWR Board members themselves! In a report to their shareholders on 26th March 1877, the MRC stated:

> 'It is with great satisfaction that the Directors announce that they have now, subject to the approval of the GWR Board, made such arrangements as will secure the immediate completion of the Railway and the best provision circumstances permit for the Company's liabilities.'

As a result of these arrangements, the Bill for further capital was withdrawn.

The new claims being made upon the MRC by Budd & Holt for alleged extra works presented a worrying situation to the struggling company, and were the last straw as far as the GWR were concerned. Although there had been some progress on the crossing lodges and the repair work at Dauntsey was nearly complete, there still remained some 12,000 cu. yds of ballasting to be done, and the whole frustrating nature of the situation was reflected in the half-yearly meeting of the company in Malmesbury Town Hall on 26th March when a large turnout of shareholders was present in the hope of being given an opening date for the railway. The Chairman, Mr. Hill, expressed the view that the line would be open by the end of July, and hoped that traffic on the line would far exceed their expectations, in compensation for the cost of the railway being a great deal more than first anticipated. Mr. Holt, one of the contractors, was present with his solicitor, no doubt expecting trouble, and proffered the view that the cause of the delay was a want of capital, but said that all present could expect an opening on 1st August. Sir Hungerford-Pollen said that they had had a great deal to suffer at the hands of the contractors, who were only too ready to censure the Board that had done its duty so faithfully to the company. Sir C. Alexander-Wood, the GWR Board's Deputy Chairman, who described how he himself had journeyed along the line to Malmesbury that very day and admired the prettiness of the route on his way to the meeting, attempted to smooth things over by assuring all that everything possible would be done to have the line open for July, but if trouble was expected in a very tense atmosphere, it came from a quite unexpected source when Walter Powell, MP and a former MRC Board member until September 1874, delivered an astonishing verbal attack on Jones & Forrester, the company's solicitors. In his tirade he accused them of creating bogus shares to represent the £11,000 the MRC had been given assent to raise through loans and capitalised rent charges, of prolonging the line's construction by arranging arbitration and running up bills to take advantage of the useful annuity with which the line provided them as long as it was unfinished, and of 'cooking' the company's accounts. He extended his vote of censure to the whole Board by suggesting that a Board of Trade auditor should come to investigate the accounts. Powell further claimed that it was only through his own intervention that the line was now almost in the hands of the GWR, and this, he said, would have been the case a year ago had it not been for the solicitors. The Chairman replied that he could not find language to express his condemnation of Powell's remarks, and Mr. Jones, for Jones & Forrester,

himself a Malmesbury man, gave a full account of the financial organisation of the company which satisfied the meeting and left a strong feeling of regret present for the unfortunate nature of the remarks made by the MP. A Mr. Deloitte, a professional accountant, was brought in later in the year as Special Auditor to examine the company's accounts, and his

Walter Powell, MP, famed balloonist and one of the original Directors of the Malmesbury Railway Company. The primary school in Great Somerford is named after him.

Athelstan Museum

report totally vindicated the solicitors' handling of the MRC's affairs.

During 1876 and 1877 the accounts of the MRC recorded regular amounts being paid by the company as solicitors and arbitrator's fees in respect of the Budd & Holt actions, and it may be that the £156 9s paid to Budd & Holt for arbitrator's fees on 14th February 1877 and a £200 paid to Jones & Forrester for solicitors' expenses over this arbitration were debits to the railway company which precipitated Powell's remarks of 26th March.

On 19th April 1877, the GWR Secretary, Fred Saunders, received a letter from Budd & Holt proposing to annul the present contract and complete the works under a new arrangement, or on certain specified conditions to give up the works altogether. The matter was referred to the MRC for their reaction, but, bearing in mind their recent agreement with the GWR for completing the line, the MRC Board referred the situation back to Paddington, drawing the GWR's attention to a suggestion by a major shareholder that it might be desirable to sell the line with its liabilities to the Great Western. As a result, Jones & Forrester were instructed to propose to the Malmesbury shareholders that they should sell their shares at 15% of their respective holdings, the arrangement being carried out before the end of the following month.

At a hastily-convened meeting of the shareholders in Malmesbury Town Hall on 25th April, the proposal for the sale of the railway to the GWR was discussed. With the contractors clearly wanting out, the prospect of taking out another expensive contract with Budd & Holt, or with anyone, clearly precipitated a general feeling of selling out, and it was agreed to do so at a sale of 30 shillings per share (so much for the promised 2½% dividend) on condition that the GWR should take over all responsibility for completion and running of the line. Most of the shareholders accepted these terms, making the line virtually the property of the GWR, but six shareholders insisted on holding on to their railway investment, so with the final outcome of the transfer delayed, it was left that Parliamentary sanction would be sought in due course to incorporate the MRC fully in the GWR, this finally taking place three years later. For the moment, all available shares and all business of the company were transferred to Paddington at a meeting in the GWR Board Room there on 31st May 1877.

Now that the GWR were fully in control, Budd & Holt's claims were referred to Sir Daniel Gooch, the GWR Chairman, for more arbitration, and the GWR inspected the line in early April and found that the remaining work was mainly ballasting. As the GWR had its own ballast and plant, it was decided that the job would be completed more speedily and economically if they, the GWR, took on the work themselves. As Budd & Holt had already offered in their letter of 18th April to relinquish their contract, it was thus terminated by mutual consent in June 1877, with all proceedings before Mr. Gregory now withdrawn and under the consideration of Sir Daniel Gooch. Following Sir Daniel's arbitration, costs of £768 were awarded against the MRC, these being finally paid on 10th June 1878, six months after the line opened. An award of £527 10s 6d was awarded to Budd & Holt owing from the MRC, and this was paid on 25th September 1877, an amount which greatly justified the resistance of the MRC to the contractors' original claim of £9,224. Richard Ward's fees as engineer were finally settled up by 6th August 1878, a payment of £500 being made to him on that date.

In July the GWR accepted a tender from George Drew of Chalford to complete the railway, and began running ballast from Westbury to Dauntsey, instructing Budd & Holt to clear the line of their materials so that the ballasting could be finished. With the greater efficiency and air of urgency that now prevailed, the section between Dauntsey and Somerford was completed during July. On 28th September, around midday, there was a near collision at Malmesbury between a contractor's locomotive and a GWR locomotive bringing in ballast trucks from Cowbridge. A now-recovered Bill Ponting, soon to take on the job of gateman at Kingsmead, prevented a serious accident by racing up the line and attracting the attention of the GWR crew so that they had time to stop before reaching the stationary locomotive.

On 20th November Colonel Yolland of the Board of Trade arrived to do a preliminary inspection of the line, which appears to have proceeded satisfactorily. Then on 29th November a special train, consisting of locomotive, one 1st class and one 2nd class carriage, came down to Malmesbury from Swindon. Aboard were Sir Daniel Gooch, Bart., MP, Mr. Lancaster Owen, the engineer who was overseeing completion of the work, and Colonel Charles Miles with his wife

and daughter, representing the MRC Board. It is uncertain whether this visit was official or not, but it appears that Sir Daniel was satisfied with what he saw. It seems that following these two inspections some traffic was authorised, because on 12th December, five days before the official opening, a special cattle train left Malmesbury for the main line at 3.30 with the first railway consignment of fatstock purchased at Malmesbury market.

On 15th December 1877, the *North Wilts Herald* published the following short account of the Board of Trade inspection, which had taken place the day before:

'Colonel Rich, Inspecting Officer of the Board of Trade, inspected the railway yesterday, in company with Mr. H. Voss, District Engineer (Southern Division), Mr. J. F. Stevenson, Engineer for Swindon District, Mr. T. Graham, Divisional Superintendent, Mr. W. Blackwell, Signal Engineer, Mr. C. F. Hart, Secretary, and other officials. Everything of importance appeared to be thoroughly examined, the bridges being tested with two powerful engines and carriages. It is believed a favourable report will be made.'

On 16th December, MRC Secretary Charles Hart received the following letter from the Board of Trade:

> Board of Trade,
> (Railway Dept.)
> London SW,
> 15 Dec., 1877.
>
> Sir,
> I am directed by the Board of Trade to transmit to you the enclosed copy of Colonel Rich's report of his inspection of the Malmesbury Railway, and to inform you that they see no objection to the opening of the Railway for Passenger Traffic, provided that it is worked in accordance with the undertaking given by the Company.
> I am
> etc.
> (sd.) C. Cecil Trevor
> To the Secretary of the Malmesbury Ry., Devizes.

Colonel Rich's handwritten report ran as follows;

> Swindon 14 Dec. 1877
>
> Sir,
> I have the honour to report for the information of the Board of Trade, that in compliance with the instructions contained in the minute of the 5th inst., I have inspected the Malmesbury Railway.
> The new line commences by a Junction with the Great Western Railway at Dauntsey and extends to Malmesbury. The only other station is Somerford.
> The railway is a single line with sidings. Land has been enclosed, and the overbridges have been constructed for a double line. The gauge is 4 ft 8½ in.
> The permanent way consists of a Vignoles pattern rail, that weighs 72 lbs to the lineal yard. It is fished and fixed with crab bolts to sleepers laid transversely at an average distance of 3ft apart. The sleepers next to the rail joints are only two feet apart. There is a junction for goods with the Great Western Railway at Dauntsey; but not a junction for Passenger Trains.
> A small portion of bridge rail that weighs 68 lbs per yard lineal is laid at this junction and a double-headed rail that weighs 80 lbs per yard lineal is used at the Stations and for the junction points of crossings. The line is well-fenced, well-ballasted, and in good running order.
> The works consist of six overbridges which are built of brick and stone, eleven underbridges that have stone abutments and wrought-iron girders. The small openings under the Railway for cattle, and floods, have wooden beams. The widest span is 60 ft. These works are sufficiently strong and the girders gave moderate deflections when loaded.

There are three crossings of public roads on the level. Lodges are provided for the gate-keepers and the gates are constructed to close across the roads and railway.

The following alterations and additions are required: Junction at Dauntsey Cabin at West end of station. No. 32 lever which works the up starting signal should not be locked for the branch goods line up to main. The platform starting signals for main up and down lines should be placed at the proper sides of the Railway (left-hand).

No. 15 lever may be allowed to work with No. 17 as requested by the Traffic Superintendent. No. 13 lever and No. 17 may be worked together; but No. 13 should be inter-locked with No. 5 starting signal.

The advance starting signal towards London is beyond the signalman's proper limits of control, and is so placed that when shunting is being done, at the east end of Dauntsey Station, engine drivers must run past the signal at danger, and consequently it is useless in its present position, for the purpose intended, of preventing them from going into the next block section.

The points and junctions at the east end of Dauntsey Station require to be worked from a separate cabin with proper signals to protect the working. When this is done an effective U-line advance starting signal can be arranged.

The platform at Dauntsey requires more gravel to raise it to the level of the curb.

The gates at the level crossing at 1 m 75 ch and at 3 m 35 ch require to have signals and lamps. The Signal Inspector proposed to place them on the gateposts, and to arrange them so as to be moved by the opening and shutting of the gates.

Small pieces of fencing are required to the wing walls of the first bridge under the Railway at the north-west end of Somerford Station. Clocks are required at each of the stations, and in Malmesbury Signal Cabin.

The Great Western Railway Company have completed the new works of this railway, and are to work it, and the officers of the Company who attended at the inspection have promised that the above requirements shall be completed at once.

I enclose an undertaking from the Malmesbury and another from the Great Western Railway Company to work the single line with only one engine in steam, or two engines coupled together which appears satisfactory, and I submit that the Board of Trade may sanction the opening of the Malmesbury Railway.

I have etc.

(sd.) F. H. Rich

Colonel Rich seems to have been well pleased with the state of the line, although it is interesting that he makes no mention of the tunnel in his summary of the major structural features of the railway. Most of the modifications he suggests were at the junction at Dauntsey, where complications were caused by the grafting of a narrow gauge branch line onto a mixed gauge layout and the existence of the goods yard both beyond the signalman's vision and beyond the limit for the mechanical operation of points allowed by the Board of Trade.

Malmesbury's railway was opened at last on Monday 17th December, at a cost up to the opening of £76,565, well above the original estimate. Final cost of the railway, not resolved until final absorption by the GWR, and bearing in mind that there was still work on the line unfinished (Somerford station, for instance), came out at £87,094 19 shillings. From the contemporary accounts of 1877 the opening day was clearly one of the greatest in the history of the town. A public holiday was observed on the suggestion of the GWR. Both the *Swindon Advertiser* and the *Wilts & Glos Standard* contained lengthy detailed accounts of the opening day's celebrations, although much of the description was rather peripheral to the actual event, recalling the 40 years of struggle to establish the town on the railway network and about who said what about whom at the evening's celebration dinner, in the style in which Victorian newspapers prosaically seemed to delight.

The *Standard* expressed the view that the single line of track would be found to be insufficient to carry on the business of the railway, hence making possible the doubling of the line, and a general appeal was made to tradesmen and others to decorate the town for the day in as festive a manner as possible. The day was blessed with fine weather, and a Union Flag flying on the tower of Dr. Kinnear's house in Oxford Street was suggestion in itself that something special was astir. Festoons of evergreens and aritificial flowers hung across the High Street, flags and bunting hung from windows, and the home of a Mr. Henry Jeston sported an elaborate device in red, white and blue proclaiming 'Success to the Malmesbury Railway', although, these apart, the result of the appeal for colour produced, in the words of the *Standard*'s reporter, 'a pretty general, though by no means elaborate or brilliant effort'. Maybe the spectre of July 1865, with all its wasted money and effort, still loomed large in some people's minds? The *Swindon Advertiser* concurred, stating 'The good people of Malmesbury were not lavish in their display of flags and bunting'. An ensign flying from the flagstaff in the Cross

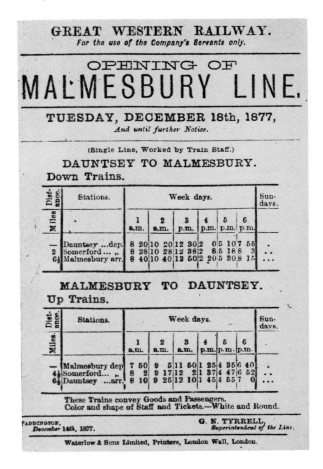

Hayes served as the rallying point at about 1.45 pm for a procession led by the Malmesbury town band which was to march down to the new station for the purpose of meeting the inaugural train. Behind the band marched a great throng which included Town Councillors and dignitaries attending in a private capacity, Directors of 'the late railway company', as the paper called it, clergy, businessmen, farmers and many more. Many flags, banners and various insignia were carried and the expenses for the day were partly borne by the GWR. At the station the crowd were met by many of the ladies of the district, who were primly waiting for both train and procession rather than march through the streets.

At 1 pm a special train arrived at Dauntsey from Swindon consisting of 14 composite coaches, a saloon and two brake vans. Unfortunately, no record has survived of the class or number of the tastefully-decorated locomotive at the head of the train, as the press simply tell us 'the engine was a very fine one'. Leading officials of the GWR were in the train, including Swindon District Engineer J. F. Stevenson, who helped Lancaster Owen supervise the completion of the branch, Western Division Superintendent T. Graham, Locomotive Supt. G. Lindsley, and Mr. Carlton, Manager of Swindon Works. The train proceeded slowly to Malmesbury, permitting a good view of the fine Wiltshire scenery through which the line passed. At the still unfinished Somerford station, the train passed through slowly without stopping, it being due to call there on the return trip. A great crowd thronged the tiny station and its approaches to watch the train pass through, a gathering described in the *Wilts Gazette & Herald* of 22nd December as including 'several choice specimens of the Wiltshire peasantry', a quaint but rather patronising description of country folk 'expressing their wonderment at the engine and attendant carriages'. It was as well that they looked intently, for they would never see its like on the line again!

At Malmesbury the train steamed slowly into the gaily-decorated and pristine station, to be greeted by a great throng on the platform. Free tickets had been issued to shareholders and promoters of the railway and their friends and families by the GWR, and about 300 people boarded the special for their free return trip to Dauntsey. Except for the accommodation of some of the ladies in the saloon, the carriages were filled without any attention to class. Those boarding included a young Jimmy Jones, later in life to be a Malmesbury Alderman who founded the Athelstan Museum in 1931. His lifetime spanned the life of the railway with a fair amount to spare, for he rode on the last passenger train 74 years later and was still alive and at home nearby when the last goods train left the station in 1962. But for now, all was euphoria, the journey out to the junction being such a trip as was never seen again on the branch, as not even the later Sunday School specials could have rivalled it for colour, excitement and splendour. Many spectators waved from the slopes of the Worthies and from the vicinity of the Abbey, the sober, grey hue of which must have contrasted timelessly with the festive atmosphere, with brightly-coloured costumes and waving handkerchiefs being in evidence at every vantage point. At Somerford, the train was joined by the Rev. Andrews and his contingent from the village of Somerford Magna, including their village band playing 'See the Conquering Hero Come', all managing to somehow cram themselves into the train – it is not recorded as to whether the band's instruments

went too! Even the unfinished station here was bedecked in flags, and the village church also sported a banner waving in the gentle breeze from its tower. The train stayed for about twenty minutes at Dauntsey, giving time for the party to inspect the facilities at the new junction, with time for some of their number to leave the station to sample the bitter at the nearby hostelry! The special then conveyed its passengers back to Malmesbury amid scenes of great jubilation.

At the evening's celebration public dinner in the King's Arms, under the presidency of Mr. T. D. Hill, MRC Chairman, praise was accorded and glasses raised to the people who had worked for many years to make the railway for which Malmesbury had waited for so long. A few words spoken by the Rev. G. W. Tucker, Vicar of Malmesbury, are worth quoting:

> 'It was indeed a novel thing to ride by that old Monastic building, the grand and Ancient Abbey, in a railway carriage – the effect of the railway will be to make that noble monument of past days better known to the world than ever.'

If a little exaggerated, the vicar's words have a sadly nostalgic ring to them now, when one thinks of the classic railway postcard view of the station with the Abbey dominating the scene from its vantage point in the background, as indeed it dominated many fine photographs taken of Malmesbury's terminus. During the evening of the 17th, townsfolk listened to the band playing in the High Street outside the King's Arms, and balloons were sent up from the Market Cross in honour of the day's events.

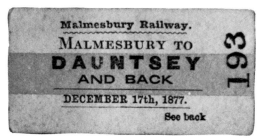

One of the complimentary tickets issued to shareholders for the opening special train. *Collection Mike Stewart*

The year 1877 was notable for the invention of the phonograph, the publication of Edward Lear's fourth nonsense book, and the adoption by Queen Victoria of the title 'Empress of India' on the suggestion of her Prime Minister, Disraeli. Victoria had already been Queen for forty years, wine could be brought for a shilling a bottle, whilst abroad Russia was knocking on the door of Constantinople. On the sporting front there was a tied Boat Race, a victory for Scotland over England by 3–1 at the Oval in the sixth annual football match between the two, and the first tennis tournament at Wimbledon. In December 1877 one Alexander Graham Bell was pushing a new invention called a telephone, whilst in Wiltshire the town of Malmesbury was opening its doors to the prosperity it hoped its new railway would bring, stimulating trade in its market and providing a modern outlet for the produce of its flourishing silk factory and the recently-established Adye & Hinwood bacon factory. Regular train service on the branch commenced on 18th December 1877, with a Monday to Saturday service of six trains each way.

The earliest known view of Malmesbury station, with the Railway Hotel just visible through the canopy support columns. The porter, third from the left, is shown holding a bell, used to herald the arrival of the branch train during the last century. The trolley probably contains large sides of bacon from the local factory. With the absence of any buildings beyond the station building itself — no parcel office or lamp hut — it seems likely that this view was taken in the mid-1880s. In early 1899 the old 'hot water house' used for preparing footwarmers for carriages was converted to a parcels office, and there is no such building visible at this stage.

Courtesy John Barnby

CHAPTER FOUR

THE OLD LINE, DAUNTSEY TO MALMESBURY 1877–1933

THE Malmesbury line began its working life on Tuesday, 18th December 1877, with a service of six trains each way daily, Sundays excepted. The branch opened in a traumatic manner for the employee in charge of the gates at Dauntsey Road Crossing, for by the time the service was underway on the Tuesday morning, these gates had been reduced to splinters by a train. Newspaper accounts and GWR records conflict over when this accident actually happened, the railway records referring to damage by an empty train on the morning prior to the opening of the line for regular traffic, the press describing the early morning branch train from Dauntsey as destroying the gates on the day after opening. It transpired that the gates had not been opened because the gateman, an elderly employee who had been in GWR service for 35 years without a single accident, couldn't reach them because the handle of the door had come off in his hand (so much for the contractors' workmanship!). Whether this incident had any bearing or not is uncertain, but the unfortunate man was replaced in January 1878 by Jabez Brain from Bristol at a wage of 18/- a week, who remained at the crossing until his retirement in May 1901. This was not the only time in the early history of the branch that trains ploughed through gates closed across the track. It is fairly certain that Kingsmead and Dauntsey road crossings were not protected by distants at this time, the Board of Trade Report on 14th December 1877, referring to the need for these crossings to be provided with signals and lamps. Thus was the point proved. Original edition Ordnance Survey maps show no distant signals for the two crossings in 1888, but they were provided at some point before 1900.

During the first year of operation, with the track requiring to settle, three permanent way gangs were employed on the line, each comprising six men plus a ganger. It was the GWR's original intention to board permanent way men in the crossing lodges on the branch, so that wives could attend to the gate duties while their husbands were out at work along the track. No rent was chargeable under this arrangement. However, P.W. men declined to occupy the cottages on these conditions, so ordinary gatemen were employed. At Kingsmead, William Ponting took on the job, having lost an arm in an accident while engaged in the construction of the branch. He remained at the crossing until his death in 1920. The crossing gates at Somerford were the responsibility of the booking porter at the station there, the first man to be employed in this capacity being 30-year-old Theodore Ironsides, a former railway policeman from Chippenham, who took on the new station at a rate of 22/- a week. No further staff were appointed at Somerford until the opening of the goods yard.

Malmesbury's first station master was Llewellyn Bradshaw, born 6th September 1850. He started work for the GWR as a passenger clerk at Wrexham in 1868 on a salary of £30 a year, moving on to a similar position at Llangollen in January 1875 before being appointed to the newly-opened station at Malmesbury for its inception at the tender age of 27, quite young for a station master on a Class 3 appointment. Following five years at Malmesbury, he was promoted to Chepstow and Clevedon, retiring in 1914. He died in Weston-Super-Mare in 1922. His station staff at Malmesbury early in 1878 was as follows;

Station master	Llewellyn Bradshaw	£100 a year
Lad clerk	George Davis	£20 a year
Passenger guard	Reuben Jeffreys	23/- a week
Shunter	Jacob Baker	20/- a week
Porter 1	unknown	18/- a week
Porter 2	John Quarrell	16/- a week
Lad porter	Harry Gregory	10/- a week

As far as is known, no signalman was ever appointed at Malmesbury, duties at the small signal box being handled by the shunter. It is probable that the 'unknown' porter was Stephen Emery, who is known to have worked as porter at Malmesbury before going on to become booking porter at Somerford, but this is unconfirmed.

With the opening of the branch, there was no longer any need for provision of conveyance at Chippenham station to meet incoming buyers on market days, and the *Wilts & Glos Standard* of 12th January, 1878, announced the following in respect of the next market day, the 16th:

'Messrs. Goulter & Rich have received instructions from Mr. Henry Long to sell by auction in the above market:
    one pair of horse omnibuses built by Perry & Son, Bristol
    one pair of horse omnibuses, as above, nearly new
    one single or pair of horse brougham
    one wagonette
    one cart used for conveyance of goods
    two sets of double harness
    three sets of single harness
    one dark brown gelding
    one bay gelding
The above have been regularly working the omnibus to and from Chippenham daily and are in good working condition.'

Long's local omnibus service was therefore an early casualty with the arrival of rail service in Malmesbury. Also advertisd were several other horses, including a brown cart mare that had been regularly employed on goods traffic from Chippenham. Thus relinquishing his transport interests, Mr. Long concentrated his living in the licensed trade, becoming a beer retailer in the High Street.

The coming of the railway brought with it a new demand for housing in the area, with a consequent increase in prices, just as did the coming of the M4 motorway a century later. A major benefit to the town was the delivery of coal direct, replacing the old pannier baskets in which laden donkeys had carried it over the rough country roads from Coalpit Heath. All branch services ran as mixed trains conveying both goods and passengers. Journey time was 20 minutes, and times, fares and connections were advertised regularly in the *Swindon Advertiser*. Although connections at Dauntsey were good, no great speed was involved in journeying to London from

Malmesbury. With the junction out at a minor station, two changes of train were usually involved, at Dauntsey and Swindon, a disadvantage not suffered by Calne, for example, where the branch joined the main line at Chippenham and outlived the Malmesbury passenger service well into the diesel age.

Industry in Malmesbury benefited greatly from the new line, a flourishing silk factory having been established, and the Adye and Hinwood bacon factory derived much success from the vast amount of trade that saw Malmesbury's market regain some of its former glory for a time. On 16th February, 1878, the *Wilts Glos. Standard* announced;

'An extra train will, we hear, run specially from Dauntsey to Malmesbury on market days at 9.32. This great desideratum has been brought about through the kindly interposition of Mr. Walter Powell, M.P., with the authorities of the Great Western Railway. The first special train will run on Wednesday next, the 20th inst.'

The result on the 20th inst was the largest attendance at Malmesbury market in more than thirty years. This first market day train was simply an extra branch service slotted in between the 9.5 ex-Malmesbury and the 10.20 ex-Dauntsey. It left Malmesbury at 9.57 as an empty train which arrived at the junction at 10.12 where the 9.10 down train from Swindon had brought down extra coaches and cattle wagons to be added to the branch set. Butchers and dealers from places as far away as Birmingham, Reading and Bristol made use of the extra accommodation and some 28 truckloads of cattle left the terminus during the day. The Cross Hayes square in the town centre was crowded with livestock and the High Street and several other available places were also occupied by buyers and sellers of many different kinds of merchandise. The *Standard*'s 25th February edition reported that:

'At about 10 a.m. streams of business people were seen wending their steps from the railway station to the Cross Hayes and the High Street, which convinces us that we are at last like our neighbours in that we can boast of railway facility and a good market.'

The market was held every third Wednesday in the month at this time, and on market days and for fairs each special train would be met by a horse-bus which would convey influential landlords, farmers and merchants to the King's Arms in the High Street for a fare of sixpence.

A letter to the Malmesbury Railway Company of 27th February, 1878, from surveyors on behalf of the Earl of Pembroke, complained that the company had not kept faith with his Lordship in the question of erecting a station at Burton Hill. The Earl owned much of the land in the Cowbridge area which would have been served by this projected station, but in his reply the company's secretary informed the surveyors that the cost of stations and the onerous conditions of working them imposed by the Board of Trade made it impossible to consider it at the present time. Indeed, Somerford station was still unfinished, although during the following month £468 was paid to contractors Brock & Bruce for its completion on 23rd March.

On Thursday, 28th March, 1878 the Malmesbury Railway Company held its half-yearly meeting at Paddington, at which the following report to the Directors was read:

'Presenting the 11th half-yearly report to the shareholders, the Directors have to congratulate them on the opening of their railway to public traffic on the 18th December last. A good train service has been arranged by the Great Western Railway Company for the development of traffic and the use that is being made of the line satisfies your Directors that it will prove a great convenience to Malmesbury and its immediate neighbourhood. A station has been erected at Great Somerford but is at present open only for passengers. Arrangements, however, are being made under which it will be available for goods and coal traffic in the course of a few months. The half-yearly statement of accounts, which are published herewith, are in accordance with the requirements of the Regulation of Railways Act of 1868, except that it has not been considered necessary to submit detailed revenue accounts for the few days the line was working under the half year to which the capital accounts refer. The receipts, in respect of share capital and debenture loans to the 31st December last have been £65,073 10s, and the expenditure for land, Parliamentary and other costs, works, stations, engineer, salaries and office disbursements have been to the same period £76,565 6s 10d, leaving a balance of £11,491 16s 10d to the debit of the account. The expenditure during the half-year included in the accounts now presented, and which is set forth in the account no. 5, has been £9,819 8s 10d. The efficient state of the permanent way, works and station buildings is made known in the Engineer's Report.

Thomas D. Hill, Chairman.'

At Dauntsey the work provided by the opening of the branch necessitated the appointment of an extra porter in April 1878, at a rate of 18/- a week. The booking porter in charge at the junction was therefore now assisted by two porters, one lad porter and a policeman. A duty chart for Dauntsey during the early 1880s describes the policeman as being responsible for the safe custody of the junction station during the night. He saw that no unauthorised person was allowed on the premises, that all night goods put off at the station were properly covered in trucks in the yard for local despatch and in the branch bay for addition to the Malmesbury train in the morning, and he locked the station yard gates after the departure of the last passenger train. He attended to all signal lamps during the night as required and cleaned the water closets, urinals and offices on the station thoroughly. He had charge of the ground frame controlling access to the goods yard at the east end of the station, and his shift of 7.25 p.m. to 8.00 a.m. carried a remuneration of 15/- a week. On alternate Sundays he would work a day turn of 1.00–8.00 p.m. with a porter, allowing the booking porter to work alternate Sundays with the porter appointed as a result of work in connection with the new branch, thus giving the station staff a free Sunday every fortnight.

Various monthly statements by the GWR during 1878 alluded to a normal increase of about £200 to £300 fortnightly in receipts for the station group of Malmesbury, Somerford, Dauntsey, Tetbury Road and Chippenham as compared with the pre-branch figures when people would have used the three last-named stations. Thus the traffic was looked at as a group situation, allowing for the fact that the two new stations on the branch would take traffic from those already existing in the area. For example, in May 1878:

'The following is a statement of the traffic of the Malmesbury Railway for the three weeks ending April 29th, from which it will be seen that the traffic at Malmesbury and Somerford and at Chippenham, Dauntsey and Tetbury Road (stations affected by the opening of the branch) this year exceeded the traffic at Chippenham, Dauntsey and Tetbury Road last year by £231, made up as follows:-

Goods traffic	£157
Passenger	£177
Total	£334

A special train service was provided for Malmesbury Market, which was held monthly in the Cross Hayes Square. The top view was taken during the 1890s, and the busier lower view during the early 1900s, the latter perhaps for a popular occasion such as the Christmas fatstock market. An interesting difference in the two views is the addition of the tower to one of the houses in Oxford Street to the right of the Town Hall. The author's wife grew up in the house just beyond the tower.

(Top) Courtesy R. Hatchwell
(Lower) Author's collection

There was a decrease in the parcel traffic of £103 giving a net increase of £231. The decrease in parcel traffic is owing to less milk being forwarded from Chippenham to London this yr than last.'

During June 1878 work proceeded at Somerford to bring the station's goods facilities into operation. Points for connection of the proposed siding to the branch were installed at a cost of £54. The works were ready for inspection by 8th July, and the following day Colonel Rich returned to the branch for this purpose on behalf of the Board of Trade. No references had been made to the state of Somerford station in his original report, so the condition of the unfinished works of that time is not precisely known. It now transpired that the down distant signal could not be seen when operating the levers in the small cabin which faced onto the platform, the signal being away beyond the river and obscured by trees, so the works were approved subject to the addition of an electric repeater in the signal room. There remained the need to complete facilities in the goods yard and widening of the embankment to accommodate the siding.

Right from the first year of its operation, special trains and excursions were an integral feature of life on the Malmesbury branch. The first known party into the town on the new line came into the station on 22nd June, 1878, Swindon coaching stock being added to an extra branch train which ran to convey members of the Swindon Band of Hope and International Order of Good Templars. The local Flower Show Committee made arrangements for a special train service to be put on for Flower Show Day, 14th August, 1878. Cheap return fares were advertised from Swindon, Wootton Bassett, Calne and Chippenham. Several extra coaches were sent from Swindon to augment the branch set and cater for the many visitors to the town for this fete, which was held in the grounds of Burton Hill House (how useful the projected Burton Hill station would have been). As the festivities ran well into the evening, the branch train made an additional late run departing from Malmesbury at 9 p.m. Although the show ceased during the Depression of 1879–82, it resumed in 1883 and ran until 1930 when the local society closed down in financial difficulties.

The MRC half-yearly meeting at Paddington on 12th September, 1878 reported that the new goods yard at Somerford was almost completed, with the embankment formed ready for the ballast and permanent way. A new weighbridge had been provided at Malmesbury. The first half-yearly accounts for the period 18th December, 1877 to 30th June, 1878, showed the following figures:

Passengers	23,776
Parcels	6,389
Horses	259
Carriages	22
Dogs	98
Head of cattle	4,819
Goods, coal and minerals	5,727 tons

Passenger receipts at Malmesbury amounted to £592, at Somerford £108, and the *Wilts & Glos Standard* of 19th October, in publishing these figures, reported 'This state of things must be very gratifying to the Chairman and his Directors'. The number of passengers booked on the branch represented an average of about twelve passengers per train in normal service, a reasonable figure for a country branch bearing in mind that this figure did not include users who had booked their tickets elsewhere on the GWR, but, more significantly, the total receipts for the line's first half year amounted to £1,350 17s 9d, a figure which did not cover general running costs. Payments to the GWR for working costs alone totalled £675 since the opening, and the MRC was still in debt to the tune of about £18,000 for land, Parliamentary and other costs, not to mention the completion of the works by the GWR, and while such money was temporarily obtained on the security of Lloyds Bonds, it was clear that traffic revenue on the branch would never be sufficient to keep the local company independent, although such independence was only nominal, as the GWR did virtually everything except pay the MRC secretary.

The goods facilities at Somerford opened on 1st January, 1879, a porter being allocated to the station to assist the booking porter in dealing with the extra work. Located behind the passenger platform, the goods yard had a loading dock and a weighing machine, access from the branch being via a single siding with points facing trains coming from the Malmesbury direction. Incoming wagons for Somerford would be conveyed towards the rear of branch trains, the guard's van being cut off at the platform with the train pulling ahead of the points which were then reversed for it to back into the siding where the wagons were detached. A very busy outward traffic in milk developed, this being despatched on the early evening mixed train which arrived from Malmesbury

shortly after 5 p.m. Principal inward goods were feed for the farms and coal; two firms established dumps at Somerford, the Malmesbury and Tetbury Coal Company, and the Chippenham firm of Harding & Son.

In 1879 the 11.50 ex-Malmesbury was brought forward to a 10.50 departure, with the 12.30 from Dauntsey coming forward to 11.20. A further alteration saw the 2 p.m. branch train from Dauntsey put back 20 minutes on the second and last Fridays in the month to wait for the 1.15 ex-Bristol which called at Dauntsey. During that year 41,000 tickets were booked at stations on the branch, yielding £1,156 in receipts, traffic in goods and livestock earning £1,263. This pattern, with the greater portion of receipts coming from goods traffic, was to continue throughout the life of the line, although passenger receipts assumed large totals through the inclusion of milk and parcels as 'passenger train traffic', earning the line around £6,000 annually by the turn of the century. However, the milk & parcel business had not really developed in 1879, earning the line only around £220 that year, this figure including the conveyance of horses and dogs!

The night of Tuesday, 2nd March 1880, saw torrential rain and powerful winds which produced hurricane-like conditions in the north of Wiltshire, flooding part of the station yard, a quite common occurrence as it was close to the Inglebourne. With the Tay Bridge disaster of the previous year still fresh in everybody's minds, these conditions created a near-disaster on the Malmesbury branch where floodwaters of the Avon had washed away part of the masonry of Poole's Bridge. Several trains used the line next morning including the 11.35 from Dauntsey which crossed the bridge safely, but by midday an end buttress had collapsed, shifting a 53 foot span several feet and sinking the girders considerably on one side. The midday train from Malmesbury had been signalled for Dauntsey at Somerford at 12.12 and was all on its way when its driver, former 'Flying Dutchman' engineman Nicholas Gray, spotted two youths running towards the train, waving their hats and shouting. Thanks to this prompt action by the boys, two 16 year olds, Montague Potter and Henry Day, in a scene not unlike the famous warning in 'The Railway Children', a terrible accident was averted. Being a straight and nearly level section of the line, the train was travelling at its greatest prescribed speed (or more) and could not possibly have stopped in time without the boy's warning. Six passengers aboard thus walked across the bridge and thence to Dauntsey. Subsequently road conveyance was hired to convey passengers between Dauntsey and Somerford until the bridge was repaired – 'a summoned engine with crane had raised the span level'. The branch train ran between Malmesbury and Somerford for the next five days until normal service was able to resume.

In 1880 the Malmesbury Railway Company was finally vested in the GWR. Final takeover of the independent concern took place with its absorption on 1st July, 1880, confirmed by an Act of 6th August. At the MRC's 16th half-yearly meeting at Paddington on 27th August, chaired by Sir Daniel Gooch, it was resolved that:

'The vesting of the undertaking of this Company in the Great Western Railway Company under the provisions of the Great Western Railway Act of 1880 upon the terms of the issue of £15 Consolidated Ordinary Stock of that Company in exchange for every ten fully paid up £10 shares of the Malmesbury Railway Company and so in proportion for any less number of such shares be and the same is hereby approved'.

The final meeting in respect of the old company took place at Paddington on 22nd March, 1881, chaired again by Sir Daniel Gooch, at which 1150 outstanding shares were declared forfeit.

Yet another major railway scheme involving Malmesbury came before Parliament and obtained its Act in 1880 without any work on it ever materialising. The South Wales & Southampton Railway sought to link the Swindon, Marlborough & Andover Railway (later the Midland & South Western Junction) at Swindon with the Stonehouse and Nailsworth Railway in the parish of Minchinhampton, which yet again involved running a line through Malmesbury and Tetbury.

The scheme included 'permanent way and works to be bought from the Malmesbury Railway Company'. Plans show the projected route running parallel with the established Malmesbury branch from Lea Fields as far as the terminus. Whether a junction was intended is not clear, but the implications of this scheme yet again suggested that Malmesbury would be on a through line. Basically an extension of the Midland's Nailsworth branch, it would have run eastwards from Malmesbury via Brinkworth and Wootton Bassett to Swindon, but as working of the line was to be in conjunction with the SMA, GWR, LSWR and the Midland, it was obviously too complicated a plan to have much hope of coming off, as one assumes that the 1863 Agreement which helped kill the Wilts & Glos Railway was still in force? It was a most interesting scheme, nevertheless, deposited in November 1879 when the MRC was still nominally independent.

During the last century various carrier services and horse omnibus operators linked Malmesbury station with the surrounding district, typically Sherston, Luckington, Crudwell and villages out along the Bristol road, some carriers running extra services into Malmesbury on market days. The GWR's goods agent for Malmesbury was James Wall of Melksham, who provided a horse and dray service for the delivery of goods around the town. An omnibus service from Tetbury connected with the 9.25 a.m. and 4.5 p.m. branch trains from Malmesbury, also meeting the incoming 10.20 a.m. and 5.45 p.m. arrivals, the branch railway between Tetbury and Kemble not being opened until 1889. The Tetbury omnibus ran until around 1910, although, with the opening of the Tetbury line, it was cut to three days a week, Monday, Wednesday, Saturday.

In March 1882 a second station master took over at Malmesbury. Thirty-seven year old Thomas Wood's GWR career began in 1864 as a passenger clerk at Bristol, progressing via similar appointments at Weymouth, Bristol again, and Wolverhampton, to the parcels office at Bath in 1874. The Malmesbury appointment now carried a £110 a year salary, and Mr Wood stayed for sixteen years to become the town's longest-serving station master.

Somerford station was the scene of a mishap on 6th May, 1882, when the 8.20 train from Dauntsey broke down through valve failure. 'Pipes feeding the boiler burst, shattering the glass in the front of the engine and damaging the funnel.' As a result, two return branch services could not run and another engine had to be sent from Swindon to Somerford to bring the stricken train to Dauntsey in time to meet the Up Weymouth. Such a procedure would have required one of the branch train crew to walk from Somerford to Dauntsey with the train staff so the rescue engine could proceed on the branch.

On 3rd June 1882 the first documented Sunday Schools' Special train was run, providing a day trip to Weymouth for a cost of 4/- per adult, 2/- per child. Townsfolk were awoken by the town band playing in the streets betwen 5 and 6 a.m., the train, 23 carriages long, leaving at 6 a.m. and collecting children from various villages at Somerford on the way. The party was swelled by more groups at Dauntsey. In these early days of the branch, it is not certain as to how these specials were organised, but it is believed that carriages were brought to Dauntsey from Swindon, where the branch locomotive would assist in double-heading them to Malmesbury. From

An early 1900s view of the Railway Hotel, Malmesbury, with its stable buildings to the right advertising accommodation for foxhunters. *Courtesy Mr & Mrs K. Iles*

reports, it would appear that the special would then run to Dauntsey, where it would run out on to the main line in order for the entire train to be adjacent to a platform. Then the passengers would change trains, crossing the tracks (no footbridge until 1885) to join the main line special connection waiting in the other platform. This was a lengthy procedure which involved blocking both lines for a time, and on this occasion around a thousand people crowded the platforms at Dauntsey.

With much of the line running along the Avon valley and Malmesbury itself surrounded by loops of the river, it was hardly surprising that the branch was susceptible to flooding, and heavy rain of October 1882 washed away considerable amounts of ballasting on the section between the Roaring Hatches and Little Somerford. The branch service was suspended on 24th October until 8.00 p.m. next day while extra permanent way men were brought in to repack the ballast over a hundred yard section. There also survives from this period a tale of how during a bad winter, the branch train was snowed up in a cutting south of Cowbridge, staying there all night and having to be dug out next morning. It is not known for certain but one assumes that it was possible for passengers to walk into Malmesbury from near Cowbridge, rather than spend the night in a snowbound train. Porter John Quarrell was working as a relief guard on this occasion; he owned a Meerschaum pipe of which he was very proud, and was upset to discover, after removal of the train from the snowdrifts, that he only had the stem of his pipe left in his mouth!

The Malmesbury branch, as far as we can tell, went through its entire life from construction to closure without a single human fatality, but there were occasional mishaps, a notable one occurring on 18th August, 1883 when employees of the Malmesbury, Sherston and Tetbury Silk Mills, around 400 of them, took a Saturday excursion to Weston-Super-Mare. This was apparently quite a gala occasion, the town band again playing through the streets and actually going on the trip, the train leaving at 6.00 a.m. to the cheers of excursionists and

onlookers! The carriages were attractively decorated and included three saloons. The *Wilts & Glos Standard* reported:

'Everything was well-organised, reflecting the greatest credit on Mr. Wood, station master, and Mr. Nixon, General Manager of the Silk Mills. The train stopped for fifteen minutes at Bath and the band played on the platform. Weston-Super-Mare was reached at 9 o'clock, and the excursionists marched through the town to the Esplanade and sands. Return was made from Weston at 8 pm, the juvenile portion bearing away with them tiny buckets of sand and shells and bundles of seaweed as souvenirs of their first visit to the seaside.'

After return to Malmesbury around 11.00 p.m., the branch crew, on this occasion driver Nicholas Gray and fireman Evan Harry, had to take the carriages back to Dauntsey the same night for collection by a Swindon engine. Unfortunately, the booking porter at Somerford, thinking his duties over for the day, had retired to bed, leaving the level crossing gates locked across the track as usual. Around 11.25 p.m. the branch engine and 23 four-wheel coaches smashed through the gates, completely demolishing them. One can picture the horrified booking porter, helpless as he heard the distant train rumbling through the night towards his station and realising his mistake.

In late 1883, with the Tetbury–Kemble scheme under way to build a branch from the Cheltenham & Great Western Union line to the old Gloucestershire market town, Malmesbury Borough Council approached the GWR to put forward a scheme to extend this line from Tetbury to Malmesbury, thus giving a direct line between Kemble and Dauntsey! Needless to say, nothing ever came of this idea.

On 26th July 1884 the station office at Malmesbury was broken into and the silver taken which was used by the clerk in giving change to early passengers in the morning. A window had been broken in the ladies' waiting room, the offenders having chosen a Saturday, the one night when no cleaner was on duty at the shed. The following Monday a detective and two GWR officials came to investigate and interview staff, but nothing ever came of it. In the same month occurred the death of Mr T. D. Hill, who had been Chairman of the old Malmesbury Railway Company. He died on 21st July and was buried at Henbury, near Bristol.

In September 1884 booking porter Robert Perrett left Somerford station to take over the new station at Highworth in a similar capacity, this new branch having been opened the previous year. The caution he received from Paddington over

Believed to be Robert Perrett, booking porter at Somerford 1879—84.
Wiltshire Library & Museum Service

the wrecking of his crossing gates had evidently not spoilt his chances of promotion! The *Swindon Advertiser* referred to the change thus:

'Inhabitants of Somerford presented Mr Perrett with a valuable silver-plated tea and coffee service at the Volunteer Inn. He won golden opinions of his general courtesy and the way he looked after the interests of passengers.'

Mr Perrett stayed twenty years at Highworth, attaining the grading of station master there in 1897.

According to GWR Working Timetables, no market day service was provided on the branch during 1883–4, but the 1885 WTT details the third Wednesday of the month arrangement quite clearly. Cattle wagons were brought down from Swindon and the branch train went out to Dauntsey for 4.25 p.m. to collect them; the branch coaches were left and the wagons brought on into Malmesbury, where arrival was timed for 4.48 p.m. The cattle train was scheduled to leave again at 4.55, not apparently giving much time to load, and it is hard to believe that everything always went like clockwork where loading of cattle was concerned. It is likely that some cattle would have been already loaded in wagons delivered earlier in the day. These would have been horse-drawn up to

the cattle pens for loading, then left on the middle road awaiting removal. Westbound cattle traffic from Malmesbury market was collected by the 9.15 a.m. Wolverhampton to Bristol express goods which called at Dauntsey just before 6 p.m. once a month for this purpose. With the loaded wagons stabled in a siding at Dauntsey awaiting collection, the branch engine then rejoined its coach set and resumed service as the 5.25 to Malmesbury.

In 1885 the Somerfords, Dauntsey, Seagry and Christian Malford Floral Society inaugurated the Annual Somerford Show, which was held in a meadow between the River Avon and the railway. The train out of Malmesbury around 5 pm was much used by visitors to this event, and a special late service was laid on, leaving Somerford at 9.45 p.m. for Dauntsey and returning to Somerford at 10.15 to take show visitors back to Malmesbury. The regular branch stock was used but with the surprising addition of four eight-wheel coaches which were sent out to Dauntsey for strengthening purposes, thus a longer than usual branch train would run during the afternoon to accommodate show traffic. A popular annual visitor to the Somerford Show was Harry Jones, landlord of the Kings' Arms and a gentleman of quite Dickensian proportions. He had formerly had charge of the Railway Hotel in Malmesbury, and always travelled to Somerford Show on a first class return ticket. It was to his constant irritation that there was no such printed first class ticket for the 12 minute ride from Malmesbury, so he had to make do with a written order!

In March 1887 a heavy snowfall caused the canopy over the Malmesbury branch bay at Dauntsey to collapse due to the decayed state of the supports. Fortunately no one was injured. During building of the branch the original tender of £482 from contractors Brock & Bruce for this canopy had been rejected in favour of a Mr Lovatt who had offered to erect and paint a second-hand structure from Landore station for £275. The work had been done in December 1877 but the payment to Lovatt was £461 as the GWR required the canopy to be continued up to the road overbridge. No doubt the cut-price approach was now regretted, the cost of its repair being £319. The repair was carried out in October 1887 by contractor Samuel Robertson.

On 10th July 1887 three pigs were killed by the 6 p.m. ex-Malmesbury near the tunnel. A drove of pigs had been grazing in a nearby field, the property of High Street butcher Mr

Malmesbury Line.

Fares from Malmesbury.				UP TRAINS.		1 2 3	1 2 p	1 2 3	1 2 3	1 2 3	1 2 3
1st	2nd	3rd	Par.								
s. d.	s. d.	s. d.	s. d.			a.m	a.m	a.m	p.m	p.m	p.m
..	..	..	..	Malmesbury	*dep.*	7 25	9 5	10 50	1 30	4 5	6 50
0 10	0 7	0 4½	0 3½	Somerford..	,,	7 35	9 17	11 0	1 42	4 17	7 2
1 4	1 0	0 8	0 6½	Dauntsey ..	*arr.*	7 43	9 25	11 10	1 50	4 25	7 10
						1 2 3	1 2 3	1 2 3			
1 4	1 0	0 8	0 6½	Dauntsey ..	*arr.*	..	9 32	11 29	1 56	4 33	7 22
2 7	2 0	1 3½	1 0½	Chippenham	*arr.*	..	9 43	11 39	2 9	4 45	7 44
16 7	12 9	9 0	7 3	Weymouth	,,	..	2 0	3 23	6 28	20	1038
6 10	5 1	3 4½	3 0½	Bristol..	,,	..	10 48	12 50	3 10	6 58	50
							1 2 3		1 2 3	1 2 3	
1 4	1 0	0 8	0 6½	Dauntsey ..	*dep.*	7 52	9 56	11 15	2 18	5 1	7 27
3 4	2 6	0 0	1 5	Swindon ..	*arr.*	8 20	10 20	11 40	2 40	5 25	7 55
16 9	12 7	8 4½	7 10	Paddington	,,	1045	12 25	2 30	5 5	8	10 1020

DOWN TRAINS.				1 2 3	1 2 3	* 1 2 3	* 1 2 3	1 2 3
		a.m	a.m	a.m	‡	p.m	p.m	
Paddington	*dep.*	..	5 30	9 0	1145	3 0	5 0	
Swindon ..	,,	..	9 10	11 5	1 30	4 55	7 8	
Dauntsey..	*arr.*	..	9 32	11 29	1 56	5 18	7 32	
		1 2 3	1 2 3		1 2 3			
Bristol ..	*dep.*	6 25	8 40	10 0	1 15	3 30	5 50	
Weymouth	,,	..	5 25	..	1025	12 0	3 25	
Chippenham	,,	7 34	9 44	11 0	2 5	4 47	7 10	
Dauntsey ..	*arr.*	7 52	9 56	11 15	2 18	5 1	7 27	
			p		1 2 3	1 2 3	p	
Dauntsey ..	*dep.*	8 10	10 0	11 35	2 30	5 25	7 40	
Somerford	,,	8 18	10 8	11 43	2 38	5 33	7 48	
Malmesbury	*arr.*	8 30	1020	11 55	2 50	5 45	8 0	

* 1st and 2nd Class only from Paddington; 3rd class at 1·45.   † 3rd Class passengers reach Paddington at 10·20p.m.
‡ 1st and 2nd class from London, 3rd class 10.30 a.m.

Timetable connections and fares, Swindon Advertiser, July 1887.

Garlick. They had quite unexpectedly run up the line to the consternation of driver Nicholas Gray who was unable to avoid running them down.

The GWR first introduced headlamp codes on its locomotives from October 1888, an arrangement of lamps at the front of an engine indicating to signalmen what class of train was approaching. With possible classifications A to F, most of the Malmesbury branch trains, according to the WTT, ran as headcode 'A' with an unlighted lamp at the base of the engine's chimney, although a later designation of 1903 showed 'B' headcode for the mixed trains on the branch as opposed to those which ran as purely 'passenger'. In 1893 a 'B' indicated a cattle train for market, with a white diamond painted on a black background on a headlamp fixed at the foot of the chimney, whereas 'D' was for branch goods trains with a lamp over the locomotive's right-hand buffer by day, showing a green light forward at night. Further changes took place through the years.

By 1890 the branch advertisements locally featured a large number of excursion fares, usually specially priced journeys which often involved the branch train in extra trips, especially for return journeys at night. Typical destinations offered from Malmesbury were Bristol, Clevedon, Portishead, Ilfracombe, Weston-Super-Mare, Weymouth or London, or to such events as a Temperance Fete at the Crystal Palace or the Bath Horse Show. On Saturday, 29th June 1889, the appearance of Blondin, the 'Hero of Niagara', performing on the high wire at Cirencester, caused a rush of excursion fares from all over the system, a 2/6d return being offered from Malmesbury to this event with a return at 10.30 p.m.

In January 1893 the GWR introduced some improvements to the goods service on the branch, with the first purely goods train on the line and a new market day service. The branch engine left its coaches at Dauntsey to run a daily goods into Malmesbury where it arrived at 4.52 p.m., leaving again at 5.5. Two cattle trains were now provided each way on market days, hauled by the branch engine, leaving the terminus at 9.53 a.m. and 2.3 p.m.

The station house at Somerford was originally single storey, built in the same style as the lodges at Kingsmead and Dauntsey Road. By the end of the 1880s Somerford house was occupied by booking porter Stephen Emery and his family. He and his wife Eliza brought four children with them when he took on the post, and in 1890 the attendant in charge was regraded 'station inspector'. By 1892 there were four more young Emerys and no doubt the family were finding the house somewhat cramped, so in November 1893 the GWR spent £127 in adding an extra storey to the house, providing two more bedrooms. Mr Emery had a long association with the branch, as it is believed that he worked for the railway at Malmesbury, remained at Somerford to attain the grading of station master there in 1897, then moved on to Dauntsey as station master in 1903, where he stayed for eleven years until his retirement, thus being associated with every station on the Malmesbury branch.

In December 1893 the people of Malmesbury made representations to the GWR asking for earlier delivery of daily papers from London. A petition was organised by Mr Hanks, a stationer on the High Street, and in February 1894 arrangements were made so that the 7.20 a.m. train from Swindon to Chippenham followed instead of preceded the London train carrying the newspapers, a move allowing the papers to be switched to the local at Swindon, dropped off at Dauntsey and brought into Malmesbury at 8.52 instead of 10.25 as previously.

Military arrivals by rail were quite a regular event in the last century at Malmesbury, providing spectacular displays. Such an event was the visit made by the 2nd Volunteer Battalion of the Wiltshire Regiment on 27th October 1894. Complete with drum, fife, bugle band, bearers and signals, 200 men came in on the 2.40 p.m. train, formed up on the station approach and marched out to Cole Park where drills were held, followed by refreshments. What a grand sight they must have made as they marched back through the town in the evening, leaving on the 6.55 train.

In November 1894 Malmesbury inhabitants again asked the GWR for a service alteration, this time for a train on market days at 3 p.m. to connect with the 3.23 up and 3.24 down trains at Dauntsey. After due consideration, the General Manager expressed the view that the 4 p.m. ex-Malmesbury on the summer service could be re-timed to leave an hour earlier and meet the needs expressed. This was duly carried out and the train altered to 2.55 p.m. out of Malmesbury.

In January 1895 a new arrangement saw a mixed train leave Malmesbury at 4.55 p.m. instead of the daily 5.5 goods on Mondays and Fridays only, and by July 1897 the mixed train completely replaced the afternoon goods, with a 3.38 mixed from Dauntsey taking over from the 3.25 goods.

An unusual timetabling of July 1895 introduced a late Saturdays only excursion run on the branch, running as empty stock from Malmesbury at 9.15 and leaving Dauntsey at 9.45 for 10 p.m. back to the terminus. This continued during the July–December timetablings until 1898, after which it ceased. Whether this train was laid on as a result of generally increasing excursion traffic on the GWR, with the need to provide a regular late connection on the branch, is not known for certain – a similar provision existed on the Calne branch at this time.

In November 1895, in opposition to the GWR, a Bill was deposited in Parliament seeking powers to build the London & South Wales Railway, a scheme promoted by members of the minor Barry Dock & Railway Company, who wished to link their line at Cardiff to the Metropolitan at Great Missenden and the Midland at Hendon. Linking South Wales and London, the projected line would have served Malmesbury, which is specifically referred to in the plans, the route passing along the northern border of the town, very close to the branch terminus. Had this line been built, Malmesbury might actually have spent half a century with two stations! However, the Bill was withdrawn after negotiations with the GWR, but this ambitious scheme did have the effect of seeing the GWR bring forward its own plans for their South Wales and Bristol Direct Bill, the fruition of which was to have very important effects for the Malmesbury branch, as we shall see.

With the authorisation of the South Wales & Bristol Direct Railway in 1896, there appeared a new opportunity to improve Malmesbury's railway service, as the projected route ran less than $2\frac{1}{2}$ miles to the south of the town. During 1897 informal discussions took place between members of the Town Council and the GWR's Chief Engineer regarding the possibility of connecting the branch with the new main line. The first sod for the Direct was cut by the Duchess of Beaufort, on 29th November 1897 at Old Sodbury and construction began on a 31-mile link between Wootton Bassett and Patchway. It was intended to shorten the London to South Wales run by ten miles, avoiding Box tunnel and the Wootton Bassett incline and relieving congestion on the original GWR line between Bathampton and Bristol which had been especially busy since the opening of the Severn tunnel in 1880.

The GWR had two possibilities to consider in respect of Malmesbury – either a deviation of the new line at Somerford to place the route nearer the town with a new station giving direct service to Swindon (an idea which the townsfolk rather naively considered might be forthcoming on presentation of a petition) or, the more likely choice, the provision of a new junction at Somerford between the branch and the Direct. The GWR would hardly have countenanced a deviation in their high-speed route, the major part of which was to be embankment or cutting, but a new junction was feasible without detracting from the purpose of the line. Of course it would render the section between Somerford and Dauntsey redundant but it was to be 36 years before this was done. The work generated by the branch saw a further porter allocated to Dauntsey in October 1897, then in January 1898 an extra porter was added to the staff at Somerford in order to reduce the hours of the authorised staff, giving one John Colley his first GWR appointment on 15/- a week. He stayed for three years before moving on to become a signal porter at Hallatrow.

During winter, bad weather conditions, particularly fog, would cause main line trains to run late and miss branch connections (loss of time through engine failure or low speed due to engineering restrictions would also cause this) and it was apparently common practice for extra trains to be pro-vided on some branch lines to honour a connection. At Christmas 1897, for example, two extra services were run on 23rd December because of the late-running 5 p.m. Paddington and the 5.5 ex-Swindon, and the day after two more were run on the Malmesbury branch to give connection for the delayed 1.35 p.m. Paddington and again the 5 p.m.

On 21st March 1898, Thomas Wood, Malmesbury's station master, departed for Bruton, in Somerset. Two coal merchants, Walter Alexander of the Malmesbury Coal Co., and Samuel Fisher, visited the station to present him with a purse containing £16 10s collected from the tradesmen of the town in recognition of his 16 years service there. Mr Wood left to take up his new appointment by the 1.15 train that afternoon, remaining at Bruton until April 1904, after which nothing further is known of him. His successor at Malmesbury was Arthur W. Lloyd, a 29 year old passenger clerk from Corsham who stayed for nine years before promotion to the Class 2 appointment at Calne, where he remained until his death in 1930.

At a Malmesbury Town Council meeting in May 1898 further discussion took place concerning the branch and the South Wales Direct. Mr Hinwood, from the local bacon factory, expressed the view that closure of the Somerford–Dauntsey section was unnecessary – it would be more advantageous to keep that open and instead have a deviation from the planned Direct route with a junction at Great Somerford! This would have provided a connection with the new line *and* a junction at Dauntsey with the existing main line. Mr Forrester, the Mayor, declared that he would contact the GWR and that a deputation would be required to see the

An 1898 view of the foundations of Somerford Viaduct taking shape on the new Direct line. The photographer must have been standing with the Malmesbury branch behind him. To the right is the temporary Kingsmead Siding which connected to the branch at some point to the right off the photograph. There appears to be some further track laid at the upper right part of the photo, and it is clear from this view that the temporary siding crossed the River Avon. *Contractors' Chronicle*

GWR Directors. One imagines that the GWR's reaction to such an idea would have been less than enthusiastic at being asked to consider re-aligning their highly-prestigious new scheme for the sake of a small town in rural Wiltshire!

A discussion at this meeting which had a more immediate outcome was over the provision of Sunday train service on the branch. Farmers in the locality were keen to obtain Sunday

been constructed in such a way as to allow the goods train locomotive to run round its train for return to Dauntsey. Also during 1898, during the January–July timetable only, a late goods train service was provided on the branch, leaving Malmesbury at 9.30 p.m., calling at Somerford on both trips and returning to Malmesbury at 11.00 p.m. It is not known why this service was put on. It could have been an effort to keep

An early century look at Malmesbury terminus, with a variety of coal company wagons attached to the branch stock at the platform. The middle road is occupied by cattle wagons, a gas-tank wagon or cordon, and the coal wagon from which the locomotive was usually coaled. The Fisher Coal Company office can be seen in the yard beyond. *Collection Robin Littlewood*

conveyance for their milk, and the council unanimously decided to back a petition to the GWR requesting a Sunday evening train for passengers and milk.

The construction of the Direct line involved extensive works at Little Somerford, with the largest embankment on the railway, nearly four miles long and containing nearly a million cubic yards of material. A viaduct of thirteen arches was to cross the River Avon and immediately east of this a new bridge, numbered 16A on the branch, was to carry the Direct over the Malmesbury line. A temporary connection was put in from the Malmesbury branch to a new siding used for delivering of building materials for the work here, and for nearly five years the branch saw a great deal of extra traffic as materials were brought to the site. Kingsmead Siding first appeared in the WTT in January 1898 and was served by one daily goods train until January 1901 when the train was cut to three days a week until the removal of the siding late in 1902 when work at the site was complete. In 1898 the goods train left Swindon at 8.00 p.m., and arrived at Kingsmead from Dauntsey at 9.36 a.m., except on market days when it was retimed to come in at 11.22, allowing the market service to run as usual every third Wednesday in the month. The precise location of Kingsmead Siding is a mystery, although clues from photographs and press accounts suggest that it left the branch at some point between Kingsmead Crossing and the new Direct, the tracks crossing the Avon to give access to storage siding space on the west side of the river. It may have

delivery of supplies and heavy core to Kingsmead Siding at an hour when it would not interfere with the normal branch timetable during the first months of use of the siding when work and requirements there in respect of the Direct were quite heavy.

West of Little Somerford, the Direct ran through a cutting near Pincombe Wood and close to where the line crossed the Chippenham road $2\frac{1}{2}$ miles south of Malmesbury, an extensive depot was installed at Kingway Barn, where a large number of navvies were housed, with missions and reading rooms provided for them. During the seven year period of construction there were many accidents, many of them fatal, and newspapers of the period regularly mention injured workers being brought in to Malmesbury Hospital from Kingway Barn.

Agitation continued for connection of the branch to the Direct line. In August 1898 Earl Cawdor, Chairman of the GWR, received the following communication from the Mayor of Malmesbury, William Forrester, Esq:

'My Lord,

The Council of this Borough have requested me to call the attention of your Lordship as Chairman of your Board of Directors to a matter of great importance affecting the welfare of this Borough. As your Lordship is no doubt aware this place is entirely dependent on the Great Western Company for its railway communication which is at present given by the branch line from Dauntsey. That line mainly follows the course of the River Avon

The classic station postcard view, depicting Malmesbury around 1903, with the ancient Abbey as ever dominating the scene from the hilltop in the background. This photograph makes an interesting comparison with page 34, as the lamp hut (bottom right corner) is now in use and behind it is the old parcels office, formerly the 'hot water house' up to 1898. *Author's collection*

A view across the station forecourt at some time prior to 1912. There is as yet no new wooden parcels office, which was provided that year to the left of the platform entrance gate. The wooden entrance porch led directly into the first class waiting room, and was only ever opened and used when VIPs were passing through the station, such as Lord Suffolk's arrival shown on page 52. *Lens of Sutton*

MALMESBURY BRANCH.

Single Line, worked by Train Staff, and only one Engine in Steam at a time (or two or more coupled).   Colour and shape of Staff, White and Round.   No Block Telegraph.

DOWN TRAINS. — WEEK DAYS.

Distances	STATIONS	1 Mixed	3 Goods	5 Goods	7 Pass.	9 Goods	11 Pass.	13 Goods	14 Pass.	15 Mixed	16 Pass.	17 Pass.	18A Pass.
M C		A.M.	A.M.	A.M.	A.M.	A.M.	A.M.	P.M.	P.M.	P.M.	P.M.	P.M.	P.M.
—	Dauntsey ... dep.	8 20	9 37	9 37	10 15	11 12	11 45	1 42	2 25	3 43	6 0	8 20	10 10
2 30	Somerford ... ,,	8 28	W	ST	10 23	ST 11 22	11 58	W	2 33	3 55	6 8	8 28	10 18
6 40	Malmesbury ... arr.	8 40	9 46	9 41	10 35	W	12 10	1 57	2 45	4 10	6 20	8 40	10 30

DOWN TRAINS. — SUNDAYS.

STATIONS	1 Pass.
	P.M.
Dauntsey ... dep.	7 20
Somerford ... ,,	7 28
Malmesbury ... arr.	7 40

UP TRAINS. — WEEK DAYS.

STATIONS	Pass.	3 Pass.	5 Goods	7 Goods	9 Pass.	11 Goods	13 Mixed	14 Goods	15 Pass.	16 Mixed	17 Pass.	18A Pass.
	A.M.	A.M.	A.M.	A.M.	A.M.	A.M.	P.M.	P.M.	P.M.	P.M.	P.M.	P.M.
Malmesbury ... dep.	7 15	9 10	10 0	9 56	10 50	11 52	1 20	2 3	2 55	4 55	6 50	9 40
Kingsmead Siding ...			X	W		W		W				
Somerford ... ,,	7 27	9 22			11 2		1 32	2 19	3 7	5 7	7 5	9 52
Dauntsey ... arr.	7 35	9 30	10 10	10 11	11 10	11 42	1 40		3 15	5 15	7 13	10 0

UP TRAINS. — SUNDAYS.

STATIONS	1 Pass.
	P.M.
Malmesbury	5 40
Somerford	5 55
Dauntsey	6 3

* Third Wednesday in month only. Same Engine
X Third Wednesday in month excepted.
W Third Wednesday in month only.
' Guard will work 3.43 p.m. Mixed on this day instead of Branch engine, and afterwards work Special Dauntsey to Swindon or Bristol as ordered.
ST Engine to perform shunting at Malmesbury if required.

July–December 1899

and adapts itself to the level. The new South Wales Direct Railway, now in course of erection, crosses this line at a right angle at Little Somerford at a higher level than the Malmesbury line, but the plans of the new railway disclose no means of connection between that and the Malmesbury line. It follows, therefore, that persons travelling from Malmesbury to Wootton Bassett or Swindon will have to go to Dauntsey and thence back to the places mentioned and those who wish to go to South Wales will be obliged to go up the line to Wootton Bassett or Swindon if they wish to avail themselves of the benefits of the new line. I need hardly point out that this state of affairs would place this town at a great disadvantage, and I am sure that you will understand that my Council feel great anxiety on this subject. The geographical position of Malmesbury has on more than one occasion marked it out as a place through which the line connecting South Wales and London should run. Several projects and schemes have intersected it, and one proposed railway, of which Mr. Fowler was the engineer, and which ran on nearly parallel lines to the railway now being constructed, touched Malmesbury. It is not my wish to unduly magnify the importance of my Borough, but it is unquestionably the largest and most populous town adjacent to the new line between Newport and Swindon. My Council and I therefore address ourselves to your Lordship and the Board to aid us in at least mitigating the line and inconvenience awaiting the town if it be absolutely deprived of a connection with the new direct railway. The station nearest to our town on that line would be at Little Somerford, about three miles from here and immediately adjacent to the point at which the line crosses the Malmesbury branch. If a short connection between the two lines could be made it would be of great advantage and I am informed that it would not be a difficult or expensive link. This town does not claim to be of great manufacturing or commercial importance but it is undoubtedly the centre of a considerable district, possessing a good residential population which bids fair to increase.'

At the same time, a letter from Mr Joe Moore, Malmesbury's Town Clerk, to the local MP, made the following points:

'It cannot be expected that when the new line which is being constructed is made the present service of trains between Malmesbury and Dauntsey will be continued. Even if it were, Malmesbury would still be at a disadvantage – a route from London and Swindon via Dauntsey is much longer than it would be via Wootton Bassett and Little Somerford, hence Malmesbury would be practically cut off from the South Wales traffic. Malmesbury even now has a considerable share of South Wales business – Cardiff is a place to which many inhabitants of Malmesbury have emigrated and to which the people here send much agricultural produce, potatoes and other vegetables. Corn, fruit, cattle and pigs are constantly sent to Cardiff. When the new line is open there will be no cattle market between Wales and Swindon equalling Malmesbury for fatstock – butchers from Cardiff even now occasionally attend the market here. If the branch line were connected with the new main line at Little Somerford there would be a great increase in hunting traffic.'

Mr Moore's comments regarding westbound traffic from the branch are quite far-sighted, and his remarks concerning the market quite ironic in view of the fact that by the time the suggested link was finally made in the interests of economy in 1933, Malmesbury's market had declined to the extent that no special train was provided for market day service on the branch. The GWR, after considering overtures from Malmesbury, were unable to recommend the Little Somerford

GWR Working Timetable, July–December 1899, showing the branch's new Sunday service, goods provision to Kingsmead Siding in conjunction with the building of the new Direct, station trucks (ST) and a late Saturday night train.

Public Record Office

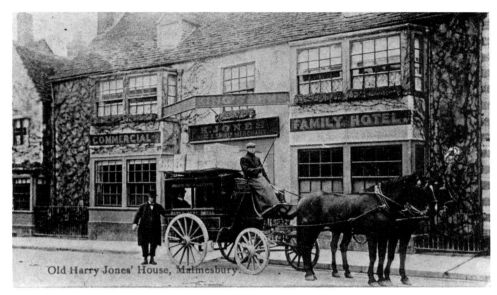

The Kings Arms horse-bus about to leave for the station, being seen off by landlord Harry Jones (referred to on page 41). The Kings Arms horse-bus met every incoming train. Surviving carriers' instruction logs from this hotel include the following:
20th Jan 1912 — one h & trap from the station to Charlton House and back to the Railway Hotel with the electric light man.
27th Jan — Brake and pair from the Station to Charlton and back with the Cricketers.
2nd Mar — one horse carriage from KA to Dauntsey Station with two commercials.
28th April — brake and pony from Station to Charlton Park with the Salisbury Police and fetch them in to the station at night.
Collection Robin Littlewood

Old Harry Jones' House, Malmesbury.

connection in 1898, the main reason appearing to be the delay it would involve to the completion of the Direct route.

The GWR's practice of running station trucks began in the 1880s – these were specially marked, covered vehicles which ran a designated daily circuit, and were used for the quick transport of perishables or other urgent traffic. It is not known for certain when Malmesbury first received its own station trucks but the 1894 WTT shows that Station Truck No. 43 was conveyed from Paddington to Swindon on the 12.50 a.m. to New Milford, a busy goods train which carried Weymouth line milk empties, goods traffic for Swindon, the Gloucester line and South Wales, and meat traffic for the Aberdare and Merthyr areas. Malmesbury's truck was dropped at Swindon at 5.00 a.m. and transferred to the 6.00 a.m. Swindon–Yeovil goods which left it at Dauntsey at 6.35 to be added to the 8.20 mixed branch train. In this way Malmesbury's master grocers received their high quality produce from London. Several STs were carried by the New Milford train, marshalled in correct order for dropping at stations and junctions en route. By 1903 No. 43 was being taken by the 11.35 p.m. Paddington–Bristol, carrying general goods traffic from Paddington and Acton for Chippenham and beyond. By July 1901 two further station trucks were shown on the branch, No. 137A to Swindon which was collected by the 2.45 ex-Bristol to Banbury Junction goods which called at Dauntsey at 6.25 p.m., and 137B to Chippenham which was collected by the 6.45 Swindon–Yeovil with milk vans off the 12.48 p.m. Paddington, leaving the Malmesbury ST at Chippenham before proceeding west. The Yeovil train took northern traffic brought down by the 3.50 a.m. from Oxley, doing local work and distributing milk cans at local stations below Witham. Both the 137 trucks went out of Malmesbury on the 4.55 p.m. mixed, probably conveying bacon, a major earner for the branch. In May 1905 the 137 STs were renumbered 171 and 172, the Swindon 171 being collected at Dauntsey at 8.25 by the Corsham stone, No. 172 for Chippenham being picked up at 6.55 by the Swindon–Dauntsey local goods. ST 43 for Malmesbury was by this time being taken on the 11.35 p.m. Paddington to Truro.

The presence of a pig on the line on the morning of Wednesday, 22nd July 1898 preceded an accident to the 9.05 train from Malmesbury. As the train emerged from the tunnel the driver caught sight of the pig and slackened speed to avoid running over it. It did not get clear of the rails, however, and, in a colourful description for normally staid Victorian news, the *North Wilts Herald* reported that 'the engine converted it into pork'. At Cowbridge, the engine, running bunker-first, jumped the rails owing to the breaking of the left-hand bogie spring. No one was hurt in the mishap, although the train ploughed for some 200 yds along the ballast before stopping. The passengers, including a GWR Director, Mr F. Davis of Ladyswood, were conveyed to Dauntsey by road, where Mr Jefford obtained an engine and some milk vans, the only vehicles available, to run on the branch and bring in passengers for Malmesbury market – they alighted at Cowbridge, and horse buses from the Kings' Arms Hotel took them on into town. A breakdown gang from Swindon arrived to clear the line, which was open again shortly after noon.

Passenger accommodation on the branch trains from Dauntsey was normally provided by a set of three four-wheel coaches, the typical stock built for branch line and suburban workings during 1890–1902. Those in use from the mid-1890s gave nearly 40 years of service in the Swindon area. The Malmesbury set comprised a brake third at each end, each with three third-class compartments, and between them a brake composite coach containing 1st and 2nd class compartments, the first class being the centre two sections. As winter approached in October 1898, passengers on the branch were pleasantly reassured by the introduction of steam heating to the coaches. The old footwarmers could nevertheless be obtained on request at some stations until 1908! It is doubtful whether this was the case at Malmesbury, however, as the old 'hot water house' in which the footwarmers were prepared was converted into a parcels office four months later at a cost of £24. Malmesbury branch stock would have been miserably cold in the winters of the early days of the line, especially in third class, as the footwarmers simply did only that. In the renovation of the branch set, the old rape-oil roof lamps were replaced by lighting from a gas cylinder carried underneath the coach, and in 1900 gas lighting was further improved by the introduction of incandescent gas mantles. As the branch train never went through to Swindon in those days, it now became necessary to keep a 'cordon' or gas tank wagon on the middle road at Malmesbury so that gas cylinders on the coaches could be readily replenished at the station when required. Oil-gas was manufactured in gasworks at Swindon, and greasers employed to travel around the system regularly to replenish gaslit coaches.

A late Saturday train was also introduced on the branch around this time and Malmesbury's Sunday train service materialised on 2nd July 1899, so that the district's milk traffic might reach London in a fresh condition. It left Malmesbury at 4.50 p.m., returning from Dauntsey at 7.20 p.m. for Malmesbury at 7.40. The service survived in more or less the same form until after closure of the original line from Dauntsey. Three weeks later two window straps were cut in the branch train by a local who boarded the last train of the day from Dauntsey in an intoxicated state. The straps were later found in a vegetable garden near Somerford station and handed in to the station master, Mr Emery. The case went to court where the defendant was fined £2 6s 0d.

From July 1900 a Mondays Only late service was introduced on the branch for the duration of the July–December timetable, later amended to July–September. Departures were from Malmesbury at 9.15 p.m. and from Dauntsey at 9.45. It is thought to have been a regular timetabled excursion run to connect with the summer Weston-Super-Mare excursion service from Swindon, the return train calling at Dauntsey at 10.7 p.m. This service lasted until 1914 and ceased with the outbreak of war.

We have observed how the building of Malmesbury's railway gave the town a more eastwards-inclined outlook, towards Swindon and London. In 1900 the Wiltshire Archaeological and Natural History Society held their 47th AGM in Malmesbury, and their subsequent report reflected this situation with the comment, 'As Malmesbury is not easily reached by rail from other parts of the county, only some 19 members were present.' Although Malmesbury's market received a great boost from the coming of the railway, there was also a counter-productive result in that people in Malmesbury could now reach larger markets by train, such as those at Swindon and Chippenham. By 1900 the Malmesbury market had again declined, despite the provision of more market day services, although the annual Christmas Fat Cattle Show was still popular. It dealt mainly in mixed agricultural products with an emphasis on livestock. Local markets in small towns retained some importance as long as livestock was difficult to transport, but the development of motor transport after the Great War saw the Malmesbury market decline to such an extent that only a small number of cattle wagons were required at the station. It is an interesting reflection of this situation that in the early years of the 20th century the GWR advertised cheap market tickets from Malmesbury and Somerford to Chippenham for the market there, at 1/4d third class, but no similar facility was readily available to Malmesbury on market day at this time.

On market days in 1902, the third Wednesday in the month (altered to the last Wednesday in May 1905), a train of cattle wagons was made up at Swindon, the 'Malmesbury Goods' in the WTT, and departed for Dauntsey at 8.05, arriving there at 8.35. After the arrival of the 9.35 branch train, the market special collected the train staff and set off for Malmesbury at 9.36, arriving at 9.51. The wagons were left at the terminus and the locomotive returned 'light' to Dauntsey where it was available for shunting duty in the yard, this allowing the branch train to resume service. At this time the market day engine was a Swindon-based pannier or saddle tank, which went into Malmesbury again at 1.42 p.m. to collect the loaded cattle wagons, which had been horse-drawn up to the pens for loading, then formed into a train on the middle road ready for the Swindon engine, which worked them out again at 2.05. According to the WTT, the Swindon engine and guard also worked the 3.43 pm mixed train into Malmesbury on market days, instead of the branch engine, and therefore must have worked the up 4.55 mixed, bearing the station trucks for Swindon and Chippenham. Back at Dauntsey, it worked market traffic to 'Bristol or Swindon, as ordered'. The branch locomotive then resumed normal service on the 6.05 passenger train from Dauntsey. All this juxtaposition of traffic conformed to the 'one engine in steam' rule in force on the branch.

The terminus at Malmesbury had to be cleared of wagons the day before market day so that the centre road at the station could be left empty for cattle wagons. Vehicles could be left out in the back road and up refuge at Dauntsey and in the siding at Somerford, although, if the expected load was not too great, the checker would do the work early on market day as the back road at the junction was usually required for milk traffic. When preparing the yard at Malmesbury for such busy periods, when maximum shunting space was required, the branch coaches would sometimes be moved temporarily out beyond the signal box or out by Lovers Lane Crossing. A push from the locomotive at the platform would be enough to send the smoothly-running stock along the very gentle gradient down towards the crossing, where the guard could hold the coaches on his hand-brake. This procedure almost caused a nasty accident to an otherwise-occupied courting couple on one occasion, surprised by the coaches moving quietly down to the crossing!

On 22nd February 1902 travellers on the branch witnessed a surprise at Kingsmead when one of the contractor's locomotives, engaged upon work in connection with the new main line, became derailed. The engine had been proceeding along the temporary line which connected the Direct with the Malmesbury branch when something went wrong at the points, it toppled over the embankment and overturned to rest with its wheels in the air. Three men had been on the engine, but were, surprisingly, unhurt.

In July 1902 Malmesbury's known staffing was as follows:

Station master	Arthur W. Lloyd	£110 a year
Lad clerk	Frederick Coates	£20 a year
Passenger guard	Reuben Jeffreys	23/- a week
Porter guard	John Quarrell	20/- a week
Shunter	Jacob Baker	20/- a week
Porter 1	Cecil Chalk	18/- a week
Porter 2	George Woodward	17/- a week
Lad porter	George Bennett	10/- a week

Known staff of the locomotive department were:

Branch enginemen	Edward Jones	6/6 a day
	Evan Harry	4/9 a day
Branch fireman	Edwin Minty	3/6 a day
Shunting fireman	Fred Wells	3/- a day

No record has been found of the cleaner.

The new viaduct at Little Somerford, looking north. Kingsmead Crossing can be seen through the third arch from the left, with the Malmesbury branch embankment visible through the large arch on the right.
Science Museum, Kensington

With Somerford Viaduct complete, some of the Direct's builders pose with Kingsmead Crossing gateman William Ponting, seen second right. He became the one serious casualty of the branch's construction when in 1875 he lost his right arm in an accident in Baskerville Cutting. Seen on the temporary Kingsmead Siding laid during construction of the Direct, *Corston*, an 0-6-0 Manning Wardle built in 1890, No. 1196, was one of 47 engines used on the Direct contract. It was known to have left the Kingsmead working by 1899.
By kind permission of Jessica Reeve

The new Direct complete, not long after 1903, looking towards Little Somerford through the Dauntsey Road railway bridge, 89 miles 29 chains from Paddington. The house visible beyond the embankment was one of a number provided in 1869 by Malmesbury's MP, Walter Powell. It was later the home of Malmesbury branch fireman Ken Stoneham.   *Author's collection*

Employment on the railway provided a secure job for its workforce as well as plenty of opportunity for promotion for those who were so inclined. Of the above staff, Jeffreys, Baker, Quarrell and Harry had been on the Malmesbury branch since the beginning, although the work of the porters at this time was very demanding and tended to serve as a useful stepping-stone to promotion. Edward Guy is a case in point – born in 1875, his first GWR employment was as a horse driver at Swindon in 1896 on 15/- a week. In January 1897 he arrived at Dauntsey as a 16/- a week porter and spent five years meeting branch and main line trains and cleaning and trimming lamps before transferring to Malmesbury in September 1902. He worked there for seven years as an 18/- a week porter, then transferred to Frome as a rail motor conductor in October 1909, a post which brought his wage up to 21/- a week. After a short period in Somerset, he went onto main line express work as a passenger guard based at Newport High Street at a wage of 23/-.

In November 1902 Malmesbury's guard since 1878, Reuben Jeffreys, retired early and his post was taken by Jacob Baker, who had been the branch shunter also since the early days. Jeffreys was born in 1847 and had been a signalman at Bristol and Box before coming to Malmesbury, and hailed from a family of twelve children, all named after biblical characters. On December 23rd his retirement was marked by a presentation in the station office at Malmesbury. After the arrival of the 12.10 train, a deputation waited upon him, comprising his successor, Jacob Baker, branch driver Ted Jones, station master Mr Lloyd, and the Mayor with members of the Town Council. The Mayor, Councillor W. Woodman, made a presentation of a purse of gold subscribed for by people of Malmesbury as 'a slight acknowledgement of his uniform civility

and courtesy to the travelling public of Malmesbury ever since the opening of the new line.' Jeffreys had indeed set a standard for impeccable efficiency, good humour and politeness on his branch train duties which was carried on by his successors, Baker and Quarrell, in a manner which is still remembered in the town today.

On 8th January 1903 the first section of the new South Wales Direct was opened for goods traffic between Wootton Bassett and Badminton. The remaining section west to Patchway was similarly opened on 1st May and the whole route opened for passenger service on 1st July 1903. The 31-mile line possessed no gradient steeper than 1 in 300 and ran via the 4444 yd Sodbury Tunnel under the main ridge of the Cotswolds. There was no formal opening of the Direct owing to the death of the GWR's General Manager, Sir Joseph Wilkinson, but the villagers of Little Somerford and other habitations along the new 'Badminton' line were treated to free rides on the first day of passenger service.

The opening of the Direct had immediate consequences for Somerford station on the Malmesbury branch. To avoid confusion with its main line neighbour, the branch station was renamed Great Somerford from 1st January 1903, an appropriate reflection of the fact that the village itself underwent several name-changes – Victorian maps of the area refer to it as Somerford Magna and Airey's Railway Map of the West of England (1886) listed the station as Broad Somerford, an appellation which appears on some village postcards.

In April 1903 Great Somerford's station master Stephen Emery moved up the line to promotion at Dauntsey, a class 4 appointment, succeeding Samuel Jefford who moved on after 21 years in charge of Dauntsey to become the first station master at the new station at Badminton on the Direct. The

Class 5 appointment at Great Somerford was taken by Jacob Rogers at a rate of 29/- a week, after varied experience as a slipper boy, policeman, signalman and porter with nine years work on the Midland Railway. At this time Rogers had four staff under his jurisdiction, the two gatemen at Dauntsey Road and Kingsmead and the two porters on his station, but following the opening of Little Somerford station, the payroll at Great Somerford was reduced by one porter. This was an expected economy in view of the fact that the new main line station would take traffic from its branch neighbour for they were less than a mile apart, and when porter John Payne moved to Yatton as a signal porter in June 1903 he was not replaced. In 1903 8,660 tickets were issued from Great Somerford, and if this represented an average of less than two passengers per train, the total station receipts of £2,595 were some twelve times the size of the wagebill of £191. During July to December 1903, a goods train, lamp code K, ran from Dauntsey at 1.38 p.m. daily to Great Somerford, returning to the junction at 2.15. It appears to have been short-lived –

perhaps for some exceptional traffic. As there was no loop at Great Somerford, it is probable that gravity was used to enable the locomotive to reach the other end of the train.

It was now recognised that there were two possible routes to Swindon and to Bristol from the locality, and the GWR agreed that passengers booking return tickets at either of the Somerford stations could travel back via either line without extra charge providing they arranged their own conveyance between the two villages. The same arrangement was allowed in the reverse direction, whereby visitors to the area from stations between Bristol and Swindon on both main lines could begin their return trip at either Great Somerford or Little Somerford. It was also agreed that holders of ordinary return or market tickets from Malmesbury to Bristol via Dauntsey could travel via Little Somerford and Badminton on the forward or return journeys if they so chose.

During 1904 the first branch train of the day was timed to leave Malmesbury at 7.05, the earliest ever in normal branch service there. The same year saw the retirement of Alfred Gale

MALMESBURY BRANCH.
Single Line, worked by Train Staff, and only one Engine in Steam at a time (or two or more coupled).

Distances. M C.	DOWN TRAINS. STATIONS.					WEEK DAYS.						
		1	2	3	4	5	6	7	8	9	10	11
		B Mixed X	K Goods	B Pass.			B Pass.		K Goods	B Pass.	B Mixed	B Pass.
		A.M.	A.M.	A.M.			A.M.		P.M.	P.M.	P.M.	P.M.
—	Dauntsey .. .. dep.	8 15	9X36	10 15	..	..	11·30	..	1X25	2X20	3 45	6 5
2 63	Great Somerford .... ,,	8 23	W	10 23	..	..	11·38	....	W	2 28	3 53	6 13
6 54	Malmesbury .... arr.	8 35	9 51	10 35	....	..	11·50	....	1 42	2 40	4 5	6 25

DOWN TRAINS STATIONS.	WEEK DAYS.			SUND'YS.		UP TRAINS. STATIONS.	WEEK DAYS.			
	12	13	14	1	2		1	2	3	4
	B Pass.	B MO		B Pass.			B Pass.	B Pass.		K Goods
	P.M.	P.M.		P.M.			A.M.	A.M.		A.M.
Dauntsey .. dep.	8 30	9 50	..	7 20	..	Malmesbury .. dep.	7 25	9 15	..	10 0
Great Somerford ,,	8 38	9 58	....	7 28	....	Great Somerford ,,	7 35	9 27	....	W
Malmesbury .... arr.	8Y50	10Y10	.	7 40	..	Dauntsey .. arr.	7 43	9X35	..	10X15

UP TRAINS STATIONS.	WEEK DAYS.										SUND'YS	
	5	6	7	8	9	10	11	12	13	14	1	2
	B Pass.		B Mixed		K Goods V	B Pass.	B Mixed V	B Pass.	D C'chs. MO		B Pass.	
	A.M.		P.M.		P.M.	P.M.	P.M.	P.M.	P M		P.M.	
Malmesbury .. dep.	10 55	...	1 3	....	2 3	2 50	4 55	6 55	9†20	..	5 50	..
Great Somerford ,,	11 7	..	1 15	....	W	3 2	5 7	7 10	—	....	6 5	....
Dauntsey .. .. arr.	11.15	....	1X23	....	2X18	3 10	5 15	7 18	9†35	..	6 13	..

V S.T. 171 Malmesbury to Swindon, 172 Malmesbury to Chippenham. **W** Last Wednesday in month only (calling at Great Somerford if required to pick up urgent traffic or foreign empties). Same Engine and Guard will work 3.45 p.m. Mixed on this day instead of Branch Engine, and afterwards work Special Dauntsey to Swindon or Bristol as ordered. **X** ST 43 Paddington to Malmesbury. **Y** Engine to perform shunting at Malmesbury.

Working timetable of July 1905, showing station truck details, market day goods service (W), and an interesting Mondays only late run in which empty coaches were taken to Dauntsey for 9.35 p.m., probably in conjunction with timetabled excursion traffic. Although specifically mixed trains are timetabled, those designated 'Pass' often in fact ran as mixed trains with extra wagons added to the passenger stock. The maximum number of vehicles allowed on branch trains at this time were 15 coal/minerals, 22 goods, 26 mixed, 30 empties.

after 17 years as ganger on the branch – a later *GWR Magazine* staff section recorded he and his wife's Golden Wedding.

No royal visits were ever made to Malmesbury by train, but the station was much used by local gentry and members of the landowning aristocracy in the days before motor cars became available. The station and branch were well looked after in those halcyon days before the great conflagration of 1914, with clean, constantly-swept stations, sparkling polished

new works were inspected by Colonel Yorke for the Board of Trade on 24th August 1906, and were passed for use immediately. Runaway catch points were ordered at a cost of £20 in December 1906.

A new station master took over at Malmesbury in January 1907, Edgar Doswell moving from the Swindon Assistant Superintendent's Office to take on the Class 3 post at £130 a year salary. Born on 17th February 1873 at Frome, he had

The arrival of the Earl and Countess of Suffolk and Berkshire, 5th January 1905, photographed on Malmesbury station forecourt. The old parcels office is visible to the right.   *Athelstan Museum*

locomotives and branch coaches with their luxuriously-upholstered first class compartments all reflecting the affluence and prestige of Malmesbury and its surroundings, an air of affluence that still exists today with the town very much a border outpost of 'Beaufortshire', the Cotswold 'Royal Triangle'.

On 5th January 1905, a notable arrival took place at Malmesbury station when the Earl and Countess of Suffolk & Berkshire arrived en route to their home at nearby Charlton Park. The Earl had just married his American bride, formerly Miss Daisy Leiter, and before leaving the station they inspected the Malmesbury Company of the Wiltshire Rifle Corps who were lined up to greet the couple's arrival on the station forecourt. The new Countess was famous for her efforts to revive the local lacemaking industry in 1908.

Following recommendations of the GWR Traffic Committee of August 1903, the Economic System of Maintenance was introduced on the branch in March 1905. This system involved modified and more economical arrangements for safe working of lines during repairs and other works incidental to maintenance of the permanent way. In January 1906 there appeared new instructions in the WTT – 'Engineers to have absolute occupation of the Malmesbury branch from 5.00 a.m. until the first train out of Malmesbury.'

In August 1906 alterations were made at Dauntsey between the branch and the main line, with the addition of slip points to provide a crossover between the up and down main lines, with consequent alterations to the signalling, upping the number of levers in use in the new signal box of 1903 to 33, with four spares. A new bay line down branch starter was installed several yards farther from the buffer stops than its predecessor and the branch run-round loop re-aligned. The

begun in 1888 as a goods clerk on £20 a year at Chippenham and progressed to Swindon via the District Superintendent's Office at Temple Meads. While at Swindon he met and courted a girl who worked at the station's famed refreshment rooms and they married shortly after his appointment to Malmesbury. Curiously, although the other stations associated with the branch possessed station houses, no such facility existed at Malmesbury for the official in charge, and after living first in the Gastons, the Doswells rented a house on Tetbury Hill. Mr Doswell's 12-year stay was a very happy one for the family, and such was the esteem in which a respected station master was held in rural communities in days gone by, that there were many gifts each Christmas from the town's tradespeople – toys for the children, a large parcel from the bacon factory, and pheasants and rabbits from farmers. Mr Doswell had a particularly fine hand which stood him in good stead for all the accountancy skills and administration required of a station master. His stay at Malmesbury was followed by a promotion to a Class 2 post at Lawrence Hill, Bristol, from where he retired in 1933. He died in 1951, the year in which Malmesbury's passenger service ceased.

In April 1908 more alterations took place at Dauntsey, this time involving extension of the platform at the east end of the station at a total cost of £1,168. The development of a huge milk traffic from the junction required provision of more loading space, so a new milk dock was built on the siding behind the passenger platform and the points forming the connections into the goods yard had to be relocated eastwards to accommodate the lengthening of the up platform. A new 11-lever ground frame was installed at the end of the down platform for working the points and crossovers to the yard, with extra levers to provide main line to main line crossover.

GREAT ✤ WESTERN ✤ RAILWAY.

Malmesbury Flower Show.

On Thursday, August 12th, 1909

CHEAP RETURN TICKETS

(First, Second and Third Class) will be issued to

MALMESBURY

AS UNDER:—

FROM.	AT	RETURN FARES.		
	p.m.	1st Class.	2nd Class.	3rd Class.
Swindon - - - -	1.53	3/7	2/4	1/10
Wootton Bassett - -	2.4	2/6	1/7	1/3
Dauntsey - - -	2.22	1/5	1/0	9d.
Chippenham - - -	2.5	2/9	1/10	1/5
Calne - - - -	1.15	3/9	2/6	2/0

Passengers return from Malmesbury by any Train the same day.

A SPECIAL LATE TRAIN will leave Malmesbury at 10.45 p.m.

Calling at Great Somerford, Dauntsey, Wootton Bassett & Swindon.

Children under Three years of age, Free; Three and under 12, Half-price.

NO LUGGAGE ALLOWED.

The Tickets are not transferable. Should a Cheap Ticket be used for any other Station than those named upon it, or by any other Train than those specified above, it will be rendered void, and therefore the Fare paid will be liable to forfeiture, and the full ordinary fare will become chargeable.

Paddington, August, 1909.

JAMES C. INGLIS, General Manager.

(Bristol—450.)   N. RIDDICK, PRINTER AND BOOKBINDER, MALMESBURY.   (B 593).

The building of the new milk dock required the demolition of a goods lock-up shed which stood in the yard prior to this work. In February 1909 'improvement of distant signals at Dauntsey' was carried out for £162.

In April 1909 second class accommodation was abolished in Britain other than on boat trains to continental ports such as Dover and Newhaven. Therefore Malmesbury's trains provided 1st and 3rd class compartments from 1909 until 1951, the change to 1st and 2nd class not coming until the mid-1950s when the French and other European nations abolished their 3rd class, by which time Malmesbury had lost its passenger service.

The years of the present century up to the Great War saw much popular use of the GWR excursion, trains which were advertised to provide a specific run at a reduced rate. In this way folk in rural areas could obtain a cheap day's visit to the capital or to the seaside, and those in urban areas could take a trip to the country, to places that had been as remote as outer space in an earlier age. The excursions introduced city folk to the delights of rural Wiltshire, and Malmesbury saw many weekend and Bank Holiday visitors in this way, the attractions of the ancient Abbey bringing many to the town by train. Midweek there was rarely any need to provide extra trains on the branch, as the normal service would suffice in daytime, but Sundays would require an extra train to run to

Dauntsey, either taking excursionists early in the morning or meeting incoming trippers from main line trains at the junction. The most popular excursions of pre-WWI years were to London, Weymouth and Weston-Super-Mare, whilst an excursion to Bristol, according to Malmesbury's great historian, Stan Hudson, could provide a Saturday night trip to the cinema with faggots and peas, Woodbines and matches, and train journey, all for less than a shilling! The GWR also provided 'specials' – another form of extra train but run for pre-set groups or organisations, such as the annual 'treats' arranged by local firms for their employees, or other organisations such as the Sunday schools. For years Malmesbury Fire Brigade booked a yearly trip by train, usually to a coastal venue such as Southampton. Both excursions and specials provided a great deal of extra work for the branch train, often augmented with extra carriages and sometimes another locomotive for double-heading from Swindon. It was usually necessary for the branch set to make a late run out to Dauntsey and back to collect the returning trippers, as return was often well after the last regular train of the night – such runs commonly took place between 11.00 p.m. and midnight, although it was not unusual for the Malmesbury train to collect excursionists in the small hours of the morning, with the branch engine being finally shedded for the night as late as 4.00 a.m.

2nd January 1911 at Malmesbury, with '517' Class 0−4−2T No. 844 at the platform with the branch set ready for the bunker-first trip to Dauntsey. Ted Jones, branch engineman 1898−1913, is seen leaning against the engine, whilst the fireman aboard is thought to be Fred Morbey. Of the remainder of the large staff group posing for the camera, it has only been possible to positively identify porter John Quarrell – the moustached gentleman seen standing on the right of the group on the platform paving slabs.   *Courtesy Mr. & Mrs. K. Iles*

In 1912 Malmesbury's Jacob Baker retired, having been employed at the station since the opening. He had moved from Chippenham (Goods) to take up the job of shunter in December 1877 on a rate of 22/- a week. For the last ten years of his working life he was branch guard, being succeeded by another GWR veteran, John Quarrell, like Baker, a servant of the branch since opening.

In 1912, the country's miners went on strike for better wages and conditions, the shortage of coal affecting the Malmesbury branch service when the GWR introduced a 'Coal Strike' timetable on 3rd March 1912. Although some branches had their trains completely cut, the important mixed traffic and the milk business on the Malmesbury branch made necessary the retention of the first train of the day and the evening 6.55 from Malmesbury, but the Sunday train was taken off. With an easing of the strike and an improvement in coal stocks, the GWR announced partial restoration of train service in the Bristol District from 14th April, and six trains each way per weekday were run on the Malmesbury line. With the termination of the strike, the Sunday train resumed and normal working returned to the branch on 29th April, but in the following July, the mid-morning 10.55 train out of Malmesbury and the 11.40 return were cut from service. A more positive development of 1912 was the authorisation of additional parcels office accommodation and the building of a new wooden parcels office by the side gate exit from the platform, costing £58.

From 1912 Malmesbury saw a great deal of military movements owing to the presence of army summer camps at Charlton Park and Easton Grey. In September 1912 it was necessary to move the Wiltshire Yeomanry 'C' Squad of the Royal Garrison Artillery to attend Army Manoeuvres at Hitchin, and empty stock was sent in to Malmesbury to collect one officer, two chargers, twenty-four men and their mounts. There was normally at least one horse-box present at Malmesbury owing to the brisk traffic associated with hunts and polo meets, but on this occasion it was necessary to send an extra three 'Mex B' horse-boxes, which could hold six troop horses each. Specials run for the Royal Wilts Yeomanry became a regular sight on the branch for several years. Horses were trained locally for the Gloucester Hussars, and during 1913 the number of horse-boxes kept at the station increased owing to the need to move horses regularly. On 9th May 1913, two 'Pacos', eight 'Mex B' and a van attached next to the engine were provided to convey six men and fifty-nine horses to Brighton for the Hussars, GWR instructions to branch staff being to 'detach smartly at Dauntsey' and transfer the traffic to a special to Swindon.

Quite the most impressive of all the military train movements on the Malmesbury branch took place on Sunday, 11th May 1913, enlivening a normally quiet day on the branch, when trains were run from Salisbury and Marlborough to convey the Royal Wiltshire Yeomanry to their summer camp at Charlton Park, during a busy period of mobilisation of Territorials to camps at Malmesbury, Amesbury, Box, Frome and Pembrey. The first of the Malmesbury trains departed Salisbury at 10.45 a.m. and was made up of a brake composite coach, two third class coaches, one 'Paco', four 'Mex B', a brake van and milk truck. A further seven 'Mex B' and two 'Pacos' were added en route at Warminster and Trowbridge, the train conveying some 87 men and a similar number of

horses to Dauntsey where arrival was at 12.35 p.m. The branch engine left Malmesbury at midday and brought the train onto the branch at 12.45 with a 1.00 p.m. arrival in Malmesbury, whereupon motor conveyance took the men out to their camp. The branch engine then returned the empty stock to the main line engine at Dauntsey and awaited the arrival of the second troop special. This train had left Westbury at 10.10 a.m. bearing a brake composite, two thirds and a brake van. It ran to Marlborough where two 'Pacos' and three 'Mex B' were added and 23 men and their mounts

Members of the Wiltshire Regiment's Territorial Battalions posing outside the entrance to Little Somerford station during local drills just prior to the Great War. The bridge behind carried the South Wales Direct of 1903 and was later widened to accommodate the re-routed Malmesbury branch to Little Somerford.
Courtesy Mrs. F. Bubb

boarded. It left Marlborough at 11.40 and called at Savernake before stopping at Patney and Chirton where a further two 'Pacos' and a six 'Mex B' were put on and a large contingent of 47 men with 50 horses and large amounts of baggage and munitions were picked up. The train then ran via Devizes, Seend and Holt Junction to Melksham, where a further detachment was collected and another two 'Mex B' added. On arrival at Dauntsey, via Chippenham, at 1.50 p.m., the branch engine again brought the train on from the junction for a 2.15 arrival in Malmesbury. The presence of some 19 vehicles on both these specials tends to suggest that double-heading might have been used on the branch for what would have been lengthy and extremely heavy trains.

In 1913, the last year before hostilities in Europe changed the face of life forever, Malmesbury was a Class 3 station with seven men on its payroll. This period was a peak for the line before, like many small branches, its business was affected by the war – the onset of huge wage rises, the eight-hour day, and the coming of increased road transport. In 1913 the annual staff payroll at Malmesbury totalled £487, a mere twenty-sixth of the total receipts for the branch of £12,750. At the terminus 17,106 tickets were issued and the handling of 66,337 parcels gave passenger traffic returns of £6,361. Total goods tonnage of 16,370, mainly received, produced goods receipts of £6,774. Outgoing traffic was brisk in milk, bacon, silk, root vegetables from the Malmesbury Commoners, much of which travelled as parcel traffic on passenger trains, and hay and straw for South Wales pit ponies and the GWR provender at Didcot. Being amidst a predominantly agricultural region, much farm produce travelled from Malmesbury on the branch trains; the Cole farm at Rodbourne Rail, for instance, sent some 900 rabbits a year to Smithfield Market. By contrast, Great Somerford had suffered a decline of some £1,000 in receipts since 1903, virtually its only parcel business being milk. It had, of course, lost out to Little Somerford on the new main line, which had handled over 20,000 parcels in 1903 and continued to rise to a peak of 41,000 by 1930.

Whitsun Bank Holiday in June 1914 proved to be the end of a golden period for rail travel at Malmesbury as hundreds of visitors from all over England came in and enjoyed the walk up to the town and Abbey from the station. In time there would be a sadder, grimmer traffic, as storm clouds gathered in Europe, hostilities precipitated by the assassination in far-off Sarajevo. On 4th August 1914, Great Britain declared war on Germany, and the following day the Government took over all the country's railways, vesting their control in a Railway Executive Committee consisting of the President of the Board of Trade and the General Managers of the principal lines. Government traffic had precedence and was to be carried without charge and there began a fortnight of mobilisation on the GWR in which 632 troop trains were run, including 186 to bring back Territorials from their summer training camps. One of these arrived in Malmesbury on 5th August, taking 30 men and their horses, stores and artillery away to war, and several more troop specials were provided during the next few days, Malmesbury station being quite an emotional place as many tearful scenes took place on the platform as the soldiers prepared to leave, many never to return. During military movements it was normal practice for the entrance to the station yard from the road to be guarded by six men with loaded carbines.

In May 1914, following the departure of Robert Chapman to Wylye, Great Somerford came under the station mastership of William Reynolds. Born in 1875, he had held no less than six such appointments in South Wales between 1899 and 1910, these moves being on account of health difficulties. In 1914, whilst in charge at Aberdylais, near Neath, he had to take medical advice and seek a post at a more quiet rural station – he thus came to Great Somerford on a wage of 35/- a week and stayed for the duration of the war. The country air seems to have benefited his health, he eventually moving on to a promotion at Patchway. He was a popular official at Somerford being a regular attender at village functions, and the family received much local bounty from the inhabitants each Christmas, notably pheasant, rabbit and partridge from the local farmers. With the outbreak of war not long after his appointment, Mr Reynolds was awakened around 2.00 a.m. one morning by a call from Divisional HQ instructing him to ensure that the level crossing gates were open for three special trains sent into Malmesbury to collect the Territorials from Charlton Park, and the family were later dimly aware of these night trains rumbling through the station just outside their bedroom windows. Autumn 1914 was particularly busy with war traffic on the branch, and Mr Reynolds' son Joe later recalled that the railway telephone seemed to be ringing all the time.

That September Belgian refugees came in to be billeted at Charlton Park and there were special trains for the Royal Field Artillery's Ammunition Column from training on Salis-

bury Plain. On 27th October the first war casualties arrived by train in Malmesbury, eight Belgians and two Frenchmen on their way to the military hospital in a converted wing of Charlton Park House. If Malmesbury was a quiet country outpost apparently unaffected by the horrors in Europe, the arrival of these hospital trains served as a grim reminder, as

William J. Reynolds, station master at Great Somerford 1914-18.
Courtesy Joe Reynolds

the branch engine drew in with the olive green ambulance coaches of the GWR, emblazoned with a red cross on a white circle. Such a train came in from Bristol on 21st November 1914, at 8.20 p.m., bearing many seriously injured British soldiers. It was a moving sight, many with bandaged heads, arms in slings and missing limbs. A large crowd met this train at the station but only Red Cross workers were allowed on the platform, the wounded being transferred to two ambulance wagons and private motor cars which had been loaned to take the men to the convalescent wing at Charlton Park.

December 1914 saw two notable incidents at Malmesbury station, one by design, the other not! On Friday, the 2nd, the Ammunition Column of the 3rd Wessex Brigade, Royal Field Artillery, left for Swindon at 2.55 to go to the continent. Their band played 'British Grenadiers' amidst patriotic scenes with relatives and friends, then the train left to the strains of 'Auld Lang Syne'. Exactly a week later, on Christmas Market day, an incoming train ran past the home signal at danger and smashed into a passenger coach and several cattle wagons left on the main track just outside the station. The branch engine had gone out to Dauntsey to fetch a train of cattle wagons to meet the extra demand for Christmas market, and on its

A postcard view of the south-east end of Malmesbury station c.1910, with a variety of goods wagons in the yard. The newly built house overlooking the terminus, 'The Cliff', dates from 1907. To the right Lovers Lane footpath can be seen coming down to the crossing just discernible through the foliage.
Author's collection

return the slippery state of the rails caused it to run into the stationary stock with such force that the wagon struck by the engine rose high, its buffers smashing the passenger coach to which it was coupled, causing serious damage to the end of the coach and sending the whole lot back through the station to hit the terminal buffers. Not surprisingly, the 517's buffers were broken! The train's fireman was blamed for the collision, having overrun the home signal in the 'on' position, although the incident does not appear to have harmed his chances of promotion, as he moved to Lydney to become a driver in 1916.

The war did not initially prevent the GWR from maintaining a full service, although excursions were suspended. Two ambulance trains were provided at Swindon, where a large number of road vehicles for artillery and general transport were constructed. Work on guns, gun carriages, shells and bombs also took place at the Swindon factory until the end of 1917, and the priority attached to this work had a direct effect on Malmesbury and other branches which received their locomotives from Swindon shed, as maintenance of locomotives there was now restricted by the more limited accommodation in the Works. Branch locomotives now spent longer on branch duties between visits to Swindon, and main line engines had to take priority. '517' Class No. 839 virtually became the branch locomotive during the war years, working from Malmesbury shed almost continuously from 1916 to 1920 (the appearance of an SECR locomotive at Malmesbury in 1918 is chronicled in Chapter 10). Fortunately these long spells without major attention had been preceded by thorough attention and care exercised at Swindon before the war, the

problem of maintenance now being compounded by shortage of manpower. By the end of August 1914 some 4,500 GWR employees had gone to war, and by the end of hostilities in 1918 some 25,479, one third of the total staff, had joined the services. 2,524 lost their lives, their places being filled by youths, women and older men.

Rail travel continued throughout the country on a huge scale, more people actually travelling on the GWR in 1916 than in 1913. It appears that by then some excursion traffic was running again, as during 1916 there are known to have been excursions from Malmesbury to London, as well as several specials – to Southampton, Portsmouth, Didcot, a Boy Scouts' Special to Birmingham, and the branch specials in connection with the Somerford Flower Show. On 5th July 1916, a troop special left Malmesbury at 7.45 a.m. for Trawsfynydd, the size of the 3rd Wessex RFA contingent requiring the sending to Malmesbury of one extra brake composite coach, two corridor thirds, one van, six 'Pacos' and five 'Scorpions'. 'Pacos' were horse-boxes of the 1880–90 era, whereas the 'Scorpions' were open carriage trucks which could carry artillery and road vehicles as long as the load was not too high or over eight tons.

However, by 1917 the demand in France for track and engines for military railways and men to work them, coupled with a need for fuel economy, made it necessary to reduce train services and restrict unnecessary passenger travel. From 1st January 1917, many expresses were taken off, passenger mileage was reduced by 9,000 miles a day and weight restrictions were imposed on parcels and luggage. Small stations and halts were closed and some unimportant branches closed to release staff and track for the war effort. The Malmesbury branch was unaffected by the cuts for a time, but from November 1917 its service was reduced to four each way with the Sunday train and the monthly market service. Trains ran from Malmesbury at 9.15, 12.05, 2.40 and 5.00, from Dauntsey at 10.20, 1.35, 3.35 and 6.10, most of them running mixed. By April 1918 the Sunday train had been axed, causing many local farmers to use road delivery to Dauntsey for their milk, and from January 1919 the market day train was taken off, although the early morning train was reinstated in July 1919 to give two passenger and three mixed trains each way on the branch daily.

Following the end of the Great War in November 1918 railwaymen were in the forefront of the battle to obtain a better deal. Government control had seriously affected the financial situation and the attitudes of the railway companies. Demands for wage increases and an eight-hour day were conceded from 1st February 1919, so that even the country porter at Great Somerford now worked a shorter day. With the increase in salaries and wage bills, the extra costs of coal and materials, the GWR's working expenses in 1919 were double that of 1913. The introduction of the eight-hour day and an increase in inflation compounded the added pressure on the railway companies' finances, and Railway Unions continued to enforce demands for larger wages and better working conditions, culminating in a nationwide railway strike on 27th September 1919, the workforce having rejected a GWR offer of 100% increase on 1914 rates with a minimum adult rate of forty shillings a day. The Malmesbury trains ceased immediately, but the company's appeal for volunteers to maintain the train service met with a good response from several retired railwaymen in the Malmesbury area who came forward to offer their services, among them former guard Reuben Jeffreys, then 17 years in retirement, whose offer to resume his old duties was gratefully accepted. It is not known, however, if Malmesbury saw any trains during what proved to be a short-lived strike – mainline service had increased as the anti-strike forces became more organised. The strike ceased on 5th October when the men accepted a minimum wage of 52 shillings a week as long as the cost of living was 110% above that of 1914, and this remained in force until October 1920 when a sliding scale of wages balanced against the cost of living came into use. The result was the addition of another £5$\frac{1}{2}$ millions to the wage bill, trebling the 1913 figure. With the heavy toll taken by the cut services and the war, the GWR now had to come to terms with changed attitudes and increased costs, shortened hours, trade depression, and above all, the increased road usage which would eventually see the decline and closure of many small branches across the system.

January 1919 saw the departure of Malmesbury's station master Edgar Doswell to Lawrence Hill. His parting shot was to recommend lodgings to his successor, George Dinham, who took the advice and moved in with a widowed Mrs Ratcliffe, whom he later married. Born at Corsham in 1882, his first GWR employment was as a clerk at Bath, then he progressed via appointments at Westbury, Frome, Castle Cary and Langport West, to attain the post of Chief Goods Clerk at Calne in 1913, where he worked under former Malmesbury station master Arthur Lloyd. During a 14-year stay he brought a quiet authority to Malmesbury station which

helped the branch to prosper for a time in the '20s after the difficult years following the Great War. He was an expert gardener, making his family virtually self-sufficient in vegetables, and was often up at 6.00 a.m. tending his garden at his eventual home at 57 Gloucester Road, near the station, before coming on duty at the station at eight. It may be perhaps surprising that Malmesbury never possessed a station garden in the tradition of many GWR stations which had staff with horticultural interests, but Mr Dinham's talent, with utilitarian gardening rather than the aesthetic, reflected the

Gateman William Ponting seen outside Kingsmead Crossing cottage with members of his family c.1918.
By kind permission of Jessica Reeve

Government encouragement to develop agriculture as much as possible to reduce purchase of food from overseas – townspeople were now encouraged to grow vegetables on allotments and also keep small livestock where practical. Railwaymen at Malmesbury rented small plots of land from the GWR and there were several meticulously kept allotments between the signal box and engine shed at the terminus, as well as on railway land along the branch in Lea Fields. Mr Dinham later moved to take over the station at Portishead, retiring in 1942 and continuing to live in the Somerset resort until his death in 1967.

In 1920 problems continued to mount for railways in general. A Ministry of Transport Act of 1919 enabled an increase of railway rates from 1st January 1920, with control of the railways passing to the Ministry on that date as a prelude to the grouping. With so many financial changes in a short period after the war, the railway was bound to suffer seriously from road competition, particularly in an area such as Malmesbury where a restricted poor service was being run with no Sunday trains. The war had provided a great boost for the internal combustion engine, giving many people the opportunity to learn how to drive, women as well as men, and many new road haulage businesses were founded which competed strongly and very successfully with the branch railways in rural areas. Such local carriers as the Sherston-based Compton & Dickensen were motorised in the early '20s long before Malmesbury station was provided with a GWR motor lorry service. A further hike in railway rates took place on 6th August 1920, passenger fares going up by some 75% on 1917 charges. By now, Malmesbury's first bus services were just over a year away.

Top: **Platform view at Malmesbury in 1922, with the ubiquitous milk churns and the typical selection of stock on the middle road — loco coal wagon, milk siphons and gas tank wagon or cordon.** *L & GRP, courtesy David & Charles*
Above: **George Dinham, station master at Malmesbury 1919–33.** *Courtesy W. G. Dinham*

An era ended on the branch with the death of Kingsmead gateman William Ponting on 20th August 1920. As previously related, he had been on the crossing duty since the very beginning, having lost an arm in an accident during the construction of the line. Before the increases of 1919, the remuneration for this continuous responsibility was 17/- a week. He and his wife Mary raised seven children at the crossing cottage, and she carried on assisted by a daughter on the gate duty until 1922 when Bill Archard took on the job. Mrs Ponting died in 1941. A humorous memory of William Ponting concerns his habit of holding horse-riders at the crossing on the pretext of an expected train, this ploy being his means of obtaining news of the outside world, the crossing work here being a quite isolated employment.

A valuable addition to Malmesbury's station staff in 1920 was Hullavington-born Victor Carter, who moved from Stoke Gifford where he had been an under shunter, to take on the job of branch porter guard. This dual role involved assisting with the work down at the goods shed and in the yard when not engaged on guard's duties on the branch train. Born in 1885, he worked for 14 years at Malmesbury, during which time he was well-known for his expert shunting work both at the terminus and at Dauntsey. On days when his wife made a shopping trip into town with their children, a favourite walk was to proceed down the Abbey steps to Lovers Lane Crossing, eagerly awaiting their father who would throw coins out to them from his guard's compartment so they could buy sweets later. Mr Carter later was promoted to Yeovil, eventually becoming yard inspector at Westbury.

Following a break of two years, Malmesbury's August Flower Show resumed on 14th August 1920, and the GWR tried out running a through train from Malmesbury to Chippenham. During the day, three extra third-class carriages were used to strengthen the branch train, starting with the 1.30 p.m. ex-Dauntsey, and a late special worked by the branch engine, left Malmesbury at 10.15 p.m., arriving at Chippenham at

10.55. The return train departed Chippenham at 11.05 and arrived back in Malmesbury at 11.45. Mr Dinham was instructed to send particulars of passengers using the service to Chippenham to the Divisional Superintendent. The arrangement was tried again in 1921 but appears to have ended there. The only other known through-working to Chippenham, or to anywhere by the branch train on the old line, was on 7th August 1922 when the branch set ran to Chippenham empty to provide a late special leaving Chippenham at 9.45 p.m. for visitors to Chippenham Flower Show. Having accomplished this, the branch train then made another run to Dauntsey at 11.15 to collect returning excursionists from Weston-Super-Mare. With the branch engine having to run around the train at Dauntsey before proceeding to Chippenham, it is probable that these through-services were not justified by the numbers that took advantage of them, regular service connections at Dauntsey being deemed sufficient, so such experiments were short-lived.

A notable staffing change took place on the branch with the retirement on 30th June 1921, of George Godby, who had worked as gateman at Dauntsey Road Crossing since 1901. Very often, gatemen on quiet branch crossings were older employees who had a particular disability resulting from injury sustained in the course of going about the company's business, and it was GWR policy to keep such men in useful

Bill Hine, crossing keeper at Dauntsey Road, 1921—33, seen outside the crossing lodge. This view was taken towards Malmesbury and features the flat-bottomed rail used on the branch.
Courtesy Mr. & Mrs. M. Drinkwater

employment by sending them to a rural crossing duty where the duties would not be too rigorous and where their wives could assist in the work. Godby had lost his leg in a shunting accident at Swindon, and was given an indoor job there as 'cloakroom porter' until the opportunity came at Dauntsey Road in June 1901. His wife Rose performed a great deal of the gate duty, often coming out in nightgown and slippers for the early train and the last one each night. Godby enjoyed a long retirement, dying in Chippenham in 1937 at the age of 87. His successor was Bill Hine, who had lost a couple of toes, also in an accident in Swindon yard. His wife Elizabeth also assisted with the gate duty. Much of the Hines' day in between trains was spent tending their allotment in the crossing cottage garden, where they also kept chickens. They stayed on in the cottage for several years after the closure of this section of the line in 1933.

The GWR's financial tribulations following the Great War, with general operating costs and the eight-hour day costing the company heavily, created a new economy-minded attitude in the management, and a GWR report published in January 1921 closely examined the operating of its stations, the first sign that there was a need to pull in the financial reins. The hours of duty for Malmesbury's station master and seven uniformed staff were published as follows:

Although the branch service still provided only five trains each way on weekdays at this time, there being three 'mixed' runs in each direction, the report alluded to Malmesbury's considerable increase in forwarded miscellaneous traffic, consisting chiefly of milk and bacon. In 1919 the 35,817 parcels forwarded brought revenue of £3,034, the figure leaping in 1920 to 68,630 with receipts of £7,849. Branch traffic was described as being 'of a general nature with figures being now practically on a pre-war footing'. If the management were considering making economies at Malmesbury, they had to look elsewhere, for such were the efforts of George Dinham and his staff to regenerate business that the report concluded:

'The porterage staff are fully occupied in their various duties. The station master and clerk are unable to carry out their duties in the hours shown on the chart and to keep the work going it is necessary for both to work overtime daily.'

The probable staffing personnel at Malmesbury in 1921 was:

Station master	–	George Dinham
Clerk	–	Lonnie Sharman
Guard	–	John Quarrell
Porter/guard	–	Victor Carter
Checker	–	George Woodward
Parcels porter	–	Cecil Moore
Porters	–	Harry Barnes
		George Ridge
Locomotive Department		
Enginemen	–	Bill Eveleigh
		Joe Halliday
Firemen	–	Redvers 'Buller' Reeve
		Dick Cooper
Cleaner	–	unknown

Malmesbury's Sunday train service was restored from 11th July 1921, and by October of that year the daily service had been increased to six each way with another return run in the mornings. Market day provision was also restored at the same time, but this was no longer provided as an extra train but simply as a mixed train facility on the 1.44 Dauntsey and the

A nostalgic view on the platform at Malmesbury in 1924, with Mr. & Mrs. Ted Jones seeing off their son Alfred and his family to Weymouth. Alfred Jones was employed on the GWR as a boy clerical officer at Reading West Signal Box until 1912 when he joined the Royal Navy. By the time of this photograph Ted Jones had enjoyed a decade of retirement since giving up his duties as branch engineman. The destination boards on the branch set were reversible, the other side reading 'Dauntsey'.   *Collection Mr. & Mrs. K. Iles*

MALMESBURY BRANCH.

Single Line, worked by Train Staff, and only one Engine in Steam at a time (or two or more coupled).

The Engineers have absolute occupation of the Malmesbury Branch each morning from 5.0 a.m. until the first train is due to leave Malmesbury.   See Appendix.

Distances.	DOWN TRAINS. STATIONS.	Ruling gradient 1 in.	Station No.	WEEK DAYS.								SUN DAYS.	
				1	2	3	4	5	6	7	8	1	2
				Mixed		Mixed	Pass.	Pass. Z	Mixed	Pass.	Pass.	Pass.	
M C.				A.M.		A.M.	A.M.	P.M.	P.M.	P.M.	P.M.	P.M.	
— —	Dauntsey .. dep.	....	1035	8 15	Mixed on last Wednesday in each month. N	10 20	11 40	1 50	3 35	6 20	7 45	7 20	....
2 53	Great Somerford ,,	94 F	1118	8 21		10 26	11 46	1 56	3 41	6 26	7 53	7 26	..
6 45	Malmesbury arr.	116 R	1149	8 33		10 36	11 56	2 6	3 53	6 36	8 3	7 38	..

	UP TRAINS. STATIONS.	Ruling gradient 1 in.	WEEK DAYS.										SUN-DAYS.	
			1	2	3	4	5	6	7	8	9	10	1	2
			Pass.	Pass.	Pass.		Mixed		Pass. Z	Mixed	Pass. D		Pass.	
			A.M.	A.M.	A.M.		P.M.		P.M.	P.M.	P.M.		P.M.	
	Malmesbury dep.	....	7 13	9 18	11 3	..	12 10	..	2 26	4 53	7 5	..	6 28	..
	Great Somerford ,,	116 F	7 23	9 28	11 13	....	12 20	....	2 37	5 4	7 20	....	6 39	....
	Dauntsey arr.	94 R	7 29	9 34	11 19	..	12 26	..	2 44	5 11	7 28	..	6 45	..

D To convey passengers, also milk for London Stations, to go forward from Dauntsey by 8.0 p.m. Chippenham Milk train.

Working timetable 1923. The service continued in this form until diversion of the branch to Little Somerford in 1933.
Public Record Office

2.25 Malmesbury on the last Wednesday in the month. Just a month previously, on 20th September 1921, the Bristol Tramways & Carriage Company had inaugurated Malmesbury's first bus service, route No. 31, between Malmesbury and Bristol. With a branch office of the omnibus company open in Swindon, the Malmesbury–Swindon service, No. 73, was first in operation a year later, and thus was the scene set for direct competition with the branch line's passenger business.

The 1921 Report showed Great Somerford station as having the minimum possible staffing – 'No reduction can be made at this station'. The station master's hours were listed as 7 a.m.–12.30 p.m. with an hour's lunch break, then 1.30–4 p.m., the hours of the one porter being 9.45–1.30/2.30–6.45. Thus breaks were staggered to ensure that someone was always on duty on the station during the day. Subsequently Great Somerford's goods yard was closed and its business transferred to Little Somerford on the nearby main line on 1st May 1922, the station being reduced to halt status at the same time, now renamed Great Somerford Halt for the remaining 11 years of its working existence. Responsibility for the halt and the crossings at Kingsmead and Dauntsey Road passed to the jurisdiction of the station master at Dauntsey from 1st August 1922, when Great Somerford's last station master, Albert Ham, transferred to Brinkworth. Great Somerford still had a small traffic in milk, 4,187 cans per year being handled as late as 1931, and the official in charge, now graded as gateman (crossing keeper) had the responsibility of collecting the milk consignment notes from farmers. Tickets for passengers were now issued and collected there by the guard on the branch train.

Work at Malmesbury station merited the reinstatement of the job of lad porter in 1923, a post which had been cut with

the war, although this appears to have been the only addition to the staff following the 1921 Report. Jim Thornbury took on the duty to commence his long association with the railway locally in a variety of capacities. Traffic figures for 1923 present a stark contrast with 1913, the last year before the Great War. The most significant increase was the almost trebling of the station wage bill over ten years, this was brought about by the pay increases of 1919 and the addition to the staff of a parcel porter to handle the vast parcels traffic, the receipts from which provided the major part of the branch's revenue. Although the 1923 takings of £18,427, some 50% up on 1913 figures, can largely be explained by the increased railway charges of 1920, it is perhaps more relevant to compare the staff paybill against the total receipts. Whereas in 1913 the wages had amounted to one twenty-sixth of the takings, by 1923 this proportion had become one-fifteenth. As time was to prove, this gap was to close ominously in the '30s, progressing to complete reversal after World War II. Dauntsey, however, showed little change in the ratio over this period, roughly one-ninth. In 1923, the 12 men employed there cost £1,705, but total takings, swelled by a huge increase in parcel traffic, had risen 150% to £16,191. Figures for Great Somerford Halt were included for Dauntsey during this period, but statistics abstracted for 1926 show the halt's modest revenue at £568, of which £174 came from passenger fares and the rest from forwarded milk traffic.

1923 is a suitable time to describe the GWR's provision of local cartage at Malmesbury, as it was in this year that the company took over parcel and goods delivery and employed its own carman in the town and another man was added to the station payroll. In the last century collection and delivery to and from the station had been carried out by a goods agent, James Wall, based at Melksham GWR station. Following the

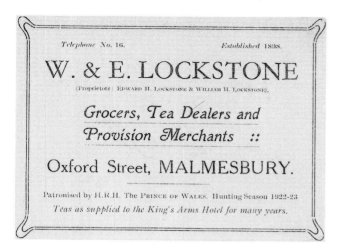

death of Mr Wall, this work was taken over on 1st April 1899, by S. C. Burt of Union Street, Bath. In 1918 their 'carman' in Malmesbury was Ernest Thornbury, who worked the town and surrounding area with a four-wheel dray hauled by a single horse. The horse was kept in the Railway Hotel stables near the station, 'Punch' being a great favourite of the carman.

Ernest Thornbury, remembered as a man who loved 'beer with all meals', was devoted to his horse with which he worked his town and country deliveries, and, although his hours were 7.00 a.m. to 5.00 p.m., he was always at the stable by 6.00 a.m. ministering to his charge, cleaning, feeding and grooming the beast so that a smart well-cared-for horse always appeared at Malmesbury goods shed ready for the first morning train in from Dauntsey. The checker helped to transfer incoming traffic to the dray. Lighter parcels for the immediate town area were taken by a lad, also employed by Burts, with a two-wheeled handcart; he would be given a tow up Gloucester Road hill to the town by the hooking up on the back of Thornbury's dray. Burts supplied horses and feed, taking commission on each parcel, a rep calling on the carman every Friday to go through the delivery sheets and assess payment. In 1923 the Bath agent went out of business, possibly bankrupted by the tough competition from those local carriers who had motorised their operations and could therefore give a more efficient service of delivery and collection over a wider area. The GWR took over the Malmesbury work from Burts, on 5th November 1923, and Ernest Thornbury hence became a railway employee. The GWR also took over the cartage operations at Melksham, Calne, Chippenham and Highworth at the same time.

Ernest Thornbury's deliveries usually began by taking leftovers from the previous night around the town in the hour or so before the first train came in. These early deliveries would be non-perishables such as wire, stone, or sleepers for the local workhouse, where the inmates chopped them up to be sold at twopence a bundle for firewood. Much of the morning was spent on more deliveries, taking commodities such as butter, cheese, groceries and other perishables to fashionable grocery businesses in the area of the High Street. The afternoon involved mainly collection, the chief ports of call being the Avon Silk Mills and the Adye & Hinwood bacon factory whose produce would be despatched on the late afternoon mixed train.

The Lockstone grocery business in Malmesbury's Oxford Street was a good example of how high quality goods continued to provide the branch with business during the '20s and '30s. Established in 1808, the family had been shareholders in the Malmesbury Railway Company in the 1870s and their traffic was typical of that of the larger master grocers in many small towns in the West. Prior to the early '20s, they employed a heavy flat horse-drawn wagon for country deliveries, with a horse and cart for town work. With the acquisition of their first Ford 'tonner', the flat wagon was sold, but the horse and cart was retained well into the '30s for local work. Large companies from whom the Lockstones bought their supplies would send their representatives to take orders, and delivery would be expected on a given train. When large consignments were delivered by rail at the station, it was a major job for a grocer to meet the train and unload the goods to their wagon in the goods yard; Somerset cheeses from Hill Bros. of Shepton Mallet were delivered to them in this way, packed in baskets of straw. Twice a year a bulk load of salt would arrive from Cheshire, large 20 or 28 lb blocks, cooking salt in tarred paper, and rock salt for cattle feeding troughs on the farms. Smaller amounts of such goods would be delivered by the GWR dray. The station truck from Paddington brought many of the Lockstone supplies well into the '30s – perishables such as bananas and lemons in cases, high quality half-cwt lots of

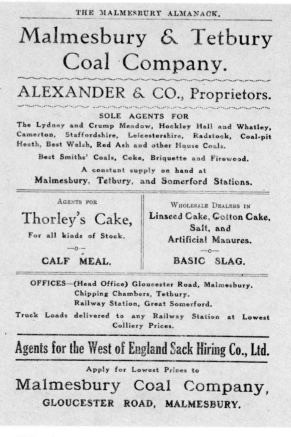

The Malmesbury Coal Company and Lockstones' Grocery provided much business for the railway.
Malmesbury Almanack 1922

Malmesbury Market Cross.

A Malmesbury Coal Company cart making deliveries to premises in the vicinity of the Market Cross.
Collection Robin Littlewood

coffee beans (generally double-packed in sacks), tea in lead-lined chests, sundries and sauces from such firms as Crosse & Blackwell, also packed in tea chests. The Lockstones employed a carter to do fortnightly or monthly deliveries around the country with their flat wagon, later the Ford, and he would usually be away on these trips for two days. His last call for the night, maybe a farm as far away as Cirencester, would give him supper, then he would wrap himself in a canvas sheet and sleep under the wagon, in the barn in the winter, with his horse put out to graze. Breakfast would be provided in the morning before continuing with the work.

Much of the Bristol traffic for Malmesbury in the '20s was delivered by GWR lorry, many supplies coming from wholesalers in Lewinsmead and Victoria Street, and manufacturers such as the Victoria Flour Company. Flour, tinned fruits, jams and preservatives, tobacco, hardware such as brushes in three gross loads, all came in by railway lorry even before the change of junction in 1933. Heavier merchandise, such as Schweppes soda siphons, were usually delivered by the larger companies' own lorries, who certainly hurt the railway with their motorisation, and, as the local carriers began to motorise and the smaller light vans started to run their more flexible routes around the countryside, a lot of the railway's trade was lost, and certainly as far as Malmesbury is concerned the GWR was slow to respond with the provision of its own local motor services.

Coal was an important source of goods revenue to the branch, arriving in open wagons by mixed train to two main dealers in the town. An early firm at both Malmesbury and Somerford stations was a Chippenham-based company, Harding & Son, established in that town in 1840. They handled coal, coke, cattle-cake, salt and hay at the branch stations until 1889 when Harding went into partnership with Mortimores at Chippenham and Calne, the Malmesbury depot being taken over by Samuel Fisher. In January 1920, this business was purchased by A. L. Curtis, including the

Somerford depot and four private owner wagons. The Curtis business went bankrupt in 1932. Its office was in the station yard adjacent to the GWR weighbridge. The company eventually became the Dolphin Coal & Coke Co. Ltd., building a loading shed in Malmesbury railway yard and also running depots at Little Somerford and Hullavington. Malmesbury offices were at both the station and in the High Street, their main customer being Malmesbury gasworks.

The Malmesbury Coal Company, listed in directories up to 1931 as the Malmesbury & Tetbury Coal Company, were originally run by Alexander & Co. with their head office and weighbridge in Gloucester Road. They also had coal dumps at Tetbury and Great Somerford. A great variety of coal was handled – Lydney and Crump Meadow, Hockley Hall and Whatley, Camerton, Staffordshire, Leicestershire, Radstock, Coalpit Heath, Best Welsh and Red Ash – as well as salt, firewood, artificial manures and cattle feed, all of which provided more goods traffic for the branch. The MCC had their own private owner wagons, black with white lettering, which were sent empty via the branch train to their suppliers, although the collieries would use railway company wagons for despatching coal if the private wagons were in short supply. In 1930 Camerton produced a cheap coal costing 5/3d per ton plus the GWR's freight charge. If a railway wagon was used, wagon hire was added, according to a scale, usually about 6d extra.

All wagons of coal coming into Malmesbury, whether in private or railway trucks, could remain in the siding at Malmesbury until the coal was collected but were charged 6d a day siding rent for any period over three days. The MCC's siding rent used to run to about £20 a month, but this was easier and cheaper for them than unloading to ground and picking up again later – it made more economic sense and involved less breakage of the coal. The Malmesbury Coal Company was taken over by Gladwins in 1937, and continued to provide business for the branch until the late '40s.

In October 1923 the evening train on the branch at last resumed, the last run of the day being the 7.45 p.m. from Dauntsey, and the branch service remained as seven each way daily, with the one Sunday return train, until the switch to Little Somerford ten years later. Malmesbury first received a town electricity supply in November 1923, and on 7th December repairs took place at Malmesbury to the station buildings to the tune of £235 – it is not known whether these works were in any way connected to each other, the alterations at the station possibly being in respect of connecting the buildings to the new supply.

The presence of horse-boxes in Malmesbury station on many old photographs is a vivid reminder of the amount of horse traffic on the branch, a reflection of Malmesbury's location in an area with a strong equestrian tradition between Badminton and the Cotswolds. Many branch trains included at least one horse-box loaded or empty in the '20s. Local gentry and landowners taking part in a Duke of Beaufort Hunt would despatch a stud groom to the station the night before to book the necessary conveyance. The next morning the horses were ridden to the station and put in the pen near the buffer-stops to await loading into horse-boxes. These vehicles were then taken on the rear of the train to Dauntsey, where the horses were unboxed and ridden to the hunt. The trip on the branch was made to save tiring the horses, and the return would usually be on the last evening train in. Substantial horse movement took place on the branch during the polo season, including many specials when American and Indian teams were featuring in polo meets at Hurlingham.

During the mid-20s the Malmesbury branch was involved in several proposed cost-saving operations as the GWR sought ways of cutting corners in the face of increased road use and competition from road transport. Road usage was now continually eroding the railway's former dominance. Motor omnibuses could provide more convenient service on short distance rural routes, local hauliers had cheap use of the roads whereas the railway had to maintain its own track and installations at great expense, and in 1923 the National Omnibus Co. in Stroud was advertising its coaches for hire for parties with charabanc outings to places as far away as Southampton, Bournemouth and the Wye Valley. With these facilities starting to encroach upon the day trip and holiday traffic, the days of long-distance express coach services between London and the West were just around the corner, and a country branch like Malmesbury with a junction at a minor station was bound to suffer. Petrol, car hire, car suppliers and repair facilities were all readily available locally, and by 1924 further bus services from Malmesbury to Stroud and Chippenham and the installation of an AA Road Service patrol office in Gloucester Street were less than three years away. Thus it was that Lord Churchill, the GWR Chairman, ominously warned of the dangers to rural lines from road competition at the GWR's AGM of February 1924:

'Many branch lines do not pay even when allowance is made for their contributive value to the rest of the system. We are considering ways and means of reducing costs of operating branch lines, but the time may come ... when branch lines ... will have to be closed up and the places on them served by road vehicles operating from the nearest trunk line station'.

Letters in the local press complained of the poor train service on the Malmesbury branch since the wartime reductions, and suggestions were made as to the possibilities of extending the branch train to Wootton Bassett or Swindon to obtain better passenger connections. One situation which no doubt prompted these ideas was the fate of anyone wishing to use the last daily branch train in the evening to travel to London – a two-hour wait was involved at Dauntsey with an arrival in the capital of 2.40 a.m.!

During 1925 the GWR conducted a survey of the working of its branch lines to determine if the most economical means of running were being used, whether those means were capable of improvement, whether substituting steam locos and heavy rolling stock with light motor rail coaches and trailers was at all practical, and, ominously, if there was any case for taking up the rails and using road motors on the routes with one man in charge of the stations attending to tickets and goods. Three areas of possible saving were quoted for the Malmesbury line, the first most obvious possibility being the question of the three gated manned crossings on the branch. The management's research showed that removal of gate-keepers, gates and signalling could save £389 a year in crossing

A sleepy view of the terminus at Malmesbury c.1930, with the station clear of traffic save for the solitary loco coal wagon in the middle road. The old brick-built parcels office is now in use as porters' quarters. The wooden structure this side of the lamp hut was a sleeper-built bunker which contained coal for station use — waiting room and office fires. Coal for personal use of railway staff came in a Malmesbury Coal Company wagon delivered to their homes by the company, the money being deducted from wages by the GWR.   *C. L. Mowat*

keepers' wages alone, and that application could be made to the Ministry of Transport for authority under the Light Railways Acts of 1896 and 1912 to work and maintain the Malmesbury and other branches as light railways. Such changes never materialised on the Malmesbury line, and one can only assume that subsequent research would have shown that although cattle guards were planned at the crossings, the sheer volume of movement along the three public roads involved, particularly in respect of local agriculture, would have created some very dangerous situations for both road and rail.

The second suggested saving concerned maintenance of the permanent way. Much essential relaying and resleepering had to be carried out on Sundays to enable essential train services to continue on weekdays. By using road transport for branch traffic between the hours of 9.00 a.m. and 5.00 p.m. and having goods and other heavy traffic moved outside these hours, maintenance work could be carried out on weekdays at ordinary rates of pay and, even allowing for the cost of the road motors, great savings effected. The quoted figure for the Malmesbury line was £49 for a day's work in this way, and the arrangement was adopted whenever such work was required.

Motive power on branch lines was an area of large expense in which possible economies were investigated. In December

The 0–4–0 Sentinel which was tested on the Malmesbury branch in October 1927. It is said that test runs were deliberately overloaded because the branch crews simply didn't want it on the line. *Great Western Railway Magazine*

1925 the GWR were in contact with the Sentinel Waggon Works of Shrewsbury with regard to trying out a Sentinel Patent Locomotive in order to test its capabilities for working branch lines as a possible successor to the ageing '517' class locomotives. With drivers on 15/- a day, firemen on 9/6d to 10/6d a day, and the high expense of coal and locomotive maintenance, there was a need for a loco with low coal consumption and which could be worked by one man instead of two, although one can easily guess at the railway unions' reaction had the latter idea been pushed. On 21st December 1925, the Sentinel Co wrote to the GWR offering their Type C.E. 100 hp 0–4–0 for trials on the Malmesbury branch, claiming it to be capable of taking a train of 25 tons weight over the line in a running time of 16 minutes including the stop at Great Somerford, or a train of 50 tons in 22 minutes. Heavier trains of 150–200 tons would naturally be at slower speeds and take up to 40 minutes. The quotation for a month's trial included the use of a Sentinel driver to instruct the GWR men. The GWR decided to try the new locomotive and an

order was placed, although there was some delay before the trial materialised.

The Report on the Working of Branch Lines was published in March 1926, and included the above figures for the Malmesbury branch over the year 1925. Even allowing for other general costs of running the line, such as advertising, printing and supervision, on first sight, Malmesbury's line appears to have been on a sound footing and one wonders if the proposed economies in the report were simply a matter of general policy by the GWR without regard for the performance of individual lines. The figures show that running costs for the branch in 1925 were well under half of the traffic receipts. However, this was the peak year for takings on the branch, and it will be noted that the passenger traffic made a very small contribution to revenue, the line's apparent viability at this time being due to the large parcels and goods business – traffic which was to be in serious decline within a few years as road competition began to bite. Further, within two months of the publication of the report, the GWR management had other problems with which to concern themselves, precipitated by the events in the coal dispute in South Wales.

At midnight on Monday 3rd May 1926, several blasts on the branch engine's whistle at Malmesbury signalled the beginning of the General Strike as the country's workforce came out in support of the miners. General Manager Sir Felix Pole appealed to GWR men not to strike, but to no avail and Malmesbury branch trains were immediately affected. According to the contemporary press, everyone worked normally in Malmesbury except the railwaymen, although one man, Ernest Thornbury, refused to come out because of his duty to keep the horses fed, watered and groomed. He had to feed them with food obtained locally as during the strike no help was forthcoming from the GWR provender store at Didcot. He received a £5 loyalty payment from the GWR for his service during the strike.

With some buses already serving Malmesbury, and a fuller bus service imminent, the strike was very damaging to branch traffic – the number of passenger tickets booked at Malmesbury fell by nearly 7,000 in 1926, and total branch receipts for the year were down by some £2,000 on 1925 figures. Important train services on the main line were maintained by some loyal staff and volunteers – with quick training of volunteers, services did improve from 194 trains run on the first day of the strike to a total of 1,517 by 14th May. At Malmesbury, Mr H. H. Halfecree offered his services as driver of the branch train, with Captain MacKirdy of Abbey House as fireman, and in many cases GWR veterans of the old days and the old values came out of retirement to assist. It eventually proved possible to run a skeleton service on the branch, but with the townsfolk clearly against the strike in an area where values and attitudes were vastly different to those of the working masses in the cities and industrial areas, the damage was done. The strike was settled on 14th May 1926, but some customers were lost forever and the coal strike continued, to the detriment of many GWR train services which had to make do with poor quality imported continental coal. In August 1927 the GWR made one of its first efforts to come to terms with its competitors by introducing 1/- a day parking for motor cars at its stations.

In October 1927 the test of the 'Sentinel' locomotive took place on the Malmesbury branch and a report produced on its performance was presented at a GWR meeting on 2nd November 1927. The first Sentinel locomotive actually taken into GWR stock was purchased in July 1926 at a cost of £1,460, but lasted only three months before being sold off following unsuccessful trials at Fowey. On its withdrawal, an earlier delivery, held pending trials, was taken into GWR stock and numbered 13, and it was this engine which came to the Malmesbury branch for tests on 2nd October 1927. The steam locomotive was fitted with a two-cylinder vertical-type engine, mounted on the frames between and above the wheel centres. Most of the working parts of the engine were enclosed in an oil bath, which excluded dirt. The boiler was of the vertical cross water-tube type, designed to give quick raising of steam and to facilitate easy cleaning and repairs. Water tank capacity was 350 gallons and the bunker held $7\frac{1}{2}$ cwts of coal. The total weight was 20 tons. The following report was produced on the trial:

TRIP No. 1 Mixed Train – Dauntsey to Malmesbury – $6\frac{1}{2}$ Miles

		Tons	Cwts
Load:	3 six-wheel coaches	36	3
	16 empty 10 ton wagons	92	6
	1 12 ton brake van	12	0

With this load the usual timing over the Branch is 16 minutes with a stop at Great Somerford.

From Dauntsey to Great Somerford – $2\frac{3}{4}$ miles – the engine was worked at its maximum power, but it took 13 minutes, to cover this distance, the maximum speed being 19 mph and the average speed 13 mph. After $\frac{1}{2}$ minute stop at Great Somerford the train proceeded on a rising gradient of 1 in 116 for about $\frac{1}{4}$ mile and this proved too much for the engine. The pressure dropped from 275 to 200 lbs with $\frac{1}{2}$″ of water in gauge glass, and the train almost stopped at the top of the incline. Over the incline the pressure was regained and for the next mile the speed averaged 12 mph but the water in gauge glass was out of sight and the pressure again fell to 200 lbs. The gradient was then up 1 in 198, which had to be negotiated with 200 lbs pressure and water low in boiler, and after proceeding a little distance at walking pace, the train finally came to a stand about $1\frac{1}{2}$ miles from Great Somerford, $14\frac{1}{2}$ minutes having been taken to cover this distance. After standing $3\frac{1}{2}$ minutes the water appeared in the gauge glass and the pressure rose to 220 lbs. The train restarted after $5\frac{1}{2}$ minutes stop with 2″ of water in gauge glass and 275 lbs pressure, and it took 14 minutes to get to Malmesbury, $2\frac{1}{4}$ miles, the maximum speed being 15 mph, average speed 10 mph, the pressure gradually falling to 220 at Malmesbury with $\frac{1}{2}$″ of water in gauge glass.

The total time for the trip was $47\frac{1}{2}$ minutes.

TRIP No. 2 Passenger Train – Malmesbury to Dauntsey

Load: 3 four wheel coaches – 34 tons 2 cwts.

On this trip the steam pressure and water level were well maintained and the time taken was $16\frac{1}{2}$ minutes, with a momentary stop at Great Somerford and a Signal Stop outside Dauntsey. Total running time of 13 minutes. The maximum speed attained was 38 mph the average between Malmesbury and Great Somerford being 25 mph and between Great Somerford and Dauntsey 27 mph.

Trip No. 3 Passenger Train – Dauntsey to Malmesbury, G W Driver

Load:-   3 four wheel coaches = 34 tons 2 cwts.

Boiler pressure and water level were well maintained on this trip. The maximum speed attained was 36 mph. The average speed between Dauntsey and Great Somerford was 23 mph and between Great Somerford and Malmesbury 28 mph.

There was a momentary stop at Great Somerford, the total time taken being $15\frac{1}{2}$ minutes with a signal stop just outside Malmesbury, so that 15 minutes could be taken as running time.

Trip No. 4 Mixed Train – Malmesbury to Dauntsey, G W Driver

Load –		
	3 – Six wheel coaches =	36 tons 3 cwts
	9 – Empty 10 tons wagons =	47 tons 12 cwts
	12 – Ton Brake Van =	12 tons 0 cwts
	Total weight	95 tons 15 cwts

This trip was made without a stop at Great Somerford. Steam and water were well maintained and an average speed of 27 mph was kept without forcing the boiler. The train was checked just outside Dauntsey, the total time on the trip being $16\frac{1}{2}$ minutes, 16 minutes running time.

The Sentinel engine was not used further on the Malmesbury line after its trials, eventually being returned to shunting work in the Park Royal Trading Estate, which was its main duty until withdrawal in May 1946. Although the engine's showing on Trips 2, 3 and 4 as given in the report was satisfactory, these journeys were made with quite light trains of the usual branch coach stock in the case of Trips 2 and 3, whereas trip 4, although with a heavier train, was made from Malmesbury, the gradients going in the Dauntsey direction being easier than on down journeys. However, Trip No. 1, with its mixed load of 140 tons, was beyond the capacity of the engine, and as the train used was more representative of the weight of normal mixed trains on the branch, it was considered that the Sentinel was not of sufficient capacity or flexibility for hauling the heavy mixed traffic of the line's regular service. Although it was capable of hauling the usual branch set of three 4-wheel coaches, it was also borne in mind that even these passenger trains often had horse-boxes and milk siphons added to them, which would have presented the little Sentinel, with its awkward 'biscuit-tin' appearance, with difficulties on regular branch service.

During the late 1920s all six axles on the coach sets typically used on the Malmesbury branch were fitted with roller bearings, the branch providing a convenient location for this experiment, being close to Swindon Works. These were the only such fittings known of on any railway at the time, and the Malmesbury stock would even start moving in high winds until application of the handbrake in the guard's van. In the words of one local railwayman, 'We could almost push those coaches ourselves.'

Even with the onslaught of increased road competition, the GWR continued to provide special trains and excursion services for all manner of occasions, offering cheap fares from all parts of its system to events both local and far afield. Some of these ran onto other companies' tracks, giving a 10/- 3rd class return to Brighton from Malmesbury or a 5/- excursion rate to Aldershot to visit the Searchlight Tattoo. A 1st class excursion fare to London was available in the late '20s for 19/9d. Sporting occasions always were the subject of many advertised extra trains – for instance, the Swindon Town v Burnley FA Cup 4th round replay of 29th January 1929, attracted special trains from all over Wiltshire and beyond. For a fare of 1/6d return from Malmesbury and 1/3d from Great Somerford Halt, you could join a football special at Dauntsey and join the throng at Swindon on its way to the County Ground, many having come off specials from Faringdon, Hullavington, Warminster, Devizes, Steventon and Bath, even from as far away as Andover Junction and Portland. Such was the interest in a 'live' event in days before violence and disrespect became rife in our society and over-use of television diluted the spontaneous thrill of occasion.

An early '30s market day scene at Malmesbury. Cattle wagons have been brought in by special goods train and left standing on the middle road waiting for horses to draw them up two at a time to the cattle pens for loading. They would then be dropped back to the shed road (where the two figures are seen standing) to await shunting by the branch locomotive, which might, on such days, leave with a 250–300 ton load.

Bertram Farmer

Ordinary folk could travel anywhere cheaply and be part of the excitement, and the local branch train took them on the first step of the way.

In June 1930 there occurred an interesting change in the arrangements for the annual Sunday School Special train which usually ran to a popular seaside resort. The old practice was to use the regular branch non-corridor set with extra stock if necessary to Dauntsey where everyone changed to a main line train. When the 1930 special was being arranged, Malmesbury's station master was on holiday and clerk John Barnby was told by his relief, a Mr Olding, 'You know all about it' and instructed him to deal with it all. The trip was to involve all the town's Sunday schools – Roman Catholic, C of E, Methodist, Baptist, Moravian, Westport C of E, and Westport Congregational, in all some 400 people. When he phoned the Bristol DSO, Mr Barnby was able to stretch the number a little and prove that the required train of non-corridor stock would require two tank engines of the normal 0–4–2 type allowed over the branch, and he suggested running the coaches as a through-train to Weston-Super-Mare along with corridor stock. He was met with the argument that this arrangement would mean blocking both main lines at Dauntsey, yet this happened anyway. The augmented branch train would have to run out to the main line platform as there was not enough room in the bay, while the connecting train stood waiting at the down platform. The throng would have to leave the branch train, crowding the narrow footbridge to reach the down side, then find their reserved accommodation, with each Sunday school compartment separately. John Barnby's idea was tried and the special came through from

Swindon as empty stock. It so happened that it rained very heavily all day and all concerned would have received a drenching at Dauntsey under the old arrangement.

1931 was the last year in which milk provided a major source of traffic on the Malmesbury branch, with 71,545 cans being handled. At this time a great deal of this business came to the station from the town's milk factory, but after 1931 the factory turned to road tankers, leaving local individual farmers to maintain a dwindling milk business on the branch until final removal to road transport in 1938. In earlier years there had been great competition between the lads who drove the milk carts to the station from the local farms, some 'Ben Hur'-like scenes resulting as each lad strove to be the first to convey the milk to the loading dock at Malmesbury platform, in time to go out on the evening train to join the Chippenham milk train at Dauntsey. Milk empties usually came back to Malmesbury on the first train from Dauntsey in the morning, along with empty siphon wagons and some empty churns in the guard's compartment. A small amount of milk still left Great Somerford Halt in 1931, 4,187 cans being handled, roughly a dozen a day, presenting a brief but heavy piece of lifting for the crossing keeper and branch guard.

By the early '30s the business from Malmesbury market was greatly reduced, a small number of cattle wagons being brought down from Swindon on market days on the pick-up goods ('the fly') and left in the sidings for the branch train to collect. Since 1921 the market day service had existed as mixed train provision on a regular branch train once a month, wagons loaded with market traffic being conveyed out to Dauntsey in the afternoon where they were collected by a

A '517' Class 0—4—2T awaiting departure with a Malmesbury branch train during 1931. Branch set coaches are brake third coaches Nos. 2654 and 2655, with first/third composite (formerly first/second) No. 6621 in the centre of the formation. The chimney visible in the left background is the milk factory.　　　　　　　　　　　　*Bertram Farmer*

Malmesbury station from the top of the starting signal in 1929, with loaded coal wagons filling the middle road.　　　　　　　　　　　　*John Barnby*

light engine from Swindon. This arrangement did not survive the change of junction, and was last used on Wednesday 29th June 1932.

By the mid-30s, larger farmers with cattle floats were tending to take all their products to the markets where they sold their corn – the livestock markets were frequented mainly by the smaller farmers. Concentration of purchases at selected markets by the Ministry of Food, the sole buyer of fatstock, had modified marketing practice, and, although official grading centres, such as Chippenham and Warminster, benefited in this way, smaller markets, such as that at Malmesbury, fell into decline.

Following the mid-20s investigations as to how the branch running costs could be reduced, the GWR at last took the obvious step of planning to re-route the Malmesbury branch into a new junction at Little Somerford, thus closing the branch southwards from Kingsmead Crossing. The GWR Board sanctioned the diversion of the branch and the abandonment of the Kingsmead–Dauntsey section in January 1932, at estimated costs of £4,920 for engineering, £1,700 for signalling and £380 for land purchase, making a total of £7,000. Work began on the 1 in 50 gradient from Kingsmead up to the Badminton Line on 9th May 1932, and on 18th and 19th May the branch was closed and motor buses substituted

Shortly before the change of junction to Little Somerford, an unidentified Collett 0–4–2T is shown hauling a branch train bunker-first towards Kingsmead Crossing with a train for Dauntsey. Official records list expenditure for the diversion of the branch to Little Somerford as £2,080 for earthwork, £105 additional fencing, £200 additional drainage, £1,200 extension of underbridge at Little Somerford, £860 alterations to permanent way, £1,525 new permanent way, £380 land and £120 cattle grids. GWR Signal Notice No. S.1562 refers to the removal of the existing crossing gates at Kingsmead and their substitution with cattle grids with warning boards in each direction. However, in the event, a new wider set of gates was installed, and the idea for the cattle grids was dropped. Although the new work was complete for February 1933 (the time when the new Collett tanks were being sent to local branches from the Swindon Works), a legal hitch prevented the use of the new junction and abandonment of the old line until July 1933, so this photograph is thought to be at some time between March and June 1933 — the new course of the branch is as yet bare of vegetation, and the older narrower crossing gates are still in use. New fence posts mark the boundary of GWR land on the new portion up the bank towards Little Somerford. There is as yet no sign of the new ground frame provided to control access to the later retained section of the old branch for storage of crippled stock, but a white-topped engineer's lever can be seen, indicating temporary arrangements in use before the final alteration.
Courtesy Bill Archard

On the final evening of services between Dauntsey and Malmesbury, 15th July 1933, the last train, the 7.56 from Dauntsey, stands ready to depart. Brake composite coach No. 6621 is seen on the right. Just visible above the leading brake third coach is the branch starting signal in the 'off' position. Dauntsey signal box is visible beyond the platform. *Public Record Office*

for the trains for two days so that work on the new spur at Kingsmead could proceed unhampered. A further similar closure took place on 24th November 1932, between 8.30 a.m. and 4.45 p.m. so that the new works might be well advanced. By the end of the year the work was almost complete, with the provision of a wider pair of gates at Kingsmead Crossing to allow for the greater deviation of the line's course at this point, but it was not brought into use at this time as Parliamentary sanction had not yet been obtained for abandonment of the line through Great Somerford. Alterations were complete for 6th February 1933, but a legal hitch over the abandonment of the old part of the line to Dauntsey delayed use of the new line until the July.

On Friday, 14th July 1933, the *North Wilts Herald* reported:

'New Train Services' – The railway loop line at Kingsmead will be opened from Monday next. The service to Swindon from Malmesbury will be via Little Somerford, and the part of the old branch line from Great Somerford to Dauntsey will not be used. Great Somerford Halt is being closed. The townsfolk will welcome a decidedly improved service which is being introduced between Malmesbury and Swindon.'

This short report reflects the quiet manner in which the old section of the branch was closed. There were no great ceremonial touches other than a photograph of staff grouped by the train at Dauntsey and the exploding of a few fog signal detonators as the last train left Dauntsey for Malmesbury at 7.56 on a dank, cloudy evening, Saturday, 15th July 1933,

Staff group at Dauntsey on the last day of the old branch. Fireman Les Jones is seen in the cab with (*left to right*) John Barnby (Malmesbury clerk), Percy Wakefield (porter, Dauntsey), Victor Carter (branch porter/guard), and Ben Hill (branch driver). As was the upper picture, the photograph was taken with an old Brownie box camera by Edgar Cross (Dauntsey porter). *Devizes Museum*

with a Collett 0–4–2 tank, probably No. 5802, crewed by Ben Hill and Dick Cooper, with guard Frank Philips. There were no crowds, no excitement, only a few passengers. If any ceremonial farewell was laid on at Great Somerford Halt, it is not recorded. During its last full year of operation, only £125 had been taken there in passenger fares, 2,780 tickets being issued, a figure which represents about one passenger for every two trains. Thereafter, Malmesbury branch trains joined the Badminton main line at Little Somerford.

CHAPTER FIVE

'DAUNTSEY, DAUNTSEY, CHANGE FOR GREAT SOMERFORD AND MALMESBURY'

WORK AT DAUNTSEY STATION IN THE TWENTIES

DAUNTSEY station, 87 miles 59 chains from Paddington, was opened on 1st February 1868 and served initially by three up and three down passenger trains. Goods facilities were provided soon after, the first wagons of coal arriving for Joseph Barnes, the coal company which was to use the station for nearly a century. Located six miles north-east of Chippenham on the GWR main line between Chippenham and Bristol, there were two through roads and a terminal bay for the Malmesbury branch on the north side of the up platform at the west end of the station. Before the building of the branch, both platforms ended below the road bridge carrying the A420 Swindon-Chippenham road. To accommodate the branch, the up side was extended beyond the road bridge, and presented the unusual appearance of two separate platforms facing the main line on this side, each having adjacent ramps facing each other below the road bridge.

The village of Dauntsey is a scattering of houses on the southern edge of Dauntsey Park, two miles to the north of the station which was placed just where the main road began to climb Clack Mount, below Dauntsey Wharf on the disused Wilts & Berks Canal. The western half of the station was in the parish of Christian Malford. Rather than simply 'Dauntsey', a more correct appellation for the station might have been 'Dauntsey and Clack' or even 'Dauntsey Lock'. At the top of the hill was the village of Clack, actually closer to the station than Dauntsey village, although access to it less easy via the steep hill and winding road from the station. Clack was later

A beautiful view of times gone by which tells its own story, the down side station nameboard in 1932, standing amidst flowering currants in the attractive rockery borders tended for many years by porter Percy Wakefield. The station master's house featured in the right background was connected to the station by a long garden path entered through a small gate. The road to Clack Mount winds its way up the hill on the left.

Photomatic

An Edwardian window on Dauntsey station, from an old postcard on which the name was mis-spelled 'Druntsey'! Looking through the road overbridge towards Chippenham, the Malmesbury branch set can be seen in the bay platform beyond the road overbridge, while the locomotive appears to be out beyond the signal box shunting milk siphons ready for the evening Chippenham milk train. The passenger footbridge was first authorised in December 1884 at a cost of £180 and erected in 1885. The small station building on the up side was a typical example of one of the designs of GWR wayside country station structures with knapped flint and limestone quoins, slate roof and a flat simple canopy. The left-hand of the two chimneys was of a particularly ornate design. The up platform presented two separate platform faces to the main line, the ramps meeting at rail level below the overbridge. Typical GWR signs are mounted on both sides of this bridge advising passengers to cross the line via the footbridge. The hedge on the left, behind the down side waiting shelter, is the northern border of the station master's garden. *Author's Collection*

VIEW FROM DAUNTSEY HILL

A postcard view looking north-west down from Clack Mount over the GWR main line and Dauntsey station. The scattered village of Dauntsey is away to the right of St. John's Farm (also on the right) from where this picture came. The round-roofed canopy of the Malmesbury branch bay is visible to the right of the telegraph pole between the houses. The Swindon–Chippenham road, passing over the station and winding away in the distance, eventually crossed the Malmesbury branch at Swallett Gate, just off the photo at left. The Peterborough Arms and the station house can be clearly seen in the group of buildings this side of the station, whilst beyond to the right of the main road is Dauntsey Creamery. The line of bushes seen to the right, running parallel to the east end of the station, marked the northern border of the Wilts & Berks Canal. The water tank at this end of the station took its supply from the canal. Leading away from the main road in the centre distance of the picture is a line of trees which marks the route of Mile Walk (see map of line). This thoroughfare was provided by the GWR as a direct link between Dauntsey House and the GWR station, although it stopped short of the Park and Dauntsey House and ran into Ridgeway Lane because the Bristol Diocese Church Commissioners would not sell the land necessary to complete the work.

Courtesy Mr. & Mrs. R. Hitchcock

Dauntsey station house c.1917, with Mrs. Hill and daughter in the well-stocked garden. The contract to build a house for the booking porter at Dauntsey was awarded to a Mr. Yeo at a cost of £240 in August 1881. The booking porter (later the station master) lived in the house at a rent of 3/- a week which was deducted through the paybill. Railway housing was usually only provided at stations which were rather remote, and, although very few were built before 1890, at Dauntsey the governing factor must have been the station's isolation from the scattered village it purported to serve.
Courtesy Derek Hayes

renamed Bradenstoke, and the station's first telephone number was 'Bradenstoke 2'.

Dauntsey's longest serving station master, although he never officially attained that rank until he moved on, was Samuel Jefford, who was in charge there from 1882–1903. Born in 1852, he spent his early working years in signalling, working at Saltford for a year in 1875, then spending three years as a switchman in Bristol. In January 1879 he took over Ashley Hill station as booking porter, moving to Dauntsey in a similar capacity on 17th April 1882, at 25/- a week. His post was regraded as station inspector in June 1890, at 30/- a week. Although his pay rose to 39/- a week during the 1890s, and though most Class 4, 5 and 6 stations had their inspector made up to a fully-fledged station master in 1897, there is no documentary evidence to prove that this was so at Dauntsey, and it appears that Jefford finally attained the rank of station master on 1st May 1903, when he moved to Badminton to take over the new station there.

Dauntsey was a Class 4 station and therefore, being without a clerk, all issuing of tickets was done by the station master or a porter. On this grading, the station master was a member of the weekly paid staff on the railway, and normally did not progress to having charge of stations graded higher than Class 4. Higher grade stations were in the charge of men who had progressed through the ranks of salaried staff. In 1923, the station staff at Dauntsey was made up thus:

Station master – Sydney Hill	7.30–1.00 and 2.00–4.30
Parcel porter – Jack Waite	9.30–1.45 and 2.45–6.30
Shunter – Fred Watson	9.30–1.30 and 2.30–6.30
Porters – Percy Wakefield	6.45–11.00 and 12.00–2.45
Edgar Cross	12.00–3.45 and 4.45–9.00
(The early and late porters' turns were alternated weekly)	
Lad porter – Albert Stanley	10.30–1.45 and 2.45–7.30
Signalmen – George Gibbs	Signalmen's shifts
Walter Mason	were 6.00am–2.00pm, 2.00–10.00pm
Jim Raymond	and 10.00pm–6.00am

From 1922, with the closure of Great Somerford's goods yard and the reduction of that station to halt status, the three gatemen on the Malmesbury branch were added to the Dauntsey payroll.

During the 1920s the early shift porter carried a great deal of responsibility for the station, and a great amount of work was provided by the requirements of the Malmesbury branch. On arrival at the station, the early man would collect the station keys from the signal box then walk back along the platform to open up the station. In the winter, fires would have to be lit in the waiting room, station office and parcels office.

During the small hours of the night an up goods would call at Dauntsey and leave a wagon labelled 'Bristol to Dauntsey and Malmesbury' in the Malmesbury branch bay. This wagon was usually close to the locomotive, and would be shunted back onto the Malmesbury branch where the locomotive would uncouple and run around the wagon in the branch train's normal manner. The wagon was then pushed into the branch bay where it would be detached by the fireman and left for the early porter, the engine returning to the head of its train and proceeding to Wootton Bassett. This wagon provided the first main duty of the day for the early turn, as all the goods labelled for Dauntsey would have to be removed and transferred to the corrugated iron shed which served as the station's goods shed. Sometimes this wagon would be an open truck covered by a tarpaulin, at other times a van, the latter being more to the liking of the porter as he could reach and sort the contents of the vehicle more easily. Either way, though, this would be a cold and solitary job on a dark winter's morning, as he worked as quickly as possible to sort the goods using a hand-lamp, peering through the gloom to make out the labels.

This was very much a period of working against the clock in the 45 minutes or so before the arrival of the first train from Malmesbury. There were general goods on this overnight wagon – iron for local blacksmiths, fruit, groceries, even luggage, the invoices being on the wagon. Once cleared of the Dauntsey goods, the vehicle would remain in the bay ready for the trip into Malmesbury on the first down branch train of the day. The branch bay would also contain empty siphon wagons ready to return to Malmesbury for the day's milk traffic, these being left off a down train around 6.40am, others usually arriving at Dauntsey around lunchtime.

The first train from Malmesbury would arrive at 7.30, and as the bay was already occupied by siphons and the overnight wagon, it would always go out to the main line, as no vehicles were allowed to stand in the bay line when a passenger train was being admitted to that platform. In any case with a bay platform of 153ft, the presence of wagons there early in the morning would have rendered it too short for passengers to alight, so the use of the up side main platform by the branch train at this time was regular practice. It was also normal procedure for Malmesbury to wire Dauntsey after the departure of every train, informing the Dauntsey signalman of the total number of vehicles on the train, and before lowering his signals for the bay line he was expected to satisfy himself that the branch bay was perfectly clear. If sent out main line, the train crossed the 'diamond' where the branch's access to the main line platform crossed the bay line access to the up main. With some milk traffic on it as well as a few early morning passengers, the branch train could therefore set down its traffic farther along the up side and closer to the footbridge for those crossing to the down side.

The train then reversed onto the branch run-round loop and started the complex operation of shunting and organising the morning mixed train for Malmesbury – what a fine sight this must have been, whether viewed from the road overbridge, platform or signal box. The branch engine would be detached from its coaches, by the guard, Malmesbury's Victor Carter being well-remembered for the speed with which he performed this duty. Although Dauntsey possessed a shunter, Fred Watson, whose post existed purely because of the work provided by the branch, he did not come on duty until 9.30am, so the branch guard always uncoupled the train first thing in the morning.

The signalman kept the staff all the time the branch train was at Dauntsey, not giving it up until the train was ready to depart for Malmesbury. The branch set of three coaches was then pushed onto the branch loop where they were held by the guard on the handbrake while the engine backed off towards the bay, then ran past on the running line and backed onto them on the loop and pushed the coaches back into the bay to link up with the siphons in the platform. The entire bay line was then cleared as the engine hauled the train back out onto the branch loop, where the siphons were left while the coaches were shunted back into the now empty bay for passengers to board. The locomotive then went out beyond the signal box into what was known as the 'back road' to collect the guard's van, which had been left overnight at the junction after the arrival of the evening mixed train. This van was shunted onto the back of the direct wagon behind the

Another view featuring the Malmesbury branch bay. Station master Sydney Hill watches as an unidentified train approaches on the up main line through Dauntsey. The 'F' under Mr. Hill was put there by one of the family, standing for 'father'.   *Courtesy Derek Hayes*

The area around the station and canal was known as Dauntsey Lock, viewed here looking east on 17th June 1913 with the First Wilts Regiment on a lunch break at the Peterborough Arms during local manoeuvres. The house in the left foreground was originally known as Lock House, whilst on the left of the photo is Wharf House, the Wilts & Berks Canal running between these two buildings. The top of the station cutting is visible across the rooftops in the centre of the photograph.   *Courtesy Mr. & Mrs. R. Hitchcock*

siphons on the loop, the engine then returning to the platform to couple up with the now-inhabited coaches, although there were never many passengers at this time of the day. The early morning passengers then experienced the strange sensation of the train leaving for Malmesbury, stopping just around the branch bend, then reversing onto the loop to couple up with the rest of the train, which then proceeded as a mixed train, the 8.10 to Malmesbury. This routine operation depended on expert teamwork between engine crew, guard and signalman, and took around half-an-hour.

Any train coming off the branch which included milk siphons, horse-boxes or goods wagons for transfer to main line trains would almost always come out onto the main line at Dauntsey. With the exception of the first morning train, branch trains running with just the three passenger coaches apparently always used the branch bay. A van of general goods was dropped off the first train from the Paddington direction each day, and the branch engine would go across to collect this from the down road. It was also common practice for the branch engine to go up and take water from the feed on the up side when using the main line, as long as there was no up express due. When a change of branch engine was required, a new engine would be sent from Swindon and the change made at Dauntsey.

Edgar Cross, who began work on the GWR at Devizes in 1913, started at Dauntsey as a porter in 1923, becoming leading porter in 1930. He was made up to Grade 1 porter upon the reitrement of Jack Waite in 1934, thus taking on more paperwork with the cessation of the post of parcel porter. Cross remained at Dauntsey until 1938, and was thus there during a period when many important changes were

An Edwardian view of the then little used Wilts & Berks Canal at Dauntsey Lock (Lock No. 12), looking east towards Swindon. Built for 35-ton boats, the canal linked the Kennet & Avon Canal at Semington with the Thames at Abingdon and was open from Semington to Dauntsey by 6th June 1800. The GWR paid the canal company an annual rental of £300 (in 1891) for water from the canal. Dauntsey Lock was 72ft long x 7ft wide, providing a level change of 8ft 8in. A basin (provided with a slipway) seen on the right beyond the lock, was used by barges of the Barnes coal business. The cart probably belonged to the Burgess coal business, the Barnes operation using the opposite side of the canal. The Dauntsey section of the Wilts & Berks was out of regular use by 1897, final closure of the canal being on 31st July 1914.

Courtesy Mr. & Mrs. R. Hitchcock

Dauntsey in 1921, looking eastwards towards Swindon with the branch bay to the left. Beneath the branch bay, passenger seating was provided and platform scales for weighing loads up to 3 cwt. The corrugated shed was the station's goods lock-up, provided in January 1902 at a cost of £38. The track on the right, terminating on the west side of the road bridge, was the down refuge siding for holding goods trains to make way for more important traffic (including fast expresses) coming down Dauntsey Bank. The capacity of this siding was 46 wagons; a similar siding on the up side had a capacity of 54.   *L & GRP, courtesy David & Charles*

taking place. He recalled how the Malmesbury branch provided much of the work for the porters at Dauntsey during the 20s. An important morning duty was to see that milk churns returned from London were transferred from the down side so farmers could collect their own. There was no public access to the down platform except via the footbridge, so this movement of churns was essential (the station master could reach the platform direct from his house just above the station via a gate). Problems could be caused if, for example, Dauntsey and Malmesbury churns were returned on an evening train in a Melksham van. The guard and late porter would have to unload these and the early turn porter next morning would be faced with the daunting task of shifting them across the main lines one at a time to the up side. At all times these churns had to be stacked well back from the platform edge, four feet being the regulation minimum. If two men were available, a trolley could be used via the boarded crossing at the east end of the station, but either way it was arduous work. The Malmesbury churns would be put in the guard's compartment on the branch train with the assistance of the guard.

At the east end of the down side was an eleven-lever ground frame which was worked by the porters for all shunting into the goods yard. There was a crossover line from the down to the up main line, with two crossovers from the up main into

a straight road, which enabled engines shunting the goods yard to run round wagons. This frame was an essential device at Dauntsey as the goods yard was obscured from the signalman's view by the road overbridge, the distance of the yard from the box also being too great for comfortable working. The ground frame was released by the signalman either for shunting on just the up side or on the up and the down, and two separate release levers in the frame were provided. When the signalman gave a release to the porter working the frame, the latter then had sole control over whichever line had been released to him until he phoned the signalman to confirm that the running lines were clear and the release could be withdrawn. Frequently, horse-boxes or coal wagons would be left by down trains in the 20s, the ground frame being brought into use to transfer such vehicles to the yard for dispersal of goods, storage or collection by the Malmesbury engine as appropriate. Dauntsey ground frame was unusual in that it worked signals as well as points, and during the use of a ground frame at the station there were known to be at least five different layouts worked from at least two different frames.

The later shift porter came on duty at midday and remained on the station until 9pm. Thus the porters' turns overlapped so that both men were on duty during the busy afternoon period before the departure of the 3.35 mixed train to Mal-

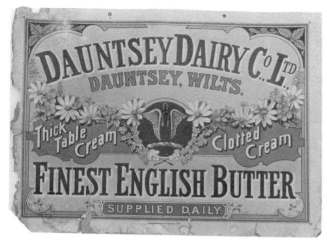

mesbury (the 1921 staff roster shows a later set of porters' times, with the early porter on duty until 4.15pm). With this train gone, the early turn porter would finish work, and the later shift man would take a tea-break down at the signal box, before work began in earnest dealing with the afternoon mixed out of Malmesbury and preparing for the heavy milk traffic which faced the station every day. Farmers would come from the surrounding region to deliver their full 17-gallon churns to the milk dock, and the loaded siphons would be left in the milk siding for collection by the Malmesbury branch locomotive, which would come off its train after bringing the evening 7.10 'milk train' out of Malmesbury to Dauntsey. This train would come out main line, then the branch engine would collect the Dauntsey milk wagons from their siding and back them onto the coaches, and then propel the whole ensemble through the station onto the up refuge, where the Malmesbury siphons would be left. The coaches were then transferred to the branch loop and the Dauntsey milk siphons put in the back road behind the signal box. The Malmesbury siphons were then shunted onto the Dauntsey vehicles in the back road ready for the Chippenham–London milk train. This completed, the engine would run round its coaches and back the train into the branch bay ready for the last run of the day into Malmesbury. The Chippenham milk train would usually arrive around 8.50pm, leaving its train in the up refuge while the engine cut off and backed into Dauntsey's back road to pick up the Dauntsey and Malmesbury milk vans. The evening porter had to assist in the marshalling of the milk train, and any loose churns on the platform which had arrived too late to be loaded would have to be added with the arrival of the train. On cold winter evenings especially, the marshalling of the milk traffic was a long and complex business, the wagons having to be matched up in the sidings with the order of destinations on the main line train. At such times the signalmen were thankful for drivers who knew the layout of the yard at Dauntsey, who could pick up their milk vans in the darkness with a minimum of lamp signals.

During the early '20s, before road services began to make inroads on the railway milk traffic, the amount of milk sent from Dauntsey and Malmesbury justified its own train from Dauntsey to depots at West Ealing, Clapham Junction and Southall (United Dairies Depots).

During this time Edgar Cross suggested to the GWR that the milk vans should have reversible labels so that the vehicles could easily be returned to Dauntsey to save continually ordering fresh rolling stock, although there were usually a couple of spare siphons at Dauntsey in case of need. Although this change was implemented, sometimes Malmesbury vans were used for empty Dauntsey churns, with the Dauntsey churns underneath Malmesbury's more often than not, therefore giving Dauntsey staff a lot of extra work in getting to the correct ones!

Some 300 churns of milk daily came from Dauntsey station alone, with a large volume coming in addition from farmers who delivered to Malmesbury and from the Wiltshire Farmers Dairy there. Around twenty farmers from Dauntsey, Foxham, Christian Malford and Sutton Benger brought their milk direct into Dauntsey station to be sent straight to their companies in London (Retail Dairymen, Mutual London, etc), paying their cheque direct to the GWR at the station for their milk conveyance. Much of the United Dairies milk came via their own creamery located just outside the station, providing the station with around 120 churns a day.

With the departure of the milk train, the evening porter had two stopping passenger trains to deal with, one in each direction, collecting tickets from any passengers and taking

Having travelled from Malmesbury on the branch train, Mark Moore and his sisters, accompanied by nanny and nurse, are seen on Dauntsey station in 1922 on their way for a West Country family holiday. *Courtesy Mark Moore*

The Malmesbury branch train at Dauntsey in 1930. The three coach branch set is headed by '517' Class 0—4—2T No. 1428. Fireman Les Jones is seen leaning from the cab whilst the guard, probably Victor Carter, leans inside to adjust some parcel traffic. No. 1428 was first put into service five months before the branch opened in 1877. She was transferred from Faringdon in January 1932 and spent the year alternating between Swindon yard and Malmesbury until being scrapped in the October.

Photomatic

any incoming parcels and putting them in the booking hall until next morning, where they would be added to the work of the early shift. After putting out the lamps, he would lock the station, take the keys to the signalman, have a short conversation, then go home.

Undoubtedly Dauntsey's best-known employee and most dependable servant was porter Percy Wakefield, who was born in 1881 and was a 16/- a week horse driver at Swindon before he moved to Dauntsey as a 17/- a week porter in 1904. He remained there for the rest of his working life until his retirement in 1943. He was an excellent gardener and kept some neat borders on the down platform, and at one time his work merited promotion to parcel porter. He found, however, that the inside and clerical work was not what he enjoyed best – he was better suited to the outdoor tasks in running a station, and a word from his wife to the station master saw him return to regular portering. His family recall him rolling two 17-gallon milk churns simultaneously along the platform, one in each hand! A feature of the station to passengers of stopping trains and those alighting at the platform were the rich Wiltshire accents of Wakefield and Edgar Cross, as well as the Dorset tones of Malmesbury guard John Quarrell, announcing the Malmesbury train. In the year the junction was switched from Dauntsey to Little Somerford, a letter appearing in a local paper ran, 'No longer shall we hear the melodious voices of the porters at Dauntsey calling, "Dauntsey, Dauntsey, change for Great Somerford and Malmesbury"'.

On quieter days a porter would be sent from Dauntsey along the Malmesbury branch if a reliefman were needed at one of the crossings, which came under the jurisdiction of the Dauntsey station master. After the rigours of Dauntsey, such work was certainly a change, but rather boring with the only duty being the opening and closing of crossing gates. On 18th October 1926 a new halt was opened on the main line between Dauntsey and Chippenham, at Christian Malford, and came under the Dauntsey station master, its platform shelters being swept and its eight oil lamps requiring daily trimming by a Dauntsey porter.

Dauntsey's lad porter in 1920 was Albert Stanley, the son of a locally-based ganger. He later worked over a wide area as a relief porter based at Challow. Working a 48-hour week for ten shillings, his main task was the cleaning and trimming of the oil lamps, as well as the usual routine of station cleaning and meeting all trains with a barrow. He worked a rostered turn of 11.30am to 8.30pm, Monday to Saturday each week, and, as he played soccer for Bradenstoke in the Chippenham & District League on Saturdays, he had to arrange with shunter Fred Watson and the station master to have the time off to play, going back in the evening to make the time up. His was a busy world of meeting branch trains, handling parcels of silk coming out of Malmesbury and seemingly-continuous cleaning. In retirement at Challow in 1982, Albert could recall the Wootton Bassett banking engine coming down to Dauntsey to assist goods trains, yards of pigs' chittlins coming out of Malmesbury from the bacon factory on

A view from the branch bay, with the last branch train from Dauntsey about to leave for Malmesbury on a wet evening, 15th July 1933. The rear van is a siphon J boarded 'To work between Malmesbury and Paddington with Milk Traffic only'. Two of these vans had been introduced the previous year, only for most of the milk from Malmesbury milk factory to be taken over by road tankers.

Bertram Farmer

A 1921 view of Dauntsey, looking east towards Swindon from the road overbridge. The first goods siding, provided for the opening of the station in February 1868 at a cost of £260, was laid using materials from a siding at the foot of the Wootton Bassett incline. The milk loading platform behind the passenger platform is just hidden behind the milk vans. A ramp and gate were provided from 1882 to facilitate loading and unloading of cattle, costing £10, but its exact up side location is uncertain here. To the left of the gated entrance to the goods yard is the 'oil house', a corrugated tin hut used for lamp trimming — station staff dealt with lamps here, but the long-burning signal and indicator lamps were under the supervision of the District Lampman from Chippenham. To the left of the gate is a heap of gravel for the Engineering Department to scatter on the roadway from the station entrance during icy conditions. The other building here is the shunters' cabin — shunter Fred Watson can be seen in the doorway. The cabin at the far end of the down platform covered the ground frame which, interlocked with the signal box, was worked by a porter. It was used to operate the points to the goods yard and the crossover road between up and down main lines in co-operation with the signalman, whose vision of this end of the station was very restricted. The Malmesbury branch engine was replenished from the water column seen at the end of the up side platform. This was fed by the water tank behind the down platform to the right of the picture. The wooden boards between the tracks in the foreground covered a drain which carried away excess rainwater and station sewage. Water came from the disused Wilts & Berks Canal higher up the hill. It was gravity fed, the flow being stemmed by an automatic cut-out. Catch points protected the station on the up side, in case any freight wagons broke loose on Dauntsey Bank. Despite the incline here, rising towards Wootton Bassett, banking engines were not kept at Dauntsey, but one could be kept in readiness at Wootton Bassett and sent when required. In 1889 a banker left Chippenham nightly at 9.30 for Dauntsey to assist trains if required up to Wootton Bassett Incline Cabin. In 1900 an engine fresh from a Calne branch passenger working would be sent to Dauntsey to be ready to assist the 'Corsham stone', the 6.40 Corsham to Paddington and various night goods destined for the London area.

L & GRP, courtesy David & Charles

the midday train, and the use of the station by two coal companies, Barnes and also Burgess, up by Dauntsey Lock.

Dauntsey's payroll included the lad porter up to 1932, when Hubert Spencer was the last person to be employed there in that capacity. During his time he worked an 11.30–8.30 day, with an hour allowed for lunch, cycling from Brinkworth to earn his 16/- shillings a week for a job, which, like Albert Stanley, principally involved polishing and trimming the 48 oil lamps on the station. In addition, like the porters, he had

the end of his shift while the porter was down in the back road assisting with the preparation of the milk train. In 1932, the post of lad porter was withdrawn when the station oil lamps were replaced with eight Tilley lamps.

A great deal of horse traffic passed through the station. Major Richardson of nearby Idover House had a training school for police horses which were sent to Imber Court, near Surbiton, in horse-boxes from Dauntsey. The porter would ring Swindon to book horse-boxes, such vehicles often being

One of Barnes Bros.'s coal wagons which were regularly seen in the goods yard from the '20s.
Gloucester Carriage & Wagon Co.

to meet every train calling at Dauntsey, and spent many hours stacking milk empties under the branch bay canopy ready for return to Malmesbury. As the signal box had no running water, he had to take cans of water down to the signalmen for their drinking and washing, as well as oil for their paraffin lamps.

Meeting the late afternoon mixed train out of Malmesbury provided a lot of hard work for the lad porter. Some milk came out on this train, but the bacon traffic sent along the branch from the Adye & Hinwood bacon factory in Malmesbury was particularly large. On one occasion, Spencer had just loaded a barrow-full of bacon from the branch train which was destined for the Spa Hotel at Bath, and was proceeding along the up side, when he saw the train on which it was supposed to go coming down Dauntsey Bank. Thinking he could beat the train and be ready on the down side with the bacon, he rushed his barrow over the east end crossover, only to lose some of the load on the track in his haste. The Swindon–Bristol stopper carved right through it – the meat was despatched as it was, hastily tied together, and no more was heard – maybe the Spa preferred its bacon ready-sliced!

Also generally responsible for the cleanliness of the station, the lad porter had to sweep out the offices and platform shelter, wipe clean the station nameboard, and during the winter clean out and make up fires ready for the next morning. Cut sleepers were sent from Bathampton and cut for firewood with an axe in the small goods shed. Firewood ready for the morning would be kept overnight in the parcels office where the early turn porter could reach it easily, to minimise his work at a time of the day when work was very hectic. During the evening the youngster would be alone on the station at

required also for hunts and shows. The Malmesbury branch engine often had to cross to the down line to collect vehicles dropped off from main line trains. It did sometimes happen that a box might arrive after the branch loco had made its last trip into Malmesbury for the night, in which case the porter and lad porter would stay on to meet it. The trains would push the box back over to the up side, then the two would push it by hand with a pinch-bar into the goods siding and into the dock behind the up platform.

The station had to send a rolling stock return every day to Controlled Rolling Stock, Swindon, to list exactly what the station had, what was to spare, and what was needed. In this way each division of the GWR knew where all its stock was at any given time.

Although the station lay at the foot of the famous Dauntsey Bank, up which heavy goods trains regularly needed a banking engine on the rear to assist them, no bankers were ever kept at Dauntsey. A Swindon engine would be kept at Wootton Bassett for this purpose, and when one was required the signalman would receive a call from Chippenham for a banker to be available. On arrival. the banking engine would wait on the bay line at Dauntsey, by the signal box, ready to be called onto the end of the train by the guard.

The station yard was a very busy place in the '20s. A carrier service was provided by Ted Burchell of Bradenstoke, who brought down milk from the Lyneham area and took away 'paid home' parcels. There was much traffic in timber, hay from the local farms for South Wales pit ponies, and cattle cake coming in for the farms. A cattle cake store was housed in a wheel-less carriage on the milk dock, with a ramp for unloading the feed into farmers' wagons. Returns were sent to the cattle feed firms detailing the amounts taken by each farmer. Much of the general merchandise coming into Dauntsey went to Wiltshire & Sons, the Bradenstoke grocery.

By far the most consistent users of the goods yard throughout the entire life of the station were the Barnes Brothers whose coal business was certainly involved with the first and last loads of coal to come into Dauntsey. When the station

Looking east from under the road bridge in 1933, with familiar advertisements for Bovril and Robertson's marmalade. Porter Percy Wakefield, the left-hand of the two figures, is seen holding a pump used to pressurise the Tilley lamps. The population of the village at this time was 370.
Courtesy Walter Wakefield

first opened, the business already existed there under Joseph & Walter Barnes, who before the opening had obtained their coal via Chippenham. The family had assisted in the building of the Malmesbury branch line, supplying horses to the railway to assist with haulage of construction materials. Coal was brought from Camerton, Radstock, Coalpit Heath and various Midland and South Wales collieries, to the coal siding at the east end of the station, where, until the '20s, they used hired wagons. Around this time they took on two 10-ton private owner wagons of their own, adding a 12-tonner in 1927. Delivery was tough work up the hill to Bradenstoke, but in the '20s they obtained a Ford Motor lorry through Ralph Barnes, who had started a motor engineering business locally in 1925. The coal business usually employed two partners and three assistants, the office being just above the station at Dauntsey Wharf.

Dauntsey seemed to breed a special kind of loyalty and identification amongst its railwaymen. Mention has been made of the long stays of Samuel Jefford and Percy Wakefield, and signalman Henry Hunt spent 30 years on the box from the early 1890s. When the station lost its junction status in 1933 there were four members of staff there who boasted between then some 140 years of company service at Dauntsey. In addition to Wakefield, these men were Jack Waite, Fred Watson and Sydney Hill.

Fred Watson began at Dauntsey in 1891 as a porter, then was appointed shunter in March 1911 on 22/- a week. He retired and the post of shunter ceased when the branch closed in 1933. Jack Waite, born in 1867, spent most of his working life there as porter and parcel porter. Sydney Hill had been at Dauntsey twenty years when he retired in 1934, the year after closure of the Malmesbury line. Hill began his railway career in 1891 and came to Dauntsey for two years as a porter in 1895. The time spent at the foot of Clack Mount obviously left its impression on him, as, after a string of small station

appointments, he was promoted to the post of Class 4 station master at Dauntsey in February 1914 on 40/- a week, remaining there until his retirement.

All branch trains arriving at Dauntsey during the '20s had connections in both directions, to London and Bristol, although three trains, the 11.03, 12.10 and 2.26 ex-Malmesbury, provided good westerly connections only as far as Chippenham. Dauntsey was served principally by stopping trains on the Swindon–Bristol local service, normally nine up and ten down on weekdays, the down service including an evening railmotor car, one class only, which left Swindon at 8.15pm, called at Dauntsey at 8.33 and arrived in Bristol at 9.43. On Sundays there were two up and four down trains, the one branch train, which existed primarily for milk, always providing a better connection for those travelling from London rather than for those going east on a Sunday. In 1930 a traveller could leave Paddington at 5.30pm, reach Swindon at 7.03, leave at 7.15 for Dauntsey, where a 7.36 arrival would give a connection with the 7.45 branch train to Malmesbury, the arrival there just after 8pm giving a good journey time of $2\frac{1}{2}$ hours with smooth connections. Those London-bound from Malmesbury, however, were faced with a 6.20 departure from Malmesbury which gave waits of 25 and 57 minutes at Dauntsey and Swindon respectively, arrival at Paddington being at 10pm.

1923 was a good year for Dauntsey station, with its fullest station staff (twelve on payroll, including the three branch gatemen), total receipts of £16,191 for the year with 16,750 tickets issued, and a very large parcel traffic – a large amount of the revenue came from parcels, which included the milk, over 90,000 churns being handled in 1925. By the time the station lost its junction status in 1933, though, its staff was reduced to seven, total receipts had dwindled to below £4,000 annually, with the decline of milk traffic seriously affecting the passenger train traffic receipts. The falling-off of goods business was not so dramatic, as it continued to be boosted by the Barnes coal operation. The loss of the branch saw a general decline continue on all fronts until the opening of Lyneham aerodrome in 1938. The changes that this and the onset of World War II brought about in the fortunes of Dauntsey station are chronicled in Appendix 0.

CHAPTER SIX

A JOURNEY ALONG
THE OLD LINE

The branch junction at Dauntsey in 1930, the line to Malmesbury curving away sharply to the right of the picture.   *C. L. Mowat*

ICTURE a summer afternoon in 1927, when the branch is in its 50th year of operation, and we have just alighted from a Bristol-bound stopping train. To the south, behind the station master's house and garden, rise the slopes of Clack Mount, to the north the meadows of the Avon valley through which our branch journey lies. There is a gently busy air about this country outpost, two miles from its village, as we cross the footbridge to the up platform, then walk under the road overbridge to the west end of the station where the connecting 'Bunk' for Malmesbury waits in the bay. The regular set of 3 four-wheel coaches at the platform is headed by a '517' class 0–4–2T, No. 540. On the footplate are driver Bill Eveleigh and fireman Dick Cooper, and as we approach the branch train, porter-guard Victor Carter is changing a reversible destination board on the centre coach to read a reassuring 'Malmesbury'. A lad porter arrives with a trolley containing some parcels from the main line train, and Carter assists him in transferring these to his compartment. The

signalman lowers the branch starting signal to 'off', the 'right away' is given, and our journey begins.

The branch to Malmesbury left the main line immediately west of the junction station, curving past the signal box where the single line token was collected, to assume a north-westerly course across Swallett Gate meadows. As the branch curved away from the junction, a cutting bank to the right partially obscured the view of Dauntsey Creamery which stood just north of the station entrance from the main road. Further on to the left, at the point where the run-round loop merged with the single running line, was a bracket bearing the up branch home signals, to the bay and main line, placed to the right for Dauntsey-bound trains for sighting purposes. Adjacent to milepost 88 from Paddington stood the protective distant signal for the junction, originally an arm worked from the box but now 'fixed' permanently at caution. The line passed over a cattle creep, bridge No. 1 on the branch, then, on a gentle falling gradient of 1 in 95 , ran into a shallow cutting

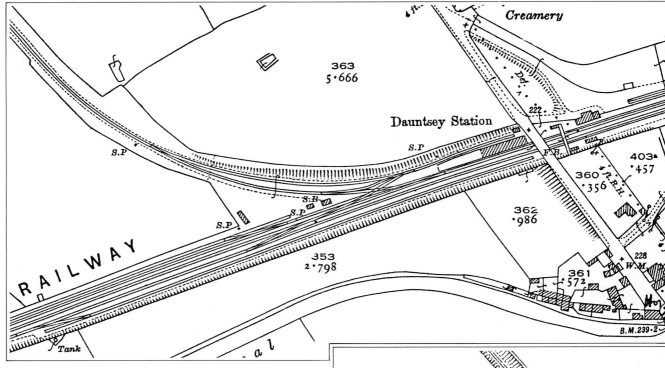

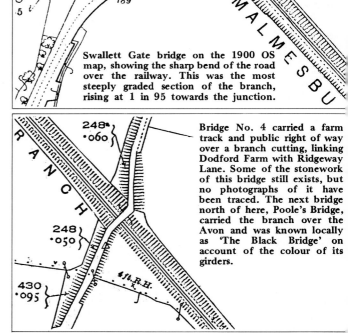

Swallett Gate bridge on the 1900 OS map, showing the sharp bend of the road over the railway. This was the most steeply graded section of the branch, rising at 1 in 95 towards the junction.

Bridge No. 4 carried a farm track and public right of way over a branch cutting, linking Dodford Farm with Ridgeway Lane. Some of the stonework of this bridge still exists, but no photographs of it have been traced. The next bridge north of here, Poole's Bridge, carried the branch over the Avon and was known locally as 'The Black Bridge' on account of the colour of its girders.

where a blast on the locomotive's whistle always indicated its approach to Swallett Gate bridge, which was constructed in stone with brick abutments and carried the main A420 road between Swindon and Chippenham. The awkward bends on the road approaches to this bridge in each direction hastened its removal after the closure of this end of the branch, at the time of our journey just six years away, enabling Wiltshire County Council to level off and straighten the highway. It was customary for the branch engine to whistle at this point, as it did for all major bridges on the line and any point, such as the crossings, where a warning of the train's approach was necessary.

On a level gradient and maintaining a straight course in a north-north-west direction, the branch passed a permanent way hut to the right and crossed Dauntsey Brook via a short single-girder span before passing over the parish boundary from Christian Malford into the parish of Dauntsey. Beyond this was a cutting, then Bridge No. 4 passed overhead carrying a farm track from nearby Idover Farm. After milepost 89 and another permanent way hut, the branch crossed the River Avon for the first time via Poole's Bridge, named after a tenant farmer, John Poole, who occupied the land here at the time of the survey of the line. Passing into the parish of Great Somerford, the gradient beyond the bridge was maintained by an embankment with four underbridges for cattle creeps and a culvert for a backstream of the Avon. Away to the right the river looped its way past Dauntsey House and the extensive grounds of Dauntsey Park, once the home of Walter Powell, MP, one of the line's original promoters. As the embankment levelled off, the train passed the down distant protecting Dauntsey Road Crossing, where the gates would be closed across the road before the train left Dauntsey, as soon as the gateman received the appropriate code on the

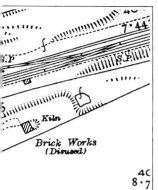

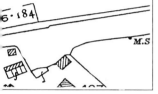

ey Lock

Dauntsey Road Crossing in 1932, looking towards Malmesbury. *Courtesy Mr. & Mrs. M. Drinkwater*

Dauntsey Road Crossing's water supply was delivered in cans and churns from Dauntsey station. Here gateman Bill Hine is seen collecting filled cans from the guard's compartment of the train's leading brake third. *Courtesy Mr. & Mrs. M. Drinkwater*

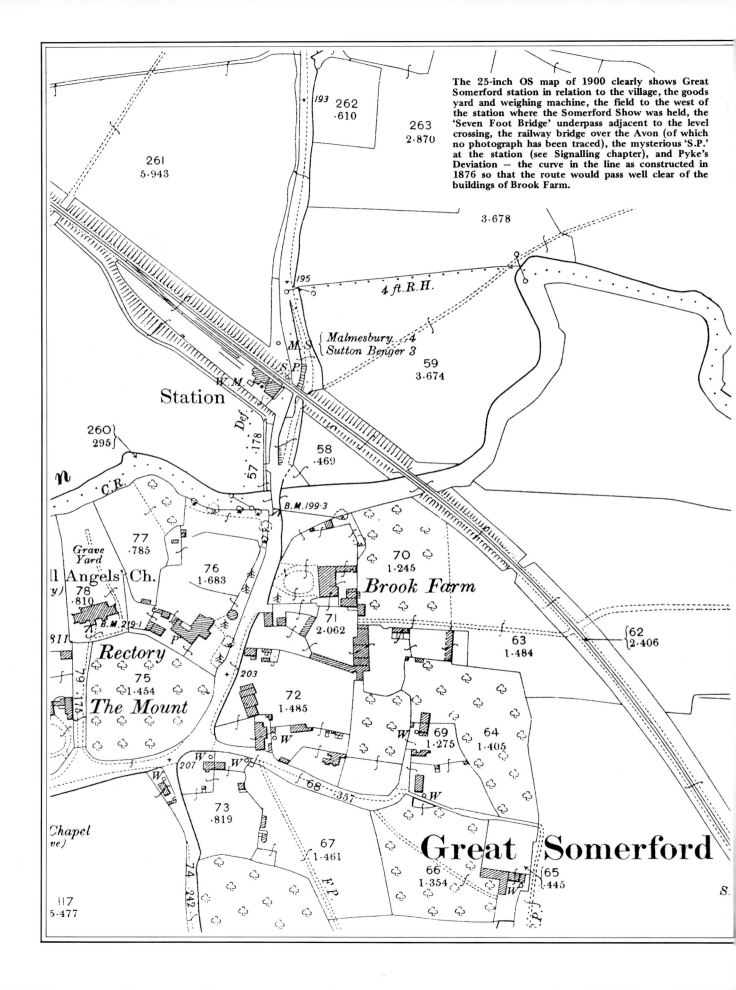

The 25-inch OS map of 1900 clearly shows Great
Somerford station in relation to the village, the goods
yard and weighing machine, the field to the west of
the station where the Somerford Show was held, the
'Seven Foot Bridge' underpass adjacent to the level
crossing, the railway bridge over the Avon (of which
no photograph has been traced), the mysterious 'S.P.'
at the station (see Signalling chapter), and Pyke's
Deviation — the curve in the line as constructed in
1876 so that the route would pass well clear of the
buildings of Brook Farm.

Looking north from the village of Great Somerford across the old road bridge over the Avon. This had stood for some 130 years before replacement in the late '20s. The station house and level crossing can be seen, with the railway embankment bringing the line in from Dauntsey on the right of the photograph. Just beyond the bridge is the start of the lane leading to the underpass which the railway were bound to provide so that cattle drives could continue when the gates at the crossing were closed across the road. At one time the well water at Great Somerford was undrinkable, so water was supplied to the station in cans from Dauntsey. It was not until 1953 that piped water reached the village.

Wiltshire Dept. of Highways & Transportation, Trowbridge

'blower' from Dauntsey signal box. In the late 'twenties the crossing lodge was occupied by Mr and Mrs Hine who shared the gate duty and kept a well-stocked garden where they would usually be when one branch train each day would halt at the crossing to deliver cans of drinking water to them. South of the crossing a wooden picket fence separated the cottage's rear garden from the railway, the front garden being fenced off by iron railings. A quiet country road between the villages of Dauntsey and Great Somerford crossed the line at this point, which was nevertheless often busy with agricultural traffic.

From Dauntsey Road the branch kept to its straight north-north-west course on a rising 1 in 348 gradient, at milepost 90 passing between two distant signals, the arm to the left warning the driver of Great Somerford crossing and station ahead, the right-hand post bearing the up distant for Dauntsey Road Crossing. The village of Great Somerford was now visible away to the left, the nearby buildings of Brook Farm serving as a reminder that the section of line from milepost 90 to the station was the stretch known to the original builders as 'Pike's Deviation'. Here, the gentle curve produced by this alteration to the original survey took the route over two small bridges, over a footpath and cattle creep respectively, then onto an embankment and Bridge No. 13 which took the line for the second time over the River Avon. No doubt at one time a local photographer would have been waiting on occasions to capture the branch train crossing the Avon bridge from the

The old three-arch river bridge, viewed from the bank in front of the railway station. It proved inconveniently narrow for traffic even in the '20s and, it is said, tended to slow down the flow of the river in flood periods so that the waters took longer to recede. There are tales extant in the village of how girls from the silk mills in Malmesbury would come out to Great Somerford on the one Sunday evening train and Somerford boys would walk them home again beside the river, starting at this point.

Courtesy Mrs. F. Bubb

The River Avon and village church viewed from the field just south of the railway station at Great Somerford.   *Courtesy Pamela Bridges*

A postcard view of Great Somerford village. 'The Folly' referred to cottages which are to the right off camera. The road bends away to the left, and some 200 yards beyond the bend was the GWR station.
Collection Ted Porter

useful vantage point afforded by the old road-bridge nearby, but unfortunately no photographs have been traced, and no plans have been found to enable adequate description of the railway structure at this point.

The village of Somerford Magna (Great Somerford) is a habitation of attractive houses occupying rising ground by the river, the name meaning simply 'summer ford' as a reference to a seasonal crossing of the waterway. As the branch train crossed the Avon here the passenger beheld a lovely view along the river to the west, where the old three-arch hump-back bridge carried the road from the village in the direction of neighbouring Little Somerford, this bridge having existed for some 130 years before replacement in the early '30s. Away to the right of the river behind the station was the meadow where the annual Somerford Show was held, with the village church overlooking the river on an eminence to the left.

Hollow Street, Great Somerford, looking west, with the village school and schoolhouse on the left. Records of the school provided useful clues in tracing families whose forebears lived in the GWR station house; the photograph of Mr. Ham on page 213 was located as a result of examination of an old school admissions register yielding the names of the station master's children in school during 1918—22.
Collection Oliver Pike

Great Somerford station in 1921, the year before it was reduced to halt status and its goods yard closed. The station here was not started until December 1877 after the GWR had taken over control from the original MRC. Costing some £200, the station building is in Italianate style with hipped roof and brick chimney. The near bay window served the signal cabin, the other two doors leading to the station master's office, booking hall/waiting room and lavatories. The small corrugated iron shed seen at the far end of the main building served as a goods shed. The single platform was lit by five oil lamps each bearing glass nameplates with 'Somerford' (the station's original name) in black letters on an opal blue background. The railway land on the opposite side of the track to the platform was occupied by floral display, bushes and allotments. Behind the platform was a single siding which joined the branch at the north-west end, with points trailing in the Malmesbury direction. Down goods trains were usually marshalled with wagons for Great Somerford at the front of the train. On arrival at the station, the brake was screwed down on the guards van, and the train left on the running line while the wagons for Somerford were uncoupled and drawn forward clear of the points. Any empties or other vehicles awaiting collection were shunted out of the siding and onto the rest of the train, then the wagons for Somerford, typically coal, were placed in the siding. The loco then rejoined its train and continued to Malmesbury. Goods trains normally only called in the down direction, outgoing vehicles from Somerford being taken into Malmesbury for the return journey. The Malmesbury Coal Company usually kept one of their wagons here and local folk would collect their ½ cwts by pram. A local carrier was paid by the GWR to deliver goods and parcels on a handcart, and local lads would often hang around the station in the hope of earning a few coppers by delivering small parcels in the village. Apart from coal, the main traffic into Great Somerford was feed and fertilizer for the farms, and supplies from Swindon and Chippenham for shops and public houses. The station master's office was often full of fishing tackle left there by members of Bristol and Birmingham fishing clubs who came for trout in the nearby Avon. At this time the Class 5 station here provided employment as porter for one George Ridler, whose middle initial was 'W' and thus noted the sonorous 'GWR' as his full initial! *L & GRP courtesy David & Charles*

The level crossing at Great Somerford. The station house was built as a single-storey dwelling in similar design to the other crossing lodges on the branch. The second storey was added in 1893. This view is looking south towards the village with the 'Seven Foot Bridge' underpass at a lower level behind the fence on the left of the picture.

Author's collection

Similarly, visitors to the church could enjoy an excellent vista of both river and railway from the rear grounds of the churchyard.

North of the river the branch continued on a short embankment, over Bridge No. 14, then immediately through Somerford level crossing and into the station. On our 1927 trip Great Somerford had been reduced to 'halt' status, the only person on duty being gateman James Hurley who occupied the station house. There would have been but a small delay here as a solitary passenger for Malmesbury booked his ticket from the guard before boarding. The level crossing was at the south end of the platform, and below the crossing, between it and the river, was a subway which the railway company of 1872 had been instructed to put in under the line so that local

The Seven Foot Bridge, looking north towards Little Somerford. The station was up behind the hedge at left. The level crossing gates are just visible to the right of the hedge.

Courtesy Mrs. Muriel Edwards

The Seven Foot Bridge underpass, viewed from the front seat of a car, looking south towards the village of Great Somerford around 1930. To quote from the Malmesbury Railway Act of 1872: ' . . . Before opening the railway for traffic the Company shall construct and complete for public use, at or near to the place where the railway crosses the said turnpike road No. 2, in the parish of Little Somerford, a bridge or archway under the railway, not less than seven feet in height, and not less than twelve feet in width'.

Courtesy Mrs. Muriel Edwards

Another view of the old road bridge over the Avon, temporarily strengthened with tiebars before being completely replaced. The station house can just be seen on the right through the trees.
Courtesy Mrs. F. Bubb

farmers could maintain cattle drives when the gates were closed across the road. Because of its low clearance, this underpass below Bridge No. 14 was known locally as the 'Seven Foot Bridge', although the track beneath it was very-prone to flooding on account of its low elevation and proximity to the river. Village legend relates how a local butcher once fell foul of the low headroom, after a midday visit to the 'Volunteer' at which he was an esteemed and regular patron. Seeing the crossing gates closed and no train in sight, he took the underpass and forgot to duck, his customers at Little Somerford finding him unconscious at the bottom of the cart when his horse, evidently used to the journey, arrived there!

This view, from the south side of the River Avon in the early '30s, shows the new bridge over the river with the station beyond. The gated path led down to the 'Seven Foot Bridge' underpass.
Collection Oliver Pike

Great Somerford Halt c.1930, looking back towards Dauntsey and with the now closed goods yard to the right. The population of the village in 1931 was 448. There was a railway telephone between Dauntsey and Malmesbury which was linked to the station office and house at Great Somerford. If the crossing keeper (from 1922) was not on the platform, the phone was always switched through to the house.
C. L. Mowat

As the parish boundary ran through the Seven Foot Bridge, the station was actually in the parish of Little Somerford, being situated at the northern extremity of its village at $2\frac{3}{4}$ miles from Dauntsey.

Northwards from Great Somerford the branch continued on a substantial embankment on a rising 1 in 116 gradient, past the up distant for Somerford level crossing, then into a deep cutting where the line swung north towards Kingsmead. At the head of this cutting a stone overbridge carried a farmer's track overhead – this structure was unusual with its three arches, the width of the centre one a reminder that the branch was built with land wide enough for double track. Denuded remains of these arches can still be found amidst reclaimed farmland here, still showing '16' painted in white on the stone.

On a falling 1 in 150 from here the Kingsmead Crossing down distant signal was passed just before milepost 91, then the branch passed under the South Wales Direct main line just east of Somerford Viaduct over which the 1903 route bridged the River Avon and its wide valley. Where the Malmesbury branch passed under the new main line, the necessary bridge, an angular brick-built structure with single girder span, was numbered 16A on the branch. Just beyond, to the left, was the pumping station which took water from the river to supply the station and water tank at Little Somerford. Once on the north side of the Direct and having confirmed that the gates ahead at Kingsmead were open to the train, the engine crew could relax and enjoy a fine view down to the Avon with Kingsmead Mill clearly visible. Gawthropp's grist mill had been open here since 1828, and it was not unusual for the railway passengers to observe a Shire-hauled wagon

Bridge No. 16 seen after closure of the old line south of Kingsmead Crossing, showing how the centre arch was wide enough for double track.

with its load of barley, cow-cake or oats standing at the crossing, or maybe one of the new motor lorries, the driver engaged in conversation with gateman Bill Archard, maybe passing on some item of world news, with Mrs Archard breaking off from tending chickens in the crossing lodge garden to wave to the engine crew. A permanent way hut stood on the south side of the gates, later removed when the line was diverted to the Direct at this point. The crossing lodge, a stone-built cottage with sandstone quoins and a wide-pitched slate roof, was constructed in a similar style to those at Dauntsey Road and Somerford (as originally built), and stood on the north side of the crossing to the left of the train.

The branch turned westwards after Kingsmead Crossing, rising at 1 in 198, then running level on a low embankment

The Malmesbury branch at Little Somerford, looking across the Avon to Somerford Viaduct and the South Wales Direct line of 1903. This photograph was taken in 1920.

L & GRP, courtesy David & Charles

Looking past Kingsmead Crossing along the Avon Valley towards Malmesbury. The up distant for the crossing can be seen in the distance, to the right of the nameboard.

E. K. Lockstone

keeping it above the Avon flood plain. Through the years this section of the branch proved to be a difficult length to maintain for the permanent way men who would often be seen at this point. In excessive wet weather, flooding of the Avon would cause subsidence of the embankment and wash-out of ballast. In December 1908 the GWR spent £61 diverting a rhine to improve the drainage here, near the branch 91½ milepost.

The Kingsmead up distant was passed to the right and several small underbridges were crossed before the course turned north-west just before another permanent way store

and occupation crossing at the end of the embankment. With the trees of Angrove Wood garlanding the valley slopes beyond the river away to the left of the train, milepost 92 heralded the entrance to Harding's Cutting, a 20-chain excavation from which 11,590 cubic yards of earth were shifted during construction – Richard Harding was the tenant farmer in occupation here during the 1870s.

As the branch train approached Cowbridge, the passenger could see the shooting range of the Wilts Rifle Corps to the north, reduced to 600 yards in length by the construction of

This aerial view gives a fine impression of the branch almost all the way from Kingsmead Crossing and Mill to Malmesbury. Just off the right of the picture a public right of way crossed the branch, giving access from the Swindon–Malmesbury road to Kingsmead Mill via Maunditts Park Farm. The hedgerow running up to the permanent way hut in the left foreground marks the western boundary of this farm. The hut still survives. Beyond it the line curves through Harding's Cutting, and the section of the Avon known as the Roaring Hatches flows close to the railway to the north of the cutting, with two bridges carrying the line over a backstream of the river. In front of the dark area of trees the branch can be seen passing the site of the projected Burton Hill station, then into a cutting and under the Swindon road at Cowbridge. The wide curve of the Lea Fields embankment can be faintly discerned away to the right of Cowbridge House, with the town of Malmesbury away off the left of the picture beyond the white building. In the far distance the agricultural land of North Wilts stretches away towards Tetbury and the Gloucestershire border.   *Courtesy the Marsh family, Maunditts Park Farm*

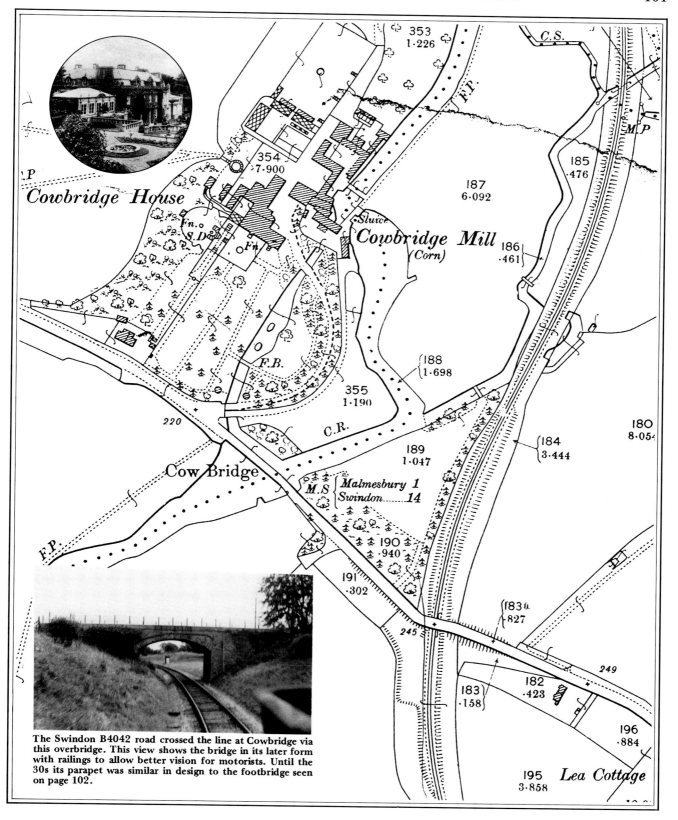

Cowbridge House

Cowbridge Mill
(Corn)

Cow Bridge

Malmesbury 1
Swindon 14

Lea Cottage

The Swindon B4042 road crossed the line at Cowbridge via
this overbridge. This view shows the bridge in its later form
with railings to allow better vision for motorists. Until the
30s its parapet was similar in design to the footbridge seen
on page 102.

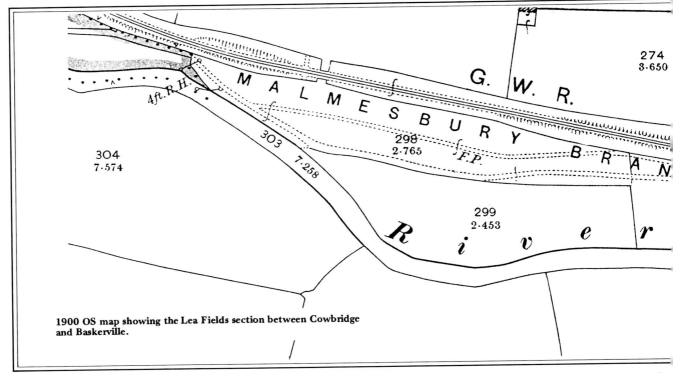

1900 OS map showing the Lea Fields section between Cowbridge and Baskerville.

the line and still in use in the '20s. Away to the left, where fields of Rodbourne Rail farm bordered the branch, young horses were often to be seen grazing and the engine would sound its whistle several times. This was an arrangement between the farmer and the crew, whereby the horses would be sent out to graze close to the line in an effort to get them used to railway noise as preparation for the milk run to Malmesbury station, On a rising 1 in 173 the route crossed briefly into the parish of Lea and Cleverton and turned north into Cowbridge cutting where the single-arch Bridge No. 27 carried the Swindon-Malmesbury B4042 road. The bridge formed a quite sharp bend over the railway, which as private motoring developed locally in the '30s became something of a black-spot for motorists, and in 1938 its parapet wall was lowered and replaced with railings to give better visibility along the road over it, a move hastened by a collision between

A mid-1930s view of a branch train, a Collett 0–4–2T with a Bristol Division B-set, heading towards Malmesbury along the Lea Fields embankment. *Author's collection*

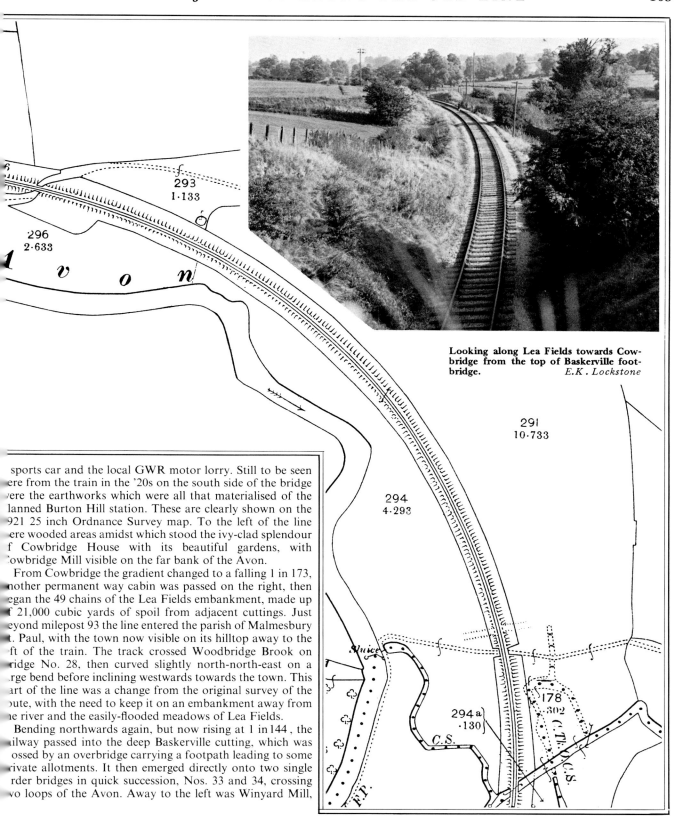

Looking along Lea Fields towards Cowbridge from the top of Baskerville footbridge. *E.K. Lockstone*

sports car and the local GWR motor lorry. Still to be seen
ere from the train in the '20s on the south side of the bridge
were the earthworks which were all that materialised of the
lanned Burton Hill station. These are clearly shown on the
921 25 inch Ordnance Survey map. To the left of the line
ere wooded areas amidst which stood the ivy-clad splendour
f Cowbridge House with its beautiful gardens, with
owbridge Mill visible on the far bank of the Avon.

From Cowbridge the gradient changed to a falling 1 in 173,
nother permanent way cabin was passed on the right, then
egan the 49 chains of the Lea Fields embankment, made up
f 21,000 cubic yards of spoil from adjacent cuttings. Just
eyond milepost 93 the line entered the parish of Malmesbury
t. Paul, with the town now visible on its hilltop away to the
ft of the train. The track crossed Woodbridge Brook on
ridge No. 28, then curved slightly north-north-east on a
rge bend before inclining westwards towards the town. This
art of the line was a change from the original survey of the
oute, with the need to keep it on an embankment away from
e river and the easily-flooded meadows of Lea Fields.

Bending northwards again, but now rising at 1 in 144, the
ailway passed into the deep Baskerville cutting, which was
ossed by an overbridge carrying a footpath leading to some
rivate allotments. It then emerged directly onto two single
rder bridges in quick succession, Nos. 33 and 34, crossing
wo loops of the Avon. Away to the left was Winyard Mill,

In Baskerville cutting, looking east through the footbridge. It was at this spot that William Ponting's serious accident occurred in 1875.
E. K. Lockstone

Looking towards Malmesbury along Baskerville cutting from the top of the footbridge.   *E. K. Lockstone*

Looking east over the town and along the branch in 1922. Baskerville bridge and cutting can be seen with the line passing along Lea Fields towards the top of the photograph.

Collection Bert Vizor

Looking north-west out of Baskerville cutting across bridges 33 and 34 towards the school footbridge and the tunnel mouth.
E. K. Lockstone

The south-east end of Malmesbury tunnel, c.1930, showing the retaining wall between the school footbridge and the tunnel mouth.
C. L. Mowat

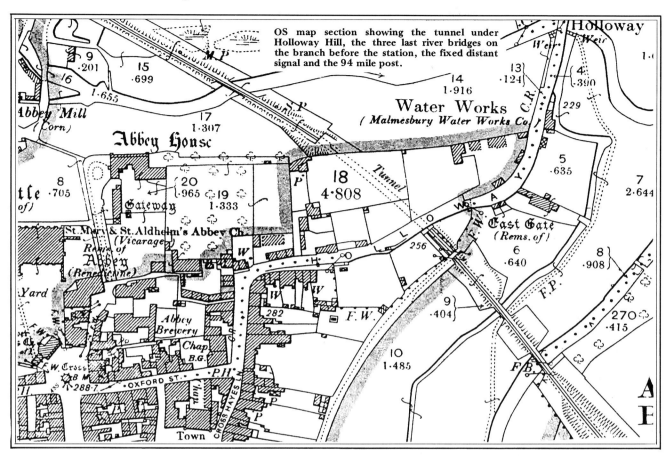

OS map section showing the tunnel under Holloway Hill, the three last river bridges on the branch before the station, the fixed distant signal and the 94 mile post.

where the line had first been projected and which had been another possible site for an intermediate station short of the town. To the right of the train could be seen the remains of the town's old East Gate, whilst to the north was Malmesbury waterworks. In 1927 an unusual incident occurred at this location concerning branch fireman Dick Cooper while working with a Swindon reliefman, Bill Joyce. As a midday train was running into Malmesbury, the driver shut off steam in Baskerville cutting to cross the two bridges, when he noticed a carriage door swing open. The train was brought to a stand between Baskerville and the tunnel and Dick Cooper alighted to run back and shut it, losing his cap as he did so. He retrieved it after dealing with the door. Days later there appeared a newspaper article headed 'Train stopped to pick up fireman's cap', which failed to explain the real reason for the stop. Not surprisingly, the Swindon driver was not pleased, and made a special visit to Malmesbury to express his views to the erring local correspondent!

On a falling 1 in 290 the railway now passed under a stone footbridge erected for the use of a nearby school, its masonry being extended into a retaining wall to mark the eastern end of Malmesbury tunnel, now in the parish of Malmesbury the Abbey. The tunnel was 105 yards long and excavated on a gentle curve through Holloway Hill. Trains emerging at the west end then passed the Malmesbury fixed signal to the right, 'wrong side', warning the driver of the approach to the station

Emerging from the tunnel at the north-west end, looking across the Inglebourne bridge, the last on the branch, before the run-in to Malmesbury station.
Austin Attewell

A view from the cab, looking over the bunker towards the north-west end of the tunnel, with Inglebourne bridge, fixed distant signal, and the 'Triangular Field' where the cutting of the sod of the failed Wilts & Glos Railway scheme took place in 1865.

North-west end of Malmesbury tunnel with fixed distant signal.   C. L. Mowat

and the need to slacken speed. The general north-west trend of the line was maintained as the Inglebourne, the Tetbury branch of the River Avon, was bridged by a large 60 foot single girder span, the largest on the line. Milepost 94 was passed shortly before Lovers Lane crossing, through which a public footpath ran between the town (in the direction of which could be seen Malmesbury Abbey in its imposing Norman grandeur through the trees at this point), and Malmesbury cricket ground, situated on a hill to the right of the railway, known as the Worthies. Tales are still extant in the town of how, many years ago, this little crossing was an unofficial boarding point for various influential people from the Oxford Street vicinity, who could walk down the Abbey steps and save themselves a walk to the station if they knew their train times and were 'in' with the crews. One doctor of note regularly used this arrangement, and no doubt some monetary appreciation would be forthcoming to engine crew and guard at Dauntsey. A popular story in the Lockstone family relates how a noted Lockstone, master grocer in Oxford Street, who regularly received high quality groceries from London and Bristol at Malmesbury station, one day walked down to Lovers Lane to avail himself of a train, only for the 'Bunk' to go straight past without stopping. Later that day it is said that both station master and guard were seen entering the grocery, caps in hand, to explain that they hadn't been able to stop on this occasion as there had been an inspector aboard!

On a level gradient into the station yard, the line passed between the coalyard and a platelayers' hut, with the home

Two contrasting views of Lovers Lane Crossing more than half a century apart. *Top :* Looking from the Worthies across the valley to the Abbey in the early years of the century. *Below :* At crossing level, looking up the footpath which led to the cricket ground. Pedestrians used the small side gates but it was rare to see the main gates opened.   *(Top) Oliver Pike collection. (Below) Don Pritchard*

Pratts Paraffin Depot for local distribution was based at Malmesbury during the late '20s — a large tank on blocks in the coal yard. Periodically, it received paraffin in a tanker wagon from Avonmouth. The tank is here seen, in April 1931, loaded on a Crocodile F ready for despatch. The light-coloured area of rubble on the left indicates the site of the depot. The corrugated shed to the left of the tank was for the coal company's horses. Mark Moore, who grew up in 'Mundens', the house directly behind the stable, recalled how he acquired an air rifle at the age of 13 and loved the metallic ring produced when he hit the roof with pellets fired from the centre upper window of this house. He was just able to reach it at about 100 yards range from his bedroom.
Bertram Farmer

Opposite page:

"I was born in 1917 at Mundens, 27 Abbey Row, Malmesbury, and that was my home for 28 years. Our large garden had two parts: the top garden on the level ground which was part of the original causeway from Westport Gate to the Abbey, and the bottom garden below the old retaining wall and sloping steeply to the river. Such was the fascination of the railway for me as a small boy that as soon as I heard the train emerge from the tunnel I would run to the end of the top garden from where there was a grandstand view covering the stretch from the goods shed to Lovers Lane Crossing. I spent many hours watching the shunting operations, sorting out the incoming mixed goods and compiling the outgoing train.

"We had a garage and stables building with access from Mill Lane, and this can be seen in the famous postcard view of the station, just to the right of the cloud of smoke above the station canopy [see page 45]. I knew the tunnel well. My older sister Joan and I often used to walk along Lea Fields and if there was ever any danger of being late home for tea, a terrible sin, we'd take a short cut home via the tunnel and Lovers Lane Crossing. Our knowledge of the timetable saved us from ever being caught by surprise, which was important because we would usually have dogs with us.

"I used to enjoy a close look at the passing train from Lovers Lane Crossing and in all those years I never saw those gates opened, although I suppose they must have been for the occasional cart or vehicle. When I had a spare penny that I could afford, I would put it on the rail here and watch it flatten and double in diameter as the engine passed over. This was a very impressive trick to show to young visiting friends.

"This view of the station was taken from the vantage point in the top garden where I would watch the shunting operations. It dates from 1930 and is very nearly the opposite view from that taken from the water tower that you showed me [page 138]. The home signal is visible here, with some goods wagons standing in the siding. In front of the engine shed are what look like cattle trucks. The weighbridge and coal company huts are visible and to the right of the loading gauge is the small white gate and the cautionary notice about the use of railway property at the end of the fenced-in footpath, which is seen again passing below the home signal on its way to Lovers Lane Crossing. The trees in the middle distance were along the old water course which would come into its own at times of severe flood but had presumably been inactive ever since the station was built, or probably earlier still when the mill was built. The river was then banked up as my picture shows, and its level controlled by the hatch gates which separated off the mill stream that flowed under the mill itself, operating a vast water-wheel. The river has now been at least doubled in width, to cope with occasional flood water now that the old water course is buried beneath the car park. A wide weir now bypasses the hatches, which are still there but silenced. If you happen to be horticulturally-minded, my picture shows from the left, asparagus beds, cucumber frames with cabbages and other greens adjoining, gooseberry bushes and neatly set out raspberry canes. That was just a small corner of a garden with a vast assortment of fruit and vegetables, tended by our omniscient gardener, a man named Weekes.

"How forcibly the photograph serves to emphasise the desecration that has resulted from the creation of Malmesbury's new 'industrial area'. I have no doubt some inhabitants of 1877 said the same when the railway itself desecrated those meadows immortalised in Turner's (rather inaccurate) painting of 1791. During a visit with my wife and an overseas visitor a few weeks ago, I was at a loss to evoke for their benefit the somnolent beauty of the country station when the train was out, the ordered activity of its return, and the lazy business of the work before the next departure, against the hideous background that we were now seeing. If I were a small boy in that garden now, how could I ever want to stand and watch?"

MARK MOORE, writing from Richmond, Surrey, October 1988

Malmesbury station yard in the early 1930s.   *Lens of Sutton*

signal 'wrong side' for viewing on the bend, and Malmesbury's cavernous goods shed looming large on the left. The engine shed and middle road tracks diverged to the right by the small signal box, and branch trains came to rest at a single terminal platform 94¼ miles from Paddington, with the ancient abbey dominating the whole scene from its commanding position on the hill south of the station. The terminus was located in the part of the town known as Westport, near the site of the Westport Gate of the old Borough, and close to the road to Tetbury in a rather unusual position, beyond the town rather than short of it as so many branch termini were.

The branch from Dauntsey was 6 miles, 4 furlongs and 1½ chains in length, taking the railway traveller to Malmesbury via 36 bridges, 11 cuttings, 12 embankments and the tunnel.

Malmesbury station on 5th July 1936 with No. 4833 inside the shed.   *W. A. Camwell*

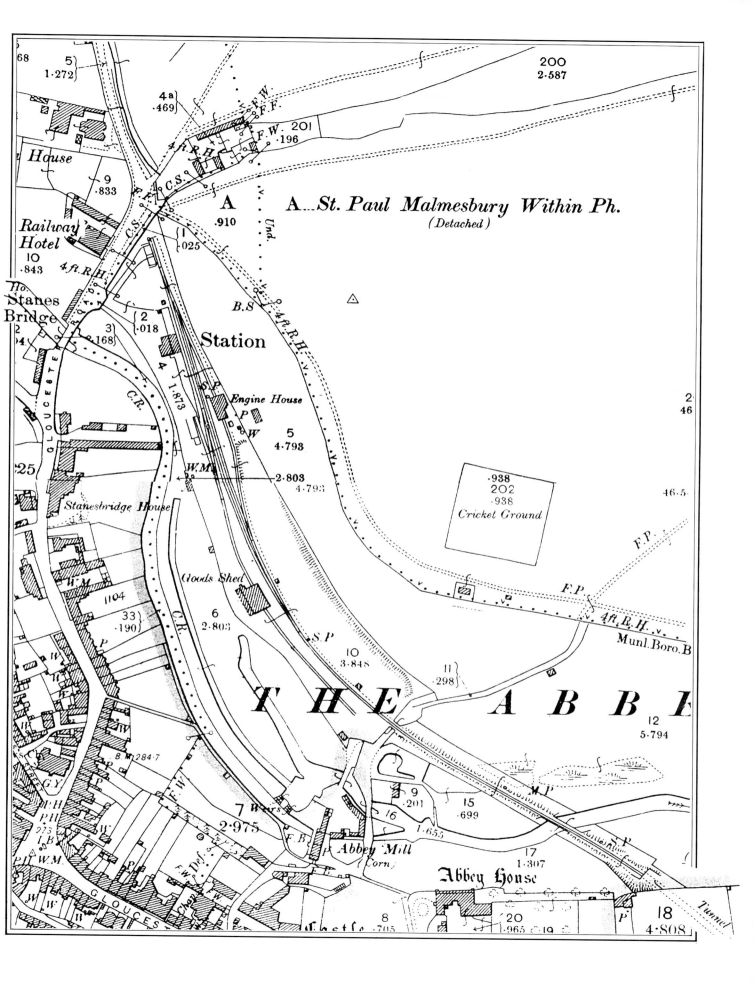

A 1929 view of the terminus from the top of the starting signal. The wagon in the foreground contains drums of 'Colas', a substance similar to tar, which was used as a spray on roads and then covered with gravel. With milk siphons alongside the loading bay on the right, spare horse-boxes and a profusion of coal and other open wagons, this view reflects the typical traffic at Malmesbury station. The loading bay siding had a rather limited capacity, so at busy times it was necessary for vehicles to be held back at Dauntsey. The Malmesbury Coal Company's mess room shed, their only base in the yard, can be seen against the boundary fence to the right of the loading gauge.

John Barnby

An unidentified 517 class 0–4–2T awaiting departure from Malmesbury c.1932 with loaded milk vans at the head of the branch coaches. The advertisement for the *Daily Telegraph* was a common appendage to many GWR station nameboards at this time.   *Lens of Sutton*

End of the journey. A tranquil scene (from the starting signal) in evening sunshine 1929, looking across the station approach to the river, with the earlier stone-built bridge and beautifully ornate hoarding similar to the one at nearby Tetbury.

John Barnby

Little Somerford station as new in 1903, even before the provision of nameboards. Passenger loops served each platform, giving four roads through the station. Gradients in each direction were a rising 1 in 300 towards Hullavington (behind the camera) and falling 1 in 400 towards Brinkworth. Platforms were originally timber and gravel surfaces, remaining so until deterioration in the '50s when they were replaced with paving. The first station master was Thomas Sorrell, appointed 12th May 1903 (Class 4) at 34/- per week.

Science Museum/Pearson collection

LITTLE SOMERFORD STATION
A WORKING PORTRAIT AND BACKGROUND
TO THE NEW JUNCTION

Before its connection with the Malmesbury branch, the station at Little Somerford existed as a village station on a busy main line, serving a small community three miles south-east of Malmesbury along the Avon valley, the village buildings including 17th-century Somerford House and a fine Early English church. It took its place on the railway map with the opening of the South Wales and Bristol Direct Line of 1903, although, as already stated, there was no formal opening owing to the death of the GWR's General Manager, Joseph Wilkinson. The new station at Little Somerford was opened for goods on the first day of 1903, and for passengers on 1st July of the same year. Passenger revenue from the station was always small, however, due both to the small population of the station's catchment and the very sparse service provided, the normal pattern being four stopping trains each way calling at all stations on the Badminton line between Swindon and Bristol.

For thirty years before it became the junction for Malmesbury, the windswept station in its exposed situation up on the embankment drew its business from brisk agricultural traffic, mainly milk and cattle. The General Strike of 1926 seriously affected parcel traffic and saw much milk business lost to road transport, and Little Somerford saw its 1930 peak of 41,539 parcels handled slump to only 2,114 in 1933. The coming of the branch in 1933 rallied the figures for a time but by 1938 a mere £82 in parcel receipts was being returned. In 1932 it was the least-used passenger station on the Badminton line, with only 1753 tickets issued in the year, yet its goods tonnage was bettered only by Chipping Sodbury and Badminton of the Direct Line stations. Although the station's passenger figures improved with its status as a junction, rising to 4,534 tickets in 1938, nearly as high as it had been in 1913, the decline of the branch service saw a steady fall in revenue which was only briefly revived by traffic during the war period. In truth, neither the branch nor the junction station were of great mutual benefit, this being reflected in the survival of the new branch as a passenger line for barely 18 years. If the switching of the Malmesbury line made life a little more

Little Somerford station, looking towards Swindon, with a Dean 0—6—0, No. 2394 passing through with a down goods about 1928. The milk churns on the up platform are awaiting collection for London.

R. D. Holt

117

Looking towards Swindon in 1922. Public and vehicle access to the station was via a long drive up from the road between the villages of Little and Great Somerford, arriving in the station forecourt, which was behind the water tower on this photograph. In the foreground is the up refuge siding of 1912 which in 1923 became part of the new Malmesbury branch. The water tower had a capacity of 14,000 gallons. It had a level indicator on the side (here showing a nearly full tank) consisting of an iron weight outside connected to a wooden float inside on a chain. The supply was maintained from a pump-house down near the Avon by Somerford Viaduct. Alongside the weighbridge office (visible through the legs of the water tower) is a galvanised iron shed which housed the generating plant for an acetylene gas lighting system for the station. This was provided by the Allen Company in January 1903 at a cost of £73. Calcium of carbide was stored here under a licence which had to be renewed annually. A miniature gas tank held five trays of carbide, with a 1cwt drum of carbide kept nearby. Porters were provided with a set of overalls to wear whilst replenishing the trays. Water dripping onto the carbide trays released the gas, causing the gas tank to rise and the whole station to light up. Shortage of carbide during World War I caused a change to oil lights for a time, but the carbide system was later reinstated and lasted until 1939 when it was replaced by oil lights.

L&GRP, courtesy David &Charles

An early 1930s view of the yard, with its brick goods lock-up and loading platform. In 1908 accommodation comprised a 6-ton crane, a mileage siding with a capacity of 25 wagons, a cattle pen siding for 9 wagons, a goods shed siding which held 17 wagons, and a shunting spur at the east end of the yard (23 wagons). The goods platform was 58ft long and had a 1-ton crane. A further siding with a capacity of 24 wagons was later provided along the northern boundary of the yard, behind the mileage siding, for the use of the Engineering Department. The platform loops were originally used as refuge for long freight trains to leave the main line clear for more important trains including the fast Paddington–South Wales expresses, but by 1912 they proved inadequate so dead-end sidings were provided at the trailing ends of each loop to increase capacity, at a cost of £338 to the Engineering Department and £85 for new signalling.

Charlie Hurley

interesting for the signalmen and helped vary the porters' routine, Little Somerford was too isolated an outpost with too poor a passenger service to be anything other than a convenient economy measure for the GWR in shortening the original branch from Dauntsey.

When the Direct line was built, a new approach road to Kingsmead Crossing on the Malmesbury branch was constructed from the village on the north side of the main line (rather than put a bridge over the old road, Mill Lane) which remained on the south side of the embankment to give access from the village to the houses which were built to accommodate the station master and signalmen. Housing was provided for two signalmen, the provision of two houses being a reflection of the 12-hour shifts which still existed for signalmen at the turn of the century. Little Somerford's first station staff comprised;

Station master	–	Thomas Sorrell	34/- a week
Porter	–	A. Edwards	17/- a week
Lad porter	–	G. Barnes	10/- a week
Signalmen	–	John Newman (transferred from Dauntsey in May 1903 at 24/- a week)	
		William Govier (transferred from Grimstone)	

Thomas Sorrell took over the station as its first station master on 12th May 1903, as a Class 4 appointment and the staff was increased in November 1905 by one porter as the station's goods and parcels business grew. By 1923 the staffing had risen to seven, the maximum it ever attained, this being made up of the station master, two porters, one lad porter and three signalmen. The post of lad porter was withdrawn by 1927 as one of his main duties, the delivery of parcels round the village in a wheelbarrow, had become unnecessary as this traffic averaged only two parcels a day by the 'twenties, and other staff were able to cover this chore! In addition to the regular work of meeting trains, cleaning platforms and attending to platform lamps, the lad porter at Little Somerford also had

to make a daily trip down the station approach and along Mill Lane to convey two ten-gallon churns of drinking water on a two-wheeler trolley to the signalmen's houses – these churns were sent down by train each day from Wootton Bassett.

Little Somerford was never provided with more than a quite sparse passenger service, four each way per day, Sundays excepted, right from the opening, and in December 1908 a petition was submitted to the GWR by the residents of the neighbourhood requesting that the 6.10 pm Paddington be stopped at Little Somerford on notice being given to the guard for passengers to alight there, to give an extra down train in the evening. The General Manager declined the request, however, and the service remained roughly the same for the entire life of the station, even the later arrival of the re-routed Malmesbury branch making little difference to the main line service.

The exiguous passenger service provided at Little Somerford was illustrated by the timetable of 1921:

Up trains

| Arrive | 8.00 | 11.36 | 1.46 | 5.36 | Goods | 2.23 |
| Depart | 8.05 | 11.38 | 1.47 | 5.48 | | 3.00 |

Down Trains — No Sunday service

| Arrive | 7.36 | 11.49 | 4.06 | 7.09 | Goods | 2.33 |
| Depart | 7.41 | 11.51 | 4.08 | 7.12 | | 3.15 |

The 5.36 up train was allowed a 12-minute stay at Little Somerford as time was required for addition of milk traffic to this train. It was rare that one would see more than two or three passengers awaiting or alighting from a train here, except on Monday mornings when Swindon cattle market was on and during the later war years. The down train that called around midday never seemed to attract anyone, beyond the occasional commercial traveller or visitor coming to see relatives in the village.

An up goods headed by a 28xx class No. 2880 rumbling through Little Somerford in June 1932.   *Photomatic*

Much cattle was handled at Little Somerford, cattle pens being located behind the main up platform, and used regularly by Newman Bros. of Lea. Saturdays in the 'twenties saw loading of bulls for conveyance to the Maiden Lane slaughterhouse serving the Bovril Company. Cattle cake came in twice weekly in a truckload, 20 tons a time, mainly from Bibby & Sons of Liverpool. The station had a goods shed (with a 58ft external platform) which in 1932 was taken over by Bibbys for use as a cattle-cake store. They rented the shed from the GWR, and several trucks would be left on the siding for off-loading there, ready for delivery or collection by the local farmers. A Bibby's rep called regularly from Swindon to check the store. With the goods shed used in this way, a brakevan body was kept on stilts next to the cattle siding for parcels and small goods consignments.

In 1926 Len Hillman came to Little Somerford as porter, staying for 11 years, during which time he saw the coming of the Malmesbury branch, later becoming parcel porter at Malmesbury. He would come on duty at 7.30 a.m., open the station, generally clean up and deal with two early trains – in his time the 7.45 up and the 8.00 down. Out across the forecourt was the weighbridge office, to which the early turn porter would go and check in any livestock and go through correspondence, before turning his attention to morning goods traffic, assisting with shunting in the yard which regularly involved organising empty coal wagons for return to collieries. There were three coal dumps at the station, Curtis of Malmesbury, the Malmesbury Coal Company and Porters

of Great Somerford. The station mainly received coal from Camerton in the Bristol direction and Derbyshire and Nottinghamshire coal on down trains.

In the '20s there was a milk train from Little Somerford each morning, which went down to Badminton, later Hullavington, then called at all stations to Wootton Bassett collecting milk for London. Most farmers would pay their carriage charges three days before the end of each month at the station, any late payments being collected by Hillman who would cycle round the farms to do this duty. Milk empties would be returned from London on a variety of trains and would be left on the down side ready for lifting across to the up side by the porters. This was heavy work involving carrying the churns across four tracks, two at a time with handles together, arms crossed at the back. Ten-gallon churns could be carried three at a time.

Cattle feed was also delivered from a store at Swindon – around 1920, Webb's hauliers of Brinkworth started a motorised business carrying the feed to the farms. They also later took over work hauling roadstone to required sites for Wiltshire County Council; this came in regularly at Little Somerford and was, up to 1931, collected by John Fishlock, a local farmer with horse and dray. Gawthropp's of Kingsmead Mill came to collect barley and wheat for the mill and there would be a steady traffic in farm implements, loading of hay to go to South Wales pit ponies, and, in addition to cattle, there was regular movement of horses, sheep and pigs. The Beaufort Hunt would use Little Somerford midweek, coming up from Badminton on a special train which set down horses and dogs on the up side. When returning to Badminton in the evening, the train would back into the up platform loop to reload, then go over the crossover to the down main to go back to Badminton.

Regular traffic into Little Somerford was received by Porters, a builder/undertaker business at Lea, near Malmesbury. Usually a truckload would come in for this business

have this finished before the station was opened by the early turn porter. Shortly after 6 a.m. a train of coal empties was due through Little Somerford, usually around 100 wagons from Old Oak Common, although its time was variable. Whenever this train had to be pulled out of the path of express passenger trains at Little Somerford, it had to be split, and both up and down loops used to stable it. These loops had capacities of 66 and 40 wagons respectively, therefore when

Little Somerford signal box in the 1930s, with Charlie Hurley in the window. Fuller details about the box are to be found in the Signalling chapter.

Courtesy Charlie Hurley

(close to the locomotive on a goods train) containing tins of paint, decorating materials and coffin timber.

In 1930 the signal box at Little Somerford had 61 levers, including spares, all of which were brought into use when the Malmesbury branch was diverted into the new junction. Was this allowance intentional? One signalman who worked the box for many years from 1930 was Charlie Hurley, who thus witnessed the change of junction and the massive alterations made in the signal box during the war.

Charlie Hurley was born in Bridgwater in 1904, starting work on the GWR in 1918 as a lad porter at Swindon Junction. He spent two years at Little Somerford as a porter, then one year as signal porter on the Midland & South Western Junction at Swindon Town. His first post as signalman was at Bleadon & Uphill, followed by a spell at Marlborough before his 14 year stay at Little Somerford. In the early '30s he lodged at Great Somerford, where he used the station on the Malmesbury branch quite frequently, often being the only passenger waiting to board on trips into Malmesbury or on monthly trips home to see his family in Somerset. When he first came to Little Somerford as signalman, the station staff consisted of station master Albert Plant and porters Len Hillman and Bill Jones, the other signalmen being Jim Hazell, who had worked the box since 1907, and Harry Clark. When the Malmesbury branch closed from Kingsmead to Dauntsey, Hazell retired and moved into the old station house at Great Somerford, where he stayed the rest of his life.

When working the morning turn during the early '30s, it was normal practice for the signalman to cook breakfast in the box quite soon after coming on duty at 6 a.m., so as to

dividing a train at Little Somerford the normal practice was for it to go straight into the down platform where 40 wagons would be detached and left, then the locomotive would take the remainder of the train past the crossover at the west end of the station and shunt the remaining wagons all the way back into the up loop. The early shift signalman was always glad to see this train through his section. On occasions when this train was late running, it had to be put over on the up main so that the early Swindon to Bristol stopper could use the platform. Another procedure was to shunt the coal train ahead of the passenger loop so that the stopper could use the platform, then alter the points so that the coal could be reversed back along the down main, enabling the local passenger service to leave for Hullavington. The coal train would have to be split again farther on down the line at Stoke Gifford as trains in excess of 100 wagons were not allowed in the Severn Tunnel. It was regular practice after 1933 for main line down goods trains to shunt wagons for Little Somerford over to the up side of the station and leave them for the Malmesbury branch locomotive to organise, thus freeing the branch crews from having to perform shunting movements over the South Wales Direct.

The first up express was due through Little Somerford around 7.50 a.m., the Boat Train from Fishguard Harbour, every day except Mondays. By this time the station master would be on duty, always going up into the signal box to take any notices, alterations or discuss any problems. He would therefore be on duty to deal with the two early morning passenger trains of the day, giving the guard of the down train the pouch with the previous day's takings to put in the travelling safe for safe custody to Bristol. This pouch bore the station's name on a brass plate and was usually returned on the early evening arrival from Bristol. The morning turn was usually quite straight-forward for the Little Somerford signalman if goods ran to schedule – these trains had to be kept out of the way of several fast expresses, including the 8.00 Pembroke, the 7.30 Carmarthen and the up 'Red Dragon'. This time was also a period for the early turn porter and station master to catch up on chores around the station, as before the coming of the branch trains there were no more trains calling at Little Somerford until nearly midday.

Between the wars Little Somerford was actually served by two direct through coaches between Bristol and York, although they were in reality part of a practice used for purposes of stock movement. The 2.45 p.m. ex-Bristol to Swindon called at Little Somerford with two extra passenger coaches, usually a brake van with 3rd class compartments and a brake composite coach. These would be Great Western and ex-Great Central stock on alternate days. They were left in the Highworth branch bay at Swindon ready to be attached to the 9.10 p.m. to York.

The various codes used by signalmen to communicate with one another were signalled on the block bell, in the case of Little Somerford, the boxes in each direction being Brinkworth (or Wootton Bassett West when Brinkworth was switched out of circuit) and Hullavington. The bell for the Hullavington direction had a particularly haunting and beautiful ring, a penetrating sound which could be clearly heard across the village in the evenings, a lost sound of a now-vanished age. As well as the aural indication of the block bell, the signalmen also operated a block telegraph, an instrument that gave a visual indication of the presence of a train on a section of line. The signalman's train register book had to be kept meticulously up-to-date, with six entries for every train, and these books were inspected by the station master every day and every month by the district inspector.

The 2.10 p.m. evening turn was not very enjoyable at Little Somerford, there being little variety in the traffic – a milk train, the down 'Red Dragon' (to Carmarthen, which passed about 7.40 p.m.), and the Boat Train to Fishguard. The arrival of the branch trains in 1933, which provided a mixed train from Malmesbury arriving at Little Somerford at 6.59, did provide more work and variation in the routine for the Little Somerford staff, but evenings were still very quiet, particularly after the loss of milk traffic. No staff increase was ever provided at the station as a result of the branch, the only addition to the Little Somerford payroll being the crossing keeper down at Kingsmead.

Oft-related is the story of how there was much excitement in Malmesbury at the thought of their local 'Bunk' travelling on the main line. On the evening trip back from Swindon it was not uncommon for the branch train driver Joe Halliday to be informed by the signalman at Brinkworth, 'Fishguard's about, Joe!' This was a cue for Halliday to exercise his sprightly style of driving, accelerating out of Brinkworth and making with all speed for the safety of the down passenger loop at Little Somerford so that the Boat Train should not be delayed.

Before working the night turn, 10 a.m.–6 p.m., the Little Somerford men would sleep from around 1 to 9 p.m. Charlie Hurley used to walk to work from Great Somerford. Once in the '20s, during his days as a porter at the station, there was an occasion when flooding of the Avon almost cut off the halt at Great Somerford from the village, and he had to ride on top of the churns on a farmer's milk wagon to reach the embankment of the old branch, then walk along the old line until he reached the Direct line embankment, along which he walked to reach his work at Little Somerford. Life as a signalman could be quite rough in winter, walking through the cold night to the lonely exposed station up on the bank, thankfully to enter the warmth of the box and enjoy some sandwiches with a mug of tea brewed on an old coal stove. Night turn was a solitary life with onerous responsibility. There was no conversation with a living soul except the man going off duty and the man who relieved you at 6 a.m., and maybe with drivers of coal trains, frustrated at being pulled in off the main line at Little Somerford to clear the road for the express goods which travelled this route during the night.

With the Swindon-Malmesbury through service being closely followed by the down Fishguard soon after 9.30 p.m., there were no passenger trains for the man on night turn to deal with, but there were several express vacuum goods (one third of the trucks/carriages linked to the engine for braking purposes) on the up line, emanating from Cardiff, Carmarthen and Fishguard, which travelled at around 60 m.p.h., and signalmen were expected to treat these as passenger trains. Thus, if a coal train from Severn Tunnel Junction was on the Hullavington to Little Somerford section, then it would have to be split and put into the loops. No passenger train was scheduled until the main line early morning stoppers, and the early branch train after '33, although there might be the occasional excursion, which would have to take its turn with the vacuum goods. There were several down express vacuum goods, including a non-stop Reading–Severn Tunnel Junction comprising around 50 wagons. A newspaper train left Paddington about 1 a.m., non-stop to Newport, passing Little Somerford around 3 a.m., and this had to be treated with respect - priority traffic for which a signalman was expected to find a clear run. After about 3.30 a.m. the Somerford man was finished with down trains for the night, there being just two up trains between then and 6 a.m. – a coal train from Severn Tunnel Junction to Reading and Old Oak Common, and a goods from St. Philip's Marsh, Bristol, to Banbury. The Saturday afternoon turn was regarded very much as cleaning duty, the furniture, levers, brasswork and windows being kept cleaned and polished to perfection, although it was a general rule that each signalman always left the cabin clean and tidy for his relief. Detonators had to be checked, and changed every month. Like all GWR boxes, the brasswork contained engraved information, while the rest of the levers (iron) were painted in the standard colour codes – black for points, blue for locking bars, red for stop signals and yellow for distants. A first-aid box was kept in the signal cabin, and one man usually made it his job to check it regularly. During Hurley's time, Harry Clark was a member of the St. John Ambulance Brigade, so he naturally took on this duty.

During the '20s and early '30s around 25 farmers sent milk to the station at Little Somerford for despatch to London, and the signalman on duty on the Saturday night had to remain on duty for an extra two hours on Sunday morning to deal with a milk train which came out from Swindon with empties around 6 a.m. In the early '30s empties were set down

Little Somerford station, looking north from the road from Great Somerford. It was a quite desolate and exposed situation up on the embankment. Both up and down buildings were erected on deep foundations going well down into the earthworks.

E. K. Lockstone

at stations as far as Hullavington, then a morning milk train started from there and called at Little Somerford, Brinkworth and Wootton Bassett and formed part of a larger train at Swindon. When this train had cleared the section in advance, usually around 8 a.m., Little Somerford box was switched out until 1.30 p.m. At this time it re-opened in order for two stopping trains to call, the down 4 p.m. with milk empties and the up 7.10, as they required diverting from the main line into the platform loop and out again. The box then switched out again until 6 a.m. Monday.

The end of milk traffic at Little Somerford came in December 1932. From a total of 39,485 churns handled at the station in 1930, the traffic slumped to 7,167 in 1932 and disappeared virtually overnight to road haulage, with no milk at all recorded for 1933. As a result, the Little Somerford signalmen no longer had to work the extra time on Sunday mornings. A limited amount of milk still came out of Malmesbury, enabling the one Sunday train on the branch, which arrived at Little Somerford at 7.03 p.m., to survive until 1935.

The station had a 14,000 gallon water tank which was used frequently by coal trains from South Wales. It was maintained by a man from Swindon Works who would come out on the early train two or three times a week to visit the pumphouse, which was located by Somerford viaduct, and fill the tank. The pumphouse contained a large steam pumping engine which took its water from the River Avon, and was linked to the Somerford tank by underground pipes. Shortly before the diverting of the Malmesbury branch to Little Somerford, the engine was replaced by a Lister engine which only required starting and would switch itself off automatically when the water tank was full. As an economy measure, the Swindon man was taken off the job, with the intention of transferring

the duty of checking the pumphouse to the Little Somerford porters – rather a strange move in light of the fact that the arrival of the branch trains created more demand for water, as the branch locomotives were invariably replenished at Little Somerford to reduce the pumping work that they otherwise had to undertake, using the locomotive to keep the Malmesbury tank full. As a result, the Somerford tank required replenishing five or six times a week. With the extra work created by the branch engine's needs, and the job of cleaning, oiling and checking the pump engine, the GWR eventually paid one of the signalmen 6/- a week extra for the pumphouse duty, although it was soon found necessary to share the duty between two signalmen, as problems could arise if the one man responsible was on duty at the box when the water tank ran down.

During Mr. Plant's time as station master, fire drill was a regular part of the station routine, and this was usually done when Bob Hillier, the Swindon man, was at the pumphouse, so as not to rob the tank of water. Regular drill enabled them to check the water pressure and the condition of the hoses, the aim being to direct the jet of water over the footbridge to reach the waiting rooms. The hydrants were by the down side toilets and between the tracks.

In February 1932 the station at Brinkworth came under the jurisdiction of Albert Plant at Little Somerford. Despite this and the 1933 elevation to junction status, Little Somerford remained a Class 4 station, although the signal box was a Class 3, a big grievance with the station master. A further source of annoyance to Mr. Plant were the wooden platforms at the station; despite his complaints that the porters had great difficulty in moving trolleys laden with milk churns on the boards, nothing was ever done, ironically, until the 1950s, when the platforms were eventually paved, long after the demise of both milk traffic and the branch passenger service.

As we have seen, although the branch created extra work for the staff at Little Somerford, particularly in respect of transferring goods traffic from the main line to branch mixed trains and vice versa, no increase in personnel at the station was deemed necessary. The former junction at Dauntsey, although also a Class 4 station, had a far better service which merited the presence of a shunter for work in connection with the branch, and a parcel porter to take on much of the paperwork, luxuries Little Somerford never experienced. It should be remembered, however, that Little Somerford became the junction for Malmesbury in changing times – it had a poor main line service, there had been a decline in its livestock traffic as well as complete loss of milk, Malmesbury market had declined in favour of larger markets elsewhere with the result that no market day special service was ever provided via the new junction, and a general growth of road haulage everywhere had severely affected the railways.

The middle and late '30s saw numerous changes in the staff at Little Somerford, particularly with regard to the porters. The *Great Western Railway Magazine* staff transfer pages contain many references to porters' comings and goings, so much so that when George Sterne alighted from a train to take up a porter's job in 1938, he was greeted by station master Henry Hill with the words, 'Have y'come to stop?' Sterne spent two years there as leading porter whilst waiting for a promotion to Chippenham, and attributed the constant

changes to the difficulty in finding suitable accommodation in the locality and to Little Somerford's being a small station with demanding work for a small staff, which made it an ideal stopping-off point for promotion. A leading porter earned £2 3s 0d a week in the mid-'30s. Little Somerford was always a very clean, well-kept station, winning many divisional prizes in later years for its neatness and gardens, and porters on later shifts spent much time cleaning the station in the evening after the station master went off duty about 5 p.m.

If many employees saw Little Somerford as a short-term post, there were men who thought otherwise, and mention should be made of Ron Thomas. He saw all the changes, worked at both Malmesbury and Little Somerford as porter, and later became signalman at the junction after Charlie Hurley. His house in the village was famous locally for many years for the signals and other railway relics in the garden. Through him the branch train staff was preserved and he donated it to Malmesbury's Athelstan Museum.

There was no bay platform for the Malmesbury branch train at Little Somerford as there had been at Dauntsey, the new branch simply ran directly into a westwards extension of the up platform loop. Based on the 1934 timetable, the first branch train of the day, the 7.21 ex-Malmesbury, would normally come to Little Somerford bunker-first, arriving at the junction at 7.30. The locomotive would run around the B-set coaches via the up main and east end crossover, then the whole train would go across 'the ladder' to the down side to collect overnight accumulated parcels. The train would then

An unidentified 'Saint' class 4—6—0 passes Little Somerford station on the Up main with a parcels train, probably during the early 'thirties. The first part of the train consists of LNE fish vans, probably destined for the 3.20 p.m. service from Swindon to Banbury, and thence onto the ex-GC line. Empty coaching stock brings up the rear of the train, possibly en route to the works. *Photomatic*

The main station building, seen from the forecourt. Like others on the main Direct, it was constructed in pressed red brick with quoins and plinths in Staffordshire blue brick. The hipped roof incorporated lantern lights and utilised Bangor slate. Window sills and chimney caps were in Forest of Dean 'Bluestone'. The main building incorporated a station master's office, parcels office, ticket office, waiting room, ladies' waiting room and lavatories. The roof awning was supported by steelwork attached to the wall of the building. The platforms were linked by an impressive covered and valanced footbridge, the enclosed areas beneath the staircases on each side being used as stores and toolsheds. Little Somerford station was constructed at a cost of £1,549 7s 7½d, the major portions of this being the near £492 spent on the buildings on the main up side, £272 on platform awnings and £540 on the timber platforms. *E. K. Lockstone*

reverse back into the up loop beyond the platform where the coaches were left, out of the way of the up train on the main line which was due to call at 8 a.m. The branch engine would then shunt the goods yard to make up a mixed train for Malmesbury. The up siding, an extension of the up platform loop, later extended in June 1941, would usually contain wagons and a Swindon brake van which had been delivered around 6 a.m. by a goods train, after which the goods loco would run light back to Swindon. These vehicles were coupled to the coaches ready for the first morning trip into Malmes-

Local Co-op employees with Charlie Porter (second from right) in the station yard at Little Somerford around 1936. Porter ran a Great Somerford-based coal business from 1924 to 1956 with its main depot and office at Little Somerford station. The weighbridge building on the right also accommodated the Porter coal office. *Courtesy Ted Porter*

bury, which crossed to the down side to provide connection for the 7.36 down and 8.00 up main line trains, leaving at 8.05.

As a through service from Swindon to Malmesbury and back was expected at 10 a.m. the 9.35 ex-Malmesbury called at Little Somerford's up platform, then left the coaches on the up loop, right up to the stop blocks. The branch engine was then free to shunt the yard, the crew being assisted by a porter and the branch guard. When the through train arrived with its Swindon crew, it called at the down side then progressed across the west end 'ladder' onto the branch. It returned to Swindon as the 11.30 ex-Malmesbury, calling at Little Somerford's up side at 11.39. With the through-train clear of the branch, the 11.50 provided connection for Malmesbury for the midday train from Swindon.

The most usual practice for branch trains at Little Somerford during the day was to use only the up platform if it was simply a case of running as a branch passenger train from terminus to junction and back, run-round taking place with coaches in the up loop beyond the platform. In later years the run-round was effected with coaches left at the platform and the locomotive using the up main. There was provision for the 1.55 ex-Malmesbury to run as a mixed train, but by the mid-'30s it did not usually do so, calling at Little Somerford at 2.04 to connect with the 1.45 ex-Swindon before using the up side back to Malmesbury at 2.10.

The 3 p.m. ex-Malmesbury ran as a through train to Wootton Bassett, giving better connections at that station. This mixed train returned to Little Somerford at 3.55 for a 4.07 arrival in Malmesbury. In the evening the 7.46 through-train to Swindon ran via Little Somerford's up side and returned via the down platform, giving a 9.23 arrival back in Malmesbury. This late run gave the opportunity for engine change at Swindon.

Broadly speaking, then, with no branch bay provision at Little Somerford, there was a variety of run-around movements available. It simply depended on main line traffic, time of day, goods and parcel traffic to be collected and the nature of the service. Sometimes a goods train in the yard, a train in the loop being held by the signalman to clear the road for a main line express, or late running on the main line, would affect the branch train's movements. In normal circumstances in the '30s the first train of the morning and the three through-trains from the Swindon direction were the services which generally used the down side before running into Malmesbury. The link from the branch direct to the up through road was rarely used, except for excursion trains which would not be calling at Little Somerford. A branch train might be turned out that way if meeting an excursion from London at Wootton Bassett, and it might occasionally be used for running-round, depending on the time of day.

The first public train for Malmesbury, the 8.10 a.m., about to leave Little Somerford's up platform on 17th July 1933. The engine is Collett 0—4—2T No. 5802, which hauled the old three-coach branch set, and tail traffic including a Mica (unrefrigerated meat van) being used here for general merchandise.
Bertram Farmer

CHAPTER EIGHT

DECLINE
MALMESBURY TO LITTLE SOMERFORD 1933–51

On the morning of 17th July 1933 the same train shown on the opposite page preparing for departure at 7.21 a.m., the first train in public service from Malmesbury to Little Somerford. Cleaner Sam Hinder can be seen on the footplate of No. 5802. *Bertram Farmer*

Following the running of the last train from Dauntsey into Malmesbury on the Saturday evening of 15th July 1933, the final connection to divert the branch to its new junction at Little Somerford was put in the next morning, Sunday the 16th. The new point was inspected by Malmesbury's station master, Richard Faull, and engineman Ben Hill, who journeyed out to Kingsmead by car early in the afternoon. It had been arranged that the one Sunday train would run solely for the conveyance of milk traffic, and at 6.55 that evening the branch train made its first run on the new line for this purpose. It is likely that a single Siphon J milk van sufficed for the milk traffic, as this was now a declining trade on the railway generally.

The first public train from Malmesbury to Little Somerford ran at 7.21 on Monday morning, the 17th, unaccompanied by any form of public fanfare. The first passengers included some Malmesbury schoolboys who rose early to ride the first train on the shortened branch, and it was one of these boys, later Cambridge University professor Bertram Farmer, who took what appear to be the only traceable photographs recording the first day on the new line.

At Little Somerford there was provision for Malmesbury branch trains to use both up and down sides, the new line joining the up passenger loop at the west end of the station. After crossing the bridge over the road between the villages of Great Somerford and Little Somerford, a structure which

had been widened to accommodate the new branch, the course ran parallel to the main lines for about 400 yards then turned north-west down a falling 1 in 50 gradient towards Kingsmead Crossing, which now found itself 700 yards from the line's new junction station. Because of the gradient and the crossing's proximity to the station, a new speed restriction of 10 mph was brought in for trains in both directions, caution boards being placed 300 yards on either side of Kingsmead.

The first Working Timetable for the new branch in July 1933 showed departures from Malmesbury at 7.21, 9.35, 11.30, 12.15, 1.55 (mixed), 3.00. 5.34, 6.50 (mixed) and 7.46, with the one Sunday departure at 6.55 p.m. Return workings from Little Somerford were at 8.05 (mixed), 10.00, 11.50, 12.40, 2.10, 3.55 (mixed), 5.55, 7.17 and 9.15, and on Sundays at 7.49. However, no indication about new through workings between Malmesbury and Swindon were given on the branch Working Timetable, and it is necessary to consult the Severn Tunnel Jct to Wootton Bassett main line services to realise that the 10.00 ex-Little Somerford and the 11.30 ex-Malmesbury were in fact branch services provided by a through train which left Swindon Junction at 9.35 and called at Wootton Bassett and Brinkworth on its way to Malmesbury. This run was made while the regular branch train was at Little Somerford, thus enabling the Swindon to proceed on the 'one engine in steam' branch and enabling the Malmesbury engine to be available for morning shunting duties in the yard at

Guard Frank Philips, driver Ben Hill and fireman Dick Cooper with the first arrival at Little Somerford from Malmesbury.   *Bertram Farmer*

Little Somerford. In the evening the 7.46 from Malmesbury ran through to Swindon, arriving at 8.30 p.m. and waiting thirty minutes before leaving on its return trip to Malmesbury where it arrived at 9.23. On Saturdays the Swindon trip was usually the opportunity for a change of engine, the branch locomotive going off to the shed for boiler wash-out and the fresh engine joining the train at the platform. A further improvement was made with the extension of the 3.00 p.m. ex-Malmesbury and the Sunday service to Wootton Bassett, where better connections could be obtained than were available with the minimal service at Little Somerford. However, although at first sight the train service along the new branch appeared to be an improvement on that provided in Dauntsey days, it is true to say that the concept of a direct service between Swindon and Malmesbury was never developed enough to make it a real success, and with the main line service at Little Somerford remaining virtually the same as it had since its opening in 1903, far fewer connections were available in each direction than had been provided via Dauntsey. The *Wilts & Glos Standard* of 22nd July 1933, was quick to note the drawbacks to the new arrangements.

> 'New Railway Service – The new railway service from Malmesbury via the loop through Little Somerford station is not an unmixed blessing. The old branch through Great Somerford and Dauntsey has been closed, so that Great Somerford is now without any railway facilities, and a serious inconvenience – and expense – is that passengers for Chippenham and Bath now have to travel via Wootton Bassett. This arrangement really places Bath and Chippenham 'off the map' from Malmesbury as regards the railway, and should lead to a further development of motor bus services. On the other hand, the services to London and Bristol are much improved.'

If the publicised better eastward connections and the increased number of branch trains, now nine each way Mondays to Saturdays, brought apparent improvements to

With run-round accomplished, the 'board' is 'off' (the starting signal seen at the end of the platform) and the same train is ready to leave with the first passenger service from Little Somerford to Malmesbury.   *Bertram Farmer*

21st July 1933 — a sunny evening in Malmesbury station. The branch train is shown here picking up milk siphons from the loading dock.
Bertram Farmer

The same train, at the platform ready to leave for Little Somerford, with Bert Reynolds and Jim Thornbury posing alongside. Within a year the old branch coaches, resplendent in new chocolate and cream paint, were sent to the scrapyards after nearly forty years of service.
Bertram Farmer

This view, taken in 1934, from the garden of station clerk John Barnby's home in Silver Street, shows the 5.55 p.m. from Little Somerford passing over bridges 33 and 34 carrying the line over the loops of the Avon on its way into Malmesbury. The old branch set of four-wheel coaches were shortly to be replaced by the new Bristol Division B-sets.   *John Barnby*

the train service from Malmesbury, the paper's reference to Chippenham was not without foundation. Not only had the old junction at Dauntsey been served by more main line stopping trains than Little Somerford (trains which continued to call for another three decades with no branch to feed them), but the railway journey between Malmesbury and Chippenham had been a much-used route. Being only ten miles apart by road, the two towns had much interchange of trade and interests, but a rail journey between the two via Wootton Bassett added twelve miles to the old route via Dauntsey. This led to an increase in omnibus service between Malmesbury, the Somerfords, Dauntsey and Chippenham. Indeed, a would-be rail traveller who required to make a morning trip to Malmesbury from Chippenham would have to endure the privations of rising at an unearthly hour to catch the up Penzance sleeper at 4.47 a.m., then wait two hours at Swindon for a connection to Little Somerford, not a recognised or appealing trip of which many could be expected to avail themselves!

The early and mid-30s were significant times of change for the Malmesbury line, as indeed they were for railways generally. If the branch lent its own unique contribution to railway history with the switching of its main line junction, with radical changes in its pattern of service and orientation towards the railway network, there were other changes, too, of both a national and local character. In the wider sense, the loss of milk traffic and market day specials, the motorisation of goods services at rural stations and the development of private motoring, road haulage and bus services, were all reflected country-wide, but there were other factors which conspired to alter the whole atmosphere of Malmesbury's line – there was no longer an intermediate station, both motive

power and coaching stock were changed within a year of each other, the permanent way gang was transferred to Little Somerford and amalgamated with the gang there to divide their attentions between the branch and a substantial section of the main line. Struggling on via the lonely outpost that was now its new junction, the branch revived its fortunes briefly, but within a short time, the whole character of the line was irrevocably altered.

During the first few months of operation via Little Somerford, delays were caused to stopping services on the main line while the Malmesbury branch train was using the up side platform. With no branch bay at the station, and because it was against the operating regulations to alter facing points within the 440 yard safety overlap beyond the first stop signal, the passenger trains from Bristol either had to be held at Hullavington, 4½ miles west, or stopped at the home signal before the facing point at Little Somerford could be reversed after the branch train had left the platform to wait in a siding. The Malmesbury train needed to be at Little Somerford to enable passengers to come off for connection and for parcel traffic to be arranged ready for transfer, so trains from Malmesbury usually arrived about eight minutes before the arrival of the main line train, at around the very time this connecting service would need to leave Hullavington.

To overcome this problem, an outer home signal was provided at Little Somerford at a cost of £285 in November 1933, this expense probably including the cost of track circuiting. This new signal enabled the Little Somerford signalmen to accept trains from Hullavington at any time and alter the points subsequently. The safety overlap of 440 yards now ended west of the facing points, with the distant signal being moved much further out on the main line, where it now had to be powerworked at more than a mile from the signal box. An additional lever was needed amongst the group of main line signal levers at the left-hand (west) end of the frame. Lever No. 1, formerly used for the up distant signal, was now allocated to the new outer home. The additional lever, now used to work the distant, was given the number '0'. Not many signal boxes had a lever numbered zero!

In 1934 the old branch set of three four-wheel coaches was replaced by the new Bristol Division 'B-sets', a pair of two-bogie brake composites which worked in permanent formation on branch and cross-country stopping services throughout the division. The old branch set was much-missed on the line – it had seen nearly forty years' regular allocation to Malmesbury, and indeed had only been repainted in 1933. The first of the new B-sets had been put into service in February 1933, displaying a bow-ended style which was superseded in 1934 by flat-ended construction. They were non-corridor stock with 1st and 3rd class compartments and electrically lit. Thus it was no longer necessary to stable a cordon in the middle road at Malmesbury to supply gas for carriage lighting.

No. 6191 was a typical coach which appeared at Malmesbury in chocolate and cream, being a bogie brake composite measuring 61' 2" by 9' 3". These heavy type 9 ft bogie vehicles had more 3rd-class compartment space than the stock they replaced, a fact that was not really appreciated until World War II. Some of the B-sets were repainted in BR maroon after nationalisation and appeared at Malmesbury in this livery. Bristol Division B-sets were also used on the main

line stoppers from Bristol and, as these runs were often used for express engines fresh out of the works after repair, it was not unusual to see a pristine 'King' at the head of a dingy B-set calling at the Malmesbury line's former junction at Dauntsey. However, this stock did not prove to be suitable for branch line work, nor was it popular with the Malmesbury staff after the roller-bearing stock of pre-33 days. Closure of branch lines after 1959 saw their final demise by August 1962 when they were finally withdrawn.

Whatever reservations one can have about the Malmesbury branch train service following the change of junction, the number of trains provided and the more direct links with Swindon made 1934 the year which can be regarded as the zenith of services on the branch. The 12.15 from Malmesbury could see a traveller in London by 2.30 p.m. with good connections at Little Somerford and Swindon. On weekday afternoons the 3 p.m. ex-Malmesbury to Wootton Bassett gave connection for Swindon with the 2.45 ex-Lawrence Hill, providing a Swindon arrival at 4.03 and a 45 min wait for the London-bound passenger to catch the 11.25 ex-Milford Haven. Various modifications to the branch service were made during the first year of operation from Little Somerford, and in 1934 two additions were made which seem to be the last positive attempts by the GWR to tap local demand at Malmesbury, with the provision of a late service from Swindon and a new Saturday afternoon train.

The new Saturday train introduced in July 1934 quickly developed as a popular service for shoppers and football fans to Swindon. Whenever Swindon Town's Division Three

MALMESBURY BRANCH.

Single Line, worked by Train Staff, and only one Engine in Steam at a time (or two or more coupled).

Distances.		DOWN TRAINS. STATIONS.	Ruling gradient 1 in.	Station No.	WEEK DAYS.										SUN-DAY
					Mixed	Pass.	Pass.	Pass.	C'ches L	Pass. SO	Mixed	Pass.	Pass.	Pass.	Pass. K
M	C.				A.M.	A.M.	A.M.	P.M.	P.M.	P.M.	P.M.	P.M.	P.M.	P.M.	P.M.
—	—	Little Somerford dep.	94 F	1118	8 10	10 26	11 50	12 40	1†40	2 10	3 55	5 55	7 5	9 15	7 49
3	60	Malmesbury arr.	116 R	1149	8 20	10 34	11 58	12 48	1†48	2 18	4 7	6 3	7 13	9 23	7 57

K Runs 35 minutes later on Thursdays and Saturdays. **L** Five minutes later on Saturdays.

	UP TRAINS. STATIONS.	Ruling gradient 1 in.	WEEK DAYS.										SUN-DAYS.
			Pass.	Pass.	Pass.	Pass.	Sw'dn Pass. SO	Mixed	Pass.	Pass.	Mixed	Sw'dn Pass.	Pass.
			A.M.	A.M.	A.M.	P.M.	P.M.	P.M.	P.M.	P.M.	P.M.	P.M.	P.M.
	Malmesbury dep.	....	7 23	9 48	11 30	12 15	1 30	1 55	3 0	5 30	6 40	7 23	6 40	..
	L. Somerford arr.	116 F	7 32	9 57	11 39	12 24	1 39	2 4	3 9	5 39	6 49	7 32	6 49	....

Little Somerford—Kingsmead Crossing.—Trains in either direction to reduce speed to 30 miles per hour.
Kingsmead Crossing—Malmesbury.—Trains in either direction to reduce speed to 10 miles per hour when approaching Caution Boards placed 300 yards from Crossing until passing over Crossing.

13 minutes to be allowed for Goods Trains over the Malmesbury Branch, in either direction, including "start" and "stop" allowances, also "Stop Board" requirements. (G. 17266).

Working Timetable for July to September 1934. Although not apparent here, the 10.26 and 9.15 from Little Somerford were in fact through trains from Swindon, the 11.30 being a return service to Swindon. The 3.00 from Malmesbury and 3.55 from Little Somerford were part of a through service between Malmesbury and Wootton Bassett.

South side were playing at home at the County Ground during the winter, a veritable throng would fill this train, so much so that it became known as the 'soccer special', although it was in fact a timetabled run. The train left Swindon at 12.20 and ran into Malmesbury while the branch train was at the junction, departing five minutes later than the usual midweek branch service, arriving in Malmesbury at 12.53 and leaving mesbury at 10.30. The branch train which arrived in Malmesbury around 7.15 on Saturdays carried the Swindon 'Football Pink', the newspapers being collected at the station by an employee of a local fishmonger who acted as the *Swindon Advertiser*'s local agent.

Following the closure of the old line from Kingsmead Crossing through to Dauntsey, the GWR decided to make

For years, as in this mid-30s view, equestrian events at the Somerford Show took place against a backdrop of crippled rolling stock on the embankment just north-west of Great Somerford station, where the old line was used as a siding for coach and wagon storage.

Courtesy Mrs. Muriel Edwards

with its full passenger load at 1.30 for a 2.10 arrival in Swindon. A cheap return adult fare cost 1/6d.

With the 'soccer' train clear of the branch and the train staff handed over, this left the branch train to make a usually empty run into Malmesbury at 1.40, in time to form the 1.55 mixed departure. However, with the Swindon occupying the branch for nearly an hour and the branch train at the junction, it was quickly found to be impractical to run the 1.55, so it was decided to take it off on Saturdays and hold its traffic back for the evening mixed – it clearly wasn't realistic to shunt Malmesbury yard and prepare a mixed train in the time available. Therefore, from 1st October 1934, a revised timetable saved the branch set an unremunerative run and it resumed branch service from Little Somerford at 2.10 p.m. It may well have been that there were protests from railway customers about the cancellation of the Saturday 1.55 mixed, as the 1935 timetables show that by then the 'soccer' train was accorded mixed status – it is probable that the Swindon locomotive shunted the yard at Malmesbury to prepare wagons to be added to the rear of the passenger coaches, usually three, sometimes four B-sets, a practice that continued until the outbreak of war.

A further alteration in September 1934 saw the departure of the evening train from Swindon put back to 10 p.m. on Thursdays and Saturdays, thus allowing Malmesburian revellers an extended evening out amidst the bright lights of Swindon! For those Saturday afternoon trippers from Malmesbury not wishing to avail themselves of a Swindon Saturday night, a train out of Swindon at 5.20 would provide connection at Little Somerford at 5.50, whilst those who stayed and caught the late service would arrive back in Mal-

use of the closed section for storing old wagons. Except for the short section between Kingsmead and bridge 16A, where a stop-block had been put in by the pumping station, no track had been lifted following closure. Access for wagon storage was therefore via Dauntsey but there was pressure from Wiltshire County Council to remove the track at the Dauntsey end of the old branch so that Swallett Gate Bridge could be demolished with a view to improving the A420 road there. Following approaches by the County, the GWR informed them in a letter of 1st February 1934 that 'The Chief Engineer is at present unable to say when the branch will no longer be required for the stabling of vehicles'.

However, further consideration by the GWR revealed that stabling requirements were unlikely to necessitate the retention of the entire $3\frac{1}{2}$ miles from Dauntsey, and on 28th March 1934, the County Council were informed of the railway's decision to put in a temporary connection at Kingsmead Crossing to link the disused branch with the new loop to Little Somerford, thus enabling them to move crippled stock onto the old branch via Little Somerford and Kingsmead. In July 1934 the track was relaid for this purpose between the pumping station and the crossing, the remains of the old branch being retained as far as the site of the old station at Great Somerford, and the remains of the old branch were thereafter referred to as Kingsmead siding (not to be confused with the Kingsmead siding of 1898–1902).

Work commenced on lifting the track from Dauntsey to Swallett Gate on 5th July 1934, the sleepers being stacked at the bridge for disposal by the WCC and the County were allowed to take ballast for a length of 600 yards from the bridge towards Dauntsey. Swallett Gate bridge was blown up

The demolition of Swallett Gate railway bridge near Dauntsey, 26th August 1934, drew a lot of interested spectators.

Great Western Railway Magazine

Removal of the old branch between Great Somerford and Dauntsey in June 1936. This view shows the loading of girder spans, thought to be from Poole's Bridge, known locally as 'the Black Bridge', south of Dauntsey Road Crossing.   *Bertram Farmer*

Shunting at Great Somerford, on the old goods siding, with the old running line to the right.   *Bertram Farmer*

Looking north towards Kingsmead, with cameraman 'riding home' with the removed girders behind a 58xx 0–4–2T.   *Bertram Farmer*

on 26th August 1934, and the road was closed for three months for straightening. The lines were left *in situ* north of the bridge until June 1936, when the track and bridge girders from Swallett Gate to Great Somerford were lifted. From there, this section of the old branch north to Kingsmead remained as a storage siding for another 25 years.

With the decline in milk traffic by rail, Malmesbury's one train each way on Sunday evenings was living on borrowed time by 1935. At this time this service was still shown in the WTT as a milk train, leaving Malmesbury at 6.45 and calling at Little Somerford and Brinkworth on its extended run through to Wootton Bassett where it arrived at 7.09, returning at 7.35 to arrive back in Malmesbury at 7.57. The Sunday service was discontinued from 3rd March 1935, the branch's milk traffic that year totalling less than 300 cans despatched from Malmesbury, much of the business from the local milk factory being taken over by road haulage. With the removal of the Malmesbury milk, the 6.10 a.m. Swindon to Little Somerford milk empties was discontinued on Monday mornings from 4th March. The cutting of the Sunday train was a negative move; despite its association with milk, many folk who visited Malmesbury at weekends used it to return east, with further connections at Swindon and Didcot seeing Sunday travellers in Paddington by 10 p.m.

With the change of junction, Malmesbury's six-man permanent way gang was transferred to Little Somerford and amalgamated with the main line gang, their length being the branch and the section of main line between Brinkworth and Rodbourne. An extra man was also allocated to the gang on

account of the large number of points and crossings to be oiled at Little Somerford. A new permanent way hut was built at the west end of the station by the branch to accommodate the larger gang and the trolley and handcar for branch use. the duties of the permanent way men were to ensure correct maintenance of the road to ensure safe running of all traffic, jobs including maintenance of gauge, oiling of points at Malmesbury and Little Somerford, hand-weeding of the track with hoes, checking of fences, snow clearance and fogging duty (only ever necessary on the branch at Kingsmead), and checking track for broken fish plates and loose or missing wooden keys. Although the thirteen-man gang would divide so that one group worked the main line and the other the branch, they would work together on such duties as rail adjustment, slacking and fish-plate oiling, jobs which required as much manpower as possible to complete promptly. The ganger would walk the branch every day to check the track, rejoining his men on the next convenient train. Twice a week two men were employed on point oiling at each end of the branch, a two-hour job at Little Somerford. The gang worked hours of 7.15 to 4.45, usually taking a breakfast break in a cabin around 8.30 and a 45-minute lunch break at 12.45. These hours were amended and breaks curtailed in order to avoid darkness, and, with the aid of shovels, hoes and ballast forks, they maintained their length in perfect condition, the only section of line which caused any great problem for them being the section between Kingsmead and Harding's Cutting, where the curve of the line often warped in hot weather and where flooding of the Avon occasionally caused ballast wash-

The Little Somerford permanent way gang c.1938 after the branch and main line gangs had been amalgamated. They looked after part of the main line and the reduced branch to Malmesbury from Little Somerford. This group, taken at Kingsmead Crossing, shows (left to right) Charlie Bubb, Jim Porter, Frank Strange, Ernest Thornbury, Albert Stoneham (ganger), Tom Scott, Elsie Archard (gateman Bill's wife), Rich Harford, Sam Scott and Harry Barnes. During the war Harford was killed by a train at Little Somerford in blizzard conditions. The two young girls are Archard family friends from the village.

Collection Bill Archard

Ian Beard and his 3½-ton
Thornycroft shortly before
his transfer to Malmesbury
in 1935.

Courtesy Ian Beard

out. In the event of any emergency and the need to stop trains, gangers' telephones were located in the same places as the permanent way huts, with one extra in Harding's Cutting.

Aware of the need to compete with local carriers in rural areas, the GWR brought Malmesbury into its motorisation scheme in July 1935. Since 1923 the GWR had provided a cartage service with horse and dray at the terminus, worked by Ernest Thornbury. In July 1935 Ian Beard was sent from Bristol with Malmesbury's first GWR motor lorry, Thornbury being eventually transferred to the permanent way gang. Beard remained at Malmesbury in charge of the motor lorry service until final closure of the branch in 1962, whereupon he was transferred to Chippenham. Born in Malmesbury in 1901, he had been based for several years at Melksham where he gained experience driving the large 3½-ton AEC Thorneycrofts.

The GWR first had a Thorneycroft steam wagon as far back as 1902, in a partnership with the Basingstoke firm which lasted beyond nationalisation of the railways. The onset of the Great War encouraged the use of mechanical transport and 1914 saw the start of bulk orders by the GWR of road vehicles from Thorneycrofts. Following the war the GWR bought 130 AEC 3½-ton lorries from army surplus stock at Slough, one of which Ian Beard used at Melksham. September 1931 saw the use of articulated vehicles begin by the GWR, and in 1933 the solid rubber tyres were replaced by pneumatic ones. Thus, motorisation of the cartage fleet had been going on for some years before it finally arrived at Malmesbury, although Beard's lorry was not the first GWR lorry to appear there, as a motor run had been made from Chippenham since 1932.

In 1932 an outward-bound wagon intended for Chippenham had been dropped from the 2.04 p.m. to Dauntsey, and the GWR put on a lorry from Chippenham to replace it. Driven regularly by a Tom Gregory, this move may have been a run-in to the 1933 change of junction. Rather than send goods to Chippenham via the new junction and Wootton Bassett, it made more economic sense to send a lorry two or three times a week, in the afternoon as required, to collect

goods going out of Malmesbury. Westbound goods taken by Gregory after 1933 were therefore going by a more direct route to Bristol, although there were still Bristol and Paddington direct wagons on the new line, the Bristol wagon running via Stoke Gifford. The Chippenham lorry continued for a short time after the arrival of Malmesbury's own motor lorry service.

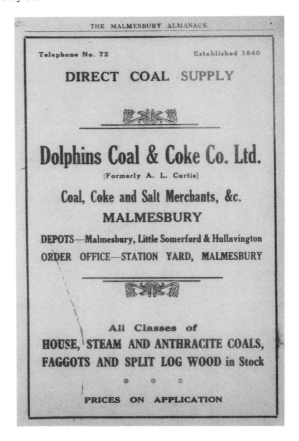

The Malmesbury lorry was stabled in the goods shed at the terminus, backed into one of the entrances so its rear was adjacent to the loading dock. Petrol for it was kept in two-gallon cans stored in a bin outside by the checker's office. In later years, with petrol companies delivering direct to pumps, the Malmesbury lorry filled up at a garage in the High Street. In the event of mechanical failure, a substitute lorry would be driven from Swindon by a mechanic who would effect the necessary repairs.

The lorry driver would collect his delivery sheets from the parcels office on the station, then proceed to the goods shed where the lorry would be loaded, after the arrival of the first train from Little Somerford, by lorry driver and checker. In the winter months, if there was a problem starting the lorry, a churn of warm water from the branch locomotive would be wheeled over to the goods shed on a trolley to supply the lorry and help get it under way; this co-operation between rail and road vehicles is a memory which evokes flavours of a long-vanished age. . . .

Ian Beard spent most of his morning around the town delivering perishables such as cheese, butter and fruits for the town groceries, beer for the public houses, and general merchandise to High Street shops. The country deliveries were made in the afternoon, mainly the distribution of cattle feed to the farms, which came in regularly from Avonmouth. The lorry route was organised so that from 4.00 p.m. onwards the time was spent on collections in and around Malmesbury, the main items being bales of silk, bacon from the local factory, and passengers' luggage in advance (PLA), all to be loaded and taken to the station ready for transferring to the evening mixed train which went out at 6.40. The lorry was then returned to the goods shed ready for the next day, ending a very busy and heavy day for its driver, with much loading and off-loading, always with deadlines in mind and careful organisation of the lorry-load to be considered.

During the mid-30s the practice of running summer specials from Malmesbury to a variety of locations continued along the 'through-special' lines first organised by John Barnby in 1930. They had been a feature of branch life since the 1880s, trains chartered specifically by a group of people or institution, booked to convey parties to a single specified destination and back, as distinct from the GWR excursion traffic, which also provided much business for the Malmesbury branch. The latter were widely advertised extra services providing special fares to different destinations and open to everyone. Of the 'specials' popular at Malmesbury, the most notable were the annual seaside trips run by the combined Sunday Schools, already referred to in Chapter 4. The 1936 one ran on 25th June with a train of ten through-corridor coaches which left Swindon at 8.50 a.m., arriving in Malmesbury behind two tank engines which had just enough room to run around the train before running it back to Little Somerford at 10.15 where it was taken over by the 'Star' class 4–6–0 No. 4062 *Malmesbury Abbey*, often appropriately used

An evocative scene at Malmesbury goods shed, 31st July 1935. On the left Tom Gregory is leaning against the Chippenham GWR motor lorry. Malmesbury porter Ron Thomas, in the centre, was assisting with loading the lorry — he later became signalman at Little Somerford. On the right is Ernest Thornbury, 'carman' with the GWR horse and dray used for goods and parcel deliveries around Malmesbury until the arrival of the town's own motor lorry not long after this photograph was taken. *Bertram Farmer*

The Sunday Schools' special train at Malmesbury, seen from the top of the water tower on Thursday, 25th June 1936. The ten bogie coaches were double-headed by two 58XX class 0–4–2Ts.

Bertram Farmer

for the main line journey on such occasions. The special ran via Filton Junction and arrived at Weston-Super-Mare's Locking Road excursion platform at 12.15. The return train left Weston at 7.22 p.m. with an 8.53 arrival back in Malmesbury and the third class return fare was 4/6d.

The excursion traffic of the GWR was a popular part of life on the branch between the wars and provided a lot of work for the railway staff at Malmesbury. Although these ran all year, August was by far the busiest month, and the most common and among the best-patronised were the Paddington to Westbury excursions which usually ran on the third Sunday in the month in the mid-30s, providing day excursions (leave before 10.00 a.m.) to a choice of Wiltshire locations, beginning in March. In 1936 the Malmesbury branch train ran out to Wootton Bassett around midday to collect those trippers who had chosen the ancient borough as their destination. There were often a good number of such folk, maybe visiting relatives or viewing the Abbey, and they brought a welcome trade to the town. Brinkworth signal box had to be opened on such days to allow the branch train to call there, and a return trip was usually made from Malmesbury in the evening to connect with the main line excursion at Wootton Bassett. Hence the third Sunday in the month during a March–December season continued to see some activity on the branch after the cessation of the Sunday milk train, the only other movements on the branch on Sundays after 1935 being the occasional visit of a weed-killer train, usually two tanks hauled by a pannier tank, or a short train of open wagons sent to collect the grass mown from cutting sides.

It was probably on the occasion of the Paddington–Westbury excursion of 25th March 1936, that an amusing incident took place at Malmesbury during the departure of a connecting excursion for Wootton Bassett. The train, crewed by Ben Hill and Dick Cooper, left Malmesbury without the train staff, and the crowd of locals who had been seeing off the train heard it stop at the other end of the tunnel and its

steady approach as it returned to the station. Clerk John Barnby, who was on duty in the station office, then discovered the train staff still hanging up on its hook in its usual place when the branch train was at the platform, immediately realising that the crew had discovered their error. Discreetly putting it inside his coat, he walked up the middle road as the train came back to the platform, and was then able to pass the staff to Cooper up on the footplate, out of sight of the crowd on the station, and hidden from those leaning mystified from the carriage windows by a convenient cloud of steam! As a result the excursion's false start was a mystery to everyone – the incident was reported in a London paper but passed without comment.

During August 1936 no less than ten excursion trains ran from Malmesbury, providing cheap day seaside trips to Paignton, Weymouth, Barry Island and Weston-Super-Mare. Unlike the Sunday Schools special, all these were run with the branch train connecting with the excursions at the nearest convenient point. Circuitous routes were often taken by the excursions in order to pick up as many people as possible, so, for example, a Frome to Barry Island excursion would pick up trippers from Malmesbury at Patchway, a Swindon Junction to Patchway service having collected them from the branch train at Little Somerford. On one Sunday that month there were two separate excursions from Malmesbury to seaside destinations, providing a busier than usual Sunday for the train crews and clerk in particular.

Many of these services returned at a very late hour, and the Malmesbury crew had to make a late run to Little Somerford or Wootton Bassett to bring home the day-trippers, the only occasions on which the branch engine would be out of its shed after midnight. The Bristol Parson Street to London excursion of Wednesday 5th August provided for return to Malmesbury at 2.12 a.m. on the Thursday, and on this occasion the branch set left the terminus at 1.35 a.m. to be in position at Little Somerford to meet those returning. In the

A 1937 Boys' National School outing about to leave Malmesbury, with families, and in the right background headmaster Ingrams.
Collection Oliver Pike

age of the private car, such travel is long a thing of the past, but before the internal combustion engine came to dominate our society such services were the only way to travel a great distance cheaply and easily, a way of getting to know the country without disturbing the common round. It is not too hard to imagine the subdued activity at Little Somerford in the small hours of the morning, with weary parents carrying sleeping children and a day's souvenirs, wearing the fashions which reflected the sober uniformity of pre-war Britain, crossing the footbridge and disappearing into the safely reassuring presence of the waiting branch train for Malmesbury, which simmered patiently at the up platform as the main line train disappeared into the night towards Bristol.

During the '30s the GWR continued to provide special trains and excursions for most events of any importance. Football matches in Bristol usually attracted an extra service or reduced fare, especially if an FA Cup match was involved – a Bristol Rovers *v* Arsenal third round tie in 1936 could be attended by folk from Malmesbury via an 11.06 branch train for 3/6d return. Cheap day tickets to Paddington every Wednesday could be purchased for 12/6d return third class, 18/9d first, travelling on the 7.23 from Malmesbury which gave a Paddington arrival at 10.37, or the 9.48 for an arrival at 12.30. Public holidays such as Whit Monday saw day excursion fares to Bristol for 3/6d third class and half-day excursion tickets

to Swindon for 1/6d return. A special excursion would be run each July for the Royal Agricultural Society Show in Bristol, and in August 1936 Malmesbury Carnival attracted an extra late service to Swindon, the branch train running at 11.00 p.m., arriving in Swindon at 11.41 and returning into Malmesbury at 12.50 a.m. A popular advertised excursion of 1937 was the GWR's half day Luncheon Car Excursion, which on Sunday, 28th February, provided an 11.15 departure from Malmesbury, changing at Little Somerford and Wootton Bassett to connect with a main line service offering a 2/6d luncheon. This train called at Reading and Ealing and arrived at Paddington at 2.00 p.m., a third class fare from Malmesbury to Paddington costing 6/6d. Passengers could return after 9.00 p.m. and a late branch train would run out to Wootton Bassett for their benefit.

Malmesbury's milk traffic disappeared almost overnight at the end of 1938, a minimal 239 cans being handled that year. The milk train, which ran daily from Little Somerford to West Ealing, was discontinued from 1st December 1938 and afterwards the small number of individual farmers, who had used Malmesbury station for their milk, delivered by road to Wootton Bassett.

In August 1939 international tension increased in Europe as storm clouds gathered with the threat of Nazi Germany, and the British Government decided to commence evacuation

MALMESBURY BRANCH.

Single Line worked by Train Staff and only one engine in steam at a time (or two or more coupled).

DOWN TRAINS.   **WEEK DAYS.**

Mile Post Distances		STATIONS.	Ruling Gradient 1 in.	Mixed	Swindon. Pass.	Pass.	Pass. **L**	Pass.	Wootton Bass'tt Mixed.	Pass.	Pass.	Swindon. Pass. **Th SX**	Swindon. Pass. **Th SO**
M C.	M C.			a.m.	a.m.	a.m.	p.m.	p.m.	p.m.	p.m.	p.m.	p.m.	p.m.
89 61	— —	Little Som. dep.	94 F.	8 10	10 26	11 48	12 36	2 13	3 55	5 50	7 3	9 15	*10 30*
93 35	8 60	Malmesbury arr.	116 R.	8 20	10 34	11 56	12 44	2 21	4 7	5 58	7 11	9 23	*10 38*

L—Nine minutes later on Saturdays.

UP TRAINS.   **WEEK DAYS.**

STATIONS.	Ruling Gradient 1 in.	Pass.	Pass.	Swindon. Pass.	Pass.	Mixed **SO**	Mixed **SX**	Wootton Bass'tt Pass.	Pass.	Mixed	Sw'd'n Pass.		
		a.m.	a.m.	a.m.	p.m.	p.m.	p.m.	p.m.	p.m.	p.m.	p.m.		
Malmesbury .. dep.	....	7 21	9 48	11 6	12 15	*1 30*	1 50	2 55	5 25	6 40	7 25	..	..
Little Somerford arr.	116 F.	7 30	9 57	11 15	12 24	*1 39*	1 59	3 4	5 34	6 49	7 34	....	....

Little Somerford—Kingsmead Crossing.—Trains in either direction to reduce speed to 30 miles per hour.
Kingsmead Crossing—Malmesbury.—Trains in either direction to reduce speed to 10 miles per hour when approaching. Caution Boards placed 360 yards from Crossing until passing over Crossing.

13 minutes to be allowed for Goods Trains over the Malmesbury Branch, in either direction, including " start " and " stop " allowances, also " Stop Board " requirements. (G. 17266.)

Working Timetable for September to July 1939, just before the wartime reductions.

An unidentified Collett 0—4—2T bringing a branch train down from the main line at Little Somerford onto the 1 in 50 gradient to Kingsmead Crossing sometime during 1936. The fireman visible is Dick Cooper.
John Barnby

of children from London and other major cities to places of comparative safety in the rural areas of Wessex and the West, much of the load falling to the GWR. The Ministry of Transport took control of the main line railways of Great Britain in an order dating from 31st August, and with the evacuation scheduled to begin on the morning of 1st September, war was precipitated on that day when Germany invaded Poland. Instructions went out over the wireless early in the morning ordering parents to start the first evacuation from the capital and report with their children to a local assembly point, usually their school, where the children were marshalled by their teachers and walked to the nearest station to journey to embarkation points in West London. Dummy runs had been practised by the schools for several days prior to 1st September, and when the order came the GWR was responsible for the safe, efficient movement of over 600,000 children from London alone. The first special train of evacuees left Ealing Broadway at 8.30 a.m., and at 11.42 that morning a ten-coach train carrying 900 children left West Ealing for Malmesbury.

Signalmen were expected to give evacuee trains a clear run through stations where they were not booked to call, to avoid confused children attempting to leave trains at the wrong place. The Malmesbury special was scheduled to change engines at Little Somerford at 1.53 p.m., for which seven minutes was allowed, and it is not hard to picture anxious yet excited, children, many out in the 'sticks' for the first time, spilling into the corridors and maybe attempting to detrain at Little Somerford. During the change of motive power, many must have wondered if this station, high on the embankment and apparently in the middle of nowhere, was their final destination. Worked by a London guard throughout, the special was double-headed on the branch by Malmesbury's engine and an extra tank locomotive sent out from Swindon, the main line locomotive remaining at Little Somerford. It is recalled by some that a third locomotive banked the train at the rear but this is unconfirmed. To accommodate the train on the branch, the 1.50 mixed from Malmesbury ran 13 minutes earlier and the 2.13 Little Somerford and the 2.55 Malmesbury were cancelled, the evacuees arriving in Malmesbury about 20 minutes behind schedule at 2.30 p.m.

On arrival at Malmesbury, the coaches were emptied separately, a procedure agreed between station master Mr. Faull, the local reception officer and the road transport officials

Looking towards Malmesbury tunnel from the vicinity of Lovers Lane Crossing during the winter of 1939-40. One of the railway allotments is shown on the left.
John Barnby

involved, then the empties were shunted out beyond the signal box and the next group brought into the platform. This procedure suggests that some non-corridor stock was included in the formation. The young Londoners included many French, Italian, Chinese, Greek and Jewish children amongst their number, and sported the pink tickets tied to their lapels which identified them as part of a school group, the tickets bearing their name, London address and school of origin. Bearing their rucksacks containing a spare change of clothes, gas mask, and tins of meat and fruit, they were met on the station by the local billeting officer with volunteers and members of the Red Cross, then taken in sixteen motor coaches up to the local secondary school where, after a cursory medical examination, they were given rations of corned beef, chocolate, biscuits and tinned milk, and taken to their new homes. Some 200 were billeted in the town itself, the rest in the surrounding rural area, their first job being to send a postcard to their parents letting them know where they were. The arrival of the evacuee train produced a great deal of work for the station staff at Malmesbury, all available personnel being on duty, much of the day's business having to be held over until the next, with the London Division stock requiring cleaning and re-equipping before being returned to Old Oak Common.

Two days later, the 3rd, the day on which Britain officially declared war on Germany, a second evacuee train from West Ealing was scheduled to arrive in Malmesbury, but although railway staff and billeting officers were on the station to meet it around 7.00 p.m., the train never materialised. It has not been possible to establish precisely the reason for this, but maybe the general efficiency of the evacuation meant that Malmesbury was not required a second time for the mothers with children and various miscellaneous groups who were moved out of London that Sunday.

Winter scene at Cowbridge, looking towards Kingsmead along the Avon Valley from the Swindon road bridge.
Collection Bert Vizor

That same Sunday also saw the last known documented excursion service to run from Malmesbury, when the branch set provided connection at Wootton Bassett with the advertised Steventon to Weymouth excursion. With this an era ended forever, as this traffic ended with the war, never to reappear when hostilities ceased. The revenue and sense of occasion which it brought to the branch was sadly missed, heralding a decline which set in all too swiftly after 1945.

The GWR's National Emergency Service was brought into operation on 25th September 1939, prompted by the need to conserve coal and rolling stock for the war effort, and, unlike the 1914–18 war, the effects on train service were far more drastic and immediate, with Malmesbury's service suffering quite seriously. The morning return run from Swindon was lost forever, and two other return passenger trains on the branch were cut, the 9.48 ex-Malmesbury and the 10.26 ex-Little Somerford, and the 12.15 and 12.36 return services. The evening mixed train was retimed to run ten minutes earlier at 6.30, and further losses were all the evening trains between Malmesbury and Swindon, with the exception of the late train on Saturday nights. These changes meant that only the early morning train out of Malmesbury had both east and westbound connections at Little Somerford, the 11.10 from Malmesbury had only a connection for Bristol with a half-hour wait, the 5.25 similarly, the 6.30 had only a connection for Swindon, while the 1.50 Saturdays excepted service apparently had no main line connection at all. At least the meagre number of stopping trains called at Little Somerford all had connections into Malmesbury, the main line stopping service being unaffected by the cuts.

A further change at this time affected the Saturdays only 'soccer' train, which no longer went from Swindon direct to Malmesbury but instead ran to Badminton, an apparently strange move in view of the fact that the main patronage for this train came from Malmesbury. The re-arranged service left Badminton at 1.18 p.m. and the Malmesbury branch set left the terminus at 1.20 to connect with the Badminton at Little Somerford at 1.30, arrival in Swindon being at 2.00 p.m. It is thought that the Saturday run from Swindon was

extended to Badminton to provide an extra train for RAF personnel at Hullavington, but it is an interesting thought that on the outbreak of war Queen Mary was moved out to the safety of Badminton, and it is possible but unconfirmed that Malmesbury's 'soccer' train could have been diverted there in order to provide an extra means of delivering Cabinet papers to the monarch in an empty train.

In January 1940 a factory was opened at Cowbridge House in Malmesbury by E. K. Cole Ltd (EKCO). Based in Southend, this followed a request from the War Ministry to open a 'shadow factory' to manufacture secret equipment for Services radio and radar use. At one time a siding was planned for the branch at Cowbridge to serve the works, the GWR going as far as to make a preliminary survey, but it never materialised, probably because the work would have involved expensive construction of a new bridge over the Avon to connect the factory with the branch. The company did not use the railway during the war, all goods being transported to and from the works by army lorries, but from 1945 the firm's business provided the branch with much new traffic, mainly in the form of the delivery to Malmesbury of electrical components as parcel traffic, some 900 people being employed at the site by 1952.

By February 1940 the afternoon run between Malmesbury and Wootton Bassett had been cut, being replaced by a 3.10 to Little Somerford, which returned as a mixed train at

Malmesbury yard during the winter of 1939-40, with the early afternoon mixed train being shunted in the yard with checker George Woodward riding on the locomotive steps. The wagons seen beyond the two coaches would have contained general merchandise.

John Barnby

3.50 p.m. The Saturdays Only train for the Swindon soccer and shopping trippers was put back to a 1.10 departure to fit in with retiming of the Badminton train. By the spring of 1940 most of the evacuees in the Malmesbury area had gradually returned to their homes, with no attacks having materialised and the situation seemingly safe, but after the Dunkirk retreat in May 1940 the whole atmosphere of the war changed in Britain. GWR stations, such as Newton Abbot, in what were considered to be 'safe' areas, were hit by German bombs, and with Britain standing alone against the enemy with the French about to capitulate in June, a fresh wave of evacuations took place. On 18th June 1940, 370 youngsters from the vulnerable docklands at Tilbury were brought to Malmesbury on a train hauled by two 4-4-0 'Dukedogs', an unusual sight on the branch, with the branch engine at the rear. Such arrivals at a quiet country terminus must have been a great sight, and a large crowd gathered outside the station to see them arrive, many of the juvenile population climbing trees in order to obtain a better view. According to eye-witness reports, unlike in 1939, the evacuees left the coaches, which stopped short of the terminal platform, by means of the wooden steps which were used for boarding and alighting on the Sunday School specials. Their food rations were issued in a marquee erected just outside the station. The nearby Westport C of E Boys School had to accommodate two extra classes with the evac-

uees' arrival, and the railway motor lorry was used to transport extra desks and chairs for the top floor of the school.

During the dark days of mid-1940, with the threat of invasion looming large, there was a real need to observe the 'blackout' which had been in force since the beginning of the war, and, located close as it was to airfields at Long Newnton, Hullavington, Lyneham, Kemble and South Cerney, Malmesbury's line could be considered to be in a vulnerable area as German air raids increased. Thus station and signal box nameboards were removed, platform lighting was restricted to those areas under cover, white lines were painted along platform edges, night work in the shed took place behind closed doors, staff were instructed to assist in closing carriage doors as quickly as possible, carriage blinds were to be kept drawn, and tarpaulins were issued to the locomotive department for use on the cab to maintain blackout conditions, for a light from an open firebox could present a tempting target for an enemy aircraft with spare ammunition after a destructive mission over the local airfields. Gas-masks were issued to engine crews and guards, and even the GWR passenger train notices for staff bore the words 'Paper is a munition of war — salvage this notice when you have finished with it.'

During the war the old siding at Kingsmead was used for the storage of ammunition wagons, and as the Blitz reached its height, relief porter Jim Thornbury worked long hours

Looking north from the site of the old Great Somerford station in 1941, with the abandoned section of the old Malmesbury branch in use for stock storage. The succession of carriage underframes were burnt-out remains following an air raid on Bristol. The old Metropolitan coach on the left, standing on the old goods siding, is thought to have been used during the war as a camp coach and mess room by soldiers when ammunition wagons were stabled on the old line away from the obvious dangers to Swindon Yard and Bristol.

Collection Eric Mountford

with an engine crew separating these vehicles to a safe distance from each other in case of bombing.

With the virtual abolition of private motoring caused by the war, nearly everyone had regular experience of rail travel during these years, and with the large number of service personnel in the area using the branch, particularly from the airbase at Long Newnton, and the frequent movement of people and materials on an albeit reduced service, the Malmesbury line's business rallied for a time. Although the parcel business was but a fraction of the 18,000 incoming parcels annually in the 1920s, both Little Somerford and Malmesbury experienced vast increases in goods tonnages which more than doubled pre-war figures, the former being particularly busy during 1941–42. A new arrival in Malmesbury which helped to account for this increase was Linolite Ltd, who in 1941 moved their operation from London to escape the bombing during the Blitz. Although manufacturers of electric light fittings, with the outbreak of war they changed over entirely to the production of hose-clips for aeroplanes and tanks. Their move to Wiltshire came on the advice of the Ministry of Aircraft Production following an air raid on the capital, as the company was the sole manufacturer of the BTR clip for the Goodrich de-icing system used in RAF bomber squadrons. The Malmesbury factory had originally been a brewery and here during the war they produced $7\frac{1}{2}$ million hose-clips, making a full return to the lighting business in 1945, purchasing their premises in 1958. Linolite used the branch for delivery of their raw materials and despatch of finished goods, with a daily collection and delivery to and from the station by the GWR lorry.

During 1941 a Canadian RAMC unit was based in the military hospital at Charlton Park, a reminder that the forces of other nations were based in Britain, there being Polish, French, Norwegian, Belgian, Dutch and Czech military units here, later joined by the Americans. With a need to assist these and our own forces, plans for improvement of railway facilities were pushed ahead in 1941 in order to give total mobility to movement of men and supplies. The needs of wartime demanded the provision of additional running loops and extensions to existing loops on double track main lines so that goods trains could be more easily accommodated when it was necessary to keep the main lines clear. In June 1941 the platform loops and siding accommodation at Little Somerford were extended, with a new frame of 78 levers being installed in the signal box, the alteration of the signalling layout and provision of a new frame being work that had been scheduled for 1935, but lack of finance had postponed the job until the war effort made it essential.

In October 1941 the late run from Swindon to Malmesbury on Saturday nights was retimed, leaving much earlier at 8.55 p.m., arriving at 9.28. On 4th May 1942, this late train was altered again, the 7.25 from Malmesbury being reduced to run only as far as Wootton Bassett, leaving there at 9.05 to return to the branch. Thus was lost any form of direct service to Swindon, with only token resumption of any such service after the war. Further alterations in October 1942 saw the 2.13 from Little Somerford altered to 2.00 p.m., and the afternoon mixed re-scheduled from 3.40 to 2.55. Malmesbury's 3.10 passenger train was retimed to 2.20, giving a 2.37 connection for Swindon on the 1.18 Lawrence Hill passenger and fish empties train. To accommodate this change

on the timetable, the 1.50 Malmesbury mixed departure was brought forward to 1.30 p.m.

In February 1943 Malmesbury's station master Richard Faull, of whom little is otherwise known, moved on to Portishead and the post was taken by Arthur Davies from Mitcheldean Road, near Ross-on-Wye. During this year Malmesbury's increased passenger business merited the appointment of an extra clerk in the booking office. The station's annual ticket issue rose to a peak of 8,564 by 1944, not a great figure, but fair in view of the curtailed service. If

Doreen Curtis on the platform at Malmesbury, during her five years as clerk.   *Courtesy Doreen Hicks*

this published total represents an average of between two and three passengers per train during the war, it should be remembered that it took no note of hundreds of service personnel travelling on passes and the many tickets booked elsewhere to Malmesbury. Therefore the line was considerably busier at this time than is suggested by recorded figures. The manpower required for the Services during the war created many more opportunities for ladies to work on the railway, and during these years several girls worked at Malmesbury as clerks, among them Sylvia Mumford, Joyce Wallington, Mary Butler and Muriel Allsopp, joining the ranks of the 16,000 women serving on the GWR in 1943 when the war effort was at its maximum intensity. Doreen Curtis spent five years at Malmesbury as clerk from 1943, going in straight from school to work at the many duties expected of the clerk at a country terminus, although the allocation of two clerks eased the workload and enabled one to come on duty for the early morning train, then go home for breakfast before returning at 9.00 a.m.

Many troop trains during the war ran with guards taken from branch line staff, thus creating vacancies at many termini for porters, and from 1940 Rose Clark was taken on in this capacity at Malmesbury. It was a very exacting life for a girl, 21 years old when she started, and in the wartime situation she was very much left to find her own way. In addition to cleaning the station, lighting the fires, climbing the ladder at the starting signal to clean out and replace the wick in the oil lamp, reporting at 6.30 to unlock the coaches, she also learned to handle the points, check goods in and make out wagon returns, and would often assist the motor driver with loading the lorry down at the goods shed, often going with him to the farms to help unload 2 cwt bags of cattle feed. Such work was useful experience which stood her in good stead when she was rewarded with the post of checker after the war upon the retirement of George Woodward.

In May 1943 the 1.30 daily mixed was taken off and its return service, the 2.00 p.m. from Little Somerford, was reduced to Saturdays only to work as a return for the 'soccer' train which ran out to Little Somerford to meet the Badminton. In October mixed train provision at the junction was transferred from the 8.12 a.m. to the 11.58, a move possibly caused by delays owing to the war. A minor branch like Malmesbury with a junction at a minor station, was very susceptible to delays caused by wartime conditions. To make stock available for the war effort, many passenger trains ran as duplicates – for example in 1943 the 12.30 Paddington to Weston-Super-Mare divided at Swindon, its rear half joining the 9.20 a.m. Sheffield to Swansea. Such manoeuvres and bad winter weather would create delays which would be magnified at an outpost like Little Somerford where the branch set had to wait for trains already late from major connecting points. Hence a Malmesbury branch train might be seen heading for home at more than its usual rate of speed, especially if Joe Halliday was the driver! Rose Clark recalled many winter occasions when she worked from 6.30 a.m. to 11.00 p.m. when required, waiting for trains well behind time in snow or fog, and spending many hours in sole charge of the station.

Doreen Curtis and Sylvia Mumford pose on parcel porter Len Hillman's motor bike outside Malmesbury station.

Courtesy Doreen Hicks

By 1943 there were signs that the war was beginning to swing towards the Allies. Americans based in a camp at Charlton Park brought their air of cheerful bravado to the area and on occasions used the station forecourt as a parade ground. Trains bearing prisoners-of-war ran on the branch in July 1943, bearing first Italians (before Italy joined the Allies in September 1943) who were taken to a camp at Easton Grey. Locals recall the special trains of six coaches standing on the run-round loop at the station until their return to Swindon, and the arrival of hired coaches from the Black & White Coach Co. of Cheltenham to transport the POWs to camp. Later, Germans were brought in by train and taken to a camp at Charlton Park, and an awesome sight on the branch was the conveyance of bombs for the airfield at Long Newnton.

The early morning train, the 7.21 out of Malmesbury, the only one of any use for travelling a long distance in one day, was often used by forces personnel going back to their units after leave, and uniforms, embraces and tearful scenes were a regular sight on the platform during this period. Many tales are extant in the area of how the branch train would be held at the platform for someone to return home to fetch a gas-mask, so a serviceman could catch the train and return to his unit on time. One tale relates how a young man in the RAF ran to the station one morning for the 7.21, only to see it already leaving. Just when he saw a chance of reaching his base at Thetford, Norfolk, the same day receding, the crew saw him, recognised him and returned their train to the platform. Local folk were used to such delays on the branch and appreciated the personal service that was possible on a country line. A local correspondent writing in the *Wilts & Glos Standard* in 1951 related what a marvellous sight was the branch train for returning service personnel as they alighted from main line trains to see the 'Bunk' pulling into the junction platform at Little Somerford.

The GWR Operating Instructions for the war years show just one special train listed from Malmesbury. On Friday, 7th January 1944, a train comprising locomotive, brake composite and brake third, was scheduled to leave Malmesbury at 9.45. After a change of engine at Little Somerford the two coaches were taken to Swindon for 10.25 where the two coaches were to be attached to the 7.45 a.m. Taunton to Paddington. No one can recall this train and it would be interesting to know if it actually ran and why.

By May 1944 the Saturday train to Swindon for the football fans and shoppers had ceased, and on 10th July 1944, the staff at Malmesbury were saddened by the death of Mr. Davies, who was in only his second year as station master there. Only in his early 50s, he had been in ill health for some time prior to his death. The terminus came under a relief station master until the following October when Percy Wood transferred from Sparkford, Somerset, to take over the station for its last seven years of passenger service.

One of the most damaging effects of World War II as far as domestic transport was concerned was the decline in standards of maintenance of track, rolling stock and fixed equipment, caused by a scarcity of labour and materials. Even so, Little Somerford was on a priority stretch of line, the vital Direct to South Wales, and during the last months of 1944 much renewal work was done in its immediate vicinity. In October £600 was spent on renewal of three signals and point and signal connections at the station; several facing point

An evocative view taken during the late '40s showing a Collett 0—4—2T with the branch set and three horse-boxes passing Abbey House and Malmesbury Abbey on its way to Little Somerford.
Courtesy Gerald and Shirley Cooper

connections were also renewed at a cost of £370 in November. The same month telegraph poles and 32 miles of telegraph wire between Little Somerford and Hullavington were replaced for £725, and in December 23 miles of wire, telegraph arms, stays and fittings were renewed for £500. The demands of war had taken their toll.

With the end of official hostilities with Germany in May 1945, a swift return to a full railway service was hoped for, but beyond a couple of minor retimings nothing happened to reinstate Malmesbury's branch service to its pre-war situation, and the delay badly affected the line's business, for within a year of the end of the war passenger revenue was down by 25% on 1944. The only regular amount of sizeable revenue was taken on winter Saturdays when Swindon Town played at home, as the 11.17 from Lawrence Hill called at Little Somerford at 12.26, providing passengers off the 12.08 Malmesbury with a Swindon arrival at 12.50, but, with over two hours to kill before the football, it was a poor substitute for the matey old 'soccer train', which now no longer even ran to Badminton. It was not long before a local coach company began offering cheap return trips to Swindon for football punters which took them in to the County Ground for the match then returned them home again, while those who travelled in by train were still hanging around draughty stations waiting for the exiguous connections to materialise. On 1st October 1945, mixed train provision returned to the 8.00 a.m. Little Somerford, so that both the morning trains into Malmesbury ran mixed.

Another sad blow struck the staff at Malmesbury with the death of Cecil Moore, on 25th August 1945. His long service on the branch is covered in Chapter 11. The railway staff at Malmesbury station in Autumn 1945 was made up thus:

Station master	–	Percy Wood
Clerks	–	Doreen Curtis, Mary Butler
Parcel porter	–	Len Hillman
Porter	–	Rose Clark
Goods porter	–	George Eldridge
Guards	–	Frank Hewlett, Bert Reynolds
Checker	–	George Woodward
Lad porter	–	Bob Neal
Motor driver	–	Ian Beard
Engine drivers	–	Ben Hill, Joe Halliday
Firemen	–	Charlie Barnes, Ken Stoneham
Cleaner	–	Norman Thornbury

At this time Malmesbury's Dick Cooper was still officially attached to Malmesbury shed, having obtained promotion to driver whilst in fact still in the Services. At the end of the war he worked as a relief driver whilst waiting for a permanent vacancy to come up at his home shed. Long-time local railwayman Jim Thornbury was at this time a relief porter based in Malmesbury, working over a wide area of the Bristol Division but also undertaking a lot of duties locally.

Little Somerford was served by five up goods trains in 1945 – a local pick-up goods from Stoke Gifford, a coal train from Aberdare to Swindon Military Sidings, a coal and goods train from Severn Tunnel Junction to London, a goods from Llandilo Junction to Swindon and the Moreton Cutting goods. One solitary down goods called at Little Somerford, the 6.50 a.m. Swindon local to Stoke Gifford, which arrived at 8.24 and departed at 9.15, having left fertiliser, cattle cake and coal. Goods tonnage forwarded and received was well down in 1945–6 after a wartime surge of business, but a fair amount of goods traffic was handled at Little Somerford for transfer to Malmesbury. During the period 1945–9, Malmesbury's lad porter Bob Neal lived at Hullavington and

Guard Frank Hewlett with a goods train shortly after arrival at Malmesbury in 1948.

Bertram Farmer

MALMESBURY BRANCH.

Single Line worked by Train Staff and only one engine in steam at a time (or two or more coupled).

DOWN TRAINS.					WEEK DAYS.									
Mile Post Distances	STATIONS.	Ruling Gradient 1 in.	Mixed	Frght	Pass.	Pass.	Pass.	Pass.	Pass.	Pass.	Swindon Pass. SO			
M C. M C.	Little		a.m.	a.m.	a.m.	p.m.	p.m.	p.m.	p.m.	p.m.	p.m.			
89 61 — —	Somerford dep.	—	8 0	10 5	11 53	12 35	2 9	2 45	6 2	7 3	10 32			
93 35 3 60	Malmesbury arr.	59 F.	8 8	10 18	12 1	12 43	2 17	2 53	6 10	7 11	10 40			

UP TRAINS.				WEEK DAYS.								
STATIONS.	Ruling Gradient 1 in.	Pass.	Empties.	Pass.	Pass.	Pass.		Pass.	Pass.	Mixed	Swindon Pass. SO	
		a.m.	a.m.	a.m.	p.m.	p.m.		p.m.	p.m.	p.m.	p.m.	
Malmesbury dep.		7 21	9 0	11 30	12 8	1 40		2 23	5 35	6 30	7 25	
Little Somerford arr.	50 R.	7 30	9 13	11 39	12 17	1 49		2 32	5 44	6 39	7 34	

Little Somerford—Kingsmead Crossing.—Trains in either direction to reduce speed to 30 miles per hour.
Kingsmead Crossing—Malmesbury.—Trains in either direction to reduce speed to 10 miles per hour when approaching Caution Boards placed 300 yards from Crossing until passing over Crossing.

13 minutes to be allowed for Freight Trains over the Malmesbury Branch, in either direction, including " start " and " stop " allowances, also " Stop Board " requirements. (G. 17266.)

This Working Timetable shows the service provided after the Second World War, May to October 1946.

Public Record Office

parcel porter Len Hillman lived at Brinkworth, and they would both take an early train to Little Somerford, where they would meet and assist with the loading of the morning parcels aboard the first morning train in Malmesbury. The Malmesbury parcel traffic usually came off the 6.30 a.m. ex-Bristol and the 7.15 ex-Swindon, and would be waiting on the platforms for them. This was a job they undertook with great care, in order to simplify the job of unloading once in Malmesbury.

In May 1946 the GWR authorised the allocation of £550 for work on improved telephone facilities on the Malmesbury line although no staff interviewed can recall the exact nature of this work. Later in the year some £400 was spent on renewal of point and signal connections in respect of the branch at Little Somerford. In the same month the GWR resumed full working, as evidenced in a Working Timetable some seven inches thick, and Malmesbury briefly enjoyed some revival of service. The late Swindon service was reinstated, Saturdays only, with the arrival back at Malmesbury (usually with a fresh locomotive) at 10.40 p.m., the latest ever timetabled train in the line's history in normal branch service. This, however, was the only Swindon through-service to resume after the war. To take pressure off the 11.58 morning mixed, a new freight service was put on to cater for the new business provided by Ekco and Linolite, a train of empties leaving Mal-

mesbury each morning at 9.00 for Little Somerford where a goods train was made up in the yard. A typical load comprised components for the above-mentioned companies, coal supplies for the RAF at Long Newnton, artificial manures, fertilisers and cattle feed for local farms and a truckload of general goods from Bristol for local shops. Parcel traffic by this time was worth only £750 a year on the branch, and could be accommodated on passenger trains in the guard's compartment or using the mixed train facility afforded by the 6.30 ex-Malmesbury. A further important improvement was the reinstatement of two early afternoon return passenger trains, but connections, unfortunately, remained less than adequate.

A very friendly and convivial atmosphere existed among the staff at Malmesbury during the last years of passenger service, working conditions which were appreciated by all who experienced them, and many former employees attribute this in no small part to the courteous and warm manner in which Mr. Wood ran the station, with an experience on the GWR dating back to the turn of the century. In 1946 checker George Woodward retired, being followed in February 1947 by engineman Joe Halliday, both men with exceptionally long service at Malmesbury.

When Percy Wood took over at Malmesbury he had been struck by how much easier a station it was to administer than

Branch driver Joe Halliday's retirement in February 1947. Minus his moustache of earlier years, Halliday is seen aboard Collett No. 5802 with fireman Jim Long in Little Somerford station. On the platform (left to right) are Dick Cooper, probably Harold Poulton, Jim Thornbury (hidden), Bert Reynolds and Little Somerford station master Bert Hunt. *Collection Bert Vizor*

A beautiful summer's evening at Malmesbury station c.1948 with the branch engine simmering on the shed road, guard's van and the customary coal wagon on the middle road and the branch set waiting at the platform.

M. E. J. Deane

had been his previous appointment at Sparkford, where his monthly balance sheet had been several times greater than that of the declining terminus for which he was now responsible – and yet Sparkford to Malmesbury represented a promotion from Class 4 to 3, gradings he could never understand! When he was appointed to Malmesbury he declined to move there as he was not offered accommodation, for there was no station house. It was three years before he was able to obtain a council house and during this time he regularly used to visit his family in Sparkford, living in lodgings in Foundry Lane. It was a condemnation of the branch's poor service that he never used it when making these weekend trips to his wife and daughter. He had permission from Bristol to go to Sparkford each Saturday and left by the 10.00 a.m. bus to Chippenham, where he would take a Weymouth train which would convey him to Castle Cary where he could change for Sparkford. He usually arrived back in Malmesbury by the same route about noon on the Monday, a practice he followed until

1947 when he was finally able to move his family to a local house, by which time the branch's final demise was about to begin. As Mr. Wood said himself:

'Malmesbury was a very quiet terminus with very poor train connections. There was never any literature available at the station as we really had nothing to offer the public. The only large amount of money we ever took was when Swindon Town were playing at home on Saturdays. During my first three years in charge, I often used to go back to the station for company after tea, then maybe to the Railway Hotel for a drink and game of darts.'

The winter of 1946/47 saw not only a coal shortage but also severe weather, which caused serious flooding in the Malmesbury area and gave the permanent way men a very hard time, one of the Little Somerford gang being killed by a train during snow clearance up on the main line. In the Spring of 1947 the GWR was forced to make drastic cuts in main line services to save coal, although the Malmesbury line escaped reduction until the summer. That July a trainload of ballast

Another view taken on the same occasion.

M. E. J. Deane

was brought into Malmesbury station and a 2 ft gauge track laid to the river bank. Small tipper trucks conveyed the ballast to the river's edge where it was used to build up the banks in an effort to repair some of the winter damage. The railway yard extended to the Inglebourne and therefore this was the GWR's responsibility.

In June 1947 the two return services, which had only been reintroduced the previous year, were taken off once more, these being the 12.08 and 1.40 from Malmesbury and the 12.35 and 2.09 from Little Somerford, leaving a serious gap in the middle of the day. Service had deteriorated to the point where even a day trip to London was not easily accomplished, being fraught with long waits at Swindon. Taking the early morning train out of Malmesbury could see a traveller in Paddington by 10.55, but with an hour's wait at Swindon. On weekdays the last branch train in from Little Somerford for a return from London was the 7.03, but this had no connection from Swindon, so one had to reach the 6.03 branch train instead. For this he had to make the 5.35 ex-Swindon, which one could only accomplish by boarding the 1.55 from Paddington which arrived in Swindon at 3.31, thus giving the day tripper about three hours in the capital with a two-hour wait at Swindon on the return journey! A longer sojourn in the capital could be achieved by leaving Paddington at 3.55 and going through to Badminton for 5.44, where a wait until 6.32 returned one to Little Somerford at 6.51 in time for the 7.03 branch train! Small wonder that printed tickets for a trip to Paddington were not apparently kept at Malmesbury at this time. There was always a substantial stock of ticket blanks in the booking office which could be made out as desired! Branch connections at Little Somerford remained much the same as in wartime, with several trains having a connecting main line service in one direction only. Main line Sunday service at Little Somerford offered only an 8.15 a.m. and 4.15 p.m. to Bristol, with just the 7.29 p.m. in the up direction. A traveller could make use of Stan Hudson's taxi service to reach Little Somerford to catch the 7.29, which by way of a Swindon connection at 8.35 provided arrival in Paddington at 10.35. With some irony, the former junction at Dauntsey still had a service of ten up and nine down trains a day, with five down and four up even on Sundays.

Although some local Malmesbury firms are known to have booked special trains for their employees after the war, Lino-lite running works outings to the Ideal Home Exhibition in London, only one Sunday Schools special took place, a trip organised through Mr. Wood in June 1947 to Barry Island, after which this outing was run by Athelstan Coaches.

The last GWR timetable retimed the Saturday Swindon run to arrive back in Malmesbury at 9.40 p.m., remaining so until closure, and following the Transport Bill of 1947 receiving the Royal Assent on 6th August, the country's railways were taken over by the Railway Executive of the British Transport Commission, the Great Western Railway became the Western Region of British Railways, and the Malmesbury line thus passed into public ownership from 1st January 1948. Rose Clark recalled being told by Mr. Wood that if answering train enquiries on the telephone (there was a phone in the checker's office) she must now say 'British Railways, Malmesbury'. One wonders if the station master's instruction was a little tongue-in-cheek, staunch GWR man that he was! Although the basic service of five trains each way on weekdays

with a daily goods and a late Saturday run to Swindon was retained by the nationalised railway, further decline set in. There was actually an increase of about 25% in the number of tickets issued from Malmesbury during 1947–9, but pay rises raised the branch's paybill expenses in 1948, and when Doreen Curtis left the booking office that year to work for the Malmesbury Coal Company she was not replaced. Mixed train provision on the branch ceased from 27th September 1948, and thereafter the 8.00 a.m. from Little Somerford and 6.30 p.m. Malmesbury ran simply as passenger trains, the goods traffic being sent on the daily freight train and the small amount of parcels being accommodated in the guard's compartment on the B-set. All mixed train facilities were removed from the Western Region a year later. Horse-box traffic and cattle wagons were now rarely seen, having virtually disappeared with the war. Less coal was now coming in by rail, although the Dolphins Coal Company still had its depot at the station and Silveys (with 'Your Burning Desire' on its lorries) had taken over the old Malmesbury Coal Company/Gladwin's business in 1947. A new stacking area, close to the running line, was authorised for Silveys in December 1948 (see page 182). Rationing of coal after the war carried on until 1952, and a regular sight at the station were the local children collecting coal by pram.

Staff group at Malmesbury in 1947. Standing (left to right): Len Hillman (parcels porter), Doreen Curtis (clerk), Frank Hewlett (guard). Seated (left to right): George Eldridge (porter), Percy Wood (station master), Bob Neal (lad porter).

Courtesy Len Hillman

No. 5805 on the branch train at Malmesbury, 7th August 1950.

W. A. Camwell

No. 5804 ready to leave for Little Somerford some time during 1949. It was unusual for any engine to run boiler-first to Little Somerford. Known and remembered locally as the 'Malmesbury Bunk', the branch train is said to have acquired this title because of the use of tank engines running bunker first. The term 'bunk' was in use on a number of other Great Western branch lines. *E. K. Lockstone*

Little Somerford, 7th August 1950, with the 11.35 train for Malmesbury departing from the down platform. Fireman Jim Long can be seen on the footplate of No. 5805, the most regular locomotive seen on the branch during the last three years of the passenger service. The coaches are B-set stock 6627/9. The flower beds, full of snapdragons, won several divisional prizes in the '50s. One of Higgs' taxis features in the background, behind the station nameboard.

W. A. Camwell

A 1949 view of an unidentified Collett 0–4–2T coming down from Little Somerford to Kingsmead Crossing. The ground frame controlled access to the old branch still used at this time for storage of damaged rolling stock from Swindon. The up fixed distant signal for Little Somerford was installed in July 1933.

John Robinson

These were quiet days on the branch, with time for engine crews to enjoy 'a cuppa' in the parcels office with station staff, having no mixed train to prepare any more. In the evening, checker George Eldridge would be in charge of the station and collect what few passenger tickets there were. It is possible that the line lost a lot of revenue through the ease with which it was possible to travel without paying on the non-corridor trains, it being very easy to evade ticket collection at Malmesbury station if the parcel porter was not on duty. When clerk Gilbert Moore left the railway in 1949, Mr Wood's daughter Sybil took on the job of clerk until the passenger service ceased.

A tale from the late '40s relates how a certain porter with a talent for playing practical jokes placed the head of a kipper in the top of the branch guard's hand lamp. When the guard lit the lamp to signal the engine driver to depart with the evening train to Little Somerford all seemed well until he entered his compartment to travel with the train. After some minutes the effect of the lighted wick on the concealed kipper polluted the van with a rotten fried fish smell, the cause of the trouble being discovered at Little Somerford and the incident providing much hilarity for a long time!

The quiet at Malmesbury station was broken during the summer months of 1949 with the dismantling of the RAF base at Long Newnton, an operation which placed heavy demands on the branch, with much movement of men and equipment, including the transport of many bombs. During

the week ending 16th July 1949, 175 wagons containing over 1,000 tons of equipment left Malmesbury for transfer to other units, and the traffic continued steadily until September, considerably boosting the line's goods tonnage to show a 50% increase over figures for 1948! A letter of 23rd July from the Adjutant at the base to the District Goods Manager at Temple Meads spoke most highly of the efforts of Mr Wood and his staff during this work;

No. 11 M.S.U. R.A.F
LONG NEWNTON,
TETBURY,
GLOS.
23.7.49.

Dear Sir,

On behalf of the Commanding Officer and myself, I wish to express our appreciation for the work of Mr. Woods and Staff of Malmesbury Station.

Great demands have been placed by this Unit on Malmesbury Station particularly during the last few weeks. It has often been impossible to give Mr. Woods any previous warning of our commitments but at all times he and his staff have provided an efficient and very willing co-operation so making our task so much lighter and happier.

It would be appreciated if our grateful thanks could be conveyed to Mr. Woods and all at Malmesbury Station for a job that has been very well done.

Yours faithfully,
(sgd) S. Benford F/O
Adjutant.
for Officer In Charge. No. 11 M.S.U.
Royal Air Force, Long Newnton.

The branch goods c.1950 and a portrait of Malmesbury's guards van No. 17501. This was attached to the rear of all goods trains, the branch guard maintaining its cabin and treating it as his own. Earlier allocations to Malmesbury were No. 35999, built in 1883 with outside wood framing and an iron underframe. It lasted in service until July 1933, the year the branch junction was changed. No. 8774 was a unique iron-bodied brake van built in 1887 and allocated to Malmesbury in February 1934. It was condemned in April 1936.

J. H. Moss

Freshly outshopped in the new British Railways all-over crimson, the branch coaches, viewed from Little Somerford signal box, are seen here with No. 5804 and fireman Jim Long.

W. A. Camwell

In 1950 the setting up of an agricultural machinery business at nearby Crudwell by A. B. Blanch & Co Ltd provided continuous business which enabled the branch to survive the 'fifties as a goods only line. Their main business was in consignments of sack and bale elevators, sending to the Scottish border country and abroad to France and Germany. The long boat-shaped well-wagons became a regular sight at the station for the handling of this machinery.

By 1950 the branch was losing a quoted figure of nearly £5,000 a year and a 50% loss of patronage was reported on the line since 1938. The line's future was now in serious doubt, and on 23rd January 1951, the press were kept out of a meeting in Malmesbury Town Hall convened to discuss the prospects for the branch's future. The meeting was attended by local councillors, members of local organisations and trade concerns in the town, and the British Railways (Western) District Commercial Superintendent Mr. H. Bolton and his deputy, Mr. G. S. Hodder. There were strong objections to the threat of closure from local farmers who used the line to send small livestock, representatives of Linolite Ltd, Electrolux Ltd, and other commercial concerns in the town, and from members of the District and Parish Councils affected. Passenger receipts for 1950 had totalled only £1,318, although the remaining business in parcels forwarded from Malmesbury boosted total passenger train traffic receipts to a nevertheless paltry £3,657 that year. Accounts for 1950 reveal only £11 worth of business in inward parcels received, a sad come down for a station that only ten years earlier had been receiving over 16,000 parcels annually. A survey was made of passenger use of the branch over a Monday to Saturday period, when the 11.35 ex-Malmesbury was found to total 23

passengers in the week, in daily totals of 4, 3, 4, 3, 4 and 5. The returning 11.58 was a very poorly-used train, a count of 14 passengers being yielded in counts of 8, 4, 1, 0, 0 and 1. Bus service alternatives now came under discussion.

The two bus routes, Malmesbury–Swindon and Malmesbury–Bristol, had been combined as Service No. 31, running as a through service between Swindon and Bristol via Malmesbury since 13th June 1948, providing a basic two-hourly service. In 1950/51 the town was served by around eight buses a day on the 295 route from Chippenham, charging a 2/- return fare. Two buses at weekends actually started their run from Malmesbury station, rather curiously as one of these ran at 4.13 p.m. on a Sunday but without any trains with which it could connect. All buses on this route called at Chippenham station. Malmesbury also benefited from the No. 223 Stroud–Trowbridge service with five buses each way daily. There were also two on Sundays on this run, a return to Trowbridge costing 3/9d, from Malmesbury to Stroud 2/9d. Malmesbury was also served by three coaches each way, seven days a week in the summer, by the Cheltenham–Bath–Portsmouth service, route No. 41 via Cirencester. With a variety of bus schedules and a high private car ownership in an affluent rural area, what need was there for a branch railway with a poor, run-down train service? For a rail journey to London it made more sense to take the bus to Chippenham as Mr. Wood had done himself, or go via Kemble if you could obtain a lift there.

In February 1951 the line's future looked even bleaker, during cuts in service imposed by a national fuel shortage and the consequent need to economise on the use of coal. On Saturday, 7th February the *Wilts & Glos Standard* announced

These views capture the changing atmosphere of the station at Malmesbury during 1950, with the new traffic provided by the Blanch agricultural machinery business of Crudwell boosting goods figures sufficiently to enable it to survive as a freight line for a further eleven years after passenger closure. Principal items for shipment appear to be straw elevators, probably destined for southern Scotland. The house where Bertram Farmer lived can be seen in the top view above the engine shed, a fine vantage-point from which to observe and develop an interest in the railway.

Bertram Farmer

'Railway Fuel Cuts Protest – Malmesbury line in the news again'. There was great resentment locally because neighbouring Tetbury had retained most of its trains during the coal shortage, but, with the exception of the daily freight, Malmesbury's service was cut completely from 12th February. Not surprisingly, lack of passengers using the line was the reason justifiably given for the temporary closure. Trains were restored on 2nd April, but only pending a decision on closure. The resumption of the passenger trains did little to cheer those few townspeople who used it, however, as the service was now reduced to a token three each way, with the extra run to Swindon on Saturdays. And yet during the last weeks of service fresh coats of brown and cream paint were seen being administered to the station buildings at Malmesbury!

On 24th May, Malmesbury Borough Council were informed that the line's passenger service would be withdrawn on 18th June, in a letter from British Railways Western Region signed by Supt. Bolton. The efforts of the council managed to succeed in staving off closure temporarily, and on 19th June, the Mayor and council journeyed to London together with local representatives of trade and industry for talks with the Railway Executive. These proved fruitless, however, and on 11th August the Executive informed the Borough Council that closure would take place on 10th September 1951.

The impending closure attracted some national attention. Early in September the *Daily Telegraph* and *Morning Post* published the following short article:

LAST TRIP OF "GHOST" TRAIN

'Malmesbury's 'ghost' train, which runs three times a day on the branch line between here and Little Somerford, 3½ miles away, will end its career on Saturday. It has been running since December 1877.

'British Railways have decided to withdraw the passenger service because it does not pay. Records over twelve months showed that the average number of passengers per train was only five.

'Up to a short time ago there were two season ticket holders. One bought a motor-cycle and now there is one. It is called the ghost train because, according to Mr. H. V. Bonner, member of Malmesbury Borough Council, "It runs nowhere and meets nothing".

'Except for an extra service on Saturday nights when it ventures into Swindon, the limit of its daily journeys is Little Somerford, on the Bristol–Swindon main line. On Sunday it rests.

'The normal journey to Swindon with a 10 or 15 minutes' wait for a connection at Little Somerford takes over an hour. Monthly return fare is 4s 8d. The two-hourly bus service does it in 50 minutes for 2s 5d return.

'The "ghost train" is also known affectionately as "The Bunk". Its first trip is 7.21 am. There is nothing more until 5.35 pm. When

LITTLE SOMERFORD AND MALMESBURY.

Single Line, worked by Train Staff, and only one engine in steam at a time (or two or more coupled).

DOWN TRAINS. WEEK DAYS.

Mile Post Distances M C.	M C.	STATIONS.	Ruling Gradient 1 in.	Pass.	Frght			Pass. SX		Pass.		Swindon Pass. SO		
89 61	—	Little Somerford .. dep.	—	a.m. 8 0	a.m. 10 5	..	..	p.m. 6 3	..	p.m. 7 3	..	p.m. 9 32	..	
93 35	3 60	Malmesbury arr.	50 F.	8 8	10 13	....	....	6 11	....	7 11	....	9 40	....	

UP TRAINS. WEEK DAYS.

STATIONS.	Ruling Gradient 1 in.	Pass.		Empties.			Pass. SX		Pass. SO	Pass. SX		Swindon Pass. SO	
Malmesbury .... dep.	....	a.m. 7 21	..	a.m. 8 30	..	..	p.m. 5 35	..	p.m. 6 21	p.m. 6 30	..	p.m. 7 25	..
Little Somerford arr.	50 R.	7 30	....	8 43	....	....	5 44	....	6 30	6 39	....	7 34	....

Little Somerford—Kingsmead Crossing.—Trains in either direction to reduce speed to 30 miles per hour.

Kingsmead Crossing—Malmesbury.—Trains in either direction to reduce speed to 10 miles per hour when approaching Caution Boards placed 300 yards from Crossing until passing over Crossing.

13 minutes to be allowed for Freight Trains over the Malmesbury Branch, in either direction, including "start" and "stop" allowances, also "Stop Board" requirements. (G. 17206.)

The rather depressing service provided by British Railways in the final days.

I made the round trip on the last train at 6.30 from Malmesbury I had the two well-kept coaches to myself. "That's nothing unusual," said Mr Hewlett, the guard, who has attended "The Bunk" for 14 years.

'We made Little Somerford in nine minutes. Mr. Benjamin Hill, 58, the driver, told me proudly of the merry days before the war, when his train shuffled breathlessly up and down the line about 14 times a day.

'An English railway died on Saturday night at 25 minutes past seven.

'She had been ill for a long time, suffering from "The Economics", a difficult disease to cure.

'Not very old, only 74, she was fairly long—six miles and 43 chains.

'Her passing was hardly noticed. She was given no State funeral and only a handful of mourners were present, including three pigs,

Last day group at Malmesbury on 8th September 1951 (left to right): Bert Reynolds with shunting pole (guard), Ken Stoneham (fireman), Dick Cooper (driver), Percy Wood (station master), George Eldridge (porter).

'He patted the sleek black boiler affectionately. "I am sorry she is going. It is a matey little train." On returning we were "crowded" with Mr. J. H. Lester, master at Malmesbury Grammar School, his wife, two children and luggage.

'Malmesbury Council and other organisations have put up a stiff fight to keep "The Bunk". An angry deputation to the Railway Executive in London failed to win a reprieve.

'When "The Bunk" whistles its last ghostly whistle next Saturday Alderman J. A. Jones, "father" of the council and a passenger on the first run in 1877, will be aboard. The last trip will be the first paying run for years.

From our SPECIAL CORRESPONDENT, Malmesbury, Wiltshire,
Sunday September 2nd, 1951.'

The 'Malmesbury Bunk' made its final run on Saturday, 8th September 1951, departing at 7.25 for all stations to Swindon. Mr. Wood took out a large number of tickets for the last run, in case he had to refill the ticket dispenser case, as he expected over a hundred passengers for the last run. In the event, only some 25 people boarded the train, some of whom only went as far as Little Somerford, and a disappointed Mr. Wood commented sadly, "People just don't seem to care any more". The train was hauled by Collett 0–4–2T No. 5805 and crewed by Dick Cooper and Ken Stoneham. Without any great ceremonial, beyond a handshake for the crew from Mr. Wood, the train left for Swindon, the trip described in somewhat sentimental fashion in the *Swindon Advertiser* the following Saturday.

two swans, a dozen children of the Modern Age, five excited women and myself.

'Mr Rowland Emmet was not present. Pity. For all his caricature he would have been sad at the closing by British Railways (Western Region) of the branch line from the township of Malmesbury to Little Somerford.

'Not even the Burgesses of Malmesbury who, be it confessed, had tried to prevent the closing of the line by the Railway Executive were there.

20-year-old engine

'There was no reverence at the passing of this famous, kindly, single-road railway. No flowers, not even a mourning band around the sleek, yet stumpy 0–4–2 engine, built in the Swindon works 20 years ago, affectionately called, by some, "The Bunk".

'Yet the engine did not need a raiment of mourning. She was black herself, with a shiny cleanliness of gleaming pistons and a cosy fussiness. She was the lovely black, prancing horse who drew the hearse, a credit to her groom, Malmesbury shedman, Pritchard.

'Soon "The Bunk", sole residuary legatee of this once delightful and prosperous line, will become lost, a drudge in sidings.

'I loved her from the moment she gave me an inviting, almost saucy, look to go aboard her footplate.

"Yes, you can come and help Dick Cooper to drive me, but I'm easy really. Just give me 120 lb of steam, open the accelerator and tell young Ken Stoneham to give a shovelful of coal now and then and I'll go anywhere you like, sedately and proudly."

'Mr R. W. ("Dick") Cooper has been with the engines since the 1914–18 war. Grey-haired, natty and clean in sky-blue jacket still encrested with the magic letters G.W.R., blunt in speech and

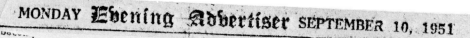

MONDAY *Evening Advertiser* SEPTEMBER 10, 1951

"THE BUNK'S" LAST RUN FROM MALMESBURY

By Melchior A. A. Sinkins
"Evening Advertiser" Special
Correspondent

AN English railway died on Saturday night at 25 minutes past seven.

prosperous line, will become lost, a drudge in sidings.

I loved her from the moment she gave me an inviting, almost saucy, look to go aboard her footplate.

"Yes, you can come and help Dick Cooper to drive

operate the passenger service between Malmesbury and Little Somerford.

But now I know why little boys become engine drivers, why grand types like Dick Cooper, 60-year-old Guard A. F. Hewlett and Stationmaster P. J. Wood and others who have lived with this little railway were sore at heart.

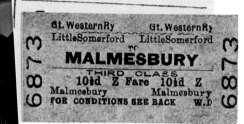

THE STATIONMASTER SAYS FAREWELL

The last train into Malmesbury, on its return from Swindon at 9.40 p.m., with local people on the bunker after souvenir lumps of coal. *Wiltshire Newspapers*

The last train from Malmesbury, the 7.25 all stations to Swindon, on 8th September 1951. Percy Wood is shaking hands with driver Dick Cooper, with Ken Stoneham looking on from the cab of No. 5805. Behind, Mr. Wood is leading porter, A. W. Archer acting as guard in the absence through illness of A. F. Hewlett. *Wiltshire Newspapers*

forthright of manner, he has earned his living for 20 years with "The Bunk". 'Course he loved her, too. You could see that.

'Dick gave a pull of the whistle lever and looked at his watch.

'It was 7.25. Our cortege moved off. Smoothly "The Bunk" and her two carriages slid away from trim, cream-and-brown, grey-stoned Malmesbury station. The last train—ever. No waving handkerchiefs. No ceremonial, nothing.

'We hissed our way along the single road, twisting, turning, past fields where cattle looked up at us and then went on chewing; past Kingsmead signal where an old man waved unhappily and Dick Cooper muttered a "cheerio" drowned in the snorting clanging of "The Bunk."'

'Into Little Somerford–and the mighty main line. Not a soul to welcome us.

'We were, for this journey, going on into Swindon.

'Brinkworth was the next stop. Here was great excitement. Two ladies and two boys cried: "What! Is this the last train we've been told about. Oh, driver, do wait!" They scooted for tickets and held up the train. "What's it matter?" said Dick Cooper. "I shan't be late."

A Service salute

'A gentleman with the R.A.F. tie reverently touched "The Bunk", saluted and shouted that he'd meet the four at Wootton Bassett in the car.

'He didn't. We were there first, and "The Bunk" chortled inwardly.

'The "Red Dragon" streaked by, screaming, to Bristol. The earth shuddered.

'Past the great sheds, a last long defiant blast on the whistle, dusk creeping over Swindon's signal boxes and rails.

'It was 7.59.

'Dick Cooper leaned from the cab. An inspector said: "Take her up 'The Loop.' ".

'No welcome. Not a murmur for the occasion. The little train lurched and disappeared into the vastness of Swindon Junction.

'The funeral was over. British Railways had officially ceased to operate the passenger service between Malmesbury and Little Somerford.

'But now I know why little boys become engine drivers, why grand types like Dick Cooper, 60-year-old Guard A. F. Hewlett and Stationmaster P. J. Wood and others who have lived with this little railway were sore at heart.'

The newspaper article omits to mention that the late run back from Swindon was made as usual, arriving back at Malmesbury on time at 9.40 p.m. A crowd of about 50 people gathered to welcome it back for the last time, the train's approach exploding several fog signal detonators which had been placed on the track. Several of the crowd climbed aboard 5805 and helped themselves to lumps of coal from the bunker as souvenirs. A last handshake for driver Cooper from Alderman Jones, who had travelled as a boy on the first ceremonial train on the line 74 years before, and Malmesbury's passenger service had ceased to be. On the following Monday, the official closure date, 5805 resumed service on the goods-only line. Dick Cooper was transferred to Oxford by the end of the year, although Ken Stoneham, Jim Long and Ben Hill continued to live locally and work the freight service. Percy Wood was redundant for a time but eventually secured a return to his native Wales the following year with his appointment to Barmouth. It is no surprise that with the curtailed train service, the temporary closure and the final cut in September, barely a thousand passenger tickets had been booked at Malmesbury during 1951, an average of just over one person per train.

Dick Cooper shaking hands with Alderman J. A. Jones, 'father' of Malmesbury Borough Council, the only person to travel on both the first and last passenger trains. As a boy in 1877 he had travelled on the first day special in the company of his father, A. Stephens Jones, a local tradesman and eminent shareholder in the Malmesbury Railway Company. *Wiltshire Newspapers*

CHAPTER NINE

AROUND MALMESBURY STATION IN LATER YEARS

The station building was built jointly by Brock & Bruce and George Drew of Chalford, the latter being paid £1,580 for his work on the building's stonework. The cobbled rockface style, achieved by the use of sandstone blocks dotted about the wall faces, was known as 'Engineers Gothic'. The quoins and window surrounds were also of sandstone. The timber porch, which has the appearance of an addition, was included on the original architect's plans, and led into a large waiting room, separated from the booking office area by a wooden counter. Off to the right was a smaller first class waiting room, which in turn led to a ladies room and lavatory. Both the general and first class waiting rooms had bay windows overlooking the forecourt. A store and gentlemen's lavatory were tucked away around the opposite corner of the building and only accessible from the platform. Staff also remember the area beneath the station being used as a cellar. The station was gas lit from the town supply, the meter being situated by the main yard gate near the large hoarding, but not until 1945 was it connected to mains water (and then only one tap!). Drinking water is said to have previously been sent from Dauntsey in churns. Although there was a well in a field which the company let for grazing, between the goods yard and the River Avon, it has not been recalled whether this was suitable drinking water. This picture was taken c.1947, but within living memory the porch was kept locked and only used for special occasions. Bert Vizor recalled an occasion in 1943 when it was used perhaps for the last time. The local train came in one lunchtime with an extra coach, from which a Union flag-draped coffin was carried through the waiting room and porch to a waiting hearse. Passengers entered and left the station through the gateway alongside the main building, but revenue was apparently lost when certain passengers apparently climbed down onto the track and walked off round the back of the train. Saturday nights were the worst time for this, especially in the dark, when they could slip away so easily while the ticket collector stood under the light.

M. E. J. Deane

A slightly later view of the station building and forecourt on 18th May 1948, very shortly after the removal of the entrance porch. The platform gates were usually left open for the arrival of mail vans and the GWR motor lorry collecting parcels, but one was closed to narrow the entrance during ticket collection.   *P. J. Garland*

A. Attewell

The brick building on the left was the old parcels office, with its larger 1912 successor alongside.

Don Pritchard

The south elevation of the station building showing Drew's sandstone embellishments to advantage. The small windows served the ladies waiting room, ladies lavatory, and the entrance behind the fence led into the gentlemen's lavatory. GWR records show that drinking water supply was not provided until July 1945, at a cost of £57 12s 0d.
J. H. Moss

The bay window in the shadowed north end wall and the window overlooking the forecourt served the general waiting room, whilst the gabled bay window section on the right, identical to the north end, enclosed the first class waiting room. The brick chimneys replaced the original stone ones which had started to crack during the mid-1920s. The £235 referred to on page 65 could have been for the chimney replacement. *J. H. Moss*

Looking towards the cattle pens and buffer stops during the final years.
A. Attewell

Malmesbury station platform in 1948, shortly after the arrival of the branch train with porter Bert Reynolds emerging from the porters room. There were no platform tickets at Malmesbury, the platform being open to the public who could stroll in to use the old VR post-box seen in the wall at this end of the building. In 1938 there were four daily collections at 10.30, 2.20, 4.45 and 7.40 but none on Sundays. The door alongside the post-box led into a tiny storeroom used for brooms and various cleaning materials. The skylight on the canopy is just discernible above the office window, and the double doorway leading into the waiting room and booking office was in shadows between the poster boards beyond the bicycles leaning against one of the platform barrows. The Bishop's cross incorporated in the decorative canopy supports was an attractive feature presumably prompted by the proximity of the Abbey. The Nestlé's chocolate machine between the barrows is fondly remembered by most people.
E.K. Lockstone

Two views of the new parcels office and its brick predecessor, originally the 'hot water hut'. Footwarmers were prepared here for the branch coaches before steam heating which had been introduced on the branch before February 1899 when £24 was authorised for the conversion of this building into a parcels office. When the larger parcels office was provided in 1912 at a cost of £58, the brick building became a porters room, apparently also used by the branch guards. There were two parcels weighing machines, a portable 30 cwt machine on wheels (No. 799) and a 5 cwt machine (No. 780) in the booking office. *A. Attewell*

The corrugated iron lamp hut housed a 40-gallon drum of paraffin on a trestle. It was filled with a tap and used to replenish signal lamps. Spare lamps and trimmings were also kept here together with roof lamps for oil-lit horse-boxes.
A. Attewell

These cattle pens were authorised in March 1895 at a cost of £230 which included a new approach. They replaced the original pens which, according to the 1889 Ordnance Survey, were situated by the loading dock behind the passenger platform. Whether this work was prompted by the need for improvement in cattle facilities or perhaps, more likely, to release the area in order to provide accommodation for milk traffic, is not recorded. However, it was certainly a distinct advantage on hectic market days to be able to deal with cattle away from the station forecourt. On market days a horse was used to haul wagons, a maximum of two at a time, from the 'middle road' to the pens for loading, then away through the engine shed to the other end of the same siding for collection by the engine. Most of the cattle traffic came from the market, which was held on the last Wednesday of the month. Up to forty wagons could be involved on these occasions when there was a steady procession of cattle drives from the Cross Hayes to the station. Just inside the main entrance, cattle were diverted to the left and through the double gates shown in the lower view. The single 5-bar gate further on divided the approach into a holding area and another enclosure immediately behind the pens. Until the 1920s the pens, constructed from old bridge rail, were limewashed when they were cleaned out, but after a change in regulations, disinfectant was used instead and applied with a hand spray. The water supply for cleaning the pens came from the water tank at the engine shed. Cattle traffic seems to have died out around 1944. The hut beyond the pens in the upper view was used for station coal (after removal of the bunker near the lamp hut), which was delivered as a wagon load about once a year. The same picture also shows the proximity of the Station Hotel. *A. Attewell*

A general view looking south from the station platform c.1949.

J. H. Moss

No. 5802 awaiting departure with the branch train on 18th May 1948. The gate on the right was used as an additional manned exit on arrival of unusually busy trains such as returning football specials; otherwise it had simply been used for empty milk churns unloaded on the platform. Before milk was lost to the roads in the 1930s, large numbers of churns from Wiltshire Farmers had been loaded alongside the dock road behind the platform. The average load was apparently two Siphon Js and about three small Siphons and sometimes an insulated van. Because of the layout of the station, milk traffic went out on the front of the train and returned as tail traffic, empty churns generally being unloaded on the platform before the vehicles were propelled back into the yard and rolled into the dock with a pinch bar.

P. J. Garland

Malmesbury engine shed was another of the structures included in the original contract drawings. Built with substantial stone walls and a slate roof, the gable ends were enclosed with timber. The internal dimensions were officially recorded as 50ft 7in long, 20ft—20ft 7in wide with a height to the ridge and wall plates of 21ft 6in and 16ft respectively. It was equipped with a full length smoke trough, which projected at each end to improve draughting, and there was a 40ft 4in long pit between the rails, the only one at the site. A long brick lean-to with slate roof, added along the west side of the building at an unknown date, provided much needed accommodation for a stores 9ft long x 8ft 3in, an office 8ft 3in long x 8ft 2in and an enginemen's cabin 8ft 4in x 8ft 4in. The height to the wall plate and ridge are recorded as 10ft and 12ft 5in. This appendage is featured on page 192.

P. J. Garland

A closer view of the northern end of the building showing the projecting end of the smoke trough and the glazing above the doors. Both of these pictures were taken on 18th May 1948.

P. J. Garland

The water tank/coaling stage and pumphouse were erected by the GWR for the opening of the line at a cost of £154 12s 0d. Measuring 12ft x 12ft x 7ft, and supported on cast iron columns, it had a capacity at 6ft 6in of 5,850 gallons. The supply came from a well alongside, water being raised by a vertical steam pump powered by steam from the branch loco. A 1907 plan describes it as a two-throw pump 5¼in x 16in. Before the Second World War the pump was connected via a swivel-jointed pipe in place of one of the whistles, but later, when the pump was changed, a flexible pipe was connected to the steam heating pipe on the engine instead. The pumphouse itself, to the right of the picture, was a wooden building 8ft 6in long by 6ft 6in wide, with heights to the ridge and wall plate of 9ft and 6ft 6in. The coal stage beneath, measuring 12ft 5in x 10ft 3in, in later years at least, was primarily used to hold a coal reserve, locos being coaled direct from a wagon stabled at the buffer stop end of the adjacent or middle siding alongside. Besides replenishing the tanks of the branch locomotive, the water tank additionally supplied a hydrant inside the shed, another on the cattle pens, and the 'Not Drinking Water' supply to the station. Although practice varied over the years, most crews would only take water here before the first train in the morning and use the Little Somerford supply during the rest of the day to save pumping at Malmesbury.

J. H. Moss

Looking south from the platform end, with the branch train arriving from Little Somerford one summer's day c.1949. Some members of staff liked to pop into the Railway Hotel, but such visits could become quite an embarrassment if the home signal was left at danger when the train arrived. The driver would keep blowing the whistle until a figure was seen flying out of the hotel and down the yard towards the signal box! Even after the branch track had been relaid, the middle road retained flat-bottomed rail spiked to the sleepers, until c.1946-7 when it had finally deteriorated to the point where it had to be replaced with the concrete block and tiebars shown. The pile of new sleepers on the left were ready for re-timbering some of the station pointwork. The ballast foot crossing was laid by the ganger by special request of the loco crews who wanted to wheel their bicycles over to the shed!   *J. H. Moss*

Two more views of the running line taken before the arrival of the train shown on the opposite page.

J . H. Moss

A leafy view of the station from the top of the Abbey c.1949. A similar view greeted visitors wandering between the grounds of the Abbey and Abbey House. *Collection M. E. J. Deane*

A view from the station yard with the Railway Hotel in the distance.   *M. E. J. Deane*

This winch was provided in later years to assist in loading Blanch's farm machinery. The cable was run via a bollard behind the station fence.   *A. Attewell*

The dilapidated coal store and office along the western boundary of the yard once occupied by A. L. Curtis and later the Dolphin Coal Company. The weighbridge and office on the right belonged to the railway, the 12-ton Pooley cart machine GW No. 3889 measuring 12 ft x 6 ft 6 in dating from 1936 when it replaced an earlier one at a cost of £120. The checker issued weigh tickets here dealing mainly with traffic coming in by rail, the weight being a vital part of many transactions. A weighbridge book was kept here to record tickets issued and gross and tare weights. The balancing and testing of the machine was also recorded, accuracy being within 3½ lb.

A. Attewell

Most wooden loading gauges had been replaced long before this one was photographed on 18th May 1948. Indeed, it would be interesting to know quite how much longer it would have survived had it not been pulled over by a high load within a few months of this picture being taken. The sign behind it is said to have warned of clearances.   *P. J. Garland*

Another view of the weigh bridge and coal offices. The guard rail was provided to deter the casual passage of vehicles over such precision equipment.

In January 1900 the GWR authorised the construction of a footpath from the town to the station. Much of it was on their land alongside the goods yard boundary. The cost was £60, the local council contributing £20 of this.

A warm June evening in 1947 and a peaceful walk from the station yard up to the Abbey and town.

Bert Vizor

Most country stations had spare land utilized as garden allotments by the staff. At Malmesbury the area between the north side of the forecourt and cattle pen approaches and land to the east of the running line, opposite the yard, were given over to cultivation. The area shown here c.1947 was also used by Jim Thornbury for poultry.

The goods shed, a comparatively commodious design for a small branch line, was built in stone with a slate roof. Inside was a wooden platform, a lock-up at the south end and two small 1½ ton cranes. Skylights illuminated the interior, which was also gas lit, and four sliding doors enclosed the rail and road entrances. Curiously, a timber-built wall enclosed the south end of the building, as shown on page 179, leaving that end of the side walls virtually free-standing. Evidently, they must have been subject to some kind of subsidence to have warranted the substantial brick buttresses on the west side of the south end of both walls. The original plans show steps leading up to the checker's office door, but, assuming they were built, they were evidently removed and access confined to the doorway from the loading area inside. The 1½ ton crane was used to unload items inside the goods shed but heavy goods were unloaded at Little Somerford and taken to Malmesbury on the Chippenham lorry. It has not been established when the doors were removed from the goods shed, leaving the contents of the building vulnerable, apart from the small lock-up, but it certainly continued to deteriorate. Broken windows in the eastern elevation were attributed to the school holidays of 1944. Those in the forecourt elevation, presumably suffering a similar fate, were eventually boarded up and, after passenger closure, the roof was felted over instead of being re-slated.   *Don Pritchard*

The desk inside the checker's office ran the length of the wall and the telephone was an extension from the booking office. The checker could ring the office for a line out. Incoming wagon labels were 'filed' on a hanging rod.   *Don Pritchard*

A grounded body was provided, perhaps during the 1930s, alongside the south end wall of the goods shed, as featured on page 174. It was used to store Portland Cement for the local agent Pontins the ironmongers, and bore an enamel sign. Railway staff apparently handed the bags out on receipt of a ticket. By the time this picture was taken in the final years, the van had gone but it is not clear whether its disappearance had any connection with damage caused when the loco pushed some wagons out of the goods shed with their doors left hinged open onto the platform, taking much of the timber wall with them! The flat wagons shown here were for Blanch's agricultural machinery.   *A. Attewell*

The forecourt elevation, looking very sorry with its boarded up windows dating from the 1930s. Locals still recall how as children they used to enter the shed and play hide-and-seek or marbles. By the 1940s it was left completely open on Sundays and children played uninterrupted amongst the parcels stacked inside. It was rare that any theft was ever reported.

Don Pritchard

The station and yard in 1949. The photograph provides a surprisingly rare glimpse of the station entrance. The manner in which the railway went beyond the town rather than stopping short of it is quite apparent here. The tomb of engineman Jones, seen on page 241, is located in Malmesbury Cemetery on the Tetbury Road, towards the top of the photograph. The Cross Hayes square and Town Hall are visible in the bottom right corner.

Hunting Aerofilms Ltd.

Samuel Fisher was running a coal business at Malmesbury around the turn of the century, operating from the office shown alongside the weighbridge office on page 44. In January 1920 the business was taken over by Arthur Curtis, a firm apparently dating from before the First World War. Curtis delivered with a horse and cart and later a Model T Ford and is thought to have had his own private owner wagons. Although these wagons were taken over by Fisher, apparently by the late '20s they were not in use. Other coal companies in Malmesbury in the period after the branch junction was switched to Little Somerford, were the Brooks Coal Co., based at the Three Cups public house in the Triangle, and Jack Giles, who it is believed took over the Brooks operation when he married into the family. Giles's lorry was kept in the Tan Yard in Dark Lane. However, as far as it has been possible to ascertain, although both these businesses used the station to collect incoming coal, neither had wharfage space there. Although it is now difficult to be precise about wharfage, the areas shown on this page, including the corrugated iron stable, were used largely by the Fisher business and its successors, although their office was farther up the yard by the weighbridge hut. Around 1933 the bankrupt Curtis business was bought up by the Dolphin Coal & Coke Co. Ltd. and the corrugated open-fronted bagging shed and store, featured in the two upper views, was erected during this time. The 1933 view on page 129 shows Dolphins' sign in place in the yard by this time. The rear of this store was supported on old sleepers and after the war the floor apparently collapsed under the weight of the coal being stored there. Afterwards it fell into disrepair and was used for the storage of empty coal sacks and bars of salt. *A. Attewell*

The Malmesbury Coal Company, earlier Alexander & Furzey, received coal at Malmesbury station, but had no office or permanent dump in the yard, only a small hut which served as a store and mess room for the coalmen. This building had been removed by the time the photos in this chapter were taken, but it is visible in the views on pages 110, 134 and 139. It was their policy to cart deliveries direct from the railway wagons to avoid double-handling and ground rent, incurring demurrage charges instead. Their main office and weighbridge was in Gloucester Road, with other depots in Tetbury and at Great Somerford station, this last being moved to Little Somerford after the junction change of 1933. The MCC are said to have had three private owner wagons, but no photographic evidence has been found to confirm their existence. They are believed to have been numbered 5, 6 and 7. In 1937 the MCC was taken over by Harold Gladwin, a baker, who had two Ford 'A' lorries for country deliveries and a horse and cart around the town, although for many years local townsfolk collected their own supplies in old prams. Gladwin's business was taken over by the Bristol-based firm of Thomas Silvey Ltd. in 1947, this firm establishing a new depot in the station yard by early 1949. Much of the coal for Malmesbury came from the Cannock Main Colliery in Staffordshire and the Camerton Coal Company. *A. Attewell*

A closer view of the corrugated iron stable, used for the Fisher/Curtis/Dolphin horses, better illustrated in the earlier view on p. 111. A hay loft was incorporated beneath the curved roof. The large coal dumps here were right against the western boundary fence which was skirted by the GWR-provided footpath to the town — a place to avoid on a dry windy day! *A. Attewell*

The southern end of the goods shed c.1947.
M. E. J. Deane

In December 1948 the GWR authorised the preparation of an 'area of approx 80 sq yds for coal stacking purposes to be taken over by Messrs. T. Silvey Ltd. at exc rate of 4s 9d per annum'. This is thought to have referred to the land to the east of the coal siding, alongside the running line as shown here. It is evident from the previous photo that this area was certainly not used before this date. Silvey's lorry can just be seen in the distance.
A. Attewell

The Pratts tank illustrated on page 111 was situated at the bottom of the yard, beyond the buffer stops. It is remembered as surrounded by a wall inside a corrugated iron fence with a 'saw tooth' top. Regular tank wagons supplied this depot from which Pratts apparently wholesaled their fuels — mainly paraffin. It is thought that the tank was removed through a centralisation of distribution at Chippenham. Unfortunately, no photographs of the Malmesbury depot have yet come to light.
A. Attewell

A closer view of Lovers Lane crossing where the footpath leading up onto the Worthies and the cricket ground crossed the line. *A. Attewell*

Looking towards the station from Lovers Lane crossing c.1948-9, showing the platelayers hut and the timber post home signal with a replacement enamel arm. The two Iron Mink vans on the end of the siding may have been condemned vehicles Nos. 37055 and 59513 which, according to GWR records, in October 1948 were prepared for use as storage vans at Malmesbury.
M. E. J. Deane

Ted Jones with '517' Class 0–4–2T No. 573 at Malmesbury c.1909. This locomotive was built at Wolverhampton and, weighing 29 tons 2 cwt empty, 36 tons 4 cwt in working order, was completed in March 1870 at a cost of £1,058. According to official allocations, 573 first appeared at Malmesbury in February 1907 from Swindon Works. During April 1908 she underwent light running repairs at Swindon, during which time No. 545 came to the branch in her place. Afterwards 573 returned, being continuously allocated to Malmesbury shed until January 1909, when she went back to Swindon and thence to the Tetbury branch. 573 was condemned in February 1915 after running 896,985 miles. The fireman on the footplate is thought to be Fred Morbey, who was 1st Class fireman at Malmesbury during 1908–13 before being promoted to driver at Swindon. By the time this photograph was taken, lamp irons had already been largely adopted over the GWR system to replace the sockets and older spigot lamps still evident here.

Courtesy Mr. & Mrs. K. Iles

CHAPTER TEN

LOCOMOTIVE DEPARTMENT
MEN, MACHINES & SHED DUTIES

IT is possible that during the first weeks of operation the branch was worked temporarily by Swindon-based crews, as Malmesbury's engineman of earliest days, Nicholas Gray, did not start until February 1878, two months after the line opened. Born in May 1826, Gray had been a passenger fireman at Paddington, during which time he had fired the GWR's crack broad gauge express, the 'Flying Dutchman', which made the run between London and Swindon in 87 minutes. He was to remain at Malmesbury for the rest of his life, living in Gloucester Street not far from the terminus and retiring on 12th February 1892. He died on 11th February 1898. His 14 years on the branch set a pattern for long service on the branch. Throughout the 73 years of the passenger service no more than ten drivers were based at Malmesbury shed.

The only other known employee at Malmesbury shed from the earliest days of the branch was an interesting character who, for the purposes of this book, must remain nameless on account of his careless handling of company stock before coming to the new line. He was a Welshman of somewhat erratic disposition and not a little irresponsible, with a liking for tobacco, alcohol and a good time, and a remarkable persistence, which explains his ability to stay in railway employment despite a catalogue of misdemeanours which would have persuaded lesser men to quit. During a six-year period in South Wales he ran up a succession of fines, reprimands, cautions and suspensions for such crimes as running a pilot engine into the Irish Goods, causing collisions through running past signals at danger and damaging engine firebox and tubes through allowing his locomotive to run short of water. He was dismissed on more than one occasion, receiving a discharge at Gellyrhaidd Junction in 1874 for the incredible faux pas of 'stopping 3 or 4 hours and going to a dancing party at a farmhouse close to the line'! Finding himself out of a job in September 1877 after a dismissal, this intrepid fellow found his way to Wiltshire where he managed to find himself work as a driver on the still nominally independent Malmesbury line, away from eagle eyes of Cardiff and Paddington, where he remained for a long time and gave the branch good service beyond the occasional failure to maintain the branch locomotive properly, and sporadic displays of initiative such as reversing his train before receiving the correct signal to do so, resulting in points being turned between coach wheels! Paddington must have turned a blind eye to his past record in view of this long service at Malmesbury, for although later tests found his sight and colour vision suspect, he was allowed to remain on branch work and advised to be 'very careful in the use of tobacco and alcohol'. With no prospects of promotion, understandably, he stayed on a fixed rate of 4/9d a day at Malmesbury, although his incident-free performance during the 1880s did earn him a rise of 3d a day in December 1889. He was undoubtedly a durable and endearing character, giving the Malmesbury line 31 years service before his retirement in January 1908. He died in 1909.

A fuller and entertaining account of the railway career of this early personality of the Malmesbury Railway can be read in Adrian Vaughan's *Grub Water & Relief.*

Branch enginemen before the Great War were often older men wishing to move to the quieter life on a country line after rigorous years on main line work. Undoubtedly the most senior of Malmesbury's drivers was James Turner, who was already 64 years of age when he succeeded Nicholas Gray as branch engineman on 25th January, 1892 on a fixed rate of 7/- a day having transferred from the Swindon shed. He stayed for six years, then on the 8th February 1898 a note was handed to him at 6.15 pm informing him that his services would not be required after he attained the age of 70, and he duly retired on his birthday the following month, 9th March, to be replaced by Edward Jones.

Edward (Ted) Jones was Malmesbury's best-known engineman of earlier years, standing out prominently on early-century photographs with his beard and heavy frame. He was born in Ruabon in North Wales on 18th March 1848, and began work on the GWR as an engine cleaner at Chester in 1870 on a daily rate of 3/6d. He became a 3rd class engineman at Newton Abbot in August 1884, progressing to 2nd Class at Bristol in December 1890 at 7/- a day. Unfortunately, owing to poor vision in his left eye and a weak colour sense, he was never able to attain 1st Class, and after his eyesight test for the top link in November 1897 proved unsatisfactory, he was taken off main line work and became a shedman in Bristol as a temporary post until a driver's vacancy came up on a branch line.

Jones was keen to remain in the Bristol area, particularly as one of his sons was apprenticed in the loco fitting department there, and in March 1898, he arrived in Malmesbury to drive the branch train for the next fifteen years and was to remain there the rest of his life. His daily rate of pay on the branch was 5/6d.

Because of his poor eyesight, Jones had to submit to a biennial eye examination and should have retired at the age of 60 in 1908, but with his excellent health, an improvement in vision and his exemplary driving record, in February 1908 GWR Supt. Churchward agreed to Jones remaining in service providing his eyesight did not deteriorate. He therefore continued until 19th March 1913.

Ted and his wife, Mary, raised four children and resided at 78, The Triangle, a short walk up Gloucester Street from the station. One of his sons, George, later became a guard on the famed 'Cheltenham Flyer'. Ted died in 1926, the local newspaper publishing a short account under the heading 'Death of old Railway Servant'. Today, in Malmesbury cemetery, a short walk from the old station site, Ted Jones's gravestone bears a '517' class locomotive carved on the stone and bearing the number '844'. This locomotive was present as the branch engine allocated to Malmesbury shed for most the year 1911, and it was during this year that one of Ted's sons, Alfred, took several photographs at the terminus

Ted Jones on the footplate of a sparkling '517' Class No. 844 by the water tower at Malmesbury in 1911. It is this engine that is depicted on Jones's tombstone (see page 241). Ted's son, George John Jones, is thought to be the young man shown here, the photograph possibly being taken to mark George's arrival at Malmesbury. Born in 1890, he worked as a cleaner at Didcot shed before promotion to fireman at Malmesbury on 1st February 1911 at 3/- a day. He moved on to Reading before the end of the year and later became a main line driver there.
Courtesy Mr. & Mrs. K. Iles

showing his father on the footplate of 844. After his death, therefore, it must have seemed appropriate to remember this particular engine on his tombstone.

Ted Jones is still remembered by older generations in the Malmesbury area – one delightful octogenarian recalled how as a girl her mother would take her to London each November for Lord Mayor's Show Day, and they would begin their journey by walking to Kingsmead Crossing where a large bearded driver with a cheerful Welsh accent would stop the train for them to board, beyond the rules of course, but this was known to happen on many a country branch, whereby people were picked up or set down near their homes rather than leave them with a long walk from a station. If Ted Jones was not a famous name at Paddington, the decorated tomb in the cemetery represents a close identification between man and the machine with which he worked, and is indicative of the pride Ted Jones took in his work, the respect he had for the GWR of which he knew he was a vital cog, and the respect and esteem in which he was held in his adopted Malmesbury.

The retirement of Ted Jones saw the arrival of a much younger man, Bill Eveleigh, who was only 31 when he arrived at Malmesbury on 20th March 1913. Born in 1882, he started work as a cleaner at Weymouth shed on 14/- a week in March 1889, becoming a shunting fireman there the following year. In January 1903 he was promoted to goods fireman, then two months later moved to Yeovil where he attained the rank of 1st class fireman in November 1911 at a rate of 5/- a day. His move to Malmesbury brought him a rise of 6d a day as 3rd group engineman, with rises and the doubling of GWR pay after the war bringing him 17/10d a day by 1921. Both at Malmesbury and elsewhere he maintained a flawless driving record and reliability which benefited the branch service, and he eventually moved back to Yeovil at his own request in August 1930, retiring voluntarily in June 1944.

Before the 1920s the job of firing on the Malmesbury branch was simply a step on the promotional ladder for younger men, although after the war and into the Depression this pattern was to change as men tended to hold on to their jobs if they were secure. However, before the Great War, a succession of firemen came and went in appointments varying from a few months to about five years. William Cambridge was such a

Ted Jones and wife Mary at home at 78 The Triangle, Malmesbury.   *Courtesy Mr. & Mrs. K. Iles*

Another 1911 view of No. 844 at Malmesbury. It is said that Ted Jones never shaved in his lifetime, the beard reaching his waist. He wore a rubber collar and when coming off duty he would wash his face, beard and collar in a bucket of hot water from the engine.

Courtesy Mr. & Mrs. K. Iles

man – he was a cleaner at Gloucester shed and came to Malmesbury in May 1894 to fire under James Turner. The only incident of note in his work at Malmesbury was an accident he sustained in January 1895 whilst working an evening train to Dauntsey – a lump of coal fell from the bunker and badly bruised his left foot, causing him to lose two days' work. He left the branch in December 1895 to return to Gloucester as a goods driver.

During the early years of the new century Ted Jones appears to have been plagued with a succession of unreliable firemen, whose unsuitability for the work was reflected in absence, epileptic fits while on duty and even refusal to work as directed. One young man, who transferred from Didcot shed to become shunting fireman in April 1905, was regularly cautioned for failure to look after equipment properly. He repeatedly neglected to clean the engine thoroughly and in May 1905 caused damage to No. 1155's whistle stem when he omitted to disconnect the pumping apparatus at the shed before moving the engine, and, when a repeat of this incident three months later caused damage to No. 545's whistle and steam pipes, he was given his notice on 13th September. He remained for a further week, during which time he refused to undertake any cleaning duties at all and was paid off and left on 22nd September. No doubt Ted Jones was glad to obtain the services of Fred Morbey, who moved from Bristol in January 1908 as a 1st class fireman on 4/6d a day at Malmesbury shed, and gave five years' consistent and reliable service before earning a promotion to 3rd group engineman at Swindon in January 1913, shortly before Jones retired.

During this period Jones' own son John spent most of 1911 as a 3/- a day fireman at Malmesbury.

As the branch locomotive required constant supervision to keep it 'in steam' all week, Malmesbury shed employed a cleaner who worked nights on the engine. Although it is fairly certain that Malmesbury shed would have employed a night man from its earliest days, no details of any cleaners have emerged from the records for the Victorian years. The earliest appointment found in documentation for Malmesbury was Alfred 'Buller' Reeve, who worked nights there from September 1917. He transferred to Lambourn in January 1918 as a 3rd group fireman, then returned to Malmesbury at his own request in May 1919, firing for driver Joe Halliday until September 1929 when he left for Swindon, eventually becoming a main line driver there. It may have been that as a result of the war there was a shortage of men to maintain locos at main sheds, so work had to be devolved onto branch sheds in order to maintain the high standard of maintenance of GWR stock. Certainly, from 1917 until 1951 the Malmesbury shed had a cleaner each night, although this was not necessary on Saturday nights after 1935 with no Sunday train.

During the dark days of World War I a young man arrived at Malmesbury shed whose career there was to extend almost until nationalisation. Joe Halliday was born in February 1887 and entered service as a cleaner at Lydney in 1904. In 1905 he moved to Alcester as a shunting fireman on 3/- a day, then in 1910 moved to the huge Tyseley depot near Birmingham as a goods fireman 3rd class, earning 3/9d a day. He excelled himself here and was promoted to 2nd class which merited a

'517' Class No. 545 with the branch train in the Malmesbury branch bay at Dauntsey in 1925. The engine crew are Joe Halliday (left, with moustache), and Buller Reeve, then fireman, later top Swindon driver. On the platform with shunting pole is long-time Dauntsey porter Percy Wakefield.
Courtesy Derek Hayes

further 1/- a day, then in August 1916 took the opportunity to work on a country branch when he attained 1st class fireman at Malmesbury, earning a daily rate of 5/-. He clearly enjoyed his time on the branch, staying there for three years, and though he went back to Lydney for promotion to 3rd group engineman in 1919, he only stayed a few months before returning to Malmesbury later in the year at his own request to become branch driver, a position now earning 12/- a day. Joe was a jovial sprightly man who drove the 'Bunk' accordingly – if he was on the footplate it was usually possible to tell, his style being characterised by the quicker manner in which his train approached the platform. He retained links with the Birmingham area, having an affinity for the Aston Villa soccer team, and carried an impeccable driving record through his entire time at Malmesbury. He retired on 22nd February 1947.

The best-loved driver of later days on the branch was Dick Cooper, but his association with the line began as early as 1919. Born in 1899, in London, he was brought up in Swindon where he started on the shed as a cleaner in June 1919, progressing there to a 9/6d a day fireman. He married a Malmesbury girl and at his own request obtained a job there as fireman in December 1919, staying in that capacity for twenty years until war broke out, firing first for Bill Eveleigh then for Ben Hill. He was a keen sportsman, being a fair boxer, and joined the Army Reserve in 1928. He was called up and went off to war on 4th September 1939, working in the railway operating service. During his absence from Malmesbury, in December 1941, his post at home was reclassed as 'temporary' and he was promoted to the rank of driver on 78/- a week. On his return from military service in December 1945 a job as relief driver was found for him in Bristol, paying 92/6d a week, pending the provision of a permanent appointment in his adopted Malmesbury. That opportunity arose with the retirement of Joe Halliday, and Dick Cooper duly returned to the branch on 7th February

'517' Class No. 217 at Malmesbury in the summer of 1930. Driver Bill Eveleigh and fireman Dick Cooper are on the footplate, with checker George Woodward just visible uncoupling the loco from the branch set.   *Bertram Farmer*

1947, where he stayed until the end of the passenger service in 1951. During the temporary cessation of passenger trains between 12th February and 2nd April 1951, he was loaned to the now British Railways' shed at Swindon, his pay as branch driver in the final year of the branch being 149/6d a week. After closure of the branch he was transferred to Oxford where he worked expresses to London, Wolverhampton and Portsmouth until his death in 1961. During his entire career his driving record was flawless.

When Bill Eveleigh transferred to Yeovil in 1930, his place was taken by Walter Anthney, a Weymouth man who had been working Channel Islands traffic, then came to Malmesbury as driver at his own request on 8th August 1930. Why he wished to come to the branch is not known, and the following month he went back to Weymouth for a short spell before returning to Malmesbury at the end of September 1930. Evidently Wiltshire did not work out for him, as he followed Bill Eveleigh to Yeovil in January 1931, eventually going back to the coast, and his position at Malmesbury was taken by Ben Hill, who stayed on the branch until long after passenger closure twenty years later.

Between the wars, unlike the pre-1914 days, the pattern of occupation altered greatly as far as Malmesbury was concerned. With pay substantially better, and a secure job harder to come by, especially as the Depression tightened its grip in the 30s, the country branch became less of a temporary training ground for young men 'shilling-chasing' in search of promotion. Especially in a pleasant rural area such as Malmesbury, men tended to value their lot and stay put, hence the firing duties on the branch in the years between the wars were undertaken almost entirely by three men, Dick Cooper, Buller Reeve and Les Jones, the last-named arriving on 24th September 1929, to replace Buller Reeve. Jones gave the branch ten years firing for Joe Halliday until promotion to Tyseley on 21st March 1938, going on to be a main line driver in the Midlands until retirement in 1965. During the war years of the '40s, firing on the branch was done by Jim Long and Charlie Barnes, the latter leaving for Salisbury in 1945 and being replaced by Ken Stoneham who worked as Dick Cooper's fireman from 1947 onwards.

Benjamin Hill arrived on the branch in January 1931 as branch driver. Born in July 1893 he, too, took the typical career road, from cleaner on Hereford shed to High Wycombe in 1923. Here he attained 1st class fireman status on the main line services, but as he worked many long distance routes, he found the strain of 'double-home' working too much and, wishing to work closer to home, transferred to Malmesbury, moved into Pool Gastons Road, earned 90/- a week and stayed to outlive the branch passenger service, retiring early in 1954 through ill-health.

In 1942 a third generation of the Thornbury family worked on the branch. Ernest had been the carman and worked on the permanent way gang, Jim had started his railway life as a lad porter at Malmesbury in the '20s and now Jim's son Norman started on the shed as the night cleaner.

WORK ON SHED

Routine maintenance work was done on the branch locomotive at night in the shed by the night cleaner and could be accomplished by the fireman on the afternoon shift. Anything more serious would require fitters being sent out from Swindon. Regular boiler washing was necessary to avoid

Joe Halliday and his fireman Les Jones (right) aboard Collett No. 5802 some time during the mid-1930s. *Courtesy Iris Jones*

build-up of scale and it is possible that in earlier days a boilersmith would have come out from Swindon once a week to do the job, assisted by the night cleaner. As cold water jets were used, it would have been necessary to cool the boiler before wash-out to avoid damaging the boiler metal when hot. There would not normally have been time to cool it, do the wash and raise steam in time for the next day's service, so could this important maintenance have been done on a Sunday, as the engine would not normally be required for Sunday service until the evening? Hot water wash-out came into use at large sheds around 1905, so it is likely that after this the Malmesbury engine would be sent off to Swindon for its boiler cleaning on a Saturday night when the last run of the day was made out to Dauntsey. There a Swindon crew would meet the branch train with a fresh temporary locomotive and take the branch's allocated engine off to the Works, usually returning it within 24 hours. Without the need to wait for the boiler to cool down, the job was thus quicker and engines re-exchanged at Dauntsey. Of course, in this way many locomotives, other than those shown in the records, must have found their way onto the Malmesbury line, not to mention the pannier tanks and goods classes which would have worked market specials.

'Buller' Reeve worked at Malmesbury shed towards the end of the Great War and recalled the routine at that time. His real name was Redvers Alfred Reeve but he was nicknamed after General Redvers Buller of the African War. Before starting on the railway he had worked for the local bacon factory, often visiting the station to collect pigs that came in by rail. They were driven along the road using a stick and kept in a small field alongside the factory before going into the slaughter house. Even before being employed, young 'Buller' had often helped to drive the pigs up to the factory.

In 1917 the railway was in need of crews and when a cleaner's vacancy arose at Malmesbury, 'Buller' applied for it. Before the curtailment of services that November, his duty started at about 10.00 p.m. but he usually arrived about 9.45 when the crew were still busy with disposal and had started to pump water.

They had arrived back at Malmesbury with the last train at 9.30 p.m., the coaches were left in the platform and the loco run onto the shed road alongside the loco coal wagon which was positioned at the end of the 'spare road'. Here the fireman began the laborious task of coaling direct from the wagon, a task which proved much easier if the wagon was empty enough to shovel coal off the bottom. It usually took about half an hour to fill the bunker, after which the engine was taken through to the farthest end of the shed to pump water, using a small vertical cylinder pumping engine powered by steam from the branch engine, which was connected by means of a steam pipe (attached to the end wall of the shed) coupled in place of one of the whistles. It took about 30–45 minutes to

Top: This doorway along the west wall inside the shed led into the cleaners' mess. Another door alongside led to the drivers' office, where, below the window, there was a desk for writing up records. Inside, another door from here led into the oil store. Crews would leave items required by the night man on the bench along the wall of the shed. Below: The fireplace that once comforted Buller Reeve and the local policeman in the small hours.
Paul Karau

View south through the shed, showing the inspection pit.

A. Attewell

fill the 3000 gallon tank which was usually only about a quarter full at this time of night.

The fire had been run down to a minimum and when the pumping was completed, the grate was cleaned and the fire thrown out. In the meantime the driver went into his office, which was always kept locked, to log the engine's mileage, etc., book any repairs and issue young 'Buller' with his cleaning equipment which included cotton waste, a flare lamp and oil, and a fire-lighter for later on. Certainly in later years, if the

would lose water, so it was sometimes better to light up an hour earlier and get the injectors on as soon as possible.

Buller recalled that locos were changed about every 7–10 days, but sometimes, if the loco needed attention, like gland packing, etc., a fitter was sent from Swindon to work in the shed overnight. This was a popular duty, for if the problem could be sorted out in a reasonable time, it was possible to spend the rest of the night asleep before returning on the first train!

This 1931 view of the station shows the brick-built lean-to office and stores built alongside the shed, contrasting with the original stone-work and displacing two of the original side windows.   *Bertram Farmer*

crew finished in time, they would lock the office/stores and retire to the Railway Hotel for a drink, leaving 'Buller' alone to carry out his cleaning duties.

'517' class No. 839 was regularly shedded at Malmesbury at this time, and 'Buller' remembered that the chimney and even the buffer heads still were being scoured, although the latter was apparently 'optional'. It was customary to start with the frames and motion which were cleaned thoroughly from the inspection pit below. The only break in this lonely duty was the usual visit from the local policeman 'from Newton and the Somerfords'. He brought his dog and called around 2.00 a.m. for a half-hour break from his patrol in the area while the town policeman was off duty. While 'Buller' had his meal break, his guest would enjoy the comfort of the cleaner's mess which adjoined the drivers' office. Facilities were simple, a table, two sizeable but hard wooden chairs, and a fire, generally kept alight by a huge lump of loco coal. 'Buller' soon found that it paid to wait until the policemen had taken his dog away before starting his sandwiches!

When 4.30 a.m. came round, it was time to light up and build the fire up so there was about 80 lb of steam 'on the clock' by the time the fireman arrived at 6.00 a.m. If a clack valve was leaking, as they apparently often did, the boiler

The driver and fireman alternated their arrival at 6.00 and 6.15 a.m., giving each other a lay-in. Buller should then have finished at 6.00 a.m. but he was usually there until 7.00 or 7.30 emptying the pit of ashes and cleaning the shed. This was unpaid overtime but he found the task was so much easier after the crew had taken the loco off shed around 6.50 a.m.

In 1942, Norman Thornbury's duty as the night man began at 10 pm, carrying a wage of 28/- for a 45-hour week. Then 16 years old, Norman lived in Bristol Street, from where he walked to the station each night and picked up the keys to the shed office from a pre-arranged spot under a stone. In winter he would light a fire in the side office and on a bench along the south wall of the shed he would find the necessary materials for the cleaning duty left out for him – lamp, oil, fire-lighters (sticks of wood), petroleum jelly and the stringy cotton waste which was sent out in bags from Swindon and used to clean the locomotives. He was not required on Saturday nights, a blessing for his social life, as there was no Sunday service at this time. It was a lonely duty, the only person he would normally see all night being a local policeman who would call in around 3 am. Five-gallon drums of the light blue cleaning oil used for locomotive cleaning and lubrication were kept in the oil store, and Norman would apply this with a pad of the cotton waste, his usual routine being to start at the smokebox and work his way round to the back. Around midnight he would break off for sandwiches and a bottle of tea. This was a squarish whisky bottle identical to one used by driver Joe Halliday – Norman's hero – who found its shape very convenient to fit on a narrow tray near the firehole door. Pre-refreshment washing facilities at the shed were quite simple – a bucket of warm water from the engine.

He would work on until around 4 am by the light of an oil flare lamp, for which a pint of paraffin was provided per night, then he'd light the engine's fire in order to have it ready for the crews coming on duty. This had to be carefully done, with two firelighters (made from eight sticks of wood) being placed in the firebox with some used waste between them. He would build up pressure to about 100 lbs of steam by 6 am, but no further as 160 lbs would risk a 'blow-off' which might wake the town at an unwelcome early hour! Night work was a boring job, often plagued by cold and draught despite the glass in the shed windows, but there was great satisfaction at the end of it with a sparkling 58XX class engine ready for the day's work. Around 6 am he would go and 'knock-up' the early turn driver, having remade the side office fire with coal from the locomotive around 5.30 so that the crew came on duty to a fresh blaze, by which they ate breakfast, typically cooking bacon on the Bunk's shovel and brewing their tea in an old milk can. When the locomotive was taken out for coaling, the cleaner removed ash which had collected in the inspection pit in the shed, and added it to the pile of clinker and ash close to the track opposite the water tower. Clinker had been removed from the locomotive by the fireman before going off duty the previous night, and every so often a wagon would be brought to the station for the removal of this accumulation for selling off to the building trade for foundation material. The smoother smokebox ash was used by Joe Halliday for his garden.

The night man's last duty was to sweep out the shed and side rooms, then he would leave the station at 7 am with the branch engine ready for service on the 7.21 am train to Little Somerford. He would sleep noon–8 pm to prepare for the next night's work. He wore the standard GWR two-piece blue overalls, with a cap which gave him some protection from the soot and dust that would often fall from the steam vents in the roof on a windy night. Occasionally, he would go out as relief fireman if one of the regulars was off sick or on vacation. As station pay packets came in on Friday afternoons, he would usually receive his wages from the driver who came on shed on Saturday mornings. Although Norman was keen to make the usual progression to fireman, he left the railway after his spell as Malmesbury's night man as he was not keen to leave his home town as one normally had to do.

During the last years of the passenger service at Malmesbury, the night man at the shed was replaced by a shedman, this normally being an older man for whom the work was not intended as a path to promotion. During this period it tended to be the smaller sheds that employed shedmen, cleaners only being retained at the larger depots. A humorous incident from Malmesbury relates how on one occasion the night man fell asleep on the job, having completed half the cleaning. When the locomotive went out next morning one side shone brightly

in complete contrast to the other side which hadn't been touched, a great source of embarrassment to him for some days thereafter!

LOCOMOTIVE POWER 1877–1933

The '517' class 0–4–2T locomotives were the mainstay of Malmesbury branch services, possibly working the branch right from the start. They were built at Wolverhampton during 1868–85 for use on GWR branch line and local services, and provided the branch's motive power almost exclusively over a period of thirty years from 1903. Our earliest recorded traced reference to a '517' at Malmesbury is December 1895 when No. 203 worked the branch. Designed by George Armstrong, Locomotive Superintendent of the GWR's Northern Division 1864–97, the early models of this class up to 1870 were built as saddle tanks, but from 1876 to 1886 these were altered to side tanks with modified framing and longer wheelbase. As only a few of the class had undergone these changes by the time the Malmesbury line had opened in December 1877 it is highly likely that some '517' saddle tanks appeared on the branch in the early days.

The history of the '517s' is very complex, being a good example of the GWR's policy of making successive improvements and modifications within one class rather than evolving completely new designs. These developments continued throughout both their first period of building and during later rebuilding, and as both Swindon and Wolverhampton works were used for subsequent work on them, they displayed many developments of framing, wheelbase, boilers, tanks, bunkers, cabs and auto-fittings. Although auto-fitted '517s' were based in large numbers at Swindon shed in the 1920s, it is unlikely that this method of working was ever used on the Malmesbury line, although it may have been tried experimentally. The '517s' were economical on coal and oil and could travel quickly, load permitting, their light axle-load making them particularly suitable for branch work. They were so good that their design was the basis for C. B. Collett's 48XX 0–4–2 tanks in 1932, several of which worked the Malmesbury branch in both their 48XX and later 14XX renumbering of the class in the 1940s.

Although the '517' class engines were the mainstay of the branch service up to 1933, it is thought that before 1902 'Metro' 2–4–0Ts would very likely have seen frequent allocation to Malmesbury shed and although no pre-1901 locomotive allocations are available for the branch, the presence of 'Metro' No. 1461 there in January 1901 tends to support this. No. 1461 had been released from a spell at the factory in February 1898 and may have worked at Malmesbury during 1898–1900. Built at Swindon during 1869–99, the name of the class derived from the Metropolitan Railway over which many of them worked, the only GWR engines to do so. Among other duties they generally worked the Reading-Paddington suburban services and gained a reputation for speed and reliability, so no doubt Ted Jones and Evan Harry were delighted to have No. 1461 in their charge around the turn of the century. This locomotive was different from earlier members of the class in having a cab and a domeless 2-ring boiler. Others of the class are reported to have worked in the Bristol Division during the 1870s, so it is reasonable to assume that 'Metros' may have featured on the Malmesbury trains during 1877–1900, especially in view of the fact that Malmesbury was close to Swindon Works and presented an ideal testing and running-in location for a newly-repaired locomotive. Many of the class continued in use into the 1930s and 1940s, some even passing into BR ownership. According to reliable local observation, some 'Metros' are known to have appeared at Malmesbury for brief spells in the 1920s, although such visits to the branch would have been very temporary, as a replacement for a failed engine, or even on a weed-killer train or Summer Sunday trains of wagons sent to the branch to collect mowings from cutting sides. They certainly don't appear in the allocations.

A rare appearance of an 0–4–4 engine on the Malmesbury branch occurred when No. 3534 of the '3521' class was reported there in December 1898, possibly on goods work to the Kingsmead siding which existed for several years in connection with the building of the South Wales Direct. Although built during 1887–9 as 0–4–2s, by May 1892 the entire class had been altered to 0–4–4 wheel arrangement, after which they undertook main line work from 1892–5 in Devon and Cornwall. An accident on one of the sharp curves between Doublebois and Bodmin Road in April 1895 heralded their end as main line locomotives, and many returned to branch and local work in the London and Bristol Divisions. They had Gooch pattern double frames, a long rigid wheelbase and an unusual arrangement of outside trailing axleboxes. It is likely that others of the class came to Malmesbury, although during 1899–1902 they were again converted, being turned back to front and reconstructed as 4–4–0 tender engines.

A look at the 1901–3 allocations for Malmesbury reveals that several members of the '850' class were based there. These were 0–6–0 saddle tanks built at the Wolverhampton Works during 1874–95, sometimes referred to as the 'terriers' of the GWR. They were well-known for their lightness and power, and in this respect were certainly superior to the '517s'. It is not known why the '850s' came to the branch during this period – it may have been simply that there weren't enough '517s' available, or perhaps it was in connection with increased freight and manoeuvring requirements to Kingsmead Siding during completion of the South Wales Direct, but this is only conjecture. Nos. 1929 and 2015 worked the branch during 1902, with 1957 transferring briefly in December from Cirencester shed, staying until 10th January 1903, when it went to Swindon, where it was refitted at the Works during a four month spell late that same year. No. 1957 was a doughty performer built in June 1888 which lasted until 1951 in service! It is likely that the '850s' featured on Malmesbury branch work in the years before 1901, but after 1903 only one allocation to Malmesbury appears in the official records. Between 1910 and 1937 they were refitted as pannier tanks, this change taking place when they were equipped with Belpaire fireboxes, the square 'shoulders' of this type of firebox not suiting the curved saddle tank.

It was never true that the Malmesbury branch had its 'own' locomotive, although it may have appeared so in the later years when the '58XX' class arrived, for, in common with many GWR branches, Malmesbury was a sub-shed of a larger depot, in this case Swindon. Locomotives were outstationed at local sheds until required elsewhere or required back at Swindon for maintenance or refitting. Malmesbury had an allocation of one locomotive at a time throughout its life, bearing the identification 'MALMES' in the allocation records and being given the code number 92. Occasionally an engine would have a long run at Malmesbury, but more usually they worked shorter spells on the branch, for, being close to Swindon Works, the Malmesbury, Faringdon and Marlborough lines would be regularly used for locomotives coming out of the Works after a heavy repair. After 'running-in' locally, they would then typically go back to the factory for a re-check before being sent out to another branch line, or very often to some far-flung part of the system in Devon or South Wales. Before the Great War Nos. 545, 552, 558, 1155 and 1443 appeared frequently at Malmesbury before 'disappearing' to another part of the network. Undoubtedly the branch's most famous '517' engine, its memory perpetuated on the gravestone in Malmesbury cemetery today, was No. 844, and its working life on the GWR must have been typical of that of many of the 0–4–2 tank engines.

No. 844 was built at Wolverhampton at a cost of £1,203 and put into service in November 1874. Its work before 1901 is not precisely known, but in 1902 she appeared at Faringdon shed, having undergone modifications to wheelbase and boiler in February 1897. During 1902 she spent three months at Swindon Works then was sent to Banbury shed where she stayed until early 1904, at which time she was allocated to Oxford to work services on the Fairford line. In November 1904 No. 844 was sent to Landovery and remained there until August 1907 when a three-month period at Swindon was necessary for repairs. Sent back to Landovery on 11th November 1907, she remained there until April 1910 – a short period was spent back in the Works, then on 9th May 1910 she arrived at Malmesbury to run out her twilight years. No. 844 became a great favourite of Ted Jones who delighted in cooking bacon on the shovel over the fire for his grandchildren, and who, like his charge, was not long for retirement. No. 844 remained at Malmesbury until February 1912, except for brief visits to Swindon during which time it was replaced by No. 520, well-known for its work on the Tetbury branch. By 1912 No. 844 was near the end of its working life and was constantly moving between the branch and Swindon, and from December 1912 she remained at the Works on light duties until scrapping in March 1913 after covering 889,892 miles and just after the retirement of Ted Jones.

As referred to in Chapter 4, during the 1914–18 war, the Swindon factory was busy producing heavy guns for long range artillery batteries, and the priorities of main line engines and the reduced accommodation in the Works meant that factory attention to branch locomotives was severely diminished, but such was the meticulous care given to its stock in the years before 1914 that many of the '517s' were able to run for long periods without trips to Swindon for repairs. No. 1161, a stalwart '517' which gave 70 years service, did not go to 'The Field' at Swindon for scrapping until 1945, and had a long run at Malmesbury during 1914–15. On 8th January 1916, No. 839 began a long period of service here which continued with only short breaks until March 1920.

From 1920–25, No. 839 appeared at Malmesbury for shorter spells, after which she was sent to Swindon, Chester, Stourbridge and Penmaenpool before being scrapped in 1932.

The needs of wartime brought about a motive power shortage on the GWR caused by the loss of locomotives to the Railway Operating Division, and in April 1917 the company requested the loan of six tank engines from the South Eastern & Chatham Railway. The following month six of the SECR's 'Q1' class were transferred to the GWR at Reading, and one of them, No. 350, actually saw branch service at Malmesbury. No. 350 was a Stirling 0–4–4T of the 'Q' class, built in 1889 and rebuilt by Wainright in 1907 to class 'Q1'. It was first sent by the GWR to Bristol, but by 1918 it had been transferred to Swindon. For a fortnight in March it worked the Malmesbury branch trains while No. 839 was being repaired at the Works, and its sombre dark grey livery must indeed have caused some comment amongst the locals, more used to the bright green of their regular engines. Maybe the dull appearance of 350 was some reflection of the austerity of life in a country now four years at war, the SECR wanderer's only relieving features being its rectangular cast iron company plate on the side of the bunker and the startling large white figures on the side tank. Its turn at Malmesbury was undoubtedly a running-in period after a spell at the Works, as was the usual GWR practice with its own locomotives. No. 350 was reported working the Avonmouth trains from Bristol during April 1918 and, according to the GWR allocations, was returned

to the SECR on 8th August 1918, the other five on loan having been returned by the spring of the following year.

By the mid-20s the '517' class engines were nearing the end of their useful life, and the years of war when so many ran without major attention may have taken their toll, reflected in the allocation to Malmesbury shed in 1925 of no less than eight different '517s' at different times during the year, although No. 839 was still giving good service and had a trouble-free year with two months at Malmesbury. By 1929 it was unusual for the class to be doing long spells at any branch shed, and, when they were not being 'farmed out' to local branches during this time, the Swindon 0–4–2s were used as carriage works pilots and station pilots at Swindon Junction, and quietly worked out their time on such duties until scrapping. No. 532 was condemned in December 1929 after performing its final duties on public service at Malmesbury, and many more of these fine tank engines made their last trips to Swindon during the early 1930s, No. 521, 529, 1158 and 1439 all seeing final work at Malmesbury during 1930. During 1930–32 there were rare appearances there of one of the '200' series of '517s', No. 217. The testing of a Sentinel locomotive in October 1927 as a possible replacement for the '517s' is chronicled in Chapter 4.

The '517s' were replaced on the Malmesbury branch shortly before the line's junction was switched to Little Somerford in July 1933. The GWR allocations for 1933 are lost, but, as the new Collett 0–4–2Ts were put into service in the Bristol

'517' Class No. 1436 at Malmesbury in September 1932, with larger 900 gallon tanks and an enclosed cab. It looks impeccable, a tribute to its cleaner. It was built in 1877, the year the branch opened, and lasted in service until 1944.   *Photomatic*

LOCOMOTIVES ALLOCATED TO MALMESBURY

Year	Number	Class	Year	Number	Class	Year	Number	Class
1901	529	517 class 0—4—2T	1923	839	517 " "	1935	5801	58XX " "
	1929	850 class 0—6—0ST		840	517 " "		5802	58XX " "
	1461	Metro class 2—4—0T		1164	517 " "		5804	58XX " "
1902	1461	Metro class 2—4—0T		519	517 " "		5805	58XX " "
	2015	850 class 0—6—0ST		1154	517 " "		5806	58XX " "
	1957	850 class 0—6—0ST	1924	1154	517 " "	1936	5802	58XX " "
	561	517 class 0—4—2T		545	517 " "		5804	58XX " "
	1929	850 class 0—6—0ST		529	517 " "		5805	58XX " "
1903	1957	850 class 0—6—0ST		1438	517 " "		5806	58XX " "
	561	517 class 0—4—2T		839	517 " "		4833	48XX class 0—4—2T
	1440	517 " "	1925	839	517 " "	1937	5800	58XX class 0—4—2T
	1155	517 " "		545	517 " "		5802	58XX " "
1904	1155	517 " "		218	517 " "		5804	58XX " "
	219	517 " "		529	517 " "		5805	58XX " "
1905	1155	517 " "		576	517 " "	1938	5800	58XX " "
	1440	517 " "		551	517 " "		5802	58XX " "
	545	517 " "		1436	517 " "		5804	58XX " "
1906	545	517 " "		1154	517 " "		5805	58XX " "
	558	517 " "	1926	551	517 " "	1939	5800	58XX " "
1907	558	517 " "		529	517 " "		5802	58XX " "
	573	517 " "		540	517 " "		5804	58XX " "
1908	573	517 " "		837	517 " "		5805	58XX " "
	545	517 " "		1477	517 " "	1940	5800	58XX " "
1909	573	517 " "	1927	217	517 " "		5802	58XX " "
	1443	517 " "		529	517 " "		5805	58XX " "
1910	1443	517 " "		539	517 " "	1941	5800	58XX " "
	844	517 " "		540	517 " "		5802	58XX " "
	541	517 " "		1427	517 " "		5805	58XX " "
1911	844	517 " "		1477	517 " "	1942	5800	58XX " "
	520	517 " "	1928	532	517 " "		5802	58XX " "
1912	844	517 " "		539	517 " "		5805	58XX " "
	520	517 " "		540	517 " "	1943	5800	58XX " "
	541	517 " "		549	517 " "		5802	58XX " "
	1154	517 " "		1477	517 " "		5804	58XX " "
	1484	517 " "	1929	529	517 " "		5805	58XX " "
1913	1484	517 " "		532	517 " "		4800	48XX class 0—4—2T
	552	517 " "		539	517 " "	1944	5800	58XX class 0—4—2T
	1476	517 " "		1158	517 " "		5802	58XX " "
1914	1161	517 " "	1930	217	517 " "		5804	58XX " "
	552	517 " "		529	517 " "		5805	58XX " "
1915	1161	517 " "		539	517 " "	1945	5800	58XX class 0—4—2T
	1443	517 " ..		1158	517 " "		5802	58XX " "
1916	1161	517 " "		1477	517 " "		5804	58XX " "
	1427	517 " "		521	517 " "		5805	58XX " "
	839	517 " "		1428	517 " "		4800	48XX class 0—4—2T
1917	839	517 " "		1439	517 " "	1946	5800	58XX class 0—4—2T
	202	517 " "	1931	217	517 " "		5802	58XX " "
1918	350	Q1 class 0—4—4T (SE & CR)		519	517 " "		5804	58XX " "
	839	517 class 0—4—2T		539	517 " "		5805	58XX " "
	1479	517 " "		835	517 " "		1453	44XX class 0—4—2T
1919	839	517 " "		1428	517 " "	1947	5800	58XX class 0—4—2T
	1446	517 " "	1932	217	517 " "		4802	58XX " "
	994	850 class 0—6—0PT		519	517 " "		5804	58XX " "
1920	994	850 " "		539	517 " "		5805	58XX " "
	839	517 class 0—4—2T		1155	517 " "		1400	14XX class 0—4—2T
	535	517 " "		1428	517 " "		1436	14XX " "
	840	517 " "		1436	517 " "		1446	14XX " "
	1154	517 " "		1478	517 " "	1948	5800	58XX class 0—4—2T
1921	840	517 class 0—4—2T	1933	519	517 " "		5802	58XX " "
1922	840	517 " "		5800	58XX class 0—4—2T		5805	58XX " "
	839	517 " "		5802	5800 " "	1949	5805	58XX " "
			1934	5801	58XX " "	1950	5805	58XX " "
				5802	58XX " "	1951	5805	58XX " "
				5804	58XX " "			
				5805	58XX " "			
				5806	58XX " "			

Collett 0—4—2T No. 5802 outside Malmesbury shed on 17th September 1947.

Collection Paul Karau

Division in January of that year, it is most likely that No. 519 was the last '517' to be allocated to Malmesbury shed, before being scrapped in April 1933. It is not known for certain which of the new Collett '58XX' class was the first of the new locomotives to be allocated to Malmesbury shed, now the only branch shed remaining open at a terminus in the entire Bristol Division, but it is known with some certainty that No. 5802 was there before the change of junction in July 1933.

The Collett 0-4-2Ts, named after the GWR's Chief Mechanical Engineer during 1922–41, were specifically built-to replace the '517s', the general design being based on the updated rebuilds of the '517' class. They had enclosed cabs which were formed flush with the sides of the tank and bunker, the extra width making larger cab windows possible. Nos. 5800–19 were built primarily for branch and shunting work, seven of them being allocated to the Bristol Division

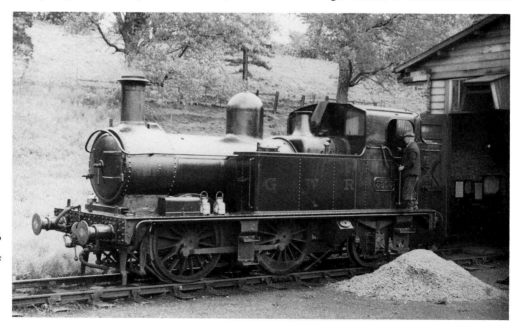

Collett 0—4—2T No. 5805 at Malmesbury c.1950.
J. H. Moss

Another picture of No. 5802 at Malmesbury, this time in goods-only days on 23rd August 1955.   *C. G. Maggs*

straight from the factory in January 1933. Of the group 5800 to 5806, only 5803 has no recorded work at Malmesbury, being normally shedded at Yatton for the Clevedon branch service. The remainder of the group were allocated elsewhere in the Bristol and Worcester divisions. No. 5801 appeared only briefly at Malmesbury, but 5802 was regularly allocated, often spending three months at a stretch there, then going to the Tetbury branch which, although only four miles away by road, was some 37 miles by rail via Swindon and Kemble! No. 5804 was regularly sent to Malmesbury, and is certainly the most photographed, but quite the most regular engine was No. 5805. This worked the branch for long stretches almost every year until passenger closure, and indeed can almost be regarded as the branch's 'own' locomotive from December 1948, hauling the last train out in 1951 and staying on to run the goods train each weekday. Unfortunately, with the closure of branch lines, there proved to be insufficient work for the '58XX' class and in February 1954 several of them, including No. 5804, were in store at Swindon, all having been withdrawn by July 1959. No. 5805 just made its quarter-century, being sent to the breaker's yard in March 1958.

Several of the Collett '48XX' class also appeared at Malmesbury, the first recorded work being by No. 4833 in July 1936. The earliest of the class to leave the factory, No. 4800 in August 1932, did not appear as Malmesbury's allocated engine until September 1943. Its spells at Malmesbury were short, never more than a month, Tetbury seeing a good deal more of it on regular service, where the '48XXs' did work as auto-trains. It is unlikely that this method of working was ever used on the Malmesbury line. In 1946 the '48XXs' were

Dick Cooper gave long service to the Malmesbury branch as fireman and driver.
Courtesy Gerald & Shirley Cooper

renovated and renumbered as '14XX' tank engines, several of them working the Malmesbury trains in their new identity during 1947. The '48XX' and '58XX' classes were identical in every respect except that the former were equipped with auto-gear and ATC apparatus and were therefore more useful and versatile than the '58XXs', and, although many of the earlier '48XXs' were withdrawn during 1956–58, many of them, as '14XXs', continued in service for some years, some, such as No. 1464, coming into Malmesbury on the daily goods run after 1951, and others such as 1441 achieving legendary fame on the auto-trains of the Chalford 'railcar' service.

CHAPTER ELEVEN

LIFE AT KINGSMEAD CROSSING
BILL ARCHARD – CROSSING KEEPER 1922–62

An undated view of Kingsmead Crossing at some stage prior to the change of junction to Little Somerford in 1933, showing the road down to Kingsmead Mill and the branch winding away in the distance towards Malmesbury. Here Bill Archard lived for 57 years, preceded only by William Ponting's family. The spring where the Archards obtained their water is by the River Avon on the left of the photograph.

Wiltshire Library and Museum Service

THE post of gateman came to be known as 'crossing keeper' in later years and involved having total responsibility for the safe operating of railway crossing gates across a public road. Bill Archard was born in Norfolk, but his family moved west during his childhood. His father was a GWR man, and Bill followed him onto the railway when he came out of the Navy at the end of the First World War. He and his wife Elsie were sent to Kingsmead Crossing on the Malmesbury branch after he sustained a fractured skull in an accident which ended his work as a shunter at Winscombe, Somerset. Through his dedication to the work, his sense of history, his appreciation of his position at the crossing as an observer of rural change, his exceptionally long service, and the support of his wife, he rehabilitated himself to fill the position with a dignity and warmth which saw him become one of the branch's best-loved characters. Even today there survive, engraved in the stonework of the crossing cottage, several historic dates and events in the history of the line, scraped in by Bill with a nail as they happened.

Bill's job was a 24-hour duty, carrying a weekly wage of 19/6d when he started at Kingsmead in 1922. He usually rose well before 7 am so as to be on duty for the first train out of Malmesbury each morning, and his hours were often extended by the late running of excursion trains. When these did not arrive back on the branch until after midnight he still had to remain up until after the train had returned to Malmesbury, then had to rise early again next morning.

Once up, his first duty would be to light the oil lamps on top of the gates. The little wooden porch at the cottage entrance contained the railway telephone, and three pips on this would be the signal that a train was leaving Malmesbury (one pip from Dauntsey, two from Great Somerford). A four-pip signal on the 'blower', as it was known, would be a signal from a station, crossing or permanent way telephone that he must pick up the receiver to take a verbal message.

Bearing in mind that there were just three miles of line on either side of Kingsmead, and that opening the gates was a manual operation, Bill would stop all road traffic as soon as the 'pips' sounded. The gates were padlocked at all times, so each one had to be unlocked, moved across the road then padlocked again, the gate farthest away from the oncoming train being moved first according to GWR regulations. He would then go to the ground frame outside his cottage and pull the distant signal to the 'off' position so that the branch train could proceed. If the distant signal was at caution, the driver had to be prepared to stop before reaching the crossing. Bill always kept a dog, which was a great help in keeping alert on the job – he had one for several years which could always sense trains just before the 'blower' sounded.

Anyone familiar with the quiet narrow road to Kingsmead Mill today would have difficulty in realising that Kingsmead was the busiest of the three crossings on the branch during the line's heyday, for as the road into Gawthropp's Mill was a dead end, what went in had to come out again. It was

Kingsmead Crossing lodge and gates, seen from the field by the Avon in the early 50s, showing the newer gates of 1933 with mushroom-head topped gateposts. Although a single-storey dwelling, the rear wall of the lodge was deeper than the front, enclosing a small cellar at the rear.
Courtesy Bill Archard

Mr. and Mrs. Archard tending their chickens outside the crossing lodge c.1924. Bill is wearing a standard GWR blue serge uniform with sleeved waistcoat.
Courtesy Bill Archard

particularly busy in the '40s when the miller, Mr. Bye, delivered meal to the farms seven days a week with a Chevrolet lorry. Many times Bill had to use his discretion when shutting the gates across the road, if the Beaufort Hunt was passing, or maybe an awkward herd of cows would cause him problems. Delivery of corn to the mill, delivery of ground corn to the farms by horse and cart, and pedestrians from Corston and Rodbourne, who came across the fields via Angrove Woods to reach the stations at the two Somerfords, provided regular traffic along the little road over Bill's crossing. The River Avon nearby was a recreational spot for local villagers and for weekend trippers out from Swindon. Thus, with agricultural, hunt and recreation traffic, vehicle and pedestrian, it was not uncommon for Kingsmead Crossing to be closed across the road with several vehicles waiting. Pedestrians could use the wicket gates on either side of the track on the south side of the crossing although there would always be a warning from Bill if a train was imminent. The sighting in either direction was not good for the gateman, train crews or people on the road, as the crossing was on a curve in respect of both road and railway, a curve that was accentuated by the change of junction of 1933, with the new spur up to Little Somerford bending out of sight up a 1 in 50 gradient. In later days, when the signalman at Little Somerford warned Kingsmead of the branch train's departure from the junction, there was far less time for Bill to do his job, and there was an occasion, during the bad winter of 1939 and with the distant signal against the train, when the engine slid down the steep gradient from the main line along the icy rails and smashed through the gates. After this incident instructions were issued to signalmen at Little Somerford that the signal was not to be cleared for a train to start until the Kingsmead gatekeeper had confirmed by phone that the gates were open.

In addition to the gates, the crossing keeper's other duties extended to maintenance of several items of important equipment. He kept paraffin, spare lamps and yellow, green and red flags in the cottage, and a set of fog signal detonators, the latter being kept to place on the tracks when an urgent warning to a train driver was required. There were two occasions in particular when Bill had to use these to stop trains, one when there were ballast slips just beyond his crossing towards Malmesbury and another where landslips in the embankment had been caused by a farmer dredging the ditch below.

Bill was responsible for filling the oil lamps on both gates every morning, and extinguishing them every night after the last train. He also replenished the signal lamps once a week, although in later years the signal lampman from Wootton Bassett would attend to the signals, bringing Bill's wages at the same time, usually on Fridays. The distants had ladders by which the arm could be reached, and a hoist on which the signal lamp could be wound down along a wire for refilling. In earlier days, when this was his duty, Bill would have to visit these signals regularly in all weathers, the distant in the Malmesbury direction being half-a-mile along the line.

It was very important for the gateman to maintain a regular routine in his duties, and whenever Bill went out of the cottage for any reason the first thing he always did was to check the indicator box on the side wall of his cottage facing the track. This was a vital piece of equipment containing repeater needles to show the on/off position of the signals, and discs indicating when the signal lamps were out. The disc normally stood in the green position, turning to red when the lamps were out and therefore in need of oil. As the up distant from the crossing was near bridge 16 and obscured from Bill's vision by the Badminton line embankment, and the down distant was out of sight around the curve towards Malmesbury, a regular look at this box was paramount in his routine. The indicators were in the top section of the box, the batteries which powered them being in the lower section. There was also a large battery box on the outside of the porch for the railway telephone, the batteries being checked and replaced whenever necessary by the Telegraph Department from Swindon every two to three weeks.

After the change of junction in 1933, at which time the gates at Kingsmead were widened to 19 feet so as to allow complete clearance for a train on the deviation of the new

An animated shot of Bill Archard clowning on the PW handcart sometime in the mid-20s. This snap provides a fine view of the crossing nameboard and the ground frame with the slanting footboards to give extra purchase on the two distant signal levers.
Courtesy Bill Archard

line, there was a point for Bill to operate, worked from a ground frame. This gave access to the remaining section of the old line now known as Kingsmead Siding (not to be confused with the Kingsmead Siding of 1898–1902). There was extra work for Bill here whenever crippled stock was being moved in or out, as all shunting movements on or off the siding had to go through the crossing. For normal branch service these points were always locked, but for access to the siding the branch train staff (with the key to the frame on the end of it) was handed to Bill, who would unlock the point after the incoming locomotive or train of old stock had cleared his gates, then reverse the lever so that shunting onto the siding could proceed. He had his flags and lamps out for this duty to stop the engine for any traffic along the road. There could be a lengthy delay for any accumulated traffic to or from the mill during such operations, so Bill had to be very alert at such times. During the second World War, when the siding was used for ammunition trucks, the continuous movement of these wagons once kept Bill at work for four days with virtually no sleep.

There was no paperwork for the gateman, unlike the signalman, except for making census returns on road traffic through the crossing. This was done about once every three years, eight hours a day, for a week. When a census was made in 1925 for a GWR Report on Working of Branch Lines the authorities doubted the accuracy of Bill's figures, for, as already mentioned, Kingsmead always showed greater traffic figures, than either Dauntsey Road or Great Somerford as any traffic for the mill had to return over the crossing.

The crossing keeper was life's quiet observer of rural ways, watching life pass by on both road and rail, and for more

Mrs. Archard in the garden c.1946.   *Courtesy Bill Archard*

than half a century Bill witnessed many changes from his vantage point at Kingsmead. He occupied a unique social position with all manner of folk, from fellow railwaymen and 'townies' from Swindon to drivers, farmers and landed gentry. The men he knew best were the permanent way workers, who regularly came past his home in the course of their work. His first contact of the day would usually be the ganger, who passed each morning on his inspection trolley before the first train. His main contact with the world beyond was his daily

Bill Archard opening the gates in favour of the road, assisted by two young nieces, c.1930. The decorative cap on the top hinge of the short gate-post characterises these older gates which were replaced in 1933 with wider examples. The oil lamps on top of the gates had to be put out every night and refilled and lit first thing in the morning. Throughout Bill's life there, the gates had to be padlocked at all times across road and rail. Bill is seen holding a can of milk and provisions from a nearby farm.
Courtesy Bill Archard

The crossing lodge at Kingsmead on 23rd August 1955.

Colin Maggs

newspaper, which the fireman on the first train into Malmesbury would throw to him each morning. It was usually caught by his dog. He had no radio until 1939, when a friend helped him set up a crystal set.

Between trains he would go for walks with his dog, collect milk or other provisions from a nearby farm, take a nap or help his wife tend the well-stocked crossing garden. During their years at Kingsmead, the Archards were completely self-sufficient in vegetables, although Mrs. Archard would obtain many other goods in the village at Little Somerford. They obtained their water from a clear spring down by the Avon, buckets being provided by the GWR for this purpose. Barrels were also provided from Swindon and kept outside the cottage for collecting rainwater. Their coal came in by rail to Malmesbury and would be dropped off to them by a mill lorry or kindly farmer.

Through the years Elsie Archard gave staunch support to her husband, undertaking his duties whenever he was ill and running the home in the tiny cottage without many of the basic amenities which we take for granted today. The cottage was lit by paraffin lamps, only replaced by electricity in the later '50s. It must have been arduous, indeed, going out on a cold dark morning to knock ice off the gates and padlock with a hammer and chisel, carrying heavy buckets of water back from the spring, sheltering from bad weather in the little porch while a train passed, tramping along the line, perhaps even in torrential rain, to the distant signal to relight the lamp. Winter conditions would emphasise the isolated position of the crossing, and on several occasions over the years the Archards lent help to digging operations to free trains trapped

in snowdrifts nearby. Holidays were short, three days a year in the '20s, with no time for more than a day trip to Bristol to buy some new clothes, or maybe to the sea at Weston-Super-Mare. When the Archards were away, a Relief Signalman from Westbury would take over at Kingsmead, although after 1933 it proved simpler to cover their absence with a porter from Little Somerford.

There were lighter moments, though, such as a summer Sunday tending their crops and flowers in the garden, talking with visitors to the nearby river or visiting with friends in the village. Sundays provided more time to relax and catch up on an odd job or two, with no trains to worry about except the evening milk run (up to 1935) and the occasional excursion or special, although after the Second World War such trains were very rare.

From 1951 to 1962, with a daily goods train in and out of Malmesbury during the week being the only regular traffic, life at the crossing became less busy, and, save for occasional movements on Kingsmead siding, Bill saw no great activity again until the line was lifted in 1963. Kingsmead Mill was bought by the Fry family (of Fry's chocolate) in 1952, and the mill continued in use until 1961, so only in the last year of the railway did traffic along the road through the crossing really cease. The mill was sold again in 1967, and with the final closure of the branch in 1962 the Somerford Fishing Association took over the crossing cottage and adjacent land until this, too, was purchased by the owners of the mill in 1980. Bill Archard remained there until 1979, having spent 57 years there and being therefore the last Malmesbury railwayman on the line. He died in Chippenham in April 1981.

Percy Wood (1890–1982), seen here 'booking up' after the departure of Malmesbury's last passenger train, 8th September 1951. Mr. Wood took out a large number of tickets for the last day of operations, in case he had to fill the dispenser, but the last day patronage was not as large as he expected, which explains the unused piles on the desk. *Wiltshire Newspapers*

MALMESBURY STATION MASTERS 1877–1951

Name	Previous post	Tenure at Malmesbury	Moved to
Llewellyn Bradshaw	Passenger Clerk, Llangollen	17th Dec. 1877 to March 1882	Chepstow
Thomas W. Wood	Parcels Office, Bath	March 1882 to 21st March 1898	Bruton
Arthur W. Lloyd	Goods Clerk, Corsham	21st March 1898 to Jan 1907	Calne
Edgar H. Doswell	Asst. Supt. Office, Swindon	Jan 1907 to 1919	Lawrence Hill
George J. Dinham	Chief Booking Clerk, Calne	1919 to 1933	Portishead
Richard Faull	Station Master, Codford	1933 to Feb 1943	Portishead
Arthur Davies	Station Master, Mitcheldean Road	Feb 1943 to 10th July 1944	Died in office, aged 52.
July to October 1944, temporary relief			
Percy Wood	Station Master, Sparkford	October 1944 to 10th Sept 1951	Barmouth

From 1951 the goods only station at Malmesbury came under the jurisdiction of the station master at Little Somerford, and from 14th Dec. 1961 until the final closure in November 1962, was under the control of the station master at Wootton Bassett.

CHAPTER TWELVE

UNIFORMED STAFF
PORTRAITS OF MALMESBURY STATION STAFF

PERCY WOOD was Malmesbury's last station master during passenger days. Born in Montgomery on 30th August 1890, he started as a 3/6d a week junior clerk at his home town station in 1904. For the summer of 1905 he worked as a seasonal telegraph clerk at 10/- a week. After a two-year spell in the goods department, he was appointed parcels clerk at a salary of £40 a year in 1907.

In 1913 he became booking clerk at Montgomery and attained his first post as station master when he took over Ynyslas on the Cambrian coast in 1921. In 1927 he transferred to Sparkford in Somerset where he remained for 17 years. On leaving this post he received a cheque for £200, a vast amount of money in those days, collected from the local public. A wallet of treasury notes was put together from all grades of railwaymen between Bristol and Weymouth, with a framed scroll containing 72 names of colleagues. Such homage is evidence of the status of the local station master in the community in days gone by, and the esteem Mr. Wood generated from both public and fellow railwaymen alike.

Percy Wood arrived at Malmesbury in October 1944, on a move which represented a rise in status from Class 4 to Class 3 and a salary of £240 a year, although once at Malmesbury he could never understand the grading, as Sparkford had been a far busier station with a higher revenue than the declining country terminus at the end of the short branch from Little Somerford. He was a keen sportsman who had played soccer for Barmouth before the Great War, having been present in their team on a great day in 1913 when they defeated mighty Aston Villa's reserves. He was also a keen cricketer, still playing for Malmesbury's club up on the Worthies above the station yard after his 60th birthday. A highly-respected and well-liked official, he was always impeccably smart on duty, being concerned to set a good example to the staff, always donning his GWR cap to leave the office and be on the platform to meet each train coming in.

In a supervisory role, his working day began at 9 am, and he was responsible as station master for all departments – passenger, goods, parcels, signalling, locomotive as well as the commercial life of the station. He was expected to visit and inspect each department daily, signing the train register in the signal box, a duty he generally undertook each morning before dealing with station correspondence. Typical paperwork would involve answering queries from local tradesmen, signing of time sheets, issuing memos and rulebook amendments to staff, and checking that public notices were up to date. Mr. Wood had a particularly good knowledge of signalling. He *was* 'the Company' to the local community, the railway's main representative to the town and district, the image of the GWR in its locality depending to a large extent on the official in charge. Mr. Wood took this responsibility very seriously, and it is fair to say that even though the branch had such a poor train service and connections during his time, he is remembered by many in the town today with great affection.

Mr. Wood's lunch break was taken between noon and 1 pm, when he would relax in the Railway Hotel and play a game of darts. He would then work an afternoon turn through to 5 pm before going home for his evening meal. He would return to work another hour after supper, usually remaining on duty until the last train of the day had arrived back from Little Somerford at 7.11 pm. With the closure of Malmesbury to passengers in 1951 and the responsibility for the goods only station transferred to the control of Little Somerford, Mr. Wood returned to his native Wales, being redundant for a time, but he eventually secured his final appointment, in charge of the Class 2 station at Barmouth on a salary of £600 a year.

Malmesbury did not let Mr. Wood go without showing him some appreciation of his seven years there, and in March 1952 he returned to attend a special presentation dinner at the Railway Hotel, where he was described as 'one of the finest station masters in the Bristol Division' and presented with a wallet of notes and a fountain pen by a large gathering of townsfolk, tradesmen and railway employees. He retired in September 1955 and moved to the small Cambrian coast town of Llwyngwril, enjoying a long and healthy retirement until his death on 26th September 1982, surviving his wife and daughter by a decade.

CLERK – JOHN BARNBY

Malmesbury's status as a Class 3 station entitled it to the inclusion of a clerk on its staff, unlike GWR stations on Class 4 and below where no such post existed. The term 'booking clerk' is sometimes used in respect of this grading, but incorrectly as far as the GWR is concerned. Whereas the term might have been appropriate at Paddington, where the chief job of such a clerk was to simply 'book' tickets (an expression going back to coaching days before there was any railway), at Malmesbury, the clerk's duties were very complex and demanding. They can be summarised as follows: to book all passenger trains, prepare monthly accounts, assist with statistical returns, record invoices, keep goods abstracts and ledgers and 'assist generally as required', this last phrase being a reflection of the fact that at a country terminus a clerk might often have to draw upon his railway experience to undertake jobs at short notice occasioned by staff absence or other eventualities. There is one instance related of how a Malmesbury clerk once took over as guard on the first branch train of the day out to Dauntsey because the regular man had overslept!

John Barnby was born in 1909, the son of a Wooburn Green and later Bridport station master. Having started as a lad clerk, passing the senior examination to attain the grade of clerk at the age of 18, he moved to Malmesbury from Maiden Newton in 1929, his eleven years there bringing some stability to the station during the difficult years of the 1930s. In fact, during the years preceding his appointment, around twenty men, usually lad clerks on their first appointment, had occupied the post at Malmesbury, over a period of 52 years. Few stayed very long, clearly using the job as a stepping-stone to larger assignments; only Alfred Clarke, who worked at Malmesbury during 1883–91, stayed there for anything like approaching John Barnby's time. Clarke put his eight years to good use, eventually going on to the Divisional Super-intendent's Office at Bristol before becoming station master at Bruton in 1905. Mr. Barnby's career proceeded similarly, moving on to the DSO as had the previous three clerks at Malmesbury, eventually taking charge of Marlborough and later Witney where he retired.

Malmesbury station provided a very wide experience in running a railway in the 'thirties, the clerk's work certainly echoing the words of the 1921 Bristol Division staffing report which stated that it was necessary for both clerk and station master to work overtime daily in order to keep the work up to date, being 'unable to carry out their duties in the hours allowed'. When John Barnby started at Malmesbury his annual salary was £90, but the question of overtime in the remunerative sense by which it is understood today hardly arose – the clerk simply worked faster. The terms of employ-ment required that a half-hour's overtime must be worked on any or every day without extra payment. Should more time be required above this, the Divisional Office had to agree, in which case the normal half-hour would be deducted. Overtime was paid for Sunday work, which still provided plenty of work for the clerk up to 1935.

During his first year at Malmesbury he worked a regular turn each day of 9 am to 7.30 pm, this including two theoretical meal-breaks and the expected half-hour, but once he grew accustomed to the duties and grew in experience he introduced an earlier day for himself of 7 am–5.30 pm.

When Mr. Faull took over the station in 1933, the earlier turn appealed to him, so in order to maintain the overlap of hours so that the station office was staffed for as long a period as possible, they worked alternate weeks on the earlier duty. They also alternated on working on Sundays in the early 'thirties when Malmesbury still had its one Sunday train each way. A half-day could be taken once a week provided the time was made up on the other weekdays.

A great deal of work had to be undertaken by Malmesbury's clerk in respect of horse-boxes. For instance, if someone rang up (tel. Malmesbury 28 in those days!) requesting a horse-box, for example, to Leicester, then the first job was to see if one was available either out in the loop or down in the yard. One usually was to be found, as the frequent horse traffic for hunts and shows meant that Malmesbury usually had several spare, but if not, Swindon Rolling Stock had to be contacted to find out from where the nearest available box could be obtained. A suitable train service then had to be arranged for despatching the vehicle, and the customer informed. Each individual booking was arranged by telegram and kept on a clip in a line along a shelf in the booking office. Traffic onto another company's tracks, such as the Southern, involved two complications – the traffic cost had to be split for a proportion of the mileage, and it was essential to order a dual-fitted horse-box if the journey went beyond the GWR network, as two types of brake system existed in the country at that time, Westinghouse and vacuum-fitted brakes. Horse-box traffic also needed to be differentiated according to the type of main line service arranged – for express trains dual-fitted horse-boxes with their long wheelbase were required.

Malmesbury's clerk was very much a cashier. In addition to receiving cash across the counter for train tickets, there was a vast amount of paperwork involved in organising a

day's takings ready for despatch to the cash office at Westbury (later Bristol). The book recording ticket issues was made up twice a day and balanced with the cash. This book was printed in columns commencing and closing with numbers and receipts in 1st Class, 3rd Class, Excursion, etc. Separate columns had to be totalled and cross-balanced. The total was then carried to the summary cash book as one, all other accounts at the station being treated in the same way. Any cash paid in by other staff, generally goods and parcels, was entered in the appropriate book, and also into the summary cash book which in every case was initialled by payer and receiver alongside the amount to prevent any dispute arising. For a station still issuing 8,379 tickets and taking £9,890 in passenger train traffic, with £5,683 goods revenue annually in 1930, such strict procedures were essential.

Thus a total was arrived at for the day's takings. A daily cash advice was made up with a carbon copy retained. The top copy was sent in a locked leather pouch in the travelling safe which left Malmesbury on the first train every morning, and the receipt portion, which was later returned, was filed for production to the Audit Clerk on his annual visit to Malmesbury, when he fully checked one month's accounts and spot-checked the others. In the days when Dauntsey was the junction, the travelling safe to Westbury started at Malmesbury, chained securely to the brake pillar in the guard's compartment and transferred to a main line train at Dauntsey, to go via Chippenham and Melksham. The safe was constructed with a double lid which allowed the cash pouches from each station maximum security under the guard's supervision. In later days, of course, the pouch, passed

John Barnby, born 1909.

to the branch guard by Malmesbury's clerk, went to Bristol via Little Somerford.

A rolling stock return had to be sent to Swindon every day to the Rolling Stock Inspector, the list being made out by the checker and passed to the clerk for despatch. Ticket stocks had to be ordered with at least a month's notice from the Audit Office at Paddington, where they were printed in a special section. A stock ticket book helped the clerk keep a record of the numbered tickets. The most used and therefore the most ordered ticket at Malmesbury was the Half-Day Excursion to Swindon (i.e. leave after 10 am – a Day Ticket was for departure *before* 10 am). A ticket order was usually placed about twice a year. Books of paper tickets were used when a journey onto another company's rails was involved, rather like a cheque book. Other regularly used tickets from Malmesbury on the old branch were to Chippenham and Bath, with relatively little to Bristol and westwards, confirming Malmesbury's eastwards-inclined emphasis alluded to in Chapter 4. Paddington Monthly and Day Returns were also well-used, the latter being another excursion ticket only issued for advertised excursion trains, as distinct from a Cheap Day Return which was for use on almost any train during the day. For obtaining other stationery from Paddington, a requisition book had to be filled in in numbered sequence. An order was placed every three months and arrived at Malmesbury in a hamper by goods wagon. It would contain headed notepaper, telegram message forms, goods invoices, envelopes, writing materials and the like.

A huge amount of work was required on the Goods Traffic, outwards invoicing and charging being a complicated job, as was the inwards recording of all invoices. 'Abstracts' are the records of all invoices to and from each and every station separately recorded, including routes. The goods traffic abstracts were the means by which remittance of revenue was ensured – the outwards abstracts of invoices of the sending station were checked with the inwards abstracts of the receiving station by the Audit Office for GWR local traffic and by the Railway Clearing House (Eversholt St, London) for intercompany traffic. Any difference whatever resulted in an inaccuracy sheet being sent to the stations being queried, when the full details had to be given – where a clerk had made an error, a debit sheet would be sent to the station and would be recorded in the inaccuracy register. Malmesbury's returns had to match up with other stations. All invoices were made out in duplicate, one copy going to the destination station. Credits and debits between stations arose on many things including in particular collection of local firms' accounts. These were dealt with by effecting credit and debit transfers with the appropriate accounts attached. Paid-home charges were often to be debited to the sending station – these were amounts caused by delivery of packages beyond the defined 'boundary' of the station's delivery area. It should be realised that in GWR accounting there were three separate categories – goods and freight, passengers, and parcel passenger traffic, the last group including milk, horses in their boxes, even elephants – John Barnby once 'handled' an elephant at Malmesbury station, during receipt and despatch of a travelling circus!

The passenger monthly returns were large sheets of paper, newspaper size, generally four double-sided sheets made up together. A balance sheet was made up and this had to balance to a penny. The monthly returns, called 'classifications', were copied out and the closing numbers brought forward as 'commencing numbers'. All tickets issued to other railway companies had to be entered for each separate station on a form with the numbers and routes. From these the Railway Clearing House worked out the division of receipts on a mileage and terminals basis.

Once a week at least, the proof book was made up, a large volume in which all issues available were entered and the closing numbers at the end of each month taken off – thus a double-entry check was made on the daily train book, which was summarised for the corresponding period. Each separate week's proof was then cross-balanced with the total issues for the month and with the daily train book summaries totalled. Thus the last day of each month was particularly busy for Malmesbury's clerk, all this on a day when he also had to collect all outstanding accounts.

The monthly returns to audit could then be prepared – these were essentially a copy of the proof book totals all separated in the same way, with all 'blank card' and 'paper ticket' issues individually entered in full. Paper tickets were in a book form with a retained carbon copy. This in fact was the old form of ticket used in coaching days when passengers were 'booked', the carbon copy replacing the earlier counterfoil system.

It was the clerk's responsibility to keep up to date on GWR practice and alterations to procedures – there were always many books of instructions and masses of circulars for Mr. Barnby to read, and both he and the station master shared the duty of passing on relevant material to the other station staff. The station master issued a GWR rulebook to staff about once every ten years, but this was constantly being amended. Most instructions were in the appendix to the rulebook, a much larger volume also being constantly amended. Vital required reading for the clerk was the Coaching Arrangements Book which was issued and updated regularly by the Railway Clearing House and contained the regulations for passenger tickets and their use.

John Barnby had to make up the timesheets and paybills of the weekly paid staff at the station, and also for the salaried staff who were paid monthly – the latter simply himself and the station master. Staff were paid on Fridays in his time, later Thursdays, although it was the station master who gave out the pay packets. Regulations required that whoever made up paybills could not pay the staff, for obvious reasons. Paybills were made out in copying ink, Malmesbury station office containing a Victorian screwpress for making copies of accounts, a device with which the clerk had to take great care, seeing that it was evenly damped with ink.

Thus Malmesbury gave the clerk the widest possible training, a fine grounding in railway administrative work for a young man with his sights set on promotion. In John Barnby's time, he simply left one task to begin another. Added to the huge amount of clerical work, of course, there were often many interruptions to the routine – tickets to issue to passengers, excess fares to charge after the arrival of a train, staff calling with wage packet queries, farmers calling with cheques for milk carriage, train enquiries to answer, both on the phone and at the booking office window, and breaking off to ensure three pips were sounded on the internal telephone to Kingsmead Crossing each time a train left the station ... then it was back to the accounting ...

Cecil Moore, 1889—1945.
Courtesy
Mr. & Mrs. C. J. Doswell

PARCEL PORTER – Cecil Moore

The work of Malmesbury's parcel porter was generally involved with all aspects of the parcels work and accounts, although, to a certain extent, his duties at a country branch terminus were, like the clerk's, much more varied than parcels work at a major station. In addition to being responsible for all checking, charging and invoicing of parcel accounts and the preparation of statistical returns for Bristol, including the busy milk traffic, he had to be on the platform ready for the arrival of every train to assume the duty of ticket collector. The parcels office from which he worked was just to the right of the usual passenger exit as people left the train, and while working at his desk he could see clearly when to move into position. His office contained a table at the rear for extra workspace, shelves for parcels and a weighing machine.

The parcel porter was expected to make up collected passenger tickets for audit, and again, being close to the relevant area of the station, assisted with cattle loading on market days. He dealt with lost property matters, regularly arranged for a supply of suitable railway vehicles for conveyance of parcel traffic and had to wire the details of outgoing perishable traffic (such as bacon and cattle) forward to each transfer point and destination. Outward parcel traffic at the station was small compared to the vast amounts coming in, typical traffic being conveyed to Hodder's Drapery, Hinwood's Outfitters and the various master grocers in the town. During Cecil Moore's long career at Malmesbury station, parcel porter's hours were 8.30 to 12.15, with an hour's lunch-break, then 2.15 to 5.30 pm, the first period of his afternoon duty being in the booking office while the clerk was at lunch, during which period he would take over the issuing of tickets and man the telephone.

As far as is known, only three men ever held the post of parcel porter at Malmesbury, although it is possible that the job existed there before Cecil Moore was appointed about 1917. Enlarged parcel office accommodation was provided at the station in 1912, and it could be that the parcel porter duty

was created at this time, but nothing has been found in the staff records to throw any light on this. Cecil Moore was born at Stoke St. Gregory in Somerset in March 1889. He started work on the GWR at Durston in 1905, then after a period at Langport East, he moved to Malmesbury as a porter about 1908. After appointment to the parcels work, long service on the branch and acquired seniority saw him become 'leading parcel porter,' during which time he built up a reputation for excellent clerical work, a standard maintained at the station by his successors, Len Hillman and Bill Archer. He was very well liked by his fellow-workers and took a great interest in all aspects of railway operating, a fact reflected in his participation in the GWR's signalling examination in 1922, which he passed with a very high mark. In the days before paid overtime, his working day often stretched well beyond the allotted hours, working from 7 am until well into the evening in order to keep the work going successfully, cheerfully turning his hand to other duties as required, be it deputising for an absent guard or porter or working the levers in the signal box – such was the spirit of the GWR in those days.

Mr. Moore was a sad loss to the branch when he died at Bath on 24th August 1945, his death being thought to have been due to an illness caused by handling foreign money at the station. Railway staff were well-represented at his funeral, in the persons of Percy Wood (Malmesbury station master), Miss D. Curtis and Miss M. Butler (clerks), Mr. B. Hunt (Little Somerford station master), Joe Halliday and Charlie Barnes (GWR locomotive department) and Frank Strange (GWR Engineering Dept). Bearers were Frank Hewlett, Jim Thornbury, Ian Beard and George Eldridge. Mr. Moore's son Gilbert later worked as clerk at Malmesbury for three years.

CHECKER – George Woodward

One of the most physically exacting jobs at a country terminus such as Malmesbury was that of checker. In the early years of the branch the station staff included a shunter, but this post was regraded as checker during the early years of the century, which meant that shunting operations were but one of his duties. In addition, the checker was responsible for

Staff group enlarged from the front cover photograph, showing (second from left) George Woodward (1882–1972) who was at this time (1908) a porter.   *Courtesy Mr. & Mrs. C. J. Doswell*

dealing with all goods traffic in and out of Malmesbury, recording goods 'unentered' and 'not to hand', working the lever frame and recording entries in the train register book in the little signal box, and making up the daily rolling stock count to send to Swindon. In 1921 the checker's hours were 8.30 to 12.30 with a break for lunch, then 1.30 to 5.30 pm.

George Woodward spent 44 years at Malmesbury station, 11 as a porter and 33 as checker. Born in 1882 at Studley, near Calne, he started on the GWR in 1901 as a lad porter at Frome and arrived at Malmesbury in March 1902 to take up duties as porter at a wage of 17/- a week. He was appointed checker in April 1913 at 21/- a week and held the post until his retirement in 1946. During this time he passed the GWR safety examination and is chiefly remembered today for the feats he used to perform in shunting and making up trains in Malmesbury yard, always seeming to have a total appreciation of the number of wagons and coaches to be handled and the length of track available. He died in 1972.

Malmesbury's checker worked from an office adjoining the goods shed where he had a telephone and was based close to that area of the terminus where he performed the bulk of his duties. Wearing a typical GWR sleeved waistcoat, from under which would extend an apron when busy with loading and unloading work, his was quite the most demanding and complex of the outdoor jobs at the terminus in days when everything went by rail. During years of Sunday service on the branch he shared alternate Sunday duties with a porter. He was responsible for working the crane in the goods shed when heavy deliveries such as machinery required careful removal from or transfer to a wagon. He assisted the carman, in later years the motor driver, in loading and unloading, and was masterly expert in the use of the shunting pole which enabled him to speedily separate wagons when needed. He was required to have a full working knowledge of the train service in and out of the station, never too difficult at Malmesbury, but nonetheless had to watch the clock and arrange his routine so that he could get across to the signal box to switch points and signals and maintain the train register.

As the checker had responsibility for the stock count, he made a point of taking this personally across to the clerk in the booking office each day – this count was Swindon's means of knowing exactly what rolling stock each station had each day, and the checker would often receive telephoned instructions to make up a set of a particular kind of wagon for transfer elsewhere, the required stock being taken to Dauntsey either by a mixed train or light engine if the timetable permitted.

Market days at Malmesbury placed great demands on the Checker. To accommodate market traffic it was necessary at one time to clear much of the rolling stock from the yard and stable it at Great Somerford and Dauntsey, taking care to leave the middle road clear so cattle trucks could be horse-drawn up to the cattle pens two at a time, loaded there and sent back through the engine shed road to form a train on the main track into the station. Horses had to be hired from the Malmesbury Coal Company for this purpose, and this, too, was the checker's responsibility. On lengthy cattle trains two brake vans were required, one next to the locomotive and one at the rear, and many times Woodward acted as emergency guard on these trains.

John Quarrell (1857–1935).
Courtesy Mr. & Mrs. W. G. Down

BRANCH GUARD – John Quarrell

Through the descendants of John Quarrell we have a vital link going back to the very beginning of the Malmesbury line in 1877. He was born in Bradpole, near Bridport in Dorset, on 8th January 1857. Finding employment difficult to secure there, he moved to Bath in November 1877 to take a 16/- a week job as porter. It is related that he arrived in Malmesbury on a platelayer's trolley before the opening of the branch, and obviously saw a good opportunity to gain not merely a job on the new line but a foothold in a community, being taken on as a porter in time to start work on the very first day of service. He set up home in Gastons Road with his wife Rosalie from Bridport, moving to Foundry Road in 1902, by which time his pay had risen to 20/- a week. He was promoted to 'passenger guard' on the branch in March 1912 on a wage of 23/-, succeeding Jacob Baker who had also been present at Malmesbury since the first day in 1877.

Malmesbury's guard was booked to start work at 6.45 am, giving him around 30 minutes to prepare for the first branch train of the day. He would call at the station office to collect his bag, which contained his red and green flags, current working timetable and appendix, oil-lit handlamp, rulebook, twelve detonators and a supply of blank train journals. In his uniform pocket would be his whistle, carriage key and company pocket watch. The three coaches were always left at the platform overnight and his first job, after putting his bag into his compartment, was to inspect the doors and check that no unauthorised persons were already aboard (it was known that the occasional vagrant would avail himself of the warmth and shelter afforded by a Malmesbury branch

A staff group on Malmesbury station in 1906. Porter John Quarrell is third from the left, but it has not been possible to positively
identify anyone else in the group.
Courtesy Mrs. Grace Whiteside

carriage whilst left unattended at night). The early turn porter would undertake any cleaning required while the guard attended to internal correspondence and brought his train journal up to date for the previous day, recording departures, stops, delays or other eventualities. When the branch engine came off shed to join its train, it would be the guard's duty to couple up and test the efficiency of the vacuum brake pipe. It was necessary to see that the brakes were releasing correctly, make checks on the lighting, communication cord, and first-aid equipment, and record the coach numbers in his journal. The destination boards on the coaches would have to be reversed from the 'Malmesbury' of the previous night to read 'Dauntsey'.

Although the routine on a country branch would be largely the same each day and involve the same crews simply alternating shifts each week, loyal staff in those days were meticulous in their application of firm discipline and organisation. Even without the watchful eye of the station master, not on duty until 9 am, it would have been a matter of honour and principle, not to mention the safety on which the GWR prided itself, that every detail of the guard's routine was rigidly adhered to, particularly on the first morning train out where it would be vital to set the tone for the working day. Thus driver and fireman's names would have to be recorded, and the crew advised of the train load (important on the 'mixed' trains), expected traffic at Great Somerford and any alterations to the usual journey.

As departure time neared, there would be passengers to reassure that this was indeed the train to Dauntsey, enquiries to answer about connections there, and late arrivals to politely hurry along. Stowage of parcels and luggage was checked to ensure safe handling, then he would make a final inspection of nearside doors, check his company-issue watch and announce 'Take your seats, please, ladies and gentlemen, the Dauntsey train is about to leave ... Right away, driver!' Then with a wave of his green flag, a blast on his whistle, he would step aboard and the train would depart.

The guard's turn at Malmesbury ended at 2.45 pm, his snack lunch usually being taken on the train, having worked four trains in each direction in normal service. The remainder of the day's services were worked by a porter guard, whose hours in 1921 were 10 am–1.15 pm and 2.15–7 pm. This man's morning turn was mainly general porterage work around the station, then on his return after lunch he would take over as guard on the 2.30 pm mixed train. From 1922 guard duties on the branch train included issuing of passenger tickets to people boarding at Great Somerford after the station's reduction to a halt, and collection of tickets for passing to the Malmesbury station master.

John Quarrell became a familiar and well-loved figure on the Malmesbury branch, to which he gave 48 years service, known for his gingery waxed moustache, his smart attire and his impeccable courtesy. Most folk in the area today still remember him with affection and respect – 'If John Quarrell came along, you made sure you were on the train – *he* was in control'. At Dauntsey, passengers alighting from main line stopping trains there would be hailed by a rich Dorset accent announcing in harmony with the Dauntsey porters, 'Dauntsey, Dauntsey, change for Great Somerford and Malmesbury'. One of those porters once recalled that Quarrell used to polish his shoes to a gleaming shine, but apparently only on the front – his stock reply to remarks on this habit was 'Oi'm a good soldier, oi never looks behoind!'

He is remembered as a gentleman in every sense, loyal to the GWR, his King and country, and proud of his work and family. His interests centred around his allotment, his chickens, bee-keeping and wine-making. He grew a special strain of gooseberries exclusively for use in his home-made wine. He was a regular winner of first prize for honey at the annual Flower Show in Malmesbury. He retired from the railway on 18th July 1925, and died in 1935, his funeral taking place at St. Mary's Church, Malmesbury, now the church hall in The Triangle. Typically, the local GWR staff were out in force at the service, being represented by station master R. Faull, parcel porter Cecil Moore, checker George Woodward, relief porter Jim Thornbury, guard Frank Philips (his successor ten years previously) and Arthur Ponting from the branch permanent way gang.

PORTER – Bill Archer

The porters at Malmesbury were always busy with all aspects of running the train service – assisting passengers, loading and unloading parcels mail and goods traffic, cleaning the station, filling in office duties when required, and working the signal box. The 1921 report on GWR duties described the porters at Malmesbury as being fully occupied in their duties, and in light of this the job of lad porter was reintroduced in 1923. Although in later years the designation 'goods porter' did exist at Malmesbury, as with other jobs at the terminus, duties often inevitably and necessarily overlapped, and porters were always heavily involved with both passenger train and goods traffic.

Bill Archer was born in Malmesbury in 1897. Like his contemporary Percy Wood, his association with the Malmesbury line began relatively late. He was initially a baker, served in World War I in the Ambulance Corps, and spent nearly 20 years in South Wales in the brewing industry. However, he longed to return to his home town, and 1939 saw him bring his family back to Malmesbury and the house in Burnivale where he was born and where he passed away in 1980. After working in the RAF Police at Hullavington for a year, Jim Thornbury advised him to go to the railway station at Malmesbury if he wanted to find work nearer home. This he did, starting work as a porter in June 1940.

In 1940 the two porters' shifts at Malmesbury were 6.45 am to 2.30 pm, and 11.00 am to 7.15 pm. On the early turn, Bill would sweep out the B-set coaches and the station office, and book any tickets for passengers who arrived for the early train, the 7.21 to Little Somerford. Although not usually a hectic period of the day, wartime movements of servicemen did produce more use of the early train, as it was the only one of the day that was any use for travelling long distance, especially for a serviceman returning from leave. The early porter was in charge of the station until about 9 am, when the station master and clerk came on duty.

Last day of passenger services, 8th September 1951. (Left to right) Bill Archer, Ken Stoneham, Percy Wood and Bert Reynolds. Ken Stoneham, b. 1925, was Malmesbury cleaner 1941–2. He moved on to Andover and Swindon, before returning to the branch in 1945 to fire for Dick Cooper. *Bert Vizor*

With the return of the train from Little Somerford into Malmesbury at 8.10, the really busy time began, even with the curtailed wartime service. Passengers would require help with luggage and the inward goods and parcels had to be quickly booked and organised so that the motor lorry could leave with its deliveries. Porters' lunch breaks were always staggered so that one was always on duty. In the afternoon the really busy time was that prior to the departure of the 5.30 pm mixed train, the busiest for outward parcels traffic.

Bill's last duties of the day would be to book tickets for the last train out to Little Somerford, and record any incoming parcels ready for delivery next morning, a complete list of everything left in the office having to be made in case of theft. As the station master and clerk usually went off duty around 5.30 pm unless it was unusually busy, it was the evening porter's job to lock the station and leave the keys in position for the morning porter to collect – this hiding place remains a trade secret!

Bill Archer was moved to Swindon in 1941 to work as a goods guard, returning to Malmesbury in 1949 as parcels porter, responsible for parcels accounts and collection of money from both consignees and collectors of parcels locally. If his duties were less heavy than 1940, more speed was required, and he was very proud of the fact that he was complimented from British Railways in London in 1950 on the standard of his book-keeping.

During the first days of September 1951, Bill worked as relief guard on the branch through the absence of Frank Hewlett, and as a result he fulfilled this duty on the last passenger train on 8th September. He recalled taking his wife and granddaughter for a last ride on the 6.30 pm to Little Somerford, but otherwise had no strong emotional response to closure – 'I had a job to do'. He stayed on as senior checker until final closure of the line to all traffic in 1962, being moved to Little Somerford until his retirement in 1965.

Len Hillman, Malmesbury parcel porter in the late '40s. *Courtesy Doreen Hicks*

Len Hillman takes Doreen Curtis for a spin on his motor bike. *Courtesy Doreen Hicks*

Herbert Sydney Hill, Dauntsey station master 1914—34. *Courtesy Derek Hayes*

Henry Jefferies Little Somerford station master 1908—21.

Edgar Doswell Malmesbury station master 1907—19. *Cty. Mr. & Mrs. C. J. Doswell*

Malmesbury station master Percy Wood with his clerks, Doreen
Curtis (right) and daughter Sybil.   *Courtesy Doreen Hicks*

Albert Ham, the last station master
at Great Somerford, employed
there 1918—22.
Courtesy Cty. Mrs. Edna Evans

Bill Archer looks on in amusement as porter Bert Reynolds tries to persuade a donkey to sample the delights of rail travel
during the removal of a complete farm from the area via Malmesbury station.   *Wiltshire Newspapers*

Jim Thornbury preparing the milk train in the late '20s.

Courtesy Jim Thornbury

LAD PORTER – E. W. ('Jim') Thornbury

The lad porter on a country station was a 'dogsbody' to everyone. The job was by its very nature a short-lived designation, as he attained adult status as porter at age 18. A lad porter's duties could be summed up in one expression – 'to assist as required'. The varied duties made for a valuable early schooling in railway life and work, and a good lad could carve himself a path to having charge of his own small station later in his career. For instance, Albert Jefferies earned 8/- a week at Malmesbury in 1889 as lad porter, and later progressed to become station master at Stanton and at Hullavington.

Jim Thornbury was born in Malmesbury in 1906. He left school at 14 and worked as a stable boy for horse dealer Bill Rich, but he proved unsuitable for this work, being a large, well-built lad, and therefore too heavy for the horses. He sought employment at the station, and was taken on as lad porter in 1923. As a child he had often assisted John Quarrell in tending his garden, and now had the opportunity to work with the long-serving guard. Jim is therefore our human link with the earliest days of the branch.

He worked an early turn of 6.30 am to 3.30 pm and a later turn of 11.15 am to 7.15 pm, these shifts being worked on an alternate weekly basis. On the morning turn he lit the fires in the station in winter, cleaned the working surfaces and toilets,

then turned his attention to the passenger coaches at the platform where they stood overnight – these would be swept out with the aid of a box fitted to the steps of each carriage flush with the floor to collect the debris. A daily task in which he took great pride was shining the coach door handles with 'Brasso'. The platform had to be swept, then he would be ready for the arrival of the morning mixed train in from Dauntsey. Fish would have to be sorted and taken across to the goods shed on a barrow, to be transferred to the GWR dray for delivery to fishmongers in the town. Over at the goods shed he would assist parcel porter Cecil Moore as a 'caller-off', collecting parcels in the shed, weighing them on the scales and calling out their weight, place of origin, charge stamp number and destination. His father, Ernest, was the local carman and Jim would assist him next, unloading trucks and filling the dray with deliveries of jam, sugar, cheese, butter, glass, fish, furniture and general merchandise, all destined for traders up in the High Street. It was normal for the lad porter to assist on the GWR delivery to the town if there was a large load, going along as vanboy to assist his father, duties also undertaken by later lad porters for the motor driver.

Other work included manning the hand pump to raise water from the river up into the water tank in the loft in the station building, and cleaning the signal lamps and the stop block lights by the cattle pens. When on the station, he would meet each train with a barrow to collect any incoming parcels, and on a busy day he might be assigned to ticket collection by the gate behind the loading bay, as two exits, one either side of the station building, would be opened on such occasions as fairs, market day or other events. Preparations for the 5.30 pm mixed train would provide him with a great deal of work, as would loading the milk as it came in from the farms and from the milk factory during the later part of the afternoon. By the time he was made up to a full porter he was earning 35/- a week, although he could boost this to £3 for one week a month by assisting with milk loading for the Sunday train.

In 1926 he left Malmesbury for short spells as a ticket collector at Weston-Super-Mare and relief porter at Badminton, then returned to Malmesbury as a porter in 1927. From this time he developed as very much a 'Jack-of-all-trades' on the railway, working from 1930 to 1951 as a relief porter based at Malmesbury. This involved going at a moment's notice to deputise for absent colleagues, and as a result he was never out of work, being able to turn his hand to carman, lorry driver, porter, shunter, signalman, guard or clerk. It was hard but varied work with a lot of travelling, going as far afield as Severn Beach or Weymouth (he was at Weymouth during the bombing in World War II). Staff illness or holidays would provide him with regular work at Malmesbury. The work carried a 3/6d a day lodging allowance, which he could save if sent to stations such as Coalpit Heath or Winterbourne along the Badminton line, for on such postings he could rise at 4.30 and cycle, in all weathers, in order to reach work at 6.30 am.

Jim and his wife raised six children at their home in Bristol Street, and he kept a railway allotment and a chicken run near the signal box at Malmesbury, renting land from the GWR at a rate of 4d per perch a year for his hundred fowl. In 1951 he became signalman at Hullavington and moved to Badminton box in 1968, retiring when it closed in 1970.

Malmesbury platform c.1930, with Cecil Moore (centre), Jim Thornbury (right) and an unidentified employee posing beside guard's van No. 35679.

Bertram Farmer

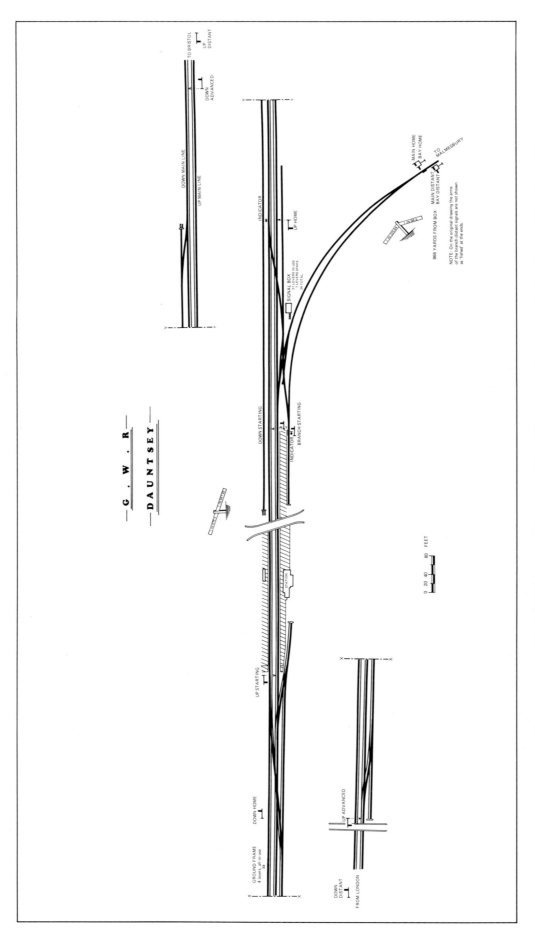

— G . W . R —

— D A U N T S E Y —

Dauntsey station, as shown on a plan sent to the BoT in 1883, a goods siding was provided to the east of the station. The points were almost certainly worked locally from ground levers. The down refuge siding on the Bristol side of the road bridge dated from 1873, and is shown on the 1883 plan as being laid to the narrow gauge only. Whether it was originally laid to mixed gauge is not known. Substantial cutting back of the clay bank was required to make space for this siding, which was provided so that slow trains could be 'recessed' while being overtaken by express traffic. It was installed before the commencement of work on building the junction for the Malmesbury branch, and the points were worked by a local lever, though some interlocking (probably by wire) was provided with the down line signals worked from levers on the platform. When the Malmesbury branch was grafted on to the existing mixed gauge layout, all the new trackage was to the narrow gauge only, including the new siding adjacent to the signal box, used primarily for stabling milk and other traffic to and from Malmesbury. As noted by the BoT Inspector in his 1877 report, there was no junction for passenger trains here, only a facility for transferring goods traffic to the main line. The goods yard at the eastern end of the station retained its mixed gauge trackwork at this time, including the 'sidestepping' so that the narrow gauge wagons were on the outside of the mixed gauge track whether on the up side or the down. There was no crossover from the up to down main lines anywhere in the station. The ground frame provided at the insistence of the BoT Inspector, who was concerned that because of the intervening bridge the signalman could not properly control movements at the London end of the station, contained just four levers.

CHAPTER THIRTEEN

SIGNALLING

THE Malmesbury branch was worked on the 'one engine in steam' principle from the outset, with the use of a train staff, round and coloured white, without which no train could proceed over the line. Semaphore signals were provided from the beginning, under the supervision of Thomas Blackall, the GWR's Signal Engineer at Reading, and although the working of the line between Dauntsey and Malmesbury and on the later truncated branch from Little Somerford was an uncomplicated business, the Board of Trade plans and pre-1900 OS maps reveal that signalling in the early days was in fact far more lavish and painstaking than that provided in later years.

Seemingly extravagant signalling existed on such branches during the last century because of the stringent requirements of the Board of Trade, and after the BoT regulations were relaxed in the early years of the 20th century much equipment was not renewed as it became life-expired. Thus on a country branch such as the Malmesbury line, rather than spend large sums on renewing unnecessary signalling equipment, those installations of the 1877 period no longer required were removed, and signal posts shown on First Edition OS maps at the level crossings and some of those at Somerford and Dauntsey stations were no longer shown on the 1900 and subsequent editions.

The date of the opening of Dauntsey signal box has not been discovered. On 13th November 1872 the GWR Board authorised construction of up line sidings at Dauntsey at a cost of £944 15s 0d. In February 1873 the Board passed authorisation for £850 to be spent on the locking of the points and signals at Dauntsey, including the provision of spare levers. Such a substantial sum of money would certainly have included the installation of a signal box. On his inspection of the new down relief siding, Captain Tyler of the Board of Trade reported on 6th June 1873: 'This siding has been laid in as a refuge in which slow trains may be placed when it is necessary to clear the line for faster trains. The siding and safety points are worked together by one lever and are wire-locked with the home signal at the Dauntsey station. The levers for working the signals are on the passenger platform, but the lever for working the points is on the ground, near the siding points.'

Captain Tyler recommended that the distant signal should be interlocked with the siding and safety points, and that this could be cheaply accomplished by means of a bar attached to the home signal, which would render it impossible for the distant to be lowered until the lever of the home signal had first been pulled over. In a further inspection by Colonel Yolland on 24th June 1873 it was noted that the locking of the distant and home signals had been provided. Apparently the signal box had not been built by this date. Since the construction of a signal box had been authorised the previous year, it is possible that Dauntsey box was built during 1874 in connection with the provision of the block telegraph, but no evidence has been found to confirm this. It is certain that the box was in existence by the time the branch opened, as the Board of Trade inspection report refers to 'Dauntsey Cabin at West end of station'. According to plans supplied to the BoT in 1883, this was a two-storey box with a 34-lever frame, 27 in use with 7 spares.

Dauntsey signal box is believed to have been built in 1877 when the layout was remodelled to accommodate the junction for Malmesbury. It was a Class 3 signal box and remained so even after closure of the branch in 1933. In 1884, before the introduction of the 8-hour day, Dauntsey signalmen worked 12-hour shifts, changing at 7 a.m. and 7 p.m., sharing a Sunday duty alternate weeks and earning 20/- a week. The signal box is contemporary with the box at Malmesbury and belongs to the same architectural style, but it is of the more usual brick-to-floor construction. No photograph has been traced, however, showing Dauntsey box in its original condition. A good number of these boxes, now referred to by the Signalling Record Society at 'Type 2', survived into the Beeching era of railway closures, but nearly all had been subjected to extensive alterations to the timber parts of the structure. Most noticeably in the case of Dauntsey, the box would have had vertical matchboarding below the windowsill down to operating floor level. The replacement of this by the new brickwork visible on the photograph does a great deal to change the appearance of the box. By this time there had also been alterations to the front windows — the central set of small panes of glass remained, but the replacement of the original and sliding windows by the later GWR '3 up, 2 down' type sashes is clearly seen. The torpedo ventilators on the roof cannot have been original as they were not introduced on GWR boxes until the 1890s. Nor is the cast iron nameplate original, the name probably being first spelt out in individual metal letters screwed directly to the woodwork. The lever frame was of the 'double twist' pattern installed in August 1903 with capacity for 37 levers. Besides its telephone links in either direction along the main line, to the boxes at Incline (up direction) and Langley Crossing (down), Dauntsey box was also linked by railway telephone with Malmesbury and the three crossing lodges on the branch. This photo was taken after closure of the Malmesbury line, fence posts to the left marking the beginning of the abandoned section of line.   *Kenneth Leach*

217

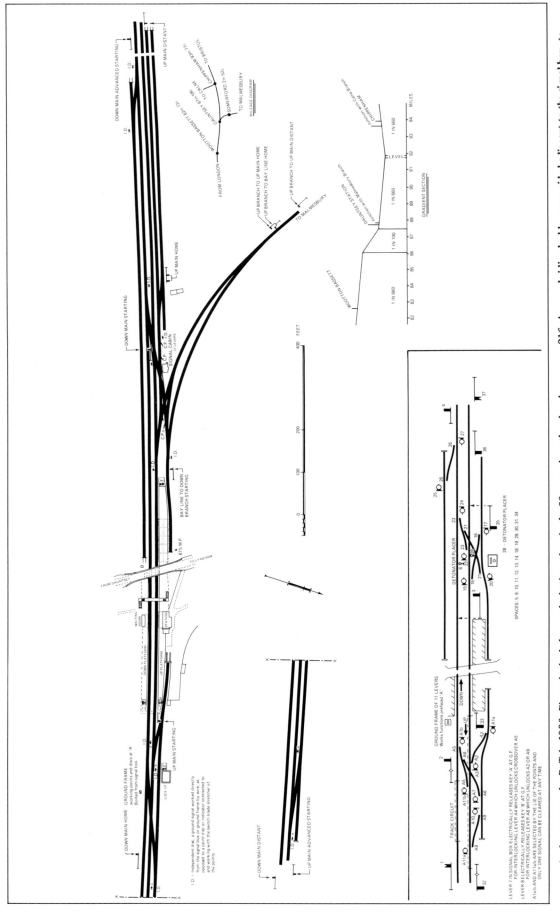

A plan sent to the BoT in 1906. Five principal changes had taken place in the 23 years since the plan shown on p. 216. A second siding had been provided adjacent to the signal box, to cater for the increased transfer traffic for the Malmesbury branch (mainly milk). A short dead-end siding, which had been provided since 1883 between the branch and main lines at the end of the bay platform, was replaced in 1906 by dual catch points. The ground frame at the London end of the station had been replaced by a second installation, several yards nearer to London, with additional levers to work the disc signals now provided at the goods yard points, as elsewhere throughout the station. A slip connection opposite the signal box now provided an up to down main crossover. To accommodate all these changes, a new frame for 37 levers was installed in the signal box, with 33 of them in use. (Inset) No numbered signal diagram for Dauntsey, while the branch was in passenger use, has been found. This diagram shows the connections beside the box after the remodelling subsequent to the closure of the branch, and also yet another alteration to the siding layout at the goods yard end. A slip connection (ground frame lever 5) was now provided, finally giving a second mains crossover and thus the ability to run round a train on the main line. To work this enlarged layout, a new (third) ground frame was installed, situated nearer the end of the down platform and more convenient for the station staff who usually had to work it. Unlike its predecessors, this ground frame was not bolted from the signal box by rods, but was unlocked by keys released electrically from instruments at the ground frame when the release levers in the signal box were pulled over. To assist in the safe working at the London end of the layout, which was largely out of view of the signalman, two track circuits had been installed.

Colonel Rich, in his Inspection Report for the Board of Trade in 1877, made some interesting references to the signalling at the new junction (see page 32), the most significant of which referred to there being a junction at Dauntsey for goods trains but not for passenger trains. Board of Trade requirements of the period dictated that junctions of all single lines intended for passenger train use were to be formed as double line junctions. To avoid this expense at Dauntsey there was no provision (as built in 1877) for passenger trains to run to or from the branch to the main lines.

The Inspecting officer's Report also stated that the points and junctions at the east end of the station had to be worked from a separate cabin. This was because the signalman's view of the far end of the station was obscured by the road overbridge. The result was that as first sited the up advanced starting signal was beyond his proper limits of control and was in a position whereby shunting engines working the yard were forced to run past it at danger into the next block section. As a result of the Report, a four-lever ground frame was provided to control movements to and from the goods yard, and the up advanced starter was placed out beyond the furthest goods yard points. The original ground frame was locked

by a rod from the signal box and located on the down side to the east of the down main home signal. Later plans reveal that during the life of the station there were successively at least three ground frames at three different sites at this end of the station. The 1906 plans show a frame apparently closer to the station, to the west of the down home signal and bolted by rods to the signal box. From this position it worked points making connections to the down main and at the east end of the up sidings, with associated independent disc signals, and a connection from the platform siding to the up main with its signals. Further alterations of 1908 saw a new ground frame installed at the east end of the down platform during enlargement of the yard facilities. This new frame was also released from the signal box by a pair of locking rods, but later the interlocking levers in the frame were electrically released from the box using key release instruments, allowing the man working the frame to take one or both keys out according to whether both up and down lines were affected or the up line only.

An interesting feature of Dauntsey's signalling was the position of the up and down main line platform starting signals. The BoT Report refers to the need for these to be

Looking eastwards from the end of the up platform, this view shows the goods yard on the left, with the up starting signal (33) prominent in the foreground. The hut beside the down line on the right contained the ground frame working all the points and disc signals for the yard. A later replacement for the down home signal (2) was fitted with a quadrant-shaped board, white on the side facing approaching drivers, to improve the sighting of the signal which was otherwise viewed against the confusing background of the station and overbridges.

placed at the 'proper sides of the railway (left hand)', an indication that these signals had been erected on the 'wrong' sides of the line for what must have been sighting purposes through the road overbridge. They were sited on the 'wrong side' so that the signalman could have an adequate view of the up starter and that drivers of down trains leaving the platform might properly view the down starter. Whether any notice was taken of the Colonel over these signals is not known, but it appears that someone may have pointed out to him the practicalities involved with this specific location, as the 1883 plan clearly shows them in place to the right of their respective lines, with the down starter on the up platform at the west of the station – a westward extension of the up side to provide a branch bay. Subsequent plans show the up main starter sited conventionally at the east end of the up platform, but photograph and diagram evidence show that the down main starting signal was located in at least three different positions during the life of the station – 1906 and 1912 plans show it between the up and down lines not far from the signal box whereas by the 1950s it had been resited again just off the end of the old branch bay platform. These changes were probably a result of trying to obtain the best possible site for driver vision of the road ahead.

At the time of opening in 1877 the branch starter at Dauntsey was located on the north side of the bay line, whilst out on the branch itself two bracket signals protected the approach to the junction. The outermost of these, 966 yards from the signal box and out beyond Swallett Gate Bridge, carried distant arms reading to the bay or main line, the innermost carrying the corresponding home signals. In August 1903 Dauntsey signal box was enlarged and a new frame of 37 levers installed, and it may have been at this time that the bracket distant was replaced by a straight post signal bearing an up branch to up main distant, located to the right ('wrong') side facing Dauntsey. At some stage between 1906 and 1923 this signal was altered from a working to a fixed distant and resited to the left just north of Swallett Gate bridge, as shown on the OS map surveyed in 1923.

In the 1877 Report both Kingsmead and Dauntsey Road crossings were reported as requiring signals and lamps. As chronicled in Chapter 4, an accident occurred at the latter place even before train service on the branch had begun, and it may have been that there were no protective signals then erected. Although the station and crossing at Somerford had the protection of distant signals, as shown in the BoT plans of 1878, there was no such provision at either Kingsmead or Dauntsey Road until much later. First Edition OS maps, surveyed in 1886, show a solitary signal post at each crossing, both in similar positions on the east side of the track and apparently on the north side of the gates. These would have been home signals to provide a stop indication when the gates were closed across the track, and were undoubtedly those provided as a result of Colonel Rich's Report, in which he referred to the need for signals and lamps which the 'Signal Inspector proposed to place on the gateposts . . . to be moved by the opening and shutting of the gates'. Unfortunately no photographic evidence has come to light to show whether these stop signals were on the gates or in fact separate posts, the OS maps of 1886 being neither clear nor conclusive on this point. What seems certain is that at some stage during the period 1886–1900 these signals were removed and distants

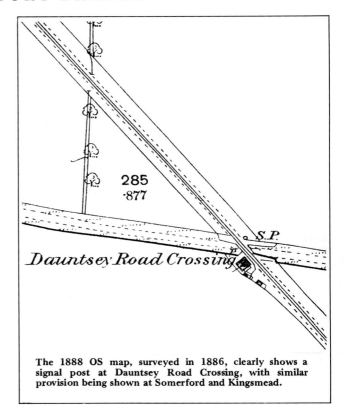

The 1888 OS map, surveyed in 1886, clearly shows a signal post at Dauntsey Road Crossing, with similar provision being shown at Somerford and Kingsmead.

installed which were controlled from ground frames at each crossing, although it is possible that the old signals and the new distants did exist simultaneously. The 1900 OS maps have been amended to show that no stop signals existed at either Kingsmead or Dauntsey Road by this time, and although BoT signalling requirements on branch lines were not relaxed until some years after this, if the OS is to be believed, it is probable that these and other signals on the branch were removed during the last years of the 19th century as they neared the end of their useful life – a cheaper expedient to maintenance or replacement.

The modest station at Somerford enjoyed substantial signalling provision in Victorian times, again a reflection of the fact that the branch was built during the period when Board of Trade regulations were very stringent. Inspection plans of June 1878 show six signals, distants, homes and starting signals in each direction, all worked from the little bay-windowed signal room in the station building. The lever frame would have had a minimum of nine working levers controlling the six signals, the goods yard point, a facing point lock and bar, and a gate lock lever (assuming interlocking with gates in the early days). Again, by the turn of the century the signalling here had been reduced with the removal of the home and starting signals, although the 1923 OS map (reproduced on page 90) still mysteriously shows a signal post in the same position as the original up starter. However, one should, in this instance, consider the map evidence as unsatisfactory, for it would have been possible for a surveyor to overlook a signal post when updating a map, and reference to the 1920s view of the crossing on page 95 indeed shows no signal at this point. A reduction in the signalling here also reflects a realisation that there were cheaper ways of signalling a 'one engine in steam' branch. With only one train at a time on the entire line and with the distants retained to protect the level crossing, the only complication at Somerford was to ensure that the goods yard point was correctly set for a train to pass. These points were no longer worked from the box in the station as they had been in earlier years but had been converted to operation from a small 2-lever ground frame. A key would have been added to the branch train staff to unlock the Somerford station points, an arrangement which was also used on the Little Somerford–Malmesbury line to gain access to the old branch at Kingsmead crossing when it was used for storage of crippled stock. The arrangement of having a key on the train staff came into use on the new branch from 31st May 1934 (nearly a year after the change of junction) following the decision to remove the old branch south of Great Somerford and use the Kingsmead-Great Somerford section as a cripple siding.

Signalling at Malmesbury itself was quite simple and does not appear to have undergone any significant alterations except the signalling reductions of the freight-only days of the

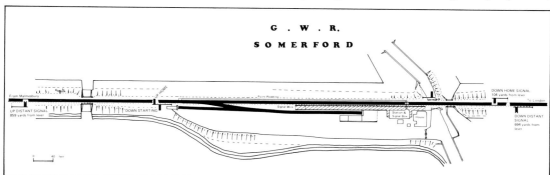

Great Somerford station signalling plan of 1878, showing clearly the full signalling provision of that period.

Great Somerford Halt in 1932, looking towards Malmesbury. The near end of the station building with the open door and bay window, served as the signal cabin, the projecting bay section offering some view along the line in each direction. Originally, Somerford signals were an up distant 859 yards from the lever frame, a down distant in Dauntsey Road direction, 884 yards, an up starter by the level crossing, a down home 104 yards towards Dauntsey Road, and a post at the north end of the platform carrying up home and down starter arms. Locking of signals at Somerford was carried out by 30th June 1878 at a cost of £54 14s 6d. During the time the Reynolds family occupied the station house during the First World War, the signalling had been much reduced, and Joe Reynolds recalled that just three levers were in use in the signal cabin — two for the distants and one for the goods yard point. *Photomatic*

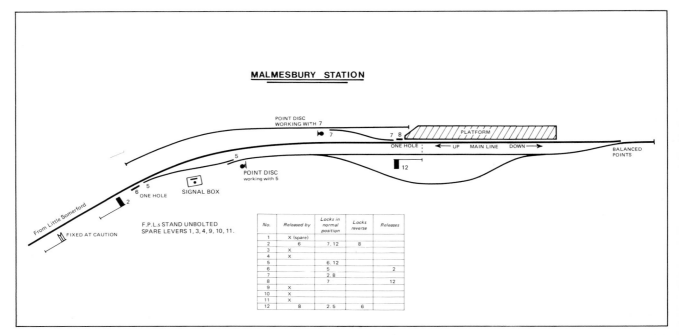

MALMESBURY STATION

No.	Released by	Locks in normal position	Locks reverse	Releases
1	X (spare)			
2	6	7. 12	8	
3	X			
4	X			
5		6. 12		
6		5		2
7		2. 8		
8		7		12
9	X			
10	X			
11	X			
12	8	2. 5	6	

Although this box is not quite like any other on the GWR, it has many features akin to the standard 'Type 2' brick boxes with hipped slate roofs built by the GWR in the mid and late 1870s. It almost certainly dates from the opening of the line in 1877 — the BoT inspection prior to opening making mention of the need for a clock to be installed in it. Clearly it was felt that the view of trains and shunting operations afforded from an elevated box was not essential at a quiet terminus such as Malmesbury, and that a ground-level structure would suffice. Having made this decision, it was sensible to build the cabin entirely from wood, but features such as the vertical boarding, small windows and shallow hipped roof betray its origin. It housed a small frame containing 12 levers.

1950s. All that was required at Malmesbury were two signals, one to let the branch train into the terminus and one to let it out again. Hence, as far as is known, signal posts were erected at only three sites there, these being a home, an up starter by the engine shed, and a distant out beyond Lovers Lane crossing to warn of the approach to the station as trains left the tunnel. Both the home and distant were located 'wrong' side for better sighting. It is probable that the distant was worked by lever No. 1 in Malmesbury signal box (shown as a spare on the signalling diagram) – distant signals were generally worked on the GWR before the Aylesbury accident of 1904 after which the company decided to fix them at danger wherever a severe speed restriction was necessary. Thus Malmesbury's distant became fixed, a permanent indication to the train driver of the approach to the stop signal outside Malmesbury station.

Malmesbury signal box, a GWR structure dating from 1877, was a simple slate-roofed hut enclosing a 12-lever frame. The single-storey edifice was designated a Class 6 box, the lowest grading. It never apparently merited the appointment of a signalman, although it is possible that there was such a post at the terminus in the early days. The staff roster listed in GWR Minutes of 1877 does not include a signalman, though, nor has such a grading been revealed in later records. Indeed, it is known from a 1921 duty roster that it was the checker's job to work the levers, although different members of the station staff apparently did so as required. Without a worked distant, a minimum 10 lever movements per train were all that was required to let a train into Malmesbury and send it out again – levers 2 and 12 controlled the home and starting signals, 5 and 7 working the points to the engine shed loop and the goods shed siding. Nos. 6 and 8 each worked a bolt with locking bar, which prevented points from being switched under a moving train. The remaining levers were

This 1949 view of Malmesbury station provides a good look at the starting signal and makes an interesting comparison with the photo on page 115. There has been complete renewal of the signal post, with a landing stage for the signal lampman, enamel pressed steel arm and a later pattern of finial (earlier finials had four-sided bases, this one has the two-sided base typical of those used latterly on concrete and late-erected wooden post signals). Also clearly visible are the standard round-section point rodding and the detector apparatus (in the foreground) in the wire run to the platform starting signal — the operating rods run transversely under the loop from the detector to the goods shed point (off to the left of the photograph). This was not a very satisfactory arrangement but unavoidable because of the position of the signal well away from its running line.   *L & GRP, cty. David & Charles*

The fixed distant at Malmesbury, placed 'wrong-side' so as to be easily seen by drivers as they emerged from the tunnel. It is made up of standard GWR components with a wooden post and yellow arm with black chevron facing the driver. The strip of metal on the arm was to prevent splitting along the fished end. There is no spectacle on the arm — the front lens of the lamp itself displays a yellow light. The signal post is fairly short in height so there is no safety hoop on the ladder. The signal is effectively derelict here with no top on the lamp or oil vessel inside.

spares which could be brought into use in the event of further sidings and signals being required at the station, developments which never materialised. Access to the engine shed from the middle road and the connection with the goods shed siding were controlled by hand with 'throw-over' levers. The points nearest the terminal buffers were a balanced set, which were forced open by the branch engine as it ran round its train, moving back into position to allow the locomotive to pass onto the shed loop. Malmesbury, then, was a relatively simple terminus to maintain, unlike the original mixed gauge layout at Dauntsey when the branch was first built, and remained in much the same form until fixed signalling at the terminus was taken out of use in 1956.

With the change of junction to Little Somerford in 1933, all the spares in the 61-lever standard 'double-twist' frame in the signal box there were brought into use to accommodate new signals and points for the branch. Down starters were required on both platform lines in order to allow access to

Little Somerford signal box. This was constructed, along with the new Badminton line, in 1903 and is a very elegant and striking example of the then standard GWR design of hipped-roof timber signal box, referred to by the Signalling Record Society as 'Type 27c'. Timber boxes were always less common than brick ones, being more susceptible to attack by the weather and insects, and were only erected where site conditions negated the use of a brick box. At Little Somerford the determining factor must have been the newly made-up ground on the embankment, which would not have had time to settle and consolidate. Similar conditions prevailed at nearby Hullavington where a box was built in the same style, whereas excavated ground at Brinkworth in the opposite direction gave solid foundations for a brick structure. Little Somerford box, graded as Class 3, was a standard 38ft x 13ft x 12ft 6in to operating floor. Oil for the signal lamps and the box was supplied from Avonmouth and stored in the oil shed on the opposite side of the station across the forecourt. The cask held 50 gallons. Signal lamps were the responsibility of the district lampman and the signalman was responsible for keeping the box itself lit. Tilley pressure lamps (which had a mantle and used less oil) were used by 1939 but these were removed for the duration of the Second World War as they gave too much illumination, particularly at an exposed main line site like Little Somerford. The lower windows illuminated the locking room, which, being the domain of the area Signal Department, was rarely used by local signalmen, except to park a bicycle, here seen outside on a fine day. This photograph was taken in 1965 when the box was nearing the end of its life; it was closed on 18th June 1967.

Graham Carey

A 1950s view of Little Somerford, looking towards Swindon with a South Wales express passing through. The up main starting signal post is of the tubular steel type, supplied from the signal works at Reading in sizes of 18, 22 and 26 feet. It appears that for some reason this post was one size larger than it need be! The arm was, of course, placed at the height that provided the best possible sight for drivers of approaching trains. The other signal was the up platform starter. *John Robinson*

the branch from both sides of the station. The provision of a new up main outer home signal at Little Somerford, resulting in a signal lever numbered 'O' at the west end of the original frame, is detailed in Chapter 8.

The internal appearance of Little Somerford signal box was altered in 1941 by the provision of a new 78-lever frame when the yard and platform loops were extended during wartime. The new installation was a second-hand frame fitted with vertical tappet 5 bar locking. There was no extension or enlargement of the box, as the spaces between the lever centres in the new frame were 4 in, as compared with $5\frac{1}{4}$ in on the original double twist frame, thus making possible the accommodation of a larger number of levers in the existing structure. In the new frame the down branch starters were worked by levers 68 and 69, the up side down branch starter actually standing on the platform. A bracket signal, controlled from levers 4 and 8, was located out on the branch 352 yards from

the box, bearing up branch to up main and up platform line home signals.

Where the Malmesbury branch tracks separated from the Badminton line, a new down distant was erected for Kingsmead Crossing, worked from the crossing ground frame. An up fixed distant signalled the approach to Little Somerford station on the 1 in 50 gradient rising from Kingsmead. A telephone message was sent to the crossing keeper by the Little Somerford signalman two minutes before the departure of every train, so that the gates could be closed across the road and the crossing down distant pulled 'off' before the branch train left the junction platform. Only on receipt of a return call from the crossing keeper would the signalman pull the down starter lever to allow the train to proceed, a necessary precaution in view of the short distance and the steep gradient down from the main line embankment to Kingsmead.

The Little Somerford–Malmesbury train staff. This was supplied by the Reading Signal Works for use on the new shortened branch, in July 1933. As originally made, there was no key on the end for unlocking the points at Kingsmead Crossing, as there was no connection to the old section of the branch at this time (see page 132). With the abandonment of the Dauntsey end of the line and the introduction of the siding access at Kingsmead, a staff fitted with a key was sent from the works from 31st May 1934. The wooden part of the staff was originally painted white but this has worn away with the years. This staff can be seen in Athelstan Museum, Malmesbury, having been owned for many years by Malmesbury railwayman Ron Thomas.

Robin Elsey

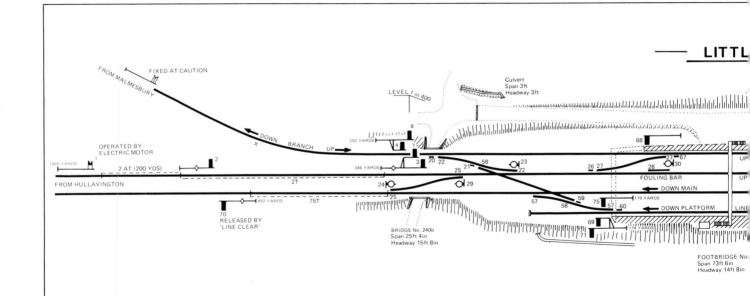

Little Somerford signalling diagram c.1942. The layout at Little Somerford was basically that of a double-tracked main line, with up and down platforms served by loop lines. This followed the GWR's practice for heavily used lines opened in latter years and allowed slow trains to be 'put inside' for faster trains to overtake. On both the up and down sides the platform loop lines were extended towards Swindon to form goods loops in which even the slower freights could be 'holed up'. A GWR reference of 31st January 1941 records the further extension of the up and down loops at Little Somerford to facilitate working of wartime traffic. Costs were £3,360 Chief Engineer, £3,500 Signal Engineer and £920 Chief Mechanical Engineer, a total of £7,780. An up stopping passenger could overtake a short freight, going in over 27 points and back out over 42. Similarly, a down 'stopper' could be turned in over 34 points and thus pass a goods train standing at No. 73 signal. The points worked by levers 50 and 66 were too far from the signal box to be worked mechanically, and so were worked by electrically operated point machines powered from a hand generator in the box. In the event of failure of the power mechanisms, the points could be wound over using special crank handles, and a telephone was provided (T) beside No. 50 points to facilitate communication between the signalman and the man on the ground. Another telephone was provided beside the trailing end of No. 66 points; this allowed the guard of a train which had arrived in the loop (up to 73 signal) to confirm to the signalman that the train had arrived complete out of the block section from Brinkworth, so that the 'train out of section' bell code could be sent by the Little Somerford man who could then accept another train after first putting 66 points to normal and set for the down main. There was track circuiting at the Brinkworth end of the layout, which was some way from the box and could be beyond vision at night or in bad weather. In accordance with GWR practice, the track circuits were numbered by reference to the levers they locked, if any — e.g. 6T occupied locked No. 6 signal lever.

Trains could be signalled on to the Malmesbury branch from either the down platform or up platform lines, but not from the down main line — the expense of providing for such a rarely needed move could never be justified. From the up platform line, 68 signal authorised movement onto the branch, this move passing over the platform end of 27 points as a facing movement, so facing lock lever No. 67 was required to prove the points set and locked. From the down platform line, signal 69 led across the 'ladder' of 57, 58 and 22 points. Any train crossing the ladder was, however, within the 440 yard overlap of signals 3 and 7, and so, to allow free acceptance of trains from Hullavington while the move was made, an outer home ('acceptance home'), No. 2 was added more than 440 yards on the approach side on 3/7 signals. This meant that the up distant signal No. 1 was too far out from the box to be properly worked by wire (it was over a mile away) so this signal (formerly numbered '0' in the old frame after the change of junction (see page 130) was electrically worked (as was the down distant No. 78).

27 points had no track circuit to prevent the signalman from reversing them to allow a train on to the up platform line before a train on the up main was pulled forward clear of the fouling point, but this was catered for by fouling bar lever 28. Before 27 lever could be moved, 28 had to be pulled first, which raised a lifting bar

into the flangeway beside the rail. Since this could not be done if the train was present, the section of the up main line just on the footbridge side of 27 points was proved clear, with no vehicles to foul a train passing over 27 into the up platform. Levers 19 and 61 worked machines to put detonators on the line quickly in the event of an emergency. There was no lever to work the up branch distant from Malmesbury, which was fixed at caution because all the routes to which it led were restricted to low speeds. Section signals 11 and 70 were released by 'line clear' having first been given by the signal box in advance. The location marked X was the site of the down distant signal for Kingsmead Crossing, controlled from the crossing ground frame by the crossing keeper.

The west end of Little Somerford station is seen here in the mid-1950s (after repaving) with an unidentified 'Hall' running through on a South Wales—Paddington express. This view shows much of signalling interest. The Malmesbury branch is on the right, forming an extension of the up platform loop, and can just be seen curving away from the main line in the distance. The layout is depicted as it existed before the 1956 alterations, when the connection from the down platform loop to the branch was removed (see page 231), Although the connection itself is obscured by the train, the fact that the down platform loop starting signal is a right-handed bracket, clearly indicates that it is still in use. The up main homes and up branch homes, which here appear to 'bridge' the branch, are both of the short-lived 'lop-sided' style of tubular bracket signal and probably replaced timber signals of similar configuration in the 1940s. The remainder of the signals visible are timber and almost certainly date from the 1933 remodelling, although the ground disc is of the pre-1918 type and would date from the opening of the line in 1903 (at that time it would have had a miniature semaphore arm; bolt-on enamel plates to make these signals more conspicuous were introduced about ten years later). This ground disc reads from the platform loop to the up main through the crossover beneath the train (this would have been a part of the original 1903 layout). The starting signal on the up platform, reading from platform loop to branch, dates from 1933. The route to the up main was not fitted with facing point locks and could only be used by non-passenger carrying trains — hence the retention of the disc; otherwise a bracket starting signal (to main and to branch) would have been provided. The facing point lock in the platform loop (foreground) bolts the points only for the branch, and a lifting bar is fitted to the left-hand switch rail only. Fitting the bar on the switch rail allows the starting signal to be placed directly adjacent to the points and gives more standing room in the platform. The metals bars at the foot of the photo are probably devices to keep the sleepers from shifting relative to one another and upsetting the working of components screwed to them. The down side water column was used by Malmesbury branch trains, although the passenger service had ceased at the time of this photograph. The large permanent way hut on the right was used by the Little Somerford gang, one of whom appears to be at work on the track beneath the bracket signals.

John Robinson

...ERFORD ——

Coal Office

Cattle Pens

MILEAGE SIDINGS

6 Ton Crane

1½ Ton Crane

Goods Shed & Platform

UP GOODS

173 YDS

DOWN MAIN UP

DOWN LOOP

SIGNAL BOX

R PLACER

23 YDS

23 YDS

173 YDS

13

50T

558 YDS

558 YDS

13AT

A11T

50

50

11

52

6T

66T

77 AT (200 YDS)

RELEASED BY 'LINE CLEAR'

14

11T

1020 YDS

TO BRINKWORTH

SPRING POINTS

POINTS 50 & 66 WORKED BY MOTOR USING A HAND GENERATOR

OPERATED BY ELECTRIC MOTOR

78

BRIDGE No. 238b
Span 14ft 2in
Headway 14ft 6in

16. 17. 18. 53. 54. 55. 56. 62. 63. 64. 65

NOT TO SCALE

Collett 0–4–2 tank No. 5802 coming into Malmesbury with the daily goods train on 23rd August 1955. The mobile crane was provided by British Railways for loading of the agricultural machinery sent from the station by A. B. Blanch of Crudwell.

Colin Maggs

CHAPTER FOURTEEN

THE LAST YEARS
GOODS ONLY 1951–62

FOLLOWING the closure of the branch passenger service, the line continued in operation for a further eleven years with a daily goods service, Sundays excepted. Working continued on the 'one engine in steam' principle, governed by the regulations of the Bristol Traffic District. Plans were made in October 1951 to close Malmesbury signal box and reduce the terminus to hand-worked

in the Western Region locomotive allocations as the final closure of the shed. Afterwards an engine was sent light from Swindon to Little Somerford, where it arrived at 9.30 am. A goods train was made up from the 7.45 am Swindon to Stoke Gifford local goods which left Little Somerford at 9.25 after thirty minutes' shunting there, and the branch goods departed for Malmesbury at 10.05. At the terminus two hours were

Another view of the train shown opposite. *Colin Maggs*

points with a stop board, but it was nearly five years before this was done. A key to the telephone huts on the branch was issued by the Little Somerford signalman to every driver who worked the line. It was returnable on leaving the branch, a necessary practice after the branch locomotive ceased to be shedded at Malmesbury, with different crews working from Swindon each week. During the October after closure, a special train travelled on the branch – a Saturday trip to Blackpool Illuminations which had been booked earlier in the year before the date of closure was announced so the booking was honoured and the 'special' went ahead. Owing to the length of the journey, arrival back in Malmesbury was in the small hours of the Sunday morning.

With the continued goods on the line and the need for the railway lorry to use the site, the station yard and approach was resurfaced in March 1952 with tarmac, Western Region bringing in an Aveling & Porter steamroller from the Pylle Hill Depot at Bristol to finish the job.

Malmesbury's last allocated locomotive, Collett tank No. 5805, continued to be based at the terminus after passenger closure, running the daily freight out to Little Somerford and back until June 1952, when the freight arrangements for the branch were altered. The Malmesbury-based engine was withdrawn, although shed facilities continued to be available to the engine on freight duty, usually a '58XX' class, '48XX' class or pannier tank, until 28th August 1953, the date given

Entering Malmesbury station during goods only days of the mid-50s, with the coal dumps now extending to the area along the main line of the branch. The stop board was installed as part of the branch's signalling rationalisation of 1956.

A quiet scene at Malmesbury on 18th August 1957, with an open wagon being loaded with Blanch machinery. The rail-built loading gauge was provided c.1949.
J. J. Davis

A hay cutter awaiting loading. The former GWR travelling crane stood on two short lengths of rail alongside the goods shed siding in the foreground.
J. J. Davis

Collett No. 5802 shunting at Malmesbury in August 1955. Senior checker Bill Archer is riding on the footboard of the guard's van with his shunting pole.
Colin Maggs

allowed to prepare a goods train which left Malmesbury at 12.15 pm, arriving at the junction at 12.28, where it joined the local from Stoke Gifford at 1.54, to reach Swindon at 2.55 pm, the branch goods locomotive assisting in double-heading if required.

Responsibility for the station at Malmesbury was transferred to the station master at Little Somerford, Mr. Hunt, whose jurisdiction also extended to Brinkworth. The substantial amounts of agricultural machinery and general merchandise which Malmesbury station still handled necessitated the retention of Bill Archer as senior checker, with the assistance of two porters, George Eldridge and Charlie Bennett. The motor lorry was, as it had been since its arrival in 1935, still Malmesbury-based under British Railways, and still driven by Ian Beard.

The year 1956 saw substantial simplification of the signalling arrangements at both ends of the branch. With no Malmesbury trains coming through from Swindon and the goods trains being made up in the goods yard at Little Somerford, on the up side of the station, the junction-crossover from the branch to the up main and the lead from the down platform to the branch were no longer required and were duly taken out of use on 8th/9th April 1956. The two redundant bracket signals were removed, the up branch homes on the branch itself and the down branch and main starters on the down platform line. They were replaced by straight post signals, a new up branch home being located on the up side of the branch 230 yards from the signal box, and a down platform starter for the down main at 174 yards. At the same time a new catch point was installed on the branch facing up trains to protect against over-running the up branch home signal. Nine of the existing ground signals for shunting were

22nd May 1954 saw the retirement of engineman Ben Hill after many years' association with the line. Here he is receiving a retirement handshake from Bert Hunt, Little Somerford station master at this time who was also in charge of Malmesbury goods station.
Peter Harding

fitted with yellow arms and lights. The 1951 proposal to reduce signalling at Malmesbury was at last carried out with the closure and demolition of the signal box on 16th September 1956. All worked signals were taken out of use, all points being worked by hand with a stop board placed by the goods shed where all incoming goods trains were to stop dead and thereafter work to hand signals. The fixed distant at the tunnel remained until final closure.

In September 1958 the practice of sending a light engine from Swindon for Malmesbury goods duty ceased when the

I. D. Beale

The south-east end of Malmesbury tunnel and the accompanying school footbridge in 1958.

The short branch goods during the final years.   *M. E. J. Deane*

7.45 Swindon to Stoke Gifford goods was cut back to run only as far as Hullavington, making its run into Malmesbury on its return trip. Since 1951 the Collett '58XX' class tank engines had remained in the Swindon area engaged upon local freight duties until one by one they were withdrawn during 1958, No. 5804 being condemned in June 1959. Local branch freight operation was taken over by the new Class 03 six-coupled diesel shunting engines, of which there were fifteen shedded at Swindon. These locomotives were very unpopular with signalmen on the main line, who found their slowness very annoying when they were anxious to clear their sections. Diesels D.2187, D.2188, D.2193 and D.2196 performed

A closer view of the short tunnel in the 1950s. The milepost shows 93 miles from Paddington via Little Somerford.   *A. Attewell*

Little Somerford station, forlorn and deserted during its final days, the large GWR nameboard now with 'Junction for Malmesbury' painted out. A humorous story from the early '50s relates how the Lockstone family of Malmesbury were entertaining company from Yorkshire who decided to return home by train and had to reach their northbound train at Bristol Temple Meads. There being no longer a passenger service from Malmesbury, they were driven to Little Somerford station to enquire about train times. The porter in the booking office had no timetable and was unable to remember the times of the sparse main line stopping service. The timetable had been loaned to a local farmer, so the porter was driven to the farm concerned so the timetable could be consulted! This done, the volume was returned to the farmer!
H. C. Casserley

regular Malmesbury trips, although during this period the occasional steam locomotive would still appear, such as 0–6–0 pannier tank No. 1621 or one of the '14XX' class, formerly the '48XX' class built in 1936.

During the final four years the Malmesbury goods service formed part of a local freight network centred upon Swindon, being worked by a 'link' of six drivers who worked a full week in turn to Kemble, Marlborough, Faringdon and Highworth, with goods trips on the old Midland & South Western Junction line, and the run to Hullavington which included the Malmesbury branch. The link of drivers included men who had worked at Malmesbury shed during passenger days, Jim Long and Ken Stoneham, and another member, Jack Neale, had fired as a reliefman for Bill Eveleigh on the branch back in the 1920s.

The Malmesbury goods run began at the old running shed at Swindon Junction, where there would be around 45 minutes allowed for preparing the engine before departure from the transfer yard at 7.45 am. Loaded wagons were dropped off at Wootton Bassett, Brinkworth and Little Somerford, with a 9.30 arrival at Hullavington. Here the empties from the previous day would be shunted, and loaded wagons collected for the return trip, departing at 10 am. At Little Somerford a run-round would be made to place the guard's van on the rear of the train for the run into Malmesbury, departing at 10.45. Arrival at the branch terminus was scheduled at 10.58 am, later than the 1952–8 period. Coal, feed for the farms, paper from Maidstone and box-vans of components for Ekco, machinery for repair to A. B. Blanch, and general merchandise were all brought in. After the return train was made up in the yard, the crew would usually take their lunch break on the engine. Wagons sent to Swindon were chiefly empties; there was never a lot of outward traffic except when Blanch agri-

cultural machinery was being sent out to depots and farms around the country. On such days a loaded goods train of over 30 wagons would leave the station. Timetabled departure was at 12.15 pm, arriving at Little Somerford at 12.28, the train often carrying permanent way men in the guard's van, whose normal routine involved walking in from their hut at Little Somerford to check the track, oiling the points at Malmesbury when required, in order to ensure smooth shunting operations, then joining the goods guard for a ride back up to the main line. The train called at Brinkworth if required, at Wootton Bassett at 2.04, and returned to Swindon at 2.43 pm.

The only passenger trains to run into Malmesbury during these last few years were special railway tours organised by enthusiasts. On 18th August 1957, the Railway Correspondence and Travel Society ran a trip from Swindon, 'The Moonraker', which comprised an old B-set hauled by one of the line's former regular engines, No. 5802, bearing an RCTS headboard and express headlamps. Its driver was former branch fireman Jim Long, who was observed on the platform at Malmesbury gleefully pointing out to the visitors the 'GWR' letters still visible under the BR repainting!

In the summer of 1958 the girder bridges over the river between Baskerville and the tunnel were replaced, the work occupying several weekends with overtime, causing much comment and conjecture amongst the local people. The replacement of these spans gave rise to hopes among the more optimistic of the town that maybe a re-opening of the passenger service was in the pipeline. The employment situation had changed in the north of Wiltshire, with new industries having been established in Swindon in particular, and the arrival of railway representatives in Malmesbury, allegedly to assess potential use of the railway from businesses, traders and folk in the town who formed a nucleus of a possible commuter traffic, raised hopes of a revival a little further.

There were other developments in the late '50s which kept alive, in some people's minds at least, the possibility of a return of passenger trains on the branch. There were plans to renew bridges along Lea Fields, and a permanent way train actually came onto the branch and unloaded girders and concrete posts by the lineside at the rear of the Ekco factory.

out of use from 24th April 1956. The line of decrepit stock stabled along the old branch to Great Somerford had been a source of annoyance to people in that village for years, resenting the railway's seemingly incomplete closure procedure especially on Show Day, when horse trials took place against a backdrop of old coaches and wagons atop the embankment. A train was sent to pick up the track, the engine propelling from the Kingsmead end. During this operation some trucks broke away and ran through the stop-blocks to end up in the

The RCTS railtour of 9th April 1961 brought large crowds and a diesel multiple unit.

The materials lay there for some time, then were re-loaded and removed – owing to spending restrictions the work was never done, and the hardware allocated to sites of greater priority elsewhere.

Probably the most tantalising sight on the branch during this period of forlorn hope was the appearance of new diesel multiple-unit sets on several occasions. As it turned out, these were on test runs from Swindon – the new stock never actually came as far as the station, usually stopping short in the vicinity of the tunnel, at which point they would apparently retreat and mysteriously vanish, taking with them any faint hopes harboured locally of a new service. The DMUs, of course, subsequently came into use and at time of writing are still in use over the BR system in many areas.

With the closure of Brinkworth signal box on 15th March 1959, British Railways introduced advance section working between Little Somerford & Wootton Bassett West. Brinkworth's siding connection to the up main line was retained, controlled by a ground frame electrically interlocked with Little Somerford station signal box by means of a key release instrument. To maintain signalling capacity, intermediate block signals, a home and distant, were installed near Brinkworth on both up and down lines. The down line signals were worked from Wootton Bassett West signal box, the up line signals from Little Somerford, each signalman therefore working two sections of line, one being ahead of his regular section.

Kingsmead siding, the remains of the old branch from Dauntsey, was dismantled in March 1959, having been taken

living room of the old station house at Great Somerford. Jim Hazell, retired signalman from Little Somerford, was fortunately asleep upstairs at the time. The station master at Little Somerford, Ralph Biggs, pressed some workmen into service, who had been working at Brinkworth, to shore up the walls of the damaged building until it could be properly repaired.

Ralph Biggs had taken over the station at Little Somerford in September 1958, on the retirement of Bertram Hunt after 16 years there. The staff still comprised station master, two porters and three signalmen, the post also including responsibility for Malmesbury and Brinkworth, with a main line passenger service of four trains each way per weekday and a large amount of goods traffic. When Stanley Mulcock succeeded Biggs in February 1960, the passenger service on the Badminton line still existed in its sparse form, much as it had since opening in 1903, but this ceased on 3rd April 1961, when the Bristol-Swindon stopping service was axed, Malmesbury's motor lorry being transferred to Chippenham at the same time. Malmesbury's Saturday goods train ceased to run from 12th June 1961. The establishment of two porters at Little Somerford was now reduced to one, and when Mulcock left in December 1961 both Little Somerford and Malmesbury again came under the control of Ralph Biggs, now station master at Wootton Bassett, his domain extending along the main line as far as Hullavington.

On Sunday, 9th April 1961, another RCTS railtour arrived at the desolate terminus at Malmesbury in two Swindon three-car DMU sets. This was the 'Berks & Wilts Rail Tour' from

Paddington, which also visited the Windsor & Eton, Highworth and Faringdon branches. The 300 passengers were met at Malmesbury by many surprised inhabitants, who were quite unused to such a large crowd on the station, and the Mayor, Mr. H. C. Avis, who greeted the party on behalf of the local corporation. Bill Archer opened the station office for the occasion.

Although the coal dump at Malmesbury station was still in use during the final years, coal was now a thin trade on the branch, most coming in by road on lorries from Badminton station. There was still an occasional appearance made by a steam locomotive on the branch – No. 5815, the last of the '58XX' class and known to be the last of the series to work into Malmesbury, was observed on freight duty as late as 29th July 1961, when it left Little Somerford hauling one coal wagon with brake van for the terminus.

Undoubtedly the main user of the station in the last years was the firm of A. B. Blanch & Co. of nearby Crudwell. Formed in 1950, the company provided the line with much business, especially in the summer months, when their machinery packed the station yard. Bale elevators, green crop loaders, hedge cutters, swarth turners, ploughs and driers stood by the tracks and on the platforms awaiting despatch along the branch. Most of these goods were destined for long distance haulage, primarily to the borders of Scotland, some 500 Blanch machines leaving the station during 1962, the line's last year. After final closure the Crudwell firm turned to Little Somerford, finally changing to road transport delivery when that station closed to goods on 10th June 1963.

In March 1962 complete closure of the branch was announced for 16th July but a protest by A. B. Blanch, who would have had to make alternative arrangements in the

0–6–0PT No. 1621 arriving in Malmesbury with the daily goods on 3rd September 1962. By this time the track serving the engine shed had been removed and the area fenced off.

Bert Vizor

Diesel shunting engines appeared first on the branch in mid-1959. Here D.2188 is shown entering Malmesbury station with a train of empties on 25th July 1962. The flat wagons were for a large consignment of Blanch machinery. *R. C. Riley*

middle of their busiest period of the year, staved off final closure until later in the year. Collapsing culverts along the line was the reason given by British Railways for the decision to close the branch, the cost of repairs being too high to warrant the expenditure. During March, also, the engine shed loop at Malmesbury was removed, the metal being sold off to a local farmer for use as cattle grids. On 31st March the branch was visited by a special for the last time when the Gloucester Railway Society ran a trip in a Bristol Division B-set hauled by pannier tank 0–6–0 No. 1658.

A Western Region News memo sheet of 31st October 1962 announced final closure for 11th November, when the traffic of Malmesbury goods station would be handled instead at Chippenham, Little Somerford and Cirencester Town stations. On that date diesel shunter D.2196 arrived at Malmesbury with the last goods train, crewed by driver Jack Neale, fireman David Titchener and guard Bob Roberts, all Swindon men. A relief station master, Mr. J. S. Walton, was brought in for the day and Bill Archer and George Eldridge received just one 'goodbye and good luck' telegram from a family who had once lived nearby. There was no great send-off, the departure of the last train being watched by a tiny group of people, the only hint of ceremony being the explosion of several fog signal detonators as the train passed over them on its way out of the terminus, passing on its way home of Alderman J. A. Jones, the only person to ride both first and last passenger trains on the branch. In 1962 he was still

The final day, 11th November 1962, with (left to right) George Eldridge, relief station master J. S. Walton, and Bill Archer.
Wiltshire Newspapers, Swindon

alive in Malmesbury, his life having spanned that of the railway with a fair amount to spare.

A short account appeared in the *Wilts Gazette & Herald* entitled 'Malmesbury's Rail Age Ends After 80 Years' – the line in fact had been in operation for almost 84 years. A local correspondent writing in the *Wilts & Glos. Standard* of 9th November had this to say in comment;

'The end of the railway at Malmesbury comes today – Friday – at about midday. The last goods train will pull in and having loaded with its final cargo, will pull out leaving Malmesbury's already derelict station and track to the weeds.

'Few will bemoan the passing of Malmesbury's railway service for the townsfolk had their say 11 years ago when the passenger rail service was withdrawn. There is no doubt that, if in those days someone had had courage enough to organise a service that went somewhere and connected with other services, this situation would not have faced Malmesbury today. Who, for example, would want to leave their homes to catch a train from Malmesbury for London shortly after 7 in the morning, stand about on a draughty platform at Little Somerford for a connection to Swindon and a further wait on an even draughtier platform, when by going to Kemble and catching a train at 9 am you could arrive in London before anyone using that early train from Malmesbury? Sounds stupid but that is the way it was. No wonder the passenger service failed. What a stupid way to run a railway.

'No, this railway closure at Malmesbury is one that that cannot be blamed on Dr. Beeching.'

Thus did Malmesbury's railway pass into history.

Top: D.2196 at Malmesbury with the final goods train, 11th November 1962. Above: The crew of the last goods train (left to right) guard Bob Roberts, driver Jack Neal, fireman or second man David Titchener. *Wiltshire Newspapers, Swindon*

POSTSCRIPT

The branch was lifted during 1963. Here the span of Bridge No. 33 is about to be removed.   *E. K. Lockstone*

THE Malmesbury branch was dismantled in October 1963, the job of track removal being undertaken by a Staffordshire firm, Pittrail Ltd., with the aid of a small diesel shunter which was delivered by road to Malmesbury. A protracted legal wrangle took place for several years for ownership of the station site, and the station buildings at Malmesbury were left in neglect, becoming a target for vandals, a haven for tramps, and a haunt for courting couples for whom the sign on the station convenience 'Please adjust your dress before leaving' was considered locally to be very apt! The station and goods yards were eventually bought by Malmesbury Borough Council on 15th March 1967, and on 21st April of that year outline planning permission was given for development of part of the site for light industry and warehousing. One acre was sold off to Wiltshire County Council for use as a new fire station and ambulance base. The attentions of vandals eventually rendered the old railway station too dangerous to leave standing, and it was duly demolished in 1968, a new road laid through the site to serve the intended industrial estate, and the new fire station opened in the summer of 1969.

Following demolition of Little Somerford station, the long loops and up sidings were taken out of use in 1966 and the signal box closed on 18th June 1967, with the introduction of the Swindon Multi-Aspect Signalling scheme. Today the Swindon-Badminton section of the main line is worked from Swindon signal box, the Badminton-Severn Tunnel section being controlled from the large modern box at Temple Meads.

To explore the present-day remains of the branch is to realise what a deep impression the railways of the past have left upon the British landscape, even where efforts have been made to build over an old line. Much of the Malmesbury branch is left for the railway enthusiast and industrial archaeologist to investigate, although it is impossible to follow the course of the line continuously owing to the removal of nearly all the bridges when the line was dismantled. This and private ownership have thus rendered long stretches of trackbed impassable. Sorties along the old course are halted amidst profuse vegetation by bare stone abutments with a sudden sheer drop to a water course or cattle track below.

At each of the old junction stations, the sad tale is the same – at Dauntsey the only sign of former activity is the station approach road by the old creamery which once supplied the station with much milk traffic, while up on the embankment at Little Somerford the station is lost forever, the only tangible reminders of it being some platform remains and one solitary edifice in the goods yard, the old brick goods lock-up. At both sites, a red light in the distance changes to green and High-Speed trains roar by in total ignorance of the long-forgotten connections for Malmesbury.

Much of the southern portion of the branch, between Dauntsey and Great Somerford, has long passed back to nature, and although sections of embankment remain, together with several bridge abutments, much of the trackbed has been reclaimed by farmland or obliterated by road improvements, the final mutilation being completed by the course of the unrelenting M4 motorway, which severs the line's course just north of Swallett Brook. The three crossing lodges on the branch all remain, each one a modernised privately occupied dwelling. At Kingsmead, Bill Archard's old home, the visitor can see where the two sections of the branch diverged, the trackbed of the original line disappearing

239

in the distance under bridge 16A which still carries the South Wales Direct of 1903, with the course of the newer spur of 1933 bending eastwards out of sight on the steep gradient up to Little Somerford. Kingsmead Crossing lodge still bears Bill Archard's scratched engravings in one of the quoins, the dates still clearly discernible and standing as a testimony to history – 'Men Line Started May 9th 1932', recording the date on which work began on the 1933 diversion of the branch, together with the dates of the opening to Little Somerford and the later closures.

From Kingsmead to Cowbridge is the most inaccessible and overgrown part of the old branch, where the track once passed along the secluded floor of the Avon valley via several bridges which are long removed. At Cowbridge there is an area of levelled earth which is a reminder of preparations for the projected station which was intended to be built by the Malmesbury Railway Company at this point, and even today the adjacent fencing contractor's yard has the air about it of a station approach and yard that never materialised. The Lea Fields embankment still describes its long curve towards Malmesbury before being truncated by the town's bypass. The deep cutting at Baskerville, engineer Ward's 'key to the works' during construction, is now completely filled in, but the tunnel still exists, as durable and timeless as when it was built, although access to it is difficult and not encouraged.

Bill Archard's nail engravings at Kingsmead Crossing lodge, recording history as it happened. An extract from a letter from Bill Archard to the author in 1980: 'I heard yesterday that my old cottage had been sold, so the passing of over 100 years has ended, but my ghost will live on there and my memories of over 70 years will still be with me. You have helped a lot to keep it alive for those who will never know of the wonderful years of steam.'   *Author*

On the small industrial estate which occupies Malmesbury's old station yard, one of the premises houses a small Lux Traffic Controls factory, ironically a firm symbolic of the town's historic association with transport and communications and also of the ascendancy of the road over the branch railway. There is some irritation locally at the underuse of the inevitable car-park here – few, it seems, are prepared to leave their cars here and walk up into the town as folk once did from the railway station. Instead, people drive all the way into the town centre with the result that the Cross Hayes is full every day, to overflowing on Saturdays. The sole railway building left here is the branch locomotive shed, again with not a little irony, housing offices and stores of a local car repair and tyre operation. After closure of the line, the postbox which was once in public use on the station was moved to the wall of the Railway Hotel's car-park, where it remained until 1984 still bearing its 'VR' inscription and the words 'Railway Station Malmesbury'. Since its disappearance with the demolition of the hostelry, a new postbox has been erected nearby, still identified as being at the 'railway station'.

A short walk up the hill towards Tetbury from the old station site brings the visitor to Malmesbury Cemetery. Here several of the well-known GWR people associated with the town's railway past are buried – Mr & Mrs Ponting of Kingsmead, station master Arthur Davies, and, most moving of all, the tomb of driver Ted Jones, bearing sculpted daffodils in honour of his Welsh heritage together with a '517' locomotive clearly showing the number '844', a wistful reminder of halcyon days when the railway ruled.

To the people of Malmesbury today, the railway is but a dim memory, recalled with an almost reluctant nostalgia by the older generations who remember its passing, whereas younger folk appear unaware that it was once possible to travel by train from the town. Although the historic centre of Malmesbury remains hemmed in by the two loops of the Avon, the town has spread over the last decade with newer developments on former agricultural land on the north-west side. The former factory of E. K. Cole has now become part of the telecommunications giant Pye TMC, today the largest employers of labour in the town. The nearest railheads are at Kemble and Chippenham, roughly ten miles equidistant in opposite directions along the A429, although no effort exists to provide a bus service to Kemble; most people who use that station are car-owners. Bus services, in the 1980s considerably reduced from those of 15 years before, today maintain the principle of the transport links fostered by the old railway, running to Swindon, Wootton Bassett and Chippenham, although the services to the last-named have never been known for their speed and ability to connect with the Paddington Bristol trains which still call there.

Little more than two miles south of Malmesbury, the Badminton line, with its fast expresses, crosses the A429 at Kingway, therefore the town is still tantalisingly close to a railway, but the closest station to the east is Swindon, and to the west Bristol Parkway. Maybe in a different transport climate, a different society of the future with new values and priorities, there might be a case for building a new station at Kingway to establish a new catchment area for this route? So might Malmesbury be re-introduced to the railway network, as Malmesbury Road, Malmesbury Kingway, or even Malmesbury Parkway to use the modern parlance? Time alone will tell...

Malmesbury Cemetery.

E. K. Lockstone

APPENDICES

COSTS OF BUILDING THE MALMESBURY LINE

	£	s.	d.
Parliamentary expenses and cost of obtaining Acts of Parliament	1,970	8	8
Land purchase and tenants' compensation	10,920	18	2
Rent charges, etc.	711	4	8
Rates, taxes, etc.	39	14	4
Construction Engineer	2,050	0	0
Construction Contractors	50,760	1	2
Stations, lodges, junctions, etc.	7,678	14	7
Interest, etc.	1,434	8	7
Salaries, Commissions, General office expenses, auditors, etc.	999	16	8
Total up to 31st December 1877	76,565	6	10

Further expenses up to 30th June 1878	£	s.	d.
Land purchase & tenants' compensation, solicitors' costs, etc.	1,260	16	4
Rent charges	47	10	10
Rents, Taxes & Tithes	15	5	9
Construction — Engineering and Surveying, Contractors, inc. arbitration costs	4,083	14	0
Stations, junctions, locking gear, station fillings, etc.	1,191	17	3
Interest on debentures	144	4	8
Salaries, printing, advertising, commissions, stationery, audit & general office disbursements	45	3	0
Total	6,788	11	10

Cost of building and completion £83,353 18 8

MALMESBURY BRANCH GRADIENT PROFILE

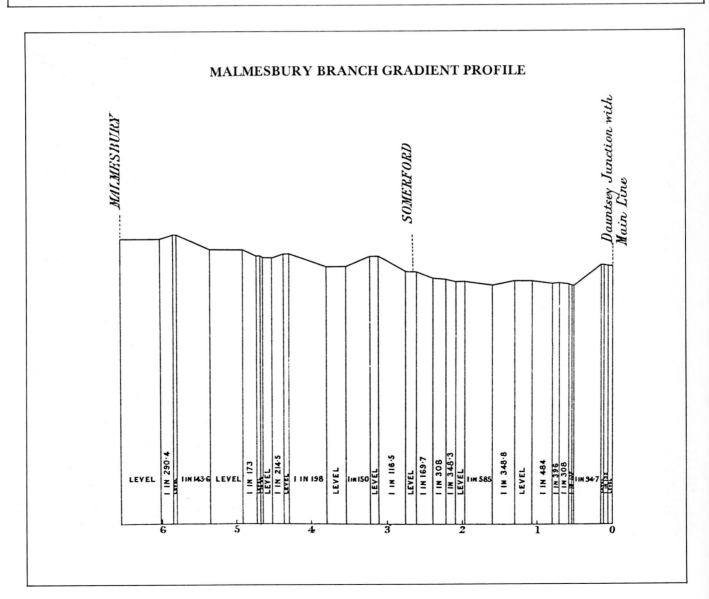

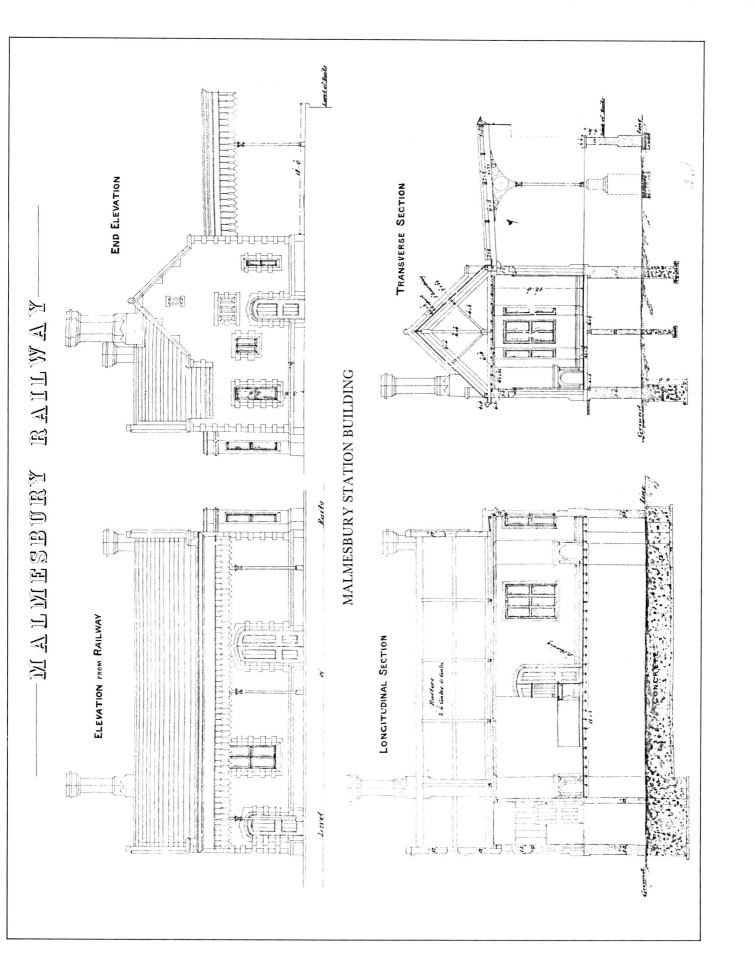

MALMESBURY RAILWAY

ELEVATION FROM RAILWAY

END ELEVATION

MALMESBURY STATION BUILDING

LONGITUDINAL SECTION

TRANSVERSE SECTION

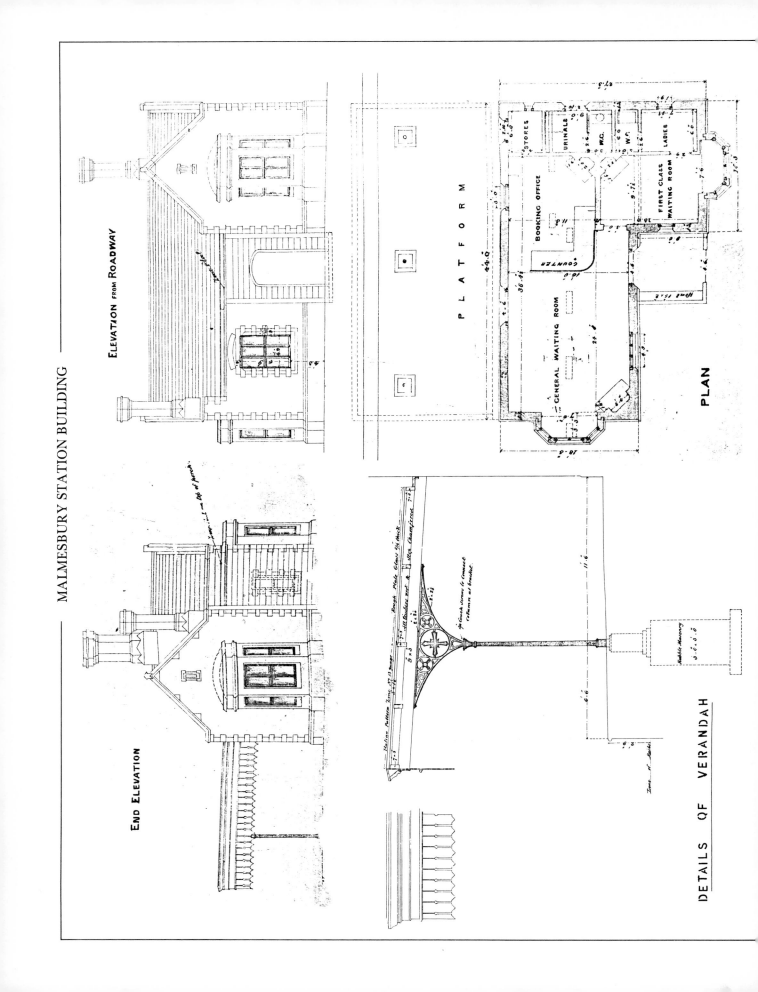

MALMESBURY STATION BUILDING

ELEVATION FROM ROADWAY

END ELEVATION

PLATFORM

PLAN

GENERAL WAITING ROOM

BOOKING OFFICE

COUNTER

STORES

URINALS

W.C.

W.C.

FIRST CLASS WAITING ROOM

LADIES

DETAILS OF VERANDAH

DETAILS OF OFFICE FITTINGS

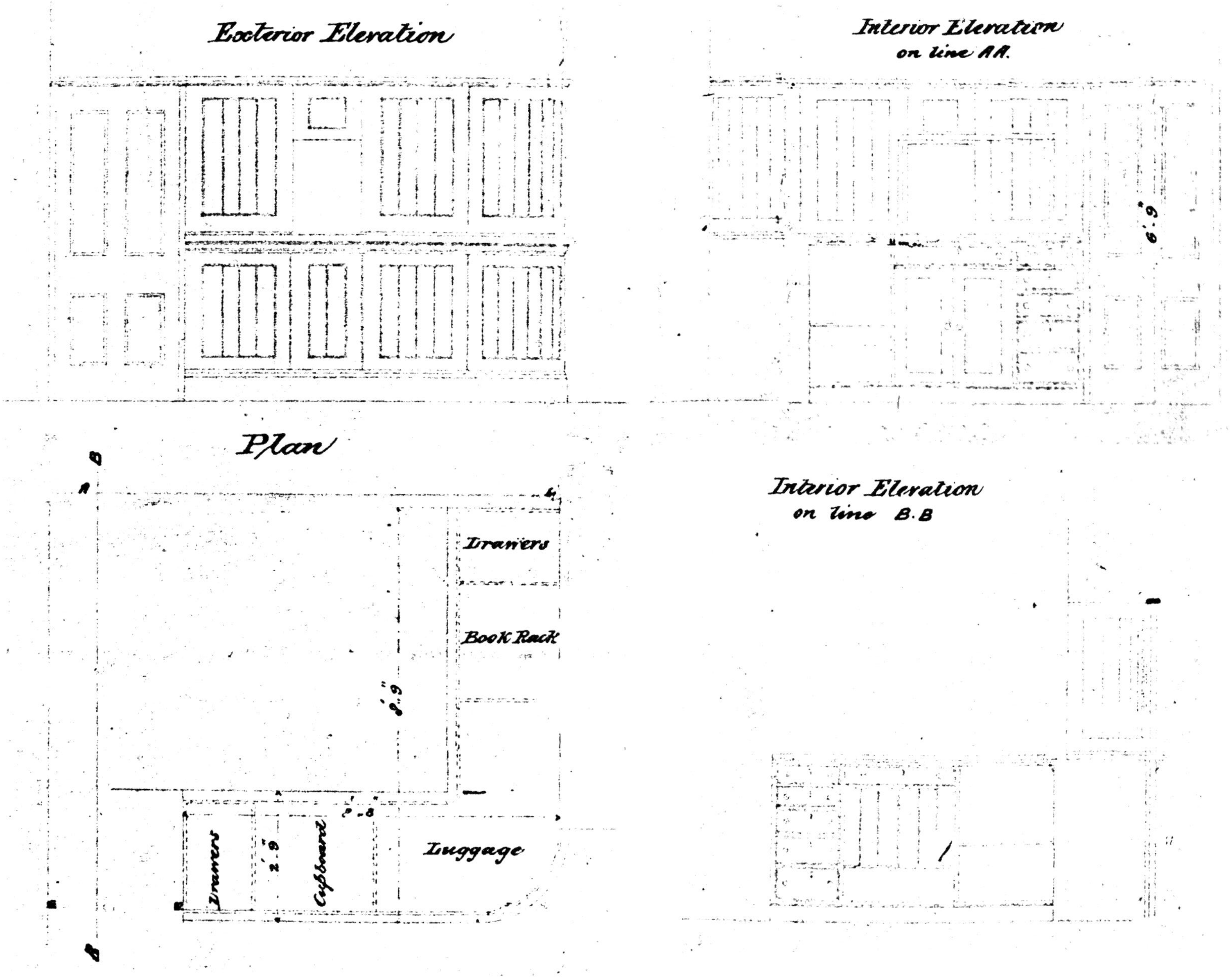

Exterior Elevation

Interior Elevation on line A.A.

6.9

Interior Elevation on line B.B

Plan

Drawers

Book Rack

8.9

Luggage

2.8

Cupboard

2.9

Drawers

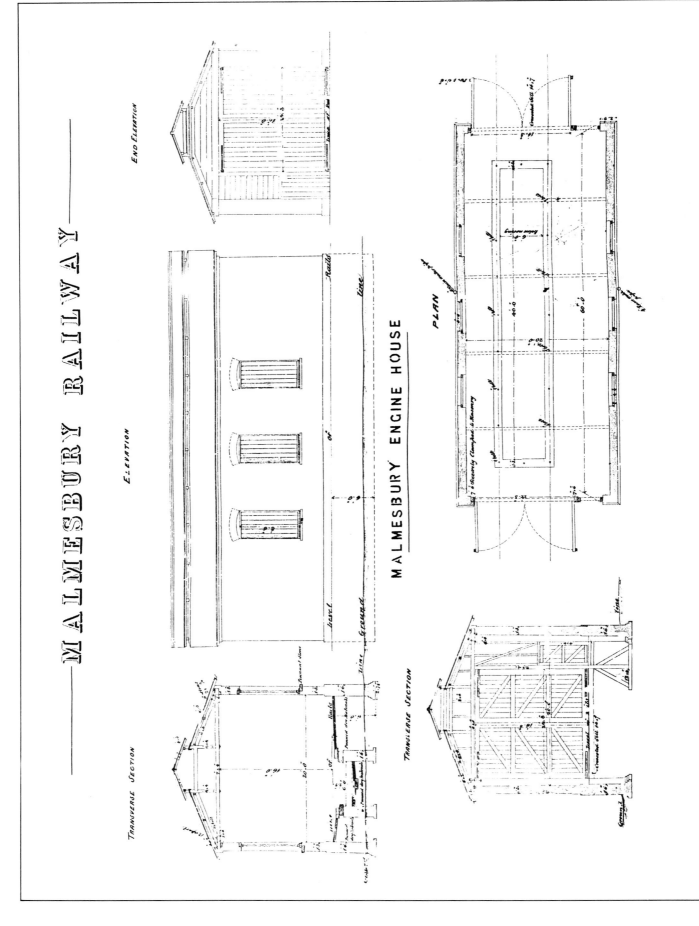

MALMESBURY RAILWAY

END ELEVATION

ELEVATION

TRANSVERSE SECTION

MALMESBURY ENGINE HOUSE

PLAN

TRANSVERSE SECTION

TRACK PLAN OF MALMESBURY 1938

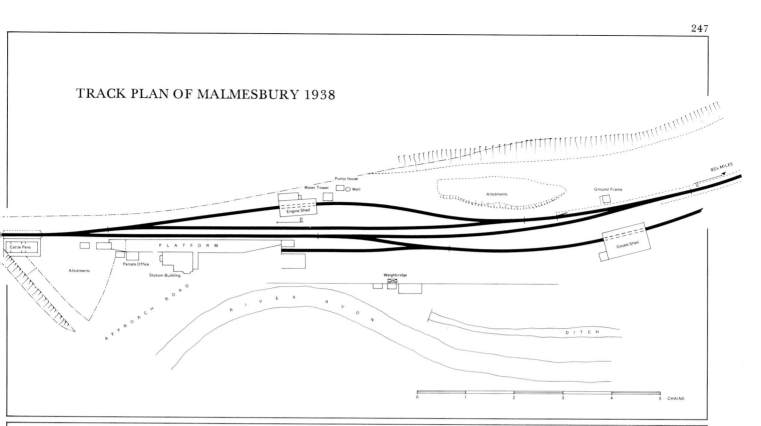

MALMESBURY STATION WATER TANK

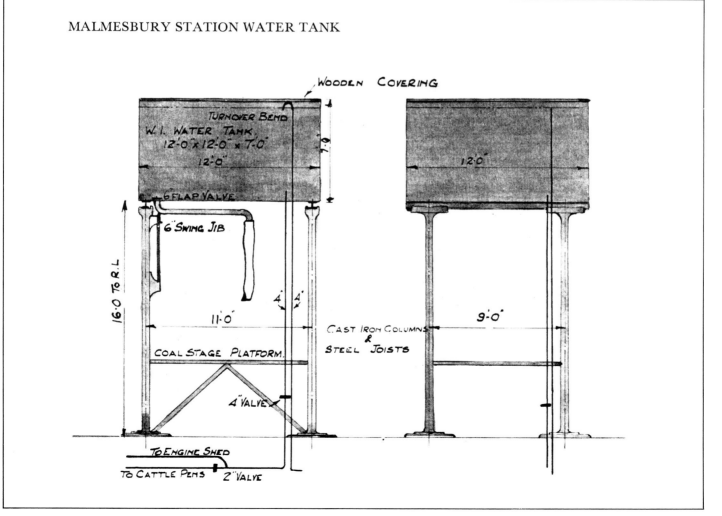

MALMESBURY GOODS SHED

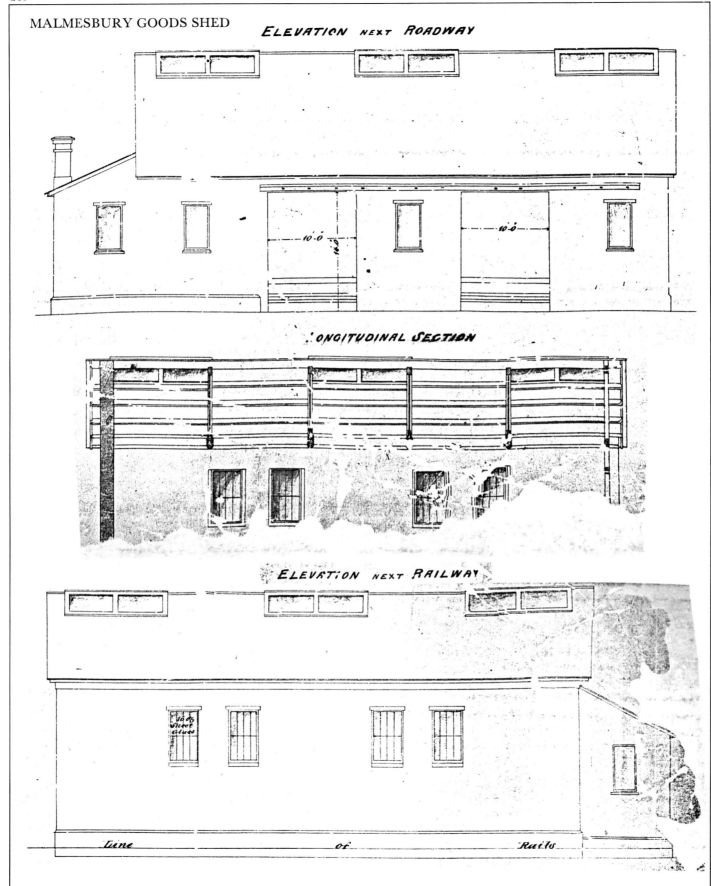

ELEVATION NEXT ROADWAY

LONGITUDINAL SECTION

ELEVATION NEXT RAILWAY

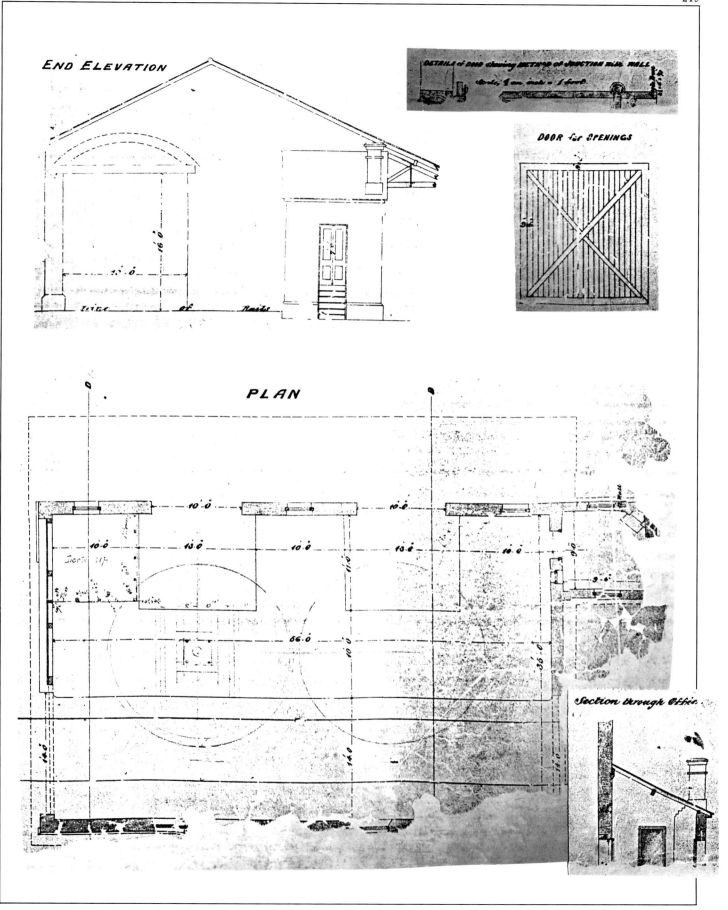

END ELEVATION

DETAILS of DOOR showing METHOD of JUNCTION with WALL

DOOR for OPENINGS

PLAN

Section through Office

MALMESBURY GOODS SHED

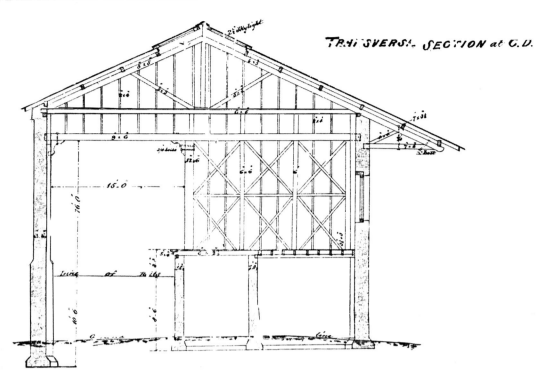

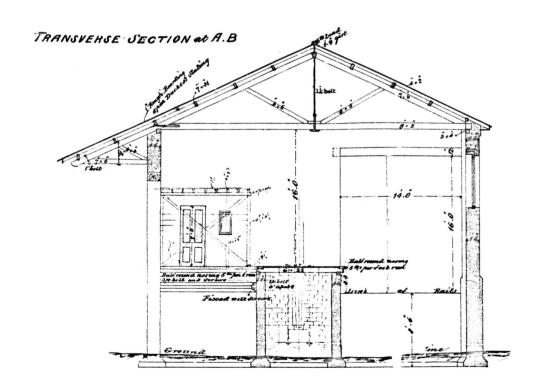

POOLE'S BRIDGE

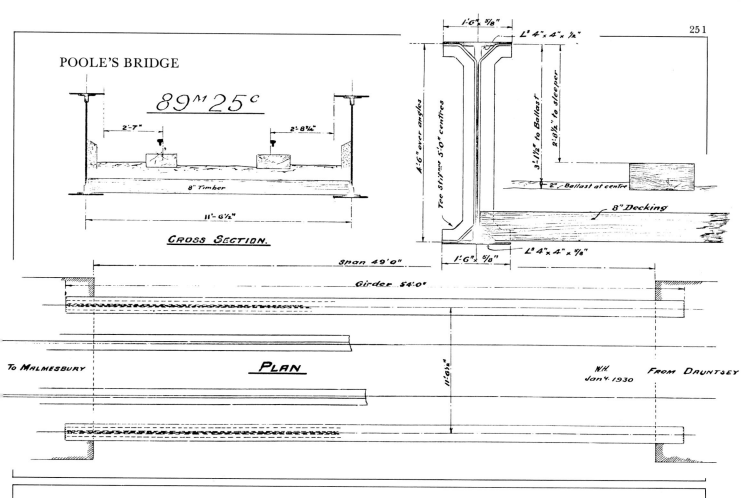

$89^M 25^C$

CROSS SECTION.

8" Timber

11'- 6½"

2'-7"   2'-8¾"

1'-6" x ⅝"

L⁴ 4" x 4" x ½"

4'-6" over angles

Tee Stif⁸ at 5'-0" centres

3'-1½" to Ballast

2'-8½" to sleeper

2" - Ballast at centre

8" Decking

L⁴ 4" x 4" x ⅝"

1'-6" x ⅝"

Span 49'0"

Girder 54'0"

PLAN

11'-6½"

To Malmesbury

N.H.
Jan⁴ 1930

From Dauntsey

THE 'SEVEN FOOT BRIDGE' AT SOMERFORD

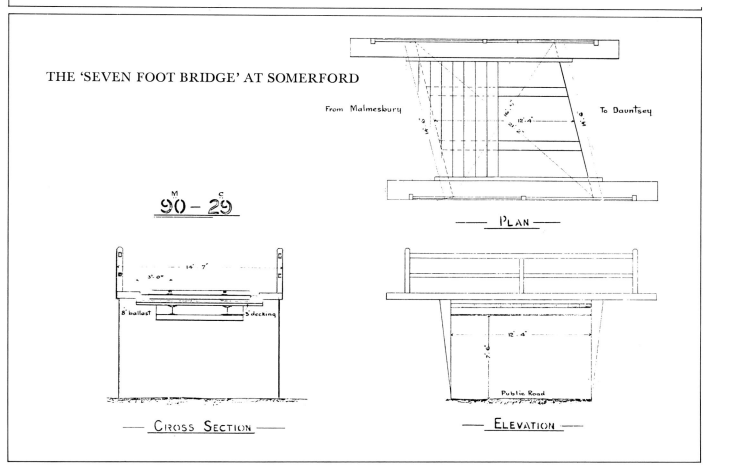

$90^M - 29^C$

From Malmesbury   To Dauntsey

12' 4"

PLAN

14' 7"

3' 0"

8" ballast   5" decking

CROSS SECTION

12' 4"

7' 6"

Public Road

ELEVATION

STAFF IN CHARGE OF COUNTRY STATIONS pre-1897

In the last century, many small country stations on the Great Western, classed 4, 5 and 6 were under the control of a booking porter rather than a station master, and this included both Dauntsey and Somerford. Before 1897, only stations graded as Class 3 and above were under a station master. When the Malmesbury branch opened in 1877, the booking porter in charge of Somerford station earned a wage of 22/- a week.

Those stations classed 1, 2 and 3 were under the control of salaried staff who had progressed through the clerical grades, whereas the smaller stations, Class 4 and below, were under an employee who was one of the 'weekly paid staff', who had typically been porters, signalmen or railway policemen, and who could not normally progress to posts in charge of stations above Class 4.

In June 1890 the posts of booking porter were all regraded as 'station inspector', examples in the records being Aynho, Portesham, Toller, Abbotsbury, Great Bedwyn, and even Kemble, a double

junction and important country station, where the regrading took place in May 1890. The records for Somerford for this period are unfortunately missing, although there is a reference in GWR Engineers' Minutes for 1893 which show that there was a 'station inspector' at Somerford. Dauntsey's attendant was regraded in June 1890 along with the rest.

In November 1897, most GWR stations under station inspectors were again reclassed, their attendants-in-charge at last receiving the title 'station master'. Examples in the GWR Staff Records include Chalford, Wylye, Shiplake and Highworth, where former Somerford booking porter Robert Perrett benefited from the regrading with a 2/- rise to 27/- a week. Again, Kemble received its regrading in May 1897, but for some reason Dauntsey was not regraded at this time and Samuel Jefford remained as station inspector until his promotion to Badminton in May 1903.

STATION MASTERS IN CHARGE OF LITTLE SOMERFORD

Name	Previous Post	Tenure at Little Somerford	Moved to
Thomas Sorrell	Lavington (SM)	12.5.1903 — 16.4.08	Pilning (SM)
Henry Jefferies	Pilning (SM)	16.4.08 — 1921	Retired
Albert Plant	Burrington (SM)	1921 — 1936	Retired
Henry J. Hill	Marlborough (SM)	1936 — 42	Relief Clerk Bristol DSO
Bertram J. Hunt	Henbury (SM)	1942 — 1958	Retired
Ralph Biggs	Dorrington (SM)	24.9.58 — 7.12.59	Wootton Bassett (SM)
	Temporary relief 7.12.59 — 24.2.60		
Stanley Mulcock	Bearley (SM)	24.2.60 — 14.12.61	Traffic Supt. Office, Bristol

Little Somerford was closed to passengers on 3rd April 1961. Stanley Mulcock remained as Station Master, with responsibility for Malmesbury and Brinkworth also, until 14th December 1961, after which date the station came under the control of the station master at Wootton Bassett. Cessation of goods service and final closure of Little Somerford took place on 10th June 1963.

STAFF IN CHARGE OF DAUNTSEY STATION, 1868 — 1965

Name & Grade	Previous Post	Tenure at Dauntsey	Moved to
William J. Kelson Booking Constable	No record of early history	Feb. 1868 — Aug. 1872	Passenger Porter, Chippenham
N. Hurford Booking Porter	Unknown	Sept. 1872 — Sept. 1873	Booking Porter Hallatrow
T. Rattue Booking Porter	Booking Porter Ashley Hill	Sept. 1873 — April 1875	Booking Porter Woolaston
H. J. Edmonds Booking Porter	Porter, Swindon	April 1875 — c.1879	Booking Porter Ely (Glam.)
Henry W. Baker Booking Porter	Unknown — no staff records found	c.1879 — April 1882	Unknown
Samuel Jefford Booking Porter	Booking Porter Ashley Hill	17.4.1882 — 1.5.03 Regraded Station Inspector June 1890	Station Master Badminton
Stephen Emery Station Master	Station Master Somerford	1.5.03 — Feb. 1914	Retired
Herbert S. Hill Station Master	Station Master Wylye	Feb. 1914 — 8.12.1934	Retired
Daniel G. Child Station Master	Station Master Marston Magna	1934 — 1945	Retired
Ernest W. Marquiss Station Master	Station Master Collingbourne	1945 — 1953	Retired
Samuel Rawle Station Master	Station Master Collingbourne	1953 — 1959	Retired
M. E. P. Weston Station Master	Cartage Section Trowbridge	1959 — 1965	Area Manager's Office, Chippenham

GREAT SOMERFORD STATION
(Class 5 station up to 1922. Class 6 1922—33)
STAFF IN CHARGE 1877—1933

Name & Grade	Previous Post	Tenure at G.S.	Moved To	
Theodore Ironsides Booking Porter	Railway Policeman Chippenham	Dec. 1877 — April 1879	Signalman Dauntsey	Somerford
Robert Perrett Booking Porter	Booking Porter Filton	April 1879 — Sept. 1884	Booking Porter Highworth	
John Emery Booking Porter	Unknown	Sept. 1884 — 1888	Unknown — Staff Records lost	
Stephen Emery Booking Porter*	Porter at Malmesbury ?	1888 to April 1903	Station Master Dauntsey	
Jacob Rogers Station Master	Station Master Winscombe	April 1903—May 1910	Station Master Henbury	Great Somerford
Robert Chapman Station Master	Station Master Grimstone & Frampton	May 1910 — Feb. 1914	Station Master Wylye	
William Reynolds Station Master	Station Master Aberdylais	25th May 1914 — 1918	Station Master Patchway	
Albert Ham Station Master	Office Messenger Bristol DSO	1918—1922	Station Master Brinkworth	
James Hurley Crossing Keeper	Goods Guard Bristol East Depot	1922—1928	Retired to live at Little Somerford	Great Somerford Halt
Thomas Strong Crossing Keeper	Signalman Chipping Sodbury	1928—1931	Retired back to Chipping Sodbury	
William Edwards Crossing Keeper	Porter Seend	Jan 1931 — March? 1933	Died in the year branch closed	
Temporary Relief Staff		March — July 1933	Until closure	

Unstaffed Halt Attendant in charge of crossing (annotation beside James Hurley through William Edwards rows)

* Stephen Emery's post of Booking Porter was regraded as Station Inspector in June 1890, then probably became Station Master in November 1897.

TRAFFIC RECORDS OF THE ORIGINAL MALMESBURY RAILWAY COMPANY

Traffic	½ yearly traffic up to 31st Dec. 1878	½ year up to 30th June 1879	½ year up to 31st Dec. 1879	½ year up to 30th June 1880
Passengers	22,593 (£646 2 0d)	19,466 (£561 5 6d)	21,539 (£595 0 0d)	18,119 (£524 18 10d)
Season tickets	£5 18 2d	£16 12 2d	£16 1 10d	£16 5 10d
Mails	£2 8 3d	£10 0 0d	£10 0 0d	£10 0 0d
Parcels, Horses, Carriages, Dogs	£77 16 7d	£105 5 0d	£115 13 6d	£133 8 2d
Goods & livestock	£542 3 6d	£611 13 5d	£651 4 4d	£593 1 7d
Total revenue	£1,274 8 6d	£1,304 16 1d	£1,387 19 8d	£1,277 14 5d
Less 50% allowance to GWR for working expenses	£637 4 3d	£652 8 0d	£693 19 10d	£638 17 3d

TRAFFIC DEALT WITH AT STATIONS.

Malmesbury Branch

STATION	YEAR	STAFF Supervisory and Wages all Grades (No.)	STAFF Pay bill Expenses (£)	TOTAL RECEIPTS (£)	Tickets issued (No.)	Season Tickets (No.)	Passenger Receipts including S.T. etc. (£)	Parcels & Misc. Number (No.)	Parcels & Misc. Receipts (£)	Total (£)	Fwd Coal & Coke "Charged" (Tons)	Fwd Other Minerals (Tons)	Fwd General Merchandise (Tons)	Recd Coal & Coke "Charged" (Tons)	Recd Other Minerals (Tons)	Recd General Merchandise (Tons)	Coal & Coke "Not Charged" Fwd & Recd (Tons)	Total Goods Tonnage (Tons)	Total Receipts excl. Coal "Not Charged" (£)	Livestock Fwd & Recd (Wagons)	Total Carted Tonnage (Tons)
Great Somerford Halt.	1903	5	191	2,505	8,066	* *	588	22,806	1,274	1,862	—	—	112	512	480	1,388	445	2,953	733	1	110
	1913	4	213	1,464	6,641		410	10,791	581	991	—	—	68	403	621	556	478	2,120	473	—	135
		Included with Dauntsey after 1922. Closed July, 1933.																			
Malmesbury	1903	8	414	12,862	20,624	* *	2,698	58,706	3,663	6,361	—	6	1,175	4,207	1,474	4,659	2,644	14,159	6,001	408	2,523
	1913	7	487	12,750	17,100	35	2,313	66,337	3,663	5,976	—	71	1,478	3,420	4,311	4,024	3,131	16,370	6,774	434	2,575
	1923	9	1,253	18,427	10,301	45	2,872	71,191	7,999	10,871	8	89	811	3,318	1,209	3,282	2,946	11,645	7,556	240	1,674
	1929	10	1,565	16,119	9,764	39	2,028	65,181	8,472	10,500	—	44	533	3,379	821	2,325	3,320	10,571	5,619	107	1,336
	1930	10	1,544	15,573	8,379	39	1,607	94,155	8,193	9,890	—	80	474	3,309	1,801	2,072	3,446	11,549	5,083	79	1,338
	1931	10	1,507	14,396	6,011	39	1,425	96,414	8,363	9,788	8	80	425	3,078	600	1,884	3,574	9,919	4,608	47	1,247
	1932	10	1,528	11,505	5,262	36	1,296	68,924	5,676	6,972	—	179	481	1,885	1,500	1,810	2,855	9,243	4,533	37	1,262
	1933	10	1,513	10,769	5,891	27	1,258	70,338	5,879	7,137	—	131	628	1,256	608	2,258	2,857	9,007	4,080	31	1,521
	1934	10	1,538	9,757	7,838	8	1,660	40,556	876	4,777	—	216	1,139	1,185	1,352	1,719	2,839	8,807	3,668	38	1,739
	1935	9	1,541	5,855	7,228	6	1,311	21,526	945	2,187	7	70	574	1,270	329	2,360	3,281	7,967	4,361	30	1,689
	1936	9	1,458	5,737	7,625	8	1,411	21,659	827	2,376	5	142	592	1,075	375	2,291	3,125	7,551	4,133	63	2,180
	1937	9	1,551	6,551	8,431	19	1,591	21,937	827	2,418	7	180	489	1,075	386	2,291	3,125	7,551	4,133	27	2,013
	1938	10	1,540	6,077	8,726	11	1,591	21,463	745	2,336	—	123	368	925	510	1,519	2,963	6,415	3,741	26	2,445

Stevenon to Dauntsey

STATION	YEAR	STAFF Supervisory and Wages all Grades (No.)	STAFF Pay bill Expenses (£)	TOTAL RECEIPTS (£)	Tickets issued (No.)	Season Tickets (No.)	Passenger Receipts including S.T. etc. (£)	Parcels & Misc. Number (No.)	Parcels & Misc. Receipts (£)	Total (£)	Fwd Coal & Coke "Charged" (Tons)	Fwd Other Minerals (Tons)	Fwd General Merchandise (Tons)	Recd Coal & Coke "Charged" (Tons)	Recd Other Minerals (Tons)	Recd General Merchandise (Tons)	Coal & Coke "Not Charged" Fwd & Recd (Tons)	Total Goods Tonnage (Tons)	Total Receipts excl. Coal "Not Charged" (£)	Livestock Fwd & Recd (Wagons)	Total Carted Tonnage (Tons)
High bridge (contd.) 1903	1903	11	601	7,145	15,028	* *	1,180	58,939	3,703	4,889	—	—	569	1,497	2,757	1,911	398	7,170	2,256	160	333
	1913	10	735	6,258	13,868	46	1,051	48,315	2,924	3,975	—	—	855	1,711	2,622	2,040	501	7,732	2,983	335	292
	1923	12	1,705	16,191	16,750	73	1,622	104,556	10,605	11,027	—	—	1,377	1,704	2,380	2,254	1,094	8,845	4,504	77	357
	1929	9	1,845	7,018	12,831	93	1,278	24,401	2,540	3,816	—	—	873	1,414	1,539	1,703	1,146	6,714	3,302	28	197
	1930	9	1,824	6,025	12,907	59	1,081	19,927	2,152	3,334	—	—	783	1,353	763	1,417	1,191	5,510	2,691	53	181
	1931	11	1,027	6,066	11,815	41	1,061	13,081	1,509	3,292	8	—	627	1,442	626	1,825	1,305	5,714	2,774	34	102
	1932	10	1,480	4,199	8,211	57	944	11,635	1,058	2,453	—	—	314	1,280	291	1,551	1,520	4,711	1,746	21	348
	1933	7	1,318	3,486	7,629	63	783	10,774	876	1,841	24	—	373	1,188	136	1,181	1,317	4,406	1,615	21	473
	1934	7	1,120	3,465	7,435	83	712	11,635	779	1,588	—	—	576	1,258	286	1,238	1,579	4,722	1,877	15	681
	1935	7	1,007	3,122	8,118	86	761	10,774	710	1,540	8	—	478	1,003	60	1,160	1,534	4,280	1,582	24	803
	1936	7	1,097	2,970	8,903	113	772	7,719	485	1,482	17	28	365	1,204	39	1,160	1,602	4,135	1,488	18	829
	1937	7	1,117	2,587	10,157	114	739	7,719	485	1,284	—	—	414	1,122	51	746	1,602	3,963	1,303	4	614
	1938	7	1,143	2,564		144	929	3,509	104	1,033	—	—	232	1,075	231	681	1,391	3,610	1,231	10	571

Little Somerford

STATION	YEAR	STAFF Supervisory and Wages all Grades (No.)	STAFF Pay bill Expenses (£)	TOTAL RECEIPTS (£)	Tickets issued (No.)	Season Tickets (No.)	Passenger Receipts including S.T. etc. (£)	Parcels & Misc. Number (No.)	Parcels & Misc. Receipts (£)	Total (£)	Fwd Coal & Coke "Charged" (Tons)	Fwd Other Minerals (Tons)	Fwd General Merchandise (Tons)	Recd Coal & Coke "Charged" (Tons)	Recd Other Minerals (Tons)	Recd General Merchandise (Tons)	Coal & Coke "Not Charged" Fwd & Recd (Tons)	Total Goods Tonnage (Tons)	Total Receipts excl. Coal "Not Charged" (£)	Livestock Fwd & Recd (Wagons)	Total Carted Tonnage (Tons)
Little Somerford.	1903	6	245	1,075	2,021	* *	245	4,124	258	503	—	—	71	340	318	1,326	270	2,334	1,172	186	57
	1913	5	373	3,862	4,662	4	778	20,827	1,212	2,020	—	—	612	212	1,068	3,146	479	7,437	1,842	130	130
	1923	7	1,003	7,574	3,704	—	661	28,633	1,954	3,388	—	17	1,104	485	1,287	2,509	839	6,714	4,236	98	175
	1929	6	1,000	5,045	2,335	—	440	36,018	1,654	2,384	—	—	213	611	399	2,077	800	4,300	2,651	230	84
	1930	6	1,041	4,729	2,071	—	350	41,539	2,246	2,596	—	14	208	309	147	3,878	855	5,405	2,133	94	85
	1931	6	683	4,715	1,937	—	306	33,333	1,750	2,066	—	12	230	289	19	4,002	977	5,693	2,669	110	74
	1932	6	976	3,373	1,753	—	269	9,246	500	769	—	28	354	311	42	4,374	1,066	6,214	2,604	80	335
	1933	7	1,027	3,479	2,853	1	374	6,924	769	488	—	34	384	286	52	4,075	1,084	6,301	2,991	82	563
	1934	7	1,143	4,008	4,176	2	472	2,827	711	1,213	—	26	422	301	114	4,443	982	6,361	2,705	57	641
	1935	7	1,122	3,721	4,609	3	449	1,822	115	666	—	13	463	412	12	3,863	1,026	5,529	3,155	156	683
	1936	7	1,190	3,783	4,050		394	1,500	127	521	—	—	242	404	43	3,202	977	5,529	3,202	222	518
									194	519	—	30	171	381	81	2,896	981	4,540	2,652	104	561

One of Malmesbury's gas-lit brake third coaches, No. 2655, derailed by the signal box in 1931. Brake thirds 2654 and 2655 were built to Diagram T34 in June 1895 and measured 31ft 0¾in by 8ft 0¾in. Height of the body was 7ft 6in, height from rail level 11ft 5¼in. The weight of each carriage was in excess of ten tons and cost of construction was in the region of £380. The brake van portion to the right accounted for about half the length of the vehicle, with a single door and observation window for the guard and double doors for the luggage and parcels accommodation. The train was formed so that the luggage section on each coach was at the outer ends, giving the same formation in either direction. The guard's compartment was all 'van' space, with brake pillar and observation window bays projecting from the coach sides. Passenger luggage and parcels traffic such as hampers, milk in churns or parcels were carried in this area. Brake composite No. 6621 was built to Diagram U5 and measured 27ft 6¾in by 8ft 0¾in with body height 7ft 6in, from rail level 11ft 5¼in. Weighing 9 tons, it was built for the Malmesbury branch train and emerged from the Swindon factory in September 1894 at a cost of £450. Coaches 2654, 2655 and 6621/2 were used for roller bearing trials on the branch, initially with chain roller bearings fitted in May 1924 and later with Skefko roller bearings fitted in October 1928. These were the only ones in GW branch line use at that time and former employees of Malmesbury station have recalled that the coaches ran so smoothly they could almost push them along the track themselves! Malmesbury staff took great pride in their coach stock, keeping their two first

class compartments meticulously clean for the local gentry. The coaches were painted chocolate and cream and the interiors were beautifully decorated, with moulded gold-coloured cornices on the ceilings, dark brown plush upholstery, buttoned binding, arm rests on each side which would stow away flush with the back upholstery, loose cushions, soft leather window straps and a brown carpet on the floor, bearing 'GWR' in a circle — 'out of this world', in the words of Malmesbury clerk John Barnby. Destination boards above the centre windows were reversible, bearing 'Dauntsey/Malmesbury'. The more utilitarian brake thirds suffered a great deal of buffeting during the time they spent on the platform running road, particularly when loose shunting. The coaches left the branch in 1934 and were condemned at the end of 1938.   *Bertram Farmer*

Walter Powell served as MP for Malmesbury from 1868—1881, being first elected at the age of 26. He was a member of the first Board of Directors of the Malmesbury Railway Company, and among his benefactions to the town were a ragged school, reading room (also provided at Great Somerford) and gas lighting for the Abbey. He was a famed balloonist, and on 11th June 1881 his balloon 'Eclipse' made an ascent from the Cross Hayes in Malmesbury, seen above. It was filled with gas via long pipes from Malmesbury Gas Works, and made a successful flight for about 45 minutes. The 2.30 train from Dauntsey was packed with around 400 people coming into town to see the spectacle. It is recorded that the branch train had an extra five carriages provided. Powell's hobby brought about his early death — he was lost over the Channel in the balloon 'Saladin' on 10th December 1881.   *Collection Oliver Pike*

DAUNTSEY STATION 1933—65

Dauntsey station's west end on 10th July 1950, looking west towards Chippenham and showing the signal box with the Malmesbury branch disused junction trackbed behind, and a siding still occupying the branch bay. *National Railway Museum*

With the closure of the Kingsmead—Dauntsey section of the Malmesbury branch in 1933, the whole character of Dauntsey station changed. With the loss of the posts of lad porter, parcel porter and shunter, the station staff was reduced to seven — station master, Grade 1 porter, two porters, and three signalmen. There was a steady decline in both passenger and goods receipts until two factors combined to change the station's fortunes. In 1938 the RAF aerodrome at Lyneham was opened, and this, coupled with the outbreak of World War II, led the station to be regraded as a Class 3, with the appointment of a booking clerk to handle the large passenger movement in RAF personnel. The grading reverted to Class 4 after the war.

There was not much goods and parcels traffic coming out from Dauntsey in later years, the only regular consignments being boxes of supplies going from Lyneham to Carlisle, often containing contraband collected by airfield customs! Inward movement, however, was heavy, particularly during the war years when the Barnes coal operation received a great boost with as many as twenty-five truckloads coming in on one occasion for the airfield. Cattle feed came in regularly for local farmers, mainly sugar beet and potatoes. This was usually collected by meal merchant Ernie Burchell and provided a lot of overtime for Dauntsey porters.

On one occasion during the war, Winston Churchill was flown into Lyneham, and spent the night in a special train on the remaining track of the Malmesbury branch. Percy Wakefield was appointed special constable.

Stores for Lyneham arrived regularly at Dauntsey, usually arriving first thing in the morning, accompanied by a bleary-eyed courier who remained with the delivery until collection. Having travelled with it overnight, his first thought would be breakfast, not easy at Dauntsey, his only immediate hope being the station master's wife! Crates for Lyneham would often come from their maintenance

unit at Carlisle, with varying degrees of priority. For instance, AOG (aircraft on ground) would be important spares for a plane. Conveyed on passenger trains as parcels traffic, much of the Lyneham traffic was destined for overseas. During the 1940s and 50s, Lyneham traffic was stored under the old canopy of the former Malmesbury bay platform until collection. Such goods would include engines, spares, boxes of shoes, repaired goods, etc. Dauntsey's station master had a pass to allow him into Lyneham Airfield for liaison concerning parcels, priority traffic, warrants and timetables.

In latter days passenger traffic at Dauntsey was largely airmen's wives who walked from the airfield caravan site at Bradenstoke for shopping trips to Chippenham, Bath and Swindon, and at weekends RAF personnel coming and going on weekend leave. Often, to avoid congestion at the station, the clerk or station master would go up to the airfield on Fridays to issue tickets. Some would go via Swindon, resulting in much paying of excess fares at Dauntsey on Sunday nights, when Reg Crockett, who worked for many years as porter and signalman, would wedge the side platform gate to restrict the exit.

A popular Friday train was the 1 p.m. off Swindon, which called at Dauntsey at 1.16 and gave connections west and north at Bristol. Servicemen would often return on Sunday nights on the 8.42 p.m. ex-Swansea which set down at Dauntsey about half-an-hour after midnight, where conveyance up to the airfield was provided by Athelstan Coaches, Barnes Taxis and Cooks of Lyneham.

Parcels traffic continued right until the end of the station's life, a Chippenham-based railway lorry calling at Dauntsey during the week at about 10 a.m. to take parcels for the villages of Dauntsey, Bradenstoke and Lyneham.

By the time the last station master, Peter Weston, took over in 1959, the Malmesbury end of the station had been dismantled, the canopy having been re-erected at Yatton in April 1956. Some goods were diverted to Calne to take pressure off Dauntsey and with the increase in dieselisation, the water troughs at the top of Dauntsey Bank were removed in 1957.

A regular visitor to the station during the last years was retired porter Percy Wakefield, who used to draw his railway pension every month in the station office and weigh himself on the parcel office scales, no doubt taking pride in the continued well-being of the station flower borders, which had continued to win prizes (usually £5 to spend on more seeds), the certificates hanging in the booking hall.

A general run-down of services forced customers to turn to road transport, and goods facilities at the station ceased on 10th June 1963. Thereafter Barnes, coal merchants, had to collect their coal from Chippenham as they had nearly a century before. By November 1963 the entire east end goods yard and the remaining rails of the Malmesbury branch had been removed. The Down refuge was removed on 24th November 1963.

During 1963 the afternoon train used by servicemen was taken off, thus forcing the RAF men to look elsewhere. This proved to be the final blow for the station, the passenger service struggling on until 4th January 1965, when the station was finally closed, along with Wootton Bassett, Christian Malford, Corsham, Box and Bathford on the main line between Swindon and Bath Spa. The signal box remained open until 25th September 1966, shortly after modernisation which involved the provision of a toilet, water supply

and stove! The crossover between Up and Down mains was removed when the box closed, the up refuge and back road having been removed the previous April.

Today the Inter-City 125s speed down Dauntsey Bank past the site of the long-forgotten junction for Malmesbury. The site of this once thriving junction is a sorry one indeed, particularly for men like Syd Jones, Dauntsey signalman 1947—57, who emigrated to Australia in 1957 and returned for a visit a quarter of a century later. With the demolition of the station building early in 1977, virtually the only reminder of former activity here is the station approach through the gateway from the road.

Syd could remember the Malmesbury branch train steaming across the fields at Swallett Gate in the '20s; he had been a lengthman based at Dauntsey in the 30s, and from his signalling days recalls the lever spaces in the signal box frame left by the 1933 closure. The sound of the block bells to Incline Box and Langley Crossing in either direction, the thrill of seeing the 'Merchant Venturer' or 'The Bristolian' passing through, or crossing light engines over to the Up main for reversal to Swindon when they came out from Swindon on tests, or even the simple pride in keeping the box immaculate, dutifully polishing the gleaming frame and levers, are all memories which must have passed through his mind as he observed the denuded wastes where there was once a living country station.

Approaching Dauntsey station at 90 mph, this picture was taken, looking west down Dauntsey Bank, from the cab of 'Castle' class 4—6—0 No. 5027 on 26th May 1961.
Kenneth Leach

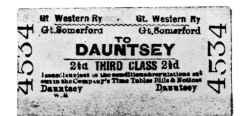
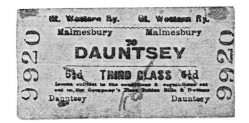
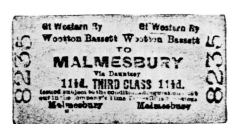